THE JEWS OF LATIN AMERICA

Latin America

Frontispiece. The southern Americas are home to 481,000,000 people, including some half-million Jews.

THE JEWS OF LATIN AMERICA

Revised Edition

Judith Laikin Elkin

HOLMES & MEIER
NEW YORK / LONDON

Published in the United States of America 1998 by
Holmes & Meier Publishers, Inc.
160 Broadway   New York, NY 10038

The author acknowledges with gratitude the courtesy of the American
Jewish Historical Society to reprint the following article which is
published in somewhat different form in this book: "Goodnight, Sweet
Gaucho: A Revisionist View of the Jewish Agricultural Experiment in
Argentina," *American Jewish Historical Quarterly* 67 (March 1978):
208–23.

Most of the photographs in this book were included in the exhibition,
"Voyages to Freedom: 500 Years of Jewish Life in Latin America and
the Caribbean," and were made available through the courtesy of the
Anti-Defamation League of B'nai B'rith. The two photographs of the
AMIA on pages 266–267 were supplied by the AMIA-Comunidad
Judía de Buenos Aires.

Typesetting by Coghill Books Typesetting, Chester, VA.
This book has been printed on acid-free paper.

Library of Congress Cataloging-in-Publication Data

Elkin, Judith Laikin, 1928–
        The Jews of Latin America / Judith Laikin Elkin. — Rev. ed.
        p.   cm.
        Rev. ed. of: Jews of the Latin American republics.   1980.
        Includes bibliographical references and index.
        ISBN 0-8419-1368-4 (cloth : alk. paper). — ISBN 0-8419-1369-2
    (pbk. : alk. paper)
        1. Jews—Latin America—History.   2. Latin America—History.
    I. Elkin, Judith Laikin, 1928–   Jews of the Latin American
    republics.   II. Title.
    F1419.J4E44   1998
    980' 004924—dc21   97-39405
                                                                CIP

Manufactured in the United States of America

TO

SARAH, TALIA, & ABIGAIL

CONTENTS

ILLUSTRATIONS

MAPS

TABLES

PREFACE TO THE REVISED EDITION

Much has happened since the first edition of this book was published. The marginalization of Jews that was a legacy of the immigration years has noticeably lessened. The continent is witness to the election of Jews to public office, the unimpeded participation of Jewish intellectuals in public life, and accelerating rates of intermarriage that bespeak ease in personal relations. Growing acceptance of a pluralistic society has occurred within social contexts that tolerate anti-Semitism and philo-Semitism alike, sometimes without distinguishing between the two or privileging one over the other.

At the same time, the brutalization of politics in Argentina, home to the largest Jewish community, exacted a horrendous price from individual citizens, including a disproportionate number of Jews. In Central America and elsewhere, Jews together with their fellow citizens have been shaken out of their homelands by revolution and the fear of pauperization. Emigration has accelerated the decrease in Jewish population size already initiated by a declining birth rate. Political and economic insecurity led to a tighter bond with the State of Israel, bringing a different set of complexities in its wake. Contemporary Latin Jews, legatees of two historically antagonistic traditions, remain balanced on the cusp of permanence or dissolution. These are some of the issues addressed in the present volume.

In 1979 I wrote of the lack of scholarly attention to the Jewish communities of Latin America. In the years since then, more research has been published on Latin American Jewry than in the previous one hundred. New scholarship fills out our knowledge of these communities and enables us to reach a fuller understanding of their status within their national societies. As the Latin American diaspora becomes visible, the range of Jewish history expands beyond its European and North American foci. At the same time, viewing Latin American societies from a Jewish perspective challenges the traditional notion of these societies as monolithic, a notion that perpetuates the nationalist view of Jews as disturbers of some uniform, ideal society, unalterably Hispanic and Catholic. It is becoming more and more apparent that non-Latin, non-Iberian immigrants played a role in the evolution of the Latin American republics, and that their societies are increasingly pluralistic in reality if not in ideology. Jews are a part of this new reality, and uncovering their life stories reveals the modernizing dynamic they brought with them.

If the earlier edition of this book was ambitious in attempting to record the Jewish presence in all Latin American countries over a period of almost five centuries, this edition may exceed the bounds of the possible in attempting to bind together under one cover the increasingly dense data and varied patterns of Jewish life in more than twenty nation-states, each with its own ecology, ethnicity, traditions, and policies that increasingly diverge from one another. Yet, that is what is undertaken here, though the risks of attempting a continent-wide analysis have multiplied over the years. The history of the Jews of Latin America is a work in progress. Recent scholarship reveals more than we knew before, but deepens its ambiguities.

Data have been updated throughout the book, based on the research of scholars whose work is cited in the text and in the expanded bibliography at the end. In some cases, new research has led to revised interpretations of events. To the extent that some topics—especially in economics—have been treated less thoroughly than might be desired, such gaps point to the need for additional primary research. New chapters have been added to this edition, including one on relations with the State of Israel and another on relations with non-Jews.

I have especially benefited from discussions with colleagues, many of which took place during the international research conferences of the Latin American Jewish Studies Association. I am also indebted to scholars who read various parts of the manuscript and generously shared their expert knowledge with me, including Professors Haim Avni, Sergio DellaPergola, Edy Kaufman, Jeff Lesser, and Victor A. Mirelman. Lois Baer Barr and David Sheinin read the entire manuscript critically. As always, I thank my husband, Sol M. Elkin, for his understanding and support.

Ann Arbor, 1997

PREFACE TO THE FIRST EDITION

Jews do not figure in the postindependence history of Latin America as currently written. Overlooked by Latin Americanists as too few and too marginal to affect the area's development, they have likewise been regarded by Jewish scholars as outside the course of Jewish history. So we find that Latin American historians omit mention of a Jewish presence within the independent republics once the fires of the Inquisition have been banked. Historians and sociologists of the Jewish people, for their part, tend to overlook Latin America, grouping its Jewish communities under "Others" after more salient groups have been investigated. The Jews of Perpignan in the thirteenth century have been the subject of a monograph, as have the Jews of Washington, D.C., in the twentieth; but there is no history of the Jews of Latin America.

Is there in fact any such entity as Latin American Jewry? The life of Jews moves within the lives of nations among whom they live, is shaped and altered by them. In the case of Latin America, without underestimating the differences that characterize the various republics, we may agree that there are also broad similarities. Cultural congruence, rooted in the phylogeny of their peoples, is the base upon which studies of such continent-wide phenomena as race, the military, the church, and the system of latifundia have all been founded. Immigration, too, is subject to continental analysis. Generally speaking, immigrants have had to integrate into societal molds that were Iberian and Catholic, that demanded of them not only conformity but complicity in a hierarchical social order that consigned them to a specialized and subordinate category. In accommodating to such social orders, Jews all over Latin America faced similar constraints and opportunities. Molded by their own cultural heritage, they made similar adaptations. The result was the emergence of an identifiable Latin American Jewry, sharing certain economic, cultural, and social characteristics that distinguish them both from their matrix populations and from the Jewries of other continents. These shared characteristics include their origin as immigrants, a distinctive demographic profile, characteristic lifestyle, and mode of acculturation. Despite differences of nuance, Latin American Jews constitute an identifiable group, the study of which enlarges our understanding of Latin America and expands the universe of the Jewish diaspora.

The reasons for Jewish invisibility have partly to do with the small number of people involved. There are probably just half a million Jews scattered through the Latin American continent and adjacent islands. In all countries save Argentina, Jews comprise less than 1 percent of the population, so that recognition of their presence may strike some as an academic nicety.°

But Jews have been numerically insignificant in all countries where they have dwelt. The vital Jewish community of seventeenth-century Amsterdam numbered no more than two thousand. Jews comprise rather less than 3 percent of the population of the United States,† yet they have profoundly influenced arts and letters, science, the economy, the administration of justice, and foreign policy, to name only major areas. Have Jews wielded a like influence within Latin America? If they have not, how may this be explained? If they have, why is this not perceived?

Emergence of a Jewish entity to take its place beside the Indian, black, and Iberian populations that have already marked out the major areas of Latin American ethnic studies is hampered by the lack of a proper name for the group. Most Spanish and Portuguese terms for "Jew" are in varying degrees impolite, pejorative, or defamatory. Usage varies in different sectors of the continent and among different population strata: *judío, israelita,* and *hebreo* may all be used benignly. Ambiguous usage reflects the ambiguous status of the Jews themselves and provides a clue to the reasons for their invisibility: one does not discuss what one cannot name.

As a concept of Latin American Jewry emerges, it becomes apparent that invisibility is a function of ambivalence in these societies that have not yet reexamined the medieval stereotype of the Jew and consequently cannot decide how to regard contemporary Jews. Traditional social structures rebuff and marginalize Jewish elements that are viewed as inconsistent with the national norm, and the evidence is that accommodation of the immigrants proceeded at a slower pace than the immigrants' own acculturation. Yet absorption of immigrants into national life must be a reciprocal process: immigrants must be willing to acculturate, society must be willing to accommodate.

How do Jews acculturate to Catholic societies that reject cultural pluralism as a valid ideal? Subjected to the cultural imperatives of Hispanic Catholicism, can Jews survive as Jews, or are they destined to assimilate or emigrate? The effort to arrange a modus vivendi between Hispanic and Judaic cultures, each containing elements historically antagonistic to the other, lends to the subject its peculiar interest.

Numerous historians, sociologists, and enthusiasts have attempted to describe particular Latin American Jewish communities, using voluminous published and unpublished materials produced, largely in Yiddish and Hebrew, by these communities themselves. For the most part, these studies present portraits of Jewish communities set uneasily upon landscapes that bear little or

---

°Within the next decade, the Jewish population of the southern Americas declined to 386,700, and Argentina's dropped below 1 percent of the total population of that country.
†The 1990 estimate is 2.2 percent.

no resemblance to reality and that emphasize Jewish detachment from national life. No scholarly attention has been focused on that large proportion of Jews who merge into the matrix populations each year, nor has any attempt been made to reconcile these apparently contradictory phenomena.

Till now, information derived from community and private surveys has not flowed into the field of Latin American studies because of the language barrier. The absence of communication between Jewish historians (for whom Latin America is peripheral) and Latin Americanists (for whom Jews are beneath the perceptual threshold) has prevented incorporation into the body of universal scholarship of that small amount of work which has been done. Here lies another reason for the invisibility of Latin American Jews. Synthesis of Jewish and Latin American data was required in order to establish the dimensions of Jewish life and to relate it to that of the national societies within which it moves.

This task is here undertaken for the first time. The present study offers data relating to Jewish life in all the Latin American republics over a span of more than two hundred years. Some of the data were generated by scholarly studies. Where these are lacking, personal reminiscences, newspaper accounts, and other subjective materials were utilized in order to present as comprehensive a picture as possible. Data were supplemented by extensive interviewing in the United States and Latin America, which served to bridge gaps and test interpretations. Needless to say, the interpretations are my own. Some, I believe, will withstand challenge; others are offered as provocations to other scholars to investigate the disjuncture between two cultures that are in ambiguous contact with each other. . . .

Ann Arbor, 1979

THE JEWS OF LATIN AMERICA

PART ONE

THE FOUNDING
OF A
NEW/OLD WORLD

CHAPTER 1

Jews in the Spanish and Portuguese Dependencies

Eden is located in the center of South America in a circle nine degrees in diameter, which amount to 160 leagues and a circumference of 460 leagues.

—Antonio de Leon Pinelo, *El paraíso en el Nuevo Mundo*

DESPITE THE ELUSIVE nature of the history of Jews and Jewish converts in the Spanish and Portuguese New World, it is appropriate to open a narrative of modern times with a glimpse into the earlier period. Only in this way can we understand the mentality of the Jews who settled in Latin America following the attainment of independence and discover the preconceptions that greeted them on their arrival.

It is a truism of Latin American history that events and ideologies of the colonial period imposed lasting patterns on the independent republics. In the case of Jews, the pattern was defined long before the imposition of Spanish and Portuguese rule in the Americas. At home, both kingdoms pursued policies that were intended to exclude Jews and the descendants of Jews from society, their purpose being to create a populace united in both political and religious allegiance. Subsequently, Jews and converted Jews were prohibited by law from entering the colonial dependencies of Spain, though, as we shall see, many of them did. Portugal tolerated the emigration of *conversos* to Brazil, but these eventually found themselves fearful for their physical survival. Because society dealt with Jews by proscribing them, Jews and their descendants figure in the history of the colonial period only as objects of legal or ecclesiastical procedures designed to reduce them to conformity, as penitents and impenitents exhibited to the people as examples of the horrors of deviance. This encounter between Jews and conversos, on the one hand, and a church-state system bent on their physical and spiritual eradication, on the other, provides the pyschological backdrop to the presence of Jews in the Latin American republics in modern times.

3

Iberia

Jews lived in the Iberian peninsula when Spain was a remote province of the Roman Empire. Before 1492, they functioned as a separate caste under Visigoths, Christians, and Moors, alternately integrated into general society and marginalized from it, subjected to periodic pogroms, but also serving as an incubator for talented individuals who then were tapped for high public office. Characteristically, special legislation ordained and circumscribed the Jews' participation in public life, protected them from excessive religious violence, and kept intact their communities in ghettos that were important sources of revenue for contending princes and princelings.

In 1391, the inflammatory preaching of religious zealots, unrestrained by the church, aroused popular zeal for the extermination of Judaism and the total Christianization of society. Pogroms erupted in Seville and, proceeding northward, forced the conversion of thousands of Jews. In 1412–15, laws requiring Jews to leave their houses and quit their professions forced a wave of "voluntary" conversions, bringing into existence a new class of person: the converso, or New Christian.[1] Mass conversion created its own momentum, leading to voluntary conversions of a considerable number of Jews, probably because conversos were able to integrate themselves into Spanish life, whereas Jews suffered heavy legal disabilities. For the rich and well educated, conversion was an open sesame into lives of influence and public service. At a time when rationalism was challenging the religious beliefs of intellectuals, it may have seemed less important to retain one's allegiance to "the dead law of Moses," as the church called Judaism, than to collaborate with the dominant society in the creation of tolerable living conditions. Intermarriage with the best families of the land became common, and by the sixteenth century there was scarcely a noble family in Spain without its converso connection.

Thousands of Spanish Jews, however, continued to adhere to their ancestral faith, and so the original body of Jewry divided into two groups living side by side: conversos and Jews. Related to each other by blood and marriage ties, the two groups found themselves cast into very different roles by society; yet their fates remained intertwined, for the church alleged that the Jews presented a threat to the adoptive faith of the conversos. In 1480, the Inquisition was formally installed in the peninsula for the purpose of inquiring into the faith of the recently converted. Riding the crest of authority accrued through their defeat of the Moors and the unification of Christian Spain, the Catholic Kings, Isabella of Castile and Ferdinand of Aragon wrested authority over the Inquisition, turning it into an instrument of the crown, not, as it was elsewhere, an instrument of the pope.

As the eight-hundred-year civil war of the Reconquest drew to its close, a thirst for religious as well as national unification gripped the victorious Catholics. Within weeks of the fall of Granada, last Moorish bastion on the peninsula, the process of sieving Jews out of Spanish life culminated in the Edict of Expulsion. The Edict, issued on March 30, 1492, forced Spain's remaining

Jews to choose between conversion to Catholicism and exile from Spain. Thousands of professing Jews now fled Spain for North Africa, Portugal, Italy, and the Ottoman Empire.[2]

Converts were allowed to stay on in Spain, and these now swelled the existing converso population. But the quality of the conversos' faith had become a matter for official inquiry. The Holy Office of the Inquisition, the institution charged with defending the Catholic religion and Spanish culture against heresy, operated on the assumption that many conversos were not true Catholics, but Judaizers, practitioners of Jewish rites in secret: in short, heretics. Motivated by religious zeal and by greed—for the property of those arrested fell forfeit to the Holy Office and to those who denounced the alleged miscreants—the Inquisition moved against the conversos with all the combined power of church and state. Arrest without a right of habeas corpus; the application of judicial torture; bounty payments to informers; interminable periods of imprisonment without opportunity to learn what charge had been brought, and by whom; all were standard operating procedure, and all were duly recorded in the *procesos* (court records) of trials. Every conceivable method for extracting confessions from prisoners was brought into play, and yet the procesos fail to answer the fundamental question of the true nature of converso belief. In fact, if it has been impossible to determine how many Jews became Christians, the number of New Christians who remained secret Jews can only be a subject for speculation.

Jewish historians who have memorialized the conversos imprisoned and tormented by the Inquisition have tended to operate on the same assumption as the Catholic establishment: these were secret Jews who had converted to save their lives and property, but they continued to practice their old religion in secret. Just who first called the conversos swine (Marranos) is uncertain, but the name stuck as a badge of honor. The Marranos are heroes in Jewish history. Conversos, however, were not at any time a cohesive group. There were beyond doubt genuine converts to Catholicism among them. Indeed, as early as 1499, the rabbis to whom such questions were addressed ruled that the Spanish conversos were voluntary converts and renegades and wrote them off as lost to Judaism.[3] The closing of Jewish religious academies, the flight of Jewish scholars abroad, the destruction of Hebrew books, all prevented conversos, whatever their inclination, from experiencing a genuine Jewish religious life. Their chief source of information about the Jewish religion came from the Bible in its Catholic version and the Edict of Faith, which the Inquisition issued periodically in order to exhort the Catholic faithful to detect and denounce Judaizers in their midst. Some stigmata noted in the Edict were bathing on Fridays and stripping the vein from the leg of an animal before cooking it. Consideration of such habits as heresy gives point to Benzion Netanyahu's remark that "the aim of the Inquisition . . . was not to eradicate a Jewish heresy from the midst of the Marrano group, but to eradicate the Marrano group from the midst of the Spanish people."[4]

Following this line of thought can lead one to the conclusion that Marranism in its origin was a myth that satisfied the very different longings of the Jews and of their tormentors: the Jews for heroes they could idealize, the Inquisition for grounds to arrest conversos and enjoy their property. Netanyahu's work on the subject opens with the question: who were the Marranos? and quickly confronts the reader with the challenging response: they were Christians.

What, then, is one to make of the unrefuted record of murderous activity directed against the Marranos by the Inquisition? Why was the Catholic Church engaged in the business of killing Catholics? It has been suggested that this came about as a result of class warfare against the rising middle class, many of whose members were conversos.[5] More precisely, as with any political movement, motives of those who harassed conversos varied between the ideological and the commercial. It is as incorrect to assume that all New Christians were crypto-Jews as it is to affirm that there were no Judaizers at all among them and that the entire case against them was conceived in paranoia and dedicated to greed.[6] Leaving this argument behind, Netanyahu suggests that rivalry with New Christians for preferment by the crown created an anti-Marrano bias that was undergirded by racism.

> Looking for a quality common to all conversos, and at the same time so negative as to support the issuance of harsh restrictive laws against them, the racial theorists believed that such a quality should be sought not in what the Marranos *did* or *believed*, but in what they *were* as human beings. This did not seem to be a difficult task. For what they were was determined by their ethnic origin—or rather, as they put it, by their *race*. Since race, they maintained, formed man's qualities and indeed his entire mental constitution, the Marranos, who were all off-spring of Jews, retained the racial makeup of their forebears. Hence ethnically they were what they (or their ancestors) had been before their conversion to Christianity; in other words, they were Jews.[7]

Whatever may have been the belief system of individuals who experienced conversion in their own flesh, any putative Judaism must have been very attenuated among their descendants of the third, fourth, fifth, sixth generation. Indeed, we know that the beliefs of individuals who admitted to Judaizing under torture were far different from the beliefs of normative Jews. Yet the definition of Jewishness has never been wholly confined within the limits of rabbinic law. While many descendants of converts embraced their new religion wholeheartedly, some who lived as Catholics retained their loyalty to Judaism for generations. Eventually, some of these crypto-Jews made their way to Holland or Italy, where they reverted openly to Judaism; such was the case with the family of the philosopher Baruch Spinoza, the rabbi-politician-seer Menasseh ben Israel, and the mercantile community of Amsterdam from which Rembrandt drew so many of his subjects. Persons who consider themselves Jews, who act upon this conviction, and who suffer punishment for it cannot be defined out of the Jewish people by legal rulings. The texture of converso religious life, like the song the sirens sang, may be beyond conjecture. The operative fact for our present history is that the ambiguity of Marrano mentality in Spain obscures the history of "Jews" in the Spanish possessions overseas because we do not really know who they were.

The case was somewhat different in Portugal. Here there was no long-drawn-out period of forced conversion alternating with voluntary conversion. In Portugal, Jews had lived in relative peace, and consequently many of the Spanish refugees of 1492 crossed over into that country. Pressures soon began to be exercised against them. When the Jews resisted conversion, hundreds of their children were kidnapped, forcibly baptized, and sent to the island of São Tomé in the Gulf of Guinea to be raised as Christians.[8] With the accession to the throne of Emanuel III (1495–1521) and his engagement to a daughter of Ferdinand and Isabella, Portugal was pressured by the Catholic monarchs to rid itself of Jews as Spain had done. But Emanuel viewed his Jews as an economic asset and did not wish to lose them. Instead, he had them all forcibly baptized. Thus, overnight in 1497, one-fifth of the Portuguese population became New Christians, *cristãos novos*. By the end of the sixteenth century, the line between Old Christian and New was so unclear that in both Europe and Latin America the names "Portuguese" and "Jew" became synonymous.

It is a peculiar paradox of history that in the century leading up to these events, the Spanish prepared for themselves a set of rules to live by that ensured the survival of the old distinction between Jew and Christian long after there were no Jews left in the kingdom. This they did by developing and elaborating the concept of *limpieza de sangre,* cleanliness of blood, according to which all Jews or descendants of Jews, or persons penanced by the Inquisition, and all their descendants, carried a taint of impurity in their blood and were to be excluded from public life.[9] Thus a caste of persons came into existence—the conversos—who were no longer Jews, but who were not accepted as Catholics either.

The preoccupation with limpieza de sangre emerged among different population sectors in the Iberian peninsula in the fifteenth century. It became official policy during the reign of Philip II (1556–98) by which time the standard of "clean blood" was being applied by the crown, the church, the military orders, the universities, and all social strata according to their circumstances to the end of excluding the descendants of Jews and Moors from public life. New Christians were barred from holding office in any corporation, public or private. They were prohibited from entering an ecclesiastical career or joining a military order; they were barred from the university and from careers in medicine or pharmacy. They could not negotiate on the stock exchange, and measures were under consideration to prevent their marrying Old Christians.

When Philip II brought Portugal under his rule, the policy of limpieza was extended to that kingdom as well as to all its dependencies overseas. By the end of the sixteenth century, it was popularly believed that neither the sacrament of baptism nor the practice of Christian virtue could change the fact of a person's Jewish origin. The ineradicable stain was in the blood, and there it stayed.[10]

Considering the pressures exerted on New Christians continually to prove and re-prove their religious orthodoxy and the increasing barriers placed in the way of their integration into national life, it would not be surprising had some of them looked abroad for new homes. As the age of exploration dawned, the newly unified Spain was ready to play a role in competition with Portugal. A vision of redemption in far-off lands, of "lost tribes settling in New Canaans," can be drawn from certain apocryphal writings, particularly the Book of Esdras. Jews who continued to live within the Judaic tradition viewed messianism with suspicion, but it would not be surprising if New Christians, who had opted out of Jewish life but who were denied access to the messianic promise of Christ, picked up on quite a different vision of messianic deliverance. The age of exploration now dawning offered a surrogate religious experience by presenting the possibility of the founding of new societies that would prefigure the nobility and innocence of paradise. In such a vision, Catholic, Protestant, and Jew could share and share alike.[11]

The money that financed Columbus's first voyage of discovery was lent to Queen Isabella by conversos who were closely associated with the court of Aragon, after the Catholic monarchs had turned down the would-be explorer "for the last time." Columbus's first letter home was written, not to the king and queen, but to two of these patrons, Luis de Santangel, secretary of the exchequer to Ferdinand of Aragon, and Gabriel Sanchez, Ferdinand's treasurer general. Both were New Christians: Santangel's cousin had been burned at the stake, and he himself was saved from the Inquisition only by the intervention of Ferdinand.

Several historians and many history buffs have tried to draw from these and other circumstances the inference that Spanish conversos were actively looking for a new land where they could live in peace, even that the alleged converso Christopher Columbus was their agent in such a search; a torrent of speculation on this subject was let loose during the Columbus Quincentenary Year.[12] Conversos had chosen Spain and exile from Judaism in preference to Judaism in exile from Spain. Now that Spain was rejecting them, some emigrated to other Mediterranean lands, while others may have looked even further abroad for a resolution to the intolerable contradictions of their lives. The theory that the discovery of the New World had a converso (even a crypto-Jewish) hidden agenda is enticing. But proof, if proof there be, has been concealed with all the cunning the conversos mustered in order to protect their identity and their lives.

The Indies

If conversos hoped that the age of discovery would open up new lands for settlement, the crown was equally intent that the new lands should remain free of any Jewish or converso taint. From the start, the monarchs attempted to apply the policy of limpieza to the Indies. As early as 1501, Queen Isabella instructed Nicolás de Ovando, governor of Hispaniola, to bar Jews, Moors, heretics, New Christians, and persons penanced by the Inquisition, and their children or grandchildren, from settling in the Indies.[13] Charles V repeated the order in 1522, singling out "recent Jewish converts." The instructions were included in the comprehensive Laws of the Indies and were repeated frequently over the next three centuries, illustrating both the continued hostility of the crown to settlers of Jewish descent and the persistence of New Christians in their efforts to share in the destiny of their homeland. Those who arrived in the New World were technically illegal immigrants who were committing a crime merely by virtue of being there, and they were subject to action by the state and by the Inquisition if they were caught. Nevertheless, the intense pressures exerted in Spain and Portugal against persons of Jewish descent resulted in the flight of numerous conversos and crypto-Jews to the New World, where the opportunity for anonymity was considerably greater than at home. Those who managed to elude the authorities in their quest for survival sought only to disappear, and consequently left no written trace. What is known of them comes from the dossiers of the Inquisition.

Seven years after Cortés landed in Mexico, the first two persons fell victim to the policy of limpieza in the New World. One of these was Hernando Alonso, a blacksmith and ship's carpenter who helped build the brigantines on which Cortés's army embarked for the siege of Tenochtitlán (Mexico City, which at that date was situated in the middle of a lake). In the ensuing years, Alonso became a rancher and purveyor of meat to the Spanish army. Denounced for having rebaptized a child in wine and for having told his wife to stay away from church while menstruating, Alonso was convicted of Judaizing and burned at the stake in 1528.[14] The actions Alonso was accused of are not Jewish customs, nor is there evidence that he embraced any Jewish beliefs. On balance, his prosecution may have been more a political than a religious ploy, an attempt by the Dominican order to tame the power of the conquistadors, bearing out the judgment of historians that "The Inquisition was the instrument for [societal] control. To be sure, the Inquisition possessed a religious function . . . but, and this is the critical element, in both the Spanish and Portuguese empires, the Inquisition was subordinated from its start to a nonreligious political agenda."[15] Characteristically, of the first "Judaizer" executed in the New World, we do not even know that he considered himself a Jew. The ambiguity of the Jewish presence within Spanish history was transferred to the New World intact.

The crown was committed to restricting immigration to the pure of blood, but like everything else that lay within the royal power to grant or withhold, permits of exemption could be bought. Exclusion was difficult enough to enforce, and exemption from the law provided a ready source of cash to the perennially empty royal treasury.[16] In 1509, the exclusion was partially lifted in consideration of a tax of 20,000 ducats. This benefit, extended for reasons of avarice, was periodically suspended for reasons of bigotry. Sometimes the effect of tightening the regulations was simply to drive up the price of the necessary certificate of limpieza. Also, because soldiers, sailors, and servants were not required to obtain a certificate, some conversos entered New Spain in these roles. Thus, despite the hazards, numerous persons of Jewish descent did in fact settle in Mexico by the mid-sixteenth century, but they lacked assurance that they could live out their lives there. What proportion of these were faithful Catholics, which ones were Judaizers, and how many remained in a state of syncretic transition is impossible to determine.

The occupations of conversos who came to the attention of the Inquisition in New Spain (a skewed sample, because not all conversos were denounced) indicate that they had come to the New World for the same reasons as everyone else: to earn a living and perhaps to strike it rich. Occupations of suspected Judaizers (*Judaizantes*) included merchant, mine owner, ship's carpenter, purveyor of meat, monk, mortician, fencing master, clogmaker, peddler, carpenter, miner, tailor, seamstress, innkeeper, breeder of pigs, pharmacist, clergyman, public scribe, confectioner, merchant to China, Dominican priest, buyer and seller of African slaves, mayor of Tecali, secretary, owner of a sugar mill, doctor, army captain, vicar general of Michoacán, dealer in cattle, farmer, silversmith, handyman, shopkeeper, juggler, weaver, jeweler, the owner of a hacienda, and the chief constable of Cuazualco.[17] The gamut of occupations reflected the conversos' earlier integration into the economy of their homeland and their subsequent integration into the economy of their adopted society, structured as it was by the Catholic Church and a system of agriculture based on slavery, which was condoned by the church and licensed by the state. It was considered less important to utilize the skills conversos brought to the new colony than to confine or expel the persons who practiced these skills. Women prisoners were listed by family relationship rather than by occupation. There is record of one who was the sister of a Jesuit priest and mother of a Dominican monk. Having been raised in a Catholic household and having raised her own children as Catholics was not a sufficient warranty that a conversa would be allowed to take her place in society.

The chief prize of the Holy Office of the Inquisition in New Spain was Luis de Carvajal y de la Cueva, conquistador, pacifier of the northern frontier, first governor of the province of Nuevo León, and faithful Catholic. He had been awarded a contract for the conquest and pacification of a vast territory stretching northwest of Mexico City; this contract, unlike most, did not specify that settlers going out with him had to produce certificates of limpieza. The governor recruited over a hundred of his relatives and friends to settle in Nuevo León, evidently ignorant of the fact that some of them were Judaizing, or perhaps calculating that, if they were, he was well advised to have them near, where he could keep an eye on them. These accompanied him, whether in the hope of improving their fortunes or in the hope that in that distant waste they could revert to their ancestral religion. Eventually, the Inquisition arrested, tortured, penanced, and executed most of the Carvajal family, including the governor's nephew and namesake, Luis de Carvajal the younger, who became a martyr to his Jewish faith. Another nephew, Gaspar, a Dominican monk and authentic Catholic, was convicted of abetting and protecting Judaizers but was allowed to repent in the privacy of his monastery. The governor, stripped of office, honor, and property, died in jail.[18]

Better known to Mexican history are conversos who succeeded in making their contributions in a Catholic mode. These may include Sor Juana Inés de la Cruz (1651–95), author of lyric and mystical poetry, who was known in Mexico as the "Tenth Muse"; and the Franciscan friar Bernardino de Sahagún, who compiled an encyclopedic work on Aztec culture that remains our primary source of information on that civilization.

The Inquisition was introduced into Peru in 1570, but found few Judaizers in its early years. During the period 1580–1640 (the so-called Babylonian Captivity, when Portugal came under the rule of Spain), numerous Portuguese entered the viceroyalty, among them conversos. Again, we find them deployed widely through the economy. According to Inquisition records, persons with the following occupations were tried for Judaizing (keeping in mind that not everyone charged with that crime was a converso): merchants, peddlers, store owners, vendors, monks, doctors, writers, scribes, lawyers, candymakers, shoemakers, silversmiths, a swordsmith, brokers of African slaves, carters, sailors, soldiers, grocers, a bailiff, a judge, a mayor, and two professional card sharks.[19]

The largest group (twenty-two) identified in Inquisition records were merchants, the next largest (thirteen) commercial travelers. In the course of time, converso merchants came to control much of the trade of South America, buying and selling in international trade and in trade among the colonies—much of which was prohibited by the mercantilist policies of the mother country. Their wealth and conspicuous lifestyle proved their undoing, for eventually their Old Christian competitors moved against them by impugning their faith. In August 1635, eighty-one persons were arrested by the Inquisition, sixty-four of these for Judaizing. All those arrested as Judaizers who survived torture appeared at the great auto-da-fé four years later, when eleven of the prisoners were burned at the stake as impenitent heretics and the rest sentenced to varying terms of imprisonment, forms of penance, or service in the galleys.[20]

This event went down in Peruvian history as "la gran complicidad" (the great conspiracy), but curiously, at the sermon delivered on the great square in Lima while the impenitents awaited their immolation, no mention was made of a conspiracy. Nor were the prisoners questioned in their cells about a conspiracy, as determined from proceso records. As all of the prisoners' considerable property fell forfeit to the Inquisition, any conspiracy that existed must have sprung from the minds of those who stood to benefit from the accusation.[21]

The destruction of the converso merchant community of Lima caused financial panic as creditors rushed to recover their debts before the Inquisition could sequester the property of those arrested, and conversos who had not been arrested fled the country. The Lima office of the Inquisition emerged as the wealthiest in the empire, but the viceroyalty was thrown into economic chaos. This was the climax of Inquisitorial activity against conversos in Peru. An office of the Inquisition was also opened in Cartagena in 1610, but it did a brisker business in witches than in Judaizers.

The southern cone of South America did not escape notice, despite its considerable distance from the metropole. Its economy may have been neglected by the Spanish crown, but the faith of its inhabitants nonetheless came under the scrutiny of the Inquisition, operating through its agents in Buenos Aires and elsewhere.[22] The most famous of its prisoners was the surgeon Francisco Maldonado de Silva of Tucumán, who was a crypto-Jew. Denounced by his pious Catholic sister, Maldonado de Silva became the most stiff-necked Jew in the dungeon of the Inquisition, writing religious tracts on scraps of paper and passing them along to other prisoners to encourage them in their resistance. Maldonado de Silva left no doubt as to his religious loyalties, for he circumcised himself, renamed himself Eli Nazareno, and fasted and prayed continually in his cell. After twelve years of imprisonment during which the Inquisitors alternately inquired into the tenets of his faith and forgot about him for long periods of time, he was taken out and incinerated along with participants in the so-called grand conspiracy of Lima.[23]

Most New Christians who came to the New World were Portuguese rather than Spanish. In Spain, conversions forced and voluntary had been going on for a century prior to the advent of America on the European consciousness, and the descendants of Jews had largely assimilated by 1580. Jews who wanted above all to retain their religious faith had already left Spain when America appeared miraculously from out of the ocean. The Jews of Portugal (who included the Jewish faithful exiled from Spain) were forcibly converted in one blow in 1497; they were assisted in this by the fact that their children were converted first and they did not want to be separated from them. Under the circumstances, the proportion who continued to practice Judaism secretly must have been large.

Confusion over identity occurred during the Babylonian Captivity, when Portuguese could freely enter Spain and the Spanish possessions. During this period, large numbers of Portuguese conversos crossed over La Plata from Brazil into present-day Argentina. From there, many worked their way northward up the smugglers' trail to Potosí (in present-day Bolivia), where rose the silver mountain that was the treasure-house of Spain and the tomb of countless Native American miners. Portuguese Jews who fled Brazil in the wake of Inquisitorial visitations built up the illegal commerce of Buenos Aires, importing West African slaves and exporting the silver of Potosí.[24] Everywhere the unwelcome commercial competition of the Portuguese won for them the contemptuous appellation *judío,* or Jew; consequently, it is unclear just how many of these merchants were in fact of Jewish or converso origin.

Considering Portugal's small population (perhaps one million at the time that colonization of Brazil began), it was sometimes deemed more expedient to banish heretics to Brazil than to forbid their going there. At various times, New Christians were prohibited or encouraged to emigrate from Portugal, each change in law being accompanied by a demand for a heavy fine on "the descendants of the New Christians of the Hebrew Nation of Portugal." The Portuguese were, after all, simultaneously trying to hold down Goa, Macao, Ceylon, and Angola. The result of this colonial policy, compounded of equal parts venality, valor, and vacillation, was that quite a few cristãos novos were enlisted in the cause of empire. These included Fernão de Noronha, who was a knight of the royal household and probably a voluntary convert and who brought an entire company of conversos to settle the land granted him by the crown; João Ramalhô, notorious fifteenth-century castaway who, together with his multitudinous halfbreed offspring, eased Portuguese penetration of the continent; Gaspar da Gama, a Polish Jew captured by Muslim traders and converted to Islam, who became a counselor to the Arab ruler of Goa, was subsequently shanghaied and baptized a Christian by Vasco da Gama, and later served with Pedro Cabral on the expedition that discovered Brazil;[25] and Tiradentes, the Toothpuller, who was a precursor of Brazilian independence and who was hanged for treason in 1789.

A large proportion of the white population of Pernambuco in the sixteenth century were probably Judaizers. They practiced a wide range of occupations: owners and managers of sugar plantations and sugar mills, farmers, owners of boardinghouses. They had a synagogue (but probably no scrolls of the law) at Camaragibe. Apparently, many officials of the Catholic Church were conversos, as we know from the royal order prohibiting their assignment to Brazil.[26] Lay conversos were not barred from Brazil, but they remained subject to the Inquisition if they reverted to Judaism. Perhaps as a result of mixed motives, Brazil never had an autonomous office of the Inquisition; instead, inspectors were sent out to Brazil periodically, and suspects were remanded to Lisbon for trial. A nuanced study of converso intellectuals such as Bento Teixeira (1561–1600), author of the epic poem *Prosopopéia* (who wound up in an Inquisition prison); and Ambrosio Fernandes Brandão, author in 1618 of the *Diálogos das Grandezas do Brazil,* provides a novel insight into their mentality. Long dismissed as a poor imitation of Camões' *Os Lusíadas,* the *Prosopopéia* may be read as a call to fellow cristãos novos to resist Portuguese oppression.[27]

Records of the Inquisition's visitation to Brazil in 1618–19 show that many Brazilian conversos were Judaizing and were in touch with the openly professing Jews of Amsterdam. That city was then a world trade center, and the relative tolerance of Calvinism had attracted Spanish and Portuguese exiles to Holland. Some families had branches in both Holland and Brazil, a factor that fostered trade between the two countries and kept the crypto-Jews of Brazil in touch with the living body of Judaism.[28] Nevertheless, it must be said that Brazilian conversos made the voluntary decision to stay where they were and to continue living as Catholics, giving point to Cohen's observation that for some Sephardim, the choice of religion was situational.

A variety of adjustments were made by cristãos novos in Brazil. Perhaps none fitted into society as smoothly as those who lived in Bahia in the mid-seventeenth century. They comprised 20 percent of the white population of eight to ten thousand and attained positions of wealth and prestige at the core of society.[29] Twenty percent of conversos who were brought before the Inquisition were owners of sugar mills (senhores de engenhos) or merchants in the lucrative international sugar trade. Although the same laws of purity of blood that excluded conversos from public life in Portugal were supposed to prevail in Brazil as well, in fact cristãos novos served on the governing Câmara and held posts in government and administration.[30] A full 32 percent of cristãos novos who were haled before the Inquisition were practicing a profession—lawyer, solicitor, scribe, judge, treasurer, tax collector—all occupations forbidden to conversos. Ownership of land and slaves conferred status, and apparently anyone who could acquire the means to live like a lord (*fidalgo*) was allowed to become one—though again, conversos were not legally allowed to become fidalgos. Intermarriage with Old Christians followed as a matter of course.

The cristãos novos were aided in their effort to assimilate by the desperate need for European manpower in the face of Native Americans who died rather than submit to regimented labor and African slaves who died of too much regimented labor—at that time, the mill owners found it cheaper to replace slaves every seven years than to feed them adequately. The distance from the homeland and the size of the territory to be subdued placed a premium on European skills, which the Portuguese were loath to see go to waste. The converso who was despised at home automatically qualified on arrival in Brazil for a higher social status owing to his white skin and European upbringing. Why be a heretic, if one could be a lord?

The conversos, of course, were neither Jews nor foreigners, but baptized Portuguese. Having been brought up in the Catholic faith, neither they nor their parents had had contact with the living Jewish tradition. After the lapse of 150 years, they differed decisively from the Jewish people from whom they originated, even though some vestiges of "Jewish" behavior may have been retained.[31] Such a vestige might amount to no more than a futile gesture of protest, such as that of the senhor de engenho who caused to be placed in a shrine a statue of St. Teresa bearing the features of his own daughter who had been burned at the stake.

About 12 percent of cristãos novos in seventeenth-century Bahia were proletarian, including shoemakers, barbers, musicians, bakers, and sailors.[32] These tended to marry into the mixed castes and disappear from the record. The people most likely to run afoul of the Inquisition were the merchants and commercial travelers, who together made up 36 percent of the converso working population. Traveling between Brazil, Portugal, Holland, and the city of Hamburg (at the time a center for the international sugar trade), they might well have chosen to remain abroad beyond the clutches of the Inquisition. But even some of those who had been penanced preferred to return to their homes in Brazil rather than exile themselves in order to live as Jews.

In the second and third decades of the seventeenth century, the Dutch West India Company conquered the rich northeast coast of Brazil. They held onto Bahia for one year only, but retained Pernambuco, Recife, and Olinda for a quarter century. In each locale, the Dutch Reform Church was established, with a sometimes grudging grant of toleration to other religions. Thus it became possible for Brazilian crypto-Jews to move to Pernambuco or Recife and openly revert to Judaism. An unknown number, but not all, New Christians did exactly this (the Dutch destroyed their records before leaving Brazil). Those who were subsequently captured by the Portuguese were either hanged as traitors or sent to Lisbon for trial as heretics.[33] When the Portuguese reoccupied their coastal cities, Inquisitorial activity was renewed with a vengeance. Brazilian "heretics" (Jews who had been baptized but subsequently reverted to Judaism) were the staple participants in Portuguese autos-da-fé until 1769. During this period, probably four hundred conversos were tried and penanced; of these, eighteen were executed but only one was burned alive.

That one was Isaac de Castro Tartas, who went from Amsterdam to Dutch Brazil and then moved on to Portuguese Bahia. An enigmatic character, de Castro had a reputation as a brilliant scholar. A secret Jew, he adopted a Catholic lifestyle in Bahia but was arrested as a heretic and sent to Lisbon for trial. His defense was that he had never been baptized. (An unbaptized Jew was not a heretic, but a Jew, and beyond the jurisdiction of the Inquisition.) His inquisitors determined to their own satisfaction that he had been baptized, and he was burned alive for it on 14 December 1647.[34] The question of why a believing Jew would move from Dutch to Portuguese jurisdiction cannot be answered satisfactorily. Perhaps he was eluding the forces of justice in Holland; perhaps, as claimed by witnesses at his trial, he wished to spread Judaism among the New Christians of Bahia. If the latter, there is no record that he made any converts.

A great loss to Portuguese literature was sustained through the execution of Antonio José da Silva, a young law student who was on his way to becoming a major playwright. Author of fables, humorous poetry, and raunchy comedies, da Silva was burned at the stake on 19 October 1739 while one of his plays was being performed at a local theater.[35]

It was left to the clever Marquis de Pombal to suggest to King José I that the distinction between Old Christian and New be officially wiped out. The destruction of records in 1773 ended the ability of government or church to discriminate, made it impossible for historians to trace the descendants of Portuguese conversos, and achieved what the Inquisition had claimed it wanted to achieve all along: the disappearance of the Jews and their descendants from Portugal and from Brazil.

Overt Jewish Communities

Identifiable Jewish life appeared during the mid-seventeenth century in regions that were captured from the Spanish or Portuguese by non-Iberian powers. When the Dutch West India Company set its sights on the northeast coast of Brazil, Jews of Holland (some of them Portuguese by birth) participated as stockholders in planning the raids, went out with the expeditions as soldiers, and settled in the conquered areas.[36] How this invasion was viewed by New Christians living on the Brazilian coast became a tortured political question; at the time, the story was put about that the capture of Bahia was caused by New Christian treachery. To some, it seemed plausible that a Dutch invasion, bringing with it the promise of religious toleration, would be welcomed by the cristãos novos; the canard was enshrined in a play by Lope de Vega. But the charge was demolished three centuries later by the Brazilian historian Anita Novinsky, who has shown that cristãos novos living in Bahia participated in the defense of their own city and of Pernambuco against the marauding heretics and their Jewish allies. Their contributions in money, manpower, and leadership were in rough proportion to their weight in the population and the economy. Furthermore, of twenty-two persons denounced by contemporaries as Dutch collaborators, just six were cristãos novos. A decade later, an inquest aimed at identifying clergy who had crossed lines during the war turned up eight Catholic priests, forty-eight Old Christians, and twenty-four New Christians.[37] Evidently, people acted according to what they conceived to be their own interests, not some preconceived notion of what was required of them as a Catholic, a Jew, or a converso. This includes the bishop of Bahia, whose premature flight from the city triggered the panic that led to Bahia's fall. Internal criticism of the bishop by those who knew what had happened "was smothered under a blanket of more public praise for his actions and simultaneous condemnation of New Christian treason."[38]

Once the Dutch established a foothold on the Brazilian coast, this New Holland attracted settlers from the homeland, including Jews. One group of two hundred Jewish settlers came out from Amsterdam in 1642 under the leadership of Rabbi Isaac Aboab. Shortly thereafter, they were able to gain official permission to establish a synagogue in Recife. A synagogue opened in Mauricia, probably another in Paraíba, and services were conducted in private homes as well.[39]

A census of Dutch Brazil taken in 1645 showed a total population of 12,703, of whom 2,899 were free white civilians. Perhaps half of these were Jews.[40] Hostility toward them began to develop as commercial competition in the little outposts became keener. Also, as Portuguese and Dutch learned each other's language, middlemen were no longer so important. Calvinist preachers who had opposed toleration from the start repeatedly urged the governor to close the synagogues. But successive Dutch administrations, intent on maximizing profitable trade, safeguarded the religious rights of their Jewish subjects—subject to the hazards of war and diplomacy. When the Dutch were driven from the Brazilian coast by the Portuguese Brazilians in 1654, the Jews had to evacuate with them. One hundred and fifty Jewish families now returned to Amsterdam; others went elsewhere in the Caribbean; and twenty-three stragglers wound up in the port of New Amsterdam, where Governor Peter Stuyvesant reluctantly admitted them on orders from his stockholders back home. This group formed the first Jewish congregation on Manhattan Island. They named it, appropriately, Shearith Israel, the Remnant of Israel.[41]

The Dutch also captured Curaçao in 1634, and some Jewish refugees from Brazil headed for that island after a brief return to Amsterdam had confirmed their preference for tropical climes. Another contingent of twelve families tried to establish a Jewish farming colony on Curaçao. Failing, they turned to commerce.[42] Jews from Italy, Guadeloupe, Suriname, and Portugal also settled on this island, located conveniently offshore of Caracas, entrepôt for the introduction of contraband into the prohibited Spanish American market.[43] Thus, the first Jews to settle openly in the Western Hemisphere were Portuguese- and Spanish-speaking Sephardim.[44] In 1715 they probably accounted for 36 percent of the white population of Curaçao. Working as sailors, navigators, merchants, slavers, and pirates, they dominated the island's shipping.[45]

This was a tightly organized community, determined to retain its religious heritage and cultural identity intact. Endogamous marriage was strongly encouraged; aloofness between different segments of society guaranteed that Jewish weddings would take place in a synagogue and that the children would be raised as Jews.[46] Cousin marriage was a continuous feature of these matches, as it was for the Portuguese of Brazil and the Sephardim of New York.[47] Despite their economic integration, Jews were still being referred to by the Dutch government as "the Portuguese Nation" 150 years after their settlement on Curaçao. It was only after the Napoleonic emancipation that the Jews, newly eligible for appointment to government positions, switched from the Portuguese language to Dutch in their synagogue.[48]

From Amsterdam, Curaçao, and other Dutch-protected areas, Sephardic merchants fanned out to other Caribbean islands and contiguous areas of the mainland, especially Suriname, which in the eighteenth century was the premier Jewish settlement in the Americas and arguably the most privileged Jewish community in the world.[49] Some settled in the British Antilles, notably Jamaica, which came under British rule in Oliver Cromwell's time and thus is not usually included in the polymorphous term "Latin America." Other groups established themselves, at least for brief periods, on Barbados, St. Croix, Nevis, St. Thomas, and St. Kitts; in Panama and Costa Rica; in New York City and in Charleston, South Carolina. By actions of 17 July 1657 and 24 September 1658, the States General of Holland recognized the Jews as Dutch citizens and defended them as such when any were captured at sea by Spaniards.[50] This became an important factor in the ability of Jews to engage freely in trade and shipping in the Caribbean area. The French monarchy granted Jews the privilege of settling in lands under French dominion in a series of *lettres patentes* issued from the sixteenth through the eighteenth century. Consequently, there were Curaçaoan Jews to be found in Guadeloupe and Martinique (where Brazilian exiles gave a stimulus to sugar manufacture), the Mississippi territory, French Santo Domingo (Haiti), and the Dominican Republic, which latter territory Spain ceded to France in 1795.[51]

Sephardic immigrants to Santo Domingo were well received, and they acculturated quickly. Arriving mostly as commercial travelers for Curaçaoan firms, they became involved in the financing of Dominican political and military ventures, particularly the war of indepence from Haiti (1844). In a letter written in 1846, the president of the republic noted that the Jews attended church and made charitable contributions through ecclesiastical authorities while at the same time the church was praying for their conversion. That, concluded the president, would be achieved not by persecution but by sweet persuasion.[52] In the atmosphere of the republic, substantially *afrancesado* due to the period of French occupation, Masonic lodges provided a neutral meeting ground for Christians and Jews. The president and the Jewish merchant in whose defense he wrote his letter of toleration were lodge brothers. Accepted by society and prospering in trade, Jews married local women and raised their children as Catholics. As the president predicted, the conversion of the Jews took place through sweet persuasion, and their descendants are traceable among upper-class Dominican families today.[53]

In these outposts of empire, Jews, as whites, belonged partially to the upper class, separated from blacks by color and by legal status; but nowhere did they enjoy the same political and social acceptance as other members of white society.[54] Their demographic profile did not differ significantly from the demographics of non-Jews, as Robert Cohen has shown for the islands of Barbados, Jamaica, and Martinique. In the seventeenth century, all lives were grimly circumscribed by early death. Jews and non-Jews did differ, however, with respect to their long-term ambitions: wealthy non-Jewish merchants moved on to New England, planters to the Carolinas. Wealthy Jews tended to remain permanently on the islands; those who left "looked to the Old World" and—like the American Confederate Judah Benjamin—retired to London, then just becoming the hub of international commerce.[55]

Those who succeeded in establishing themselves under Dutch jurisdiction prospered as traders, middlemen, interpreters, and brokers of slaves. The Dutch West India Company monopolized the import of slaves, but private entrepreneurs ran the slave auctions. Among the latter were conversos, who also provided the credit that owners of sugar mills needed until the crop was brought in. In assuming the role of broker in the slave trade, Jews and conversos were operating within a system of international trade licensed by governments and sanctioned by the Catholic Church. Following Aristotelian thought, Catholics of the period accepted the division of humankind into superior and inferior races, the latter brought into being in order to serve the former. The Spanish, Portuguese, Dutch, French, and English governments all sold licenses (*asientos*) allowing entrepreneurs to engage in the transatlantic slave trade. The expensive license was eagerly sought after by traders, the great majority of whom were Old Christians. This ideological dehumanization presumably enabled slave traders to sleep at night.

Later generations, repelled by slavery, quite rightly condemn the system from which European wealth was generated. But within the context of their times, the New Christians and Jews who participated at the margins of the trade were operating within a system they had not created and which they had no power to change. The fact that the Catholic Church approved of slavery (indeed, itself owned slaves) and that governments licensed it cannot be used to demonstrate the moral depravity of particular individuals without demonstrating also the distance humankind has come in the past 300 years in recognizing the sacredness of all human life.

Many Sephardim who settled on Caribbean islands achieved substantial commercial success. This has been ascribed by Yosef Haim Yerushalmi to two major factors. The first of these was the maintenance of family ties between New Christians and avowed Jews; the second, that these family linkages facilitated access to mutually hostile areas of the colonial world, then being fought over by Spain, Portugal, Holland, and England:

> Within world Jewry from the sixteenth through the eighteenth centuries the Sephardic and Marrano diasporas constituted, in both a metaphoric and an actual sense, a huge extended family. Acutely conscious of sharing a common origin, historic fate, and collective identity, geographical distance alone could not loosen the close and intricate web of relationships that bound them together. Quite often these were real ties of blood and kinship. Within a given family some members might be living openly as Jews in Turkey and the Balkans, Italy and North Africa, while others were still "New Christians," whether believing Catholics or crypto-Jews, in the Iberian Peninsula, in the New World, or in Portuguese India. The links among them transcended all the religious and geopolitical boundaries that divided the Christian and Muslim worlds, or Protestant from Catholic countries. In this international solidarity lay at least one of the major sources of Sephardic mercantile success.[56]

Scattered as they had been by the hazards of expulsion, inquisition, and toleration, Sephardim grasped the opportunities for trade that were presented to them in the sixteenth century by the hostility between Christian Europe and the Ottoman Empire, and in the seventeenth century by the Dutch challenge to the Spanish/Portuguese hegemony in the New World.[57] The family linkages among Sephardim (of all religions or none) enabled them to navigate treacherous political currents to emerge as successful merchants at a time when international trade was still trammeled by the mercantilist policies of the great powers. Naturally, there was from time to time a price to be paid: Jews of St. Eustatius were banished and their property confiscated because they forwarded supplies to the American patriots during the War of Independence against Britain.[58]

Latin America Achieves Independence

Jews remained hesitant to enter Spanish America proper, even after attainment of independence in the first quarter of the nineteenth century. There existed for some years the real possibility of a Spanish intervention to regain control of the chaotic republics, in which case the Inquisition might have been reinstituted, as had been the case when the Portuguese retook the Brazilian coast from the Dutch. The independent governments moved with more or less deliberation to abolish the office of the Inquisition within their own boundaries, but it was more difficult to abolish the Inquisition mentality, which had had free rein in the dependencies for four centuries. What was abolished was the institutionalization of limpieza, the legal qualification for permanent residence and for holding office. Also abolished was the incitement to denunciation that the Inquisition had provided by rewarding informers with a percentage of the property taken from those they denounced. What remained was the stigma, embedded in the very language people spoke. Some usages that remain common in Spanish today include *judío* to mean a miser, *hebreo* as a synonym for usurer, *Cohen* to mean a sorcerer or a bawd, and *sinagoga* to imply a conspiracy.[59] In similar vein, the *Pequeno Dicionário Brasileiro da Lingua Portuguêsa* defines *Judeu* as "Homem mau, individuo avarento ou negocista" [an evil man, avaricious person, one given to sharp practices]. The Portuguese-English Dictionary published by Stanford University Press defines *Judeu* simply as "Jew."

The Christian legend on which Iberian society had based its drive for purification was that there existed two inexorable enemies of Christ: the devil and the Jews.[60] Inevitably, it was assumed there was an alliance between the two. This ancient legend, transmitted to Latin America by missionaries sent to evangelize the Native Americans, was imposed upon pagans who had never seen a Jew, producing a situation where the concepts "judío" and "diablo" came to be synonyms.[61] European-derived peoples may be aware of countervailing, pro-Judaic legends, but in Mexican villages today, Easter continues to feature ritualized warfare between the forces of light and the forces of darkness, the latter personified by nude men painted as devils, who are called, plainly enough, "judíos."

The standard term for "Jew" in government documents in modern times is *israelita,* a term that is regarded by some as a circumlocution comparable to the old-fashioned use of "Hebrew" in the United States; this term, too, is pejorative in Central America. In Peru, "the word Jew has been considered an insult," said the president of the Zionist Federation in 1974. "We therefore avoid the word Jew in public and use instead the term Israelite." Shortly thereafter, the Jewish community of Peru let it be known that they preferred *judío* after all to avoid unfortunate confusion between Peruvian Jews and citizens of Israel. The confusion reflects the public's continuing hesitation, if not aversion, to addressing fellow citizens who are Jews.

As the nineteenth century progressed, Sephardic merchants moved outward from their homes in Curaçao, Suriname, Jamaica, Barbados, and other portions of the Antilles into other Caribbean islands and the countries of the Spanish Main. Surprisingly, a few individual traders and even some families of Curaçaoan Jews took up residence in two dozen Venezuelan towns in the mid-nineteenth century. Five Colombian locations can also be documented.[62] Many of these Sephardim intermarried, passing along their characteristic names to their Catholic descendants. Sephardic peregrinations were premodern in the sense that they constituted a mobile merchant class at home anywhere in the Caribbean; they retained their ties to Curaçao, returning there to marry or to die. Because of the number of males who married abroad, a surplus of unmarried Sephardic women remained on the island. This was one factor that kept the size of the mother community small; it numbered no more than a thousand at its height.[63] Folklore identifies Portuguese Sephardim as the founders of most contemporary Latin American Jewish communities. This is probably true for the circum-Caribbean. Their numbers were never sufficient, however, to sustain the omnipresence attributed to them.

Folklore has it that Marranos who survived the colonial period were the progenitors of contemporary Jewish communities. This is not in fact the case. Descendants of those who were not killed may well have survived physically, some even with memories of Jewish tradition, however distorted by the secrecy imposed upon them. But they survived as Catholics. A case in point is the family of Juan López, burned at the stake in Lisbon for Judaizing. His family fled first to Valladolid, Spain, and then to Tucumán in present-day Argentina, where his son, Diego López de Lisboa, became *regidor del cabildo,* or secretary to the town. Diego ultimately became chaplain and majordomo to the archbishop of Lima, Fernando Arías de Ugarte. One of his sons, Diego de León Pinelo, became rector of the University of San Marcos in that city. Another son, Antonio de León Pinelo, became *procurador* of Buenos Aires in 1621 and later was chosen to compile the official registry of all the laws of the Indies. There is no way the crown or the church would have tolerated in positions of trust these men, who were known to be New Christians, had their Catholic faith been in any doubt whatever. In 1650, Antonio completed his masterwork, *El paraíso en el nuevo mundo* (Paradise in the New World), in which he proved from the writings of ancient church fathers that the Garden of Eden is located on the banks of the Marañon, near the region of Iquitos.[64] For the Pinelos at least, the statement was true.

Contemporary Latin American Jews are the product of nineteenth- and twentieth-century migrations. The intermittent retrieval of Jewish ritual articles from forgotten corners of grandparents' homes have fed stories of a continuing Marrano presence; but these family heirlooms are often found to be memorabilia of nineteenth-century immigrants who discovered that discretion was the better part of valor, yet who hesitated to throw away the candelabra and the ram's horns that symbolized their tradition. Consequent on the activities of the Inquisition and relentless pursuit of the chimera of clean blood, all overt manifestations of a Jewish presence had been extinguished by the time the immigrants arrived.

As victims of Spanish bigotry, Jews always attracted the sympathy of anti-Spanish and anticlerical factions. Individuals in revolt against their peninsular heritage and seeking to escape the subordinate status decreed by their Native American heritage may fashion themselves a new identity through activating their empathy with others who suffered at the hands of their common fatherland. For example, it is customary to observe that El Inca Garcilaso de la Vega, son of a Spanish conquistador and an Inca princess who was set aside in favor of a Spanish wife, came to terms with his ambiguous heritage by writing the monumental *Royal Commentaries of the Inca.* But Garcilaso's first published work was a translation from Italian into Spanish of the *Dialoghi d'Amore,* a book by the platonic philosopher Leon Hebreo, né Judah Abravanel, a Spanish Jew whose family had been expelled from Spain in 1492. The young José Martí, later to become the liberator of Cuba, wrung from the University of Saragossa the right to offer Hebrew as his foreign language. There is a persistent story that descendants of conversos still living in Spain in the nineteenth century lent their talents and their fortunes to the achievement of Cuban independence.

The theme of the Jew who is not a Jew, the Catholic who is not that either, is woven throughout Latin American history. At the end of the seventeenth century, one would have been hard put to distinguish New Christian from Old, due to intermarriage, disappearance beyond the frontier, and destruction of records. But even after the Inquisition ceased to function, the possibility that some people possessed a secret dual identity fostered suspicion. Throughout Latin America, aspiration to public office was certain to trigger an inquiry into one's limpieza, and no one could be sure what a thorough investigation of his lineage might turn up. The charge of racial impurity was viewed as a valid political ploy, and it retained its sting through the twentieth century.[65]

By the time independence had been achieved all across the continent, Marranos, conversos, cristãos novos, and "Portuguese" all were passing into the realm of mythology from which historians are only now rescuing them. But the era left a distinctive heritage. No Jew would henceforth enter the Spanish- and Portuguese-speaking republics without being aware of what had happened here in the past. The new republics would have to achieve independence, not just from Spain and Portugal but from the temporal power of the Catholic Church, before Jewish immigrants would be attracted to their shores. And when the match had been made once more between the Jewish and Iberian cultures, the nature of the relationship would be colored ineluctably by what had gone before.

Jews declared Spain anathema after the Expulsion, vowing never to return to the land that had treated them so hardly. Conversos, for their part, made so profound an identification with the majority population that they disappeared as a separate entity—though handfuls of them are now emerging from underground to reveal their distinctive mix of Catholic and Jewish customs. The name "Marrano," intended to be pejorative, took on overtones of undying loyalty to the Jewish people, which, of course, was the very essence of the Inquisition charge against them.

How much of this ambiguity would be transferred to American lands of Iberian culture? How closely would prospective immigrants identify contemporary Argentina or Mexico or Peru with the actions and attitudes of the Spanish Inquisition? Did fear of a recurrence of religious fanaticism deter potential Jewish immigrants? Obviously, the motivations of all immigrants to the New World cannot be divined. We know that many were seeking religious freedom. What can be said with certainty is that very few Jews settled in Latin America during the first century of that continent's independence.

PART TWO

THE IMMIGRATION YEARS

CHAPTER 2

The First Jewish Immigrants to the Independent Republics, 1830–1889

As Argentina opened its doors to immigration for the first time, its readiness to receive Jewish immigrants exceeded by far the interest of Jews in settling there.

—Haim Avni

JEWS COULD NOT have settled in the Latin American republics had not radical changes overtaken the colonies on their road from dependence to autonomy. These changes legitimated the presence of Jews, yet never led to rejection of the belief system that had formerly mandated their exclusion. Consequently, the life of Jews of the Latin American republics moves in a different context from the life of Jews in the Spanish and Portuguese dependencies; but it is a context shaped by ideas rooted in the earlier era.

Immigration Debates: Tradition versus Modernization

The exclusivism of Spanish and Portuguese rule and the desire either to sustain or to reject it was the starting point for both proponents and opponents of immigration. The merits and drawbacks of recruiting European immigrants were debated all over the continent in the middle decades of the nineteenth century, and always the touchstone was the preexisting value system and whether to retain or to modify it. Certain central issues, overlapping but with differences of nuance, surfaced at slightly different times and in somewhat different terms in each of the republics. But wherever they were debated, the attitudes expressed by legislators, journalists, and molders of public opinion helped determine the type of legislation that would be passed and therefore determined also the type of immigrant the country would eventually receive. Viewed with hindsight, it is clear that the attitudes expressed during the debates over immigration spelled out the limits of accommodation the republics would be willing to offer their immigrants.

The debates centered on certain universal themes that appeared in precincts of the continent that were quite unlike one another in other respects: (a) the need to break the Catholic monopoly of faith in order to attract new immigrants (preferably from northern Europe) versus the desire to retain a Catholic standard that was intrinsic to the way of life of the elite and that many did not desire to see changed; (b) the desire for large-scale immigration of farm and factory hands for the purpose of supplying a reservoir of labor, its wages continually depressed by the arrival of new boatloads of the unemployed, versus the fear that large cohorts of immigrants would make economic and social demands that would destabilize society; (c) the hope that European immigration would provide the impetus for modernization of the economies versus the fear that introduction of modernizing elements would upset existing social arrangements; (d) the desire to remake the nation biologically, to "regenerate the race" by large-scale interbreeding with Europeans, versus the fear that large, unassimilated groups of aliens would impede formation of a firm national identity in the infant republics. Economic growth was desired by all, but the prospect of social change was problematic.

The dialectic of the immigration debate was drawn from the social philosophy of positivism, which came increasingly into vogue in Latin America of the nineteenth century. An outgrowth of the rationalist philosophy of Auguste Comte, positivism in its Latin American manifestation held that scientific observation of society could yield knowledge of the laws that governed it. These laws, which were objectively verifiable, could be manipulated for the betterment of mankind, leading to material and moral progress somewhat along utilitarian lines of "the greatest good for the greatest number." Good government consisted of developing economic and social policies in conformity with proven principles.[1] In combination with economic liberalism, positivism came to imply support for policies calculated to increase the international mobility of labor, investment capital, and entrepreneurial skills. It was increasingly urged that these commodities be imported from Europe in order to initiate economic development in the young Latin American republics.

All of these trends did not appear full-blown or simultaneously in all precincts of the continent, but many educated Latin Americans saw in positivism a means of attaining their intellectual emancipation, of choosing a rational vision of the world to replace the old one, which had been based on faith and a hierarchical vision of world order. As national polities and problems varied, so versions of positivism varied as between Argentina and Mexico, Brazil and

Cuba. Nevertheless, varieties of positivism became the dominant philosophy of governing elites in the latter half of the nineteenth century.

What type of immigrant should Latin America recruit? In contemporary terms, all races were not created equal. The white lineage of the upper classes was more highly prized than the Indian, African, and mixed blood of the lower classes. In fact, the kindest thing one could do for the dark-skinned poor was to whiten them.[2] Mestizos were commonly regarded as inferior to their criollo fathers; nevertheless, over the course of time it should be possible to create a new and superior race if only enough immigrants could be persuaded to lend themselves to the operation. A subtheme in the immigration literature was the comparative value of different ethnic groups (usually referred to as "races") as whitening agents. Some preferred Anglo-Saxons and Germans, believing them to have a superior work ethic; others opted for Spaniards and Italians, who as Catholics and Latins were less likely to disrupt existing institutions.

During the last quarter of the nineteenth century, race came increasingly to be discussed in Social Darwinist terms, following the teachings of such "scientific" racists as Joseph Arthur de Gobineau, Houston Chamberlain, and Gustave Le Bon. As might be expected, the propagation of racist ideas had a deleterious effect upon the image of the Jew. That these ideas were not indigenous to Latin America but imported from Europe is suggested by their prevalence in the most Europeanized of the republics, Argentina and Chile. The same intellectuals who idealized the English, the German, the Italian, or the Spaniard tended to regard the Syrian, Jewish, or Asian immigrant with disgust. The latter were frequently characterized by the press as immoral, slothful, and diseased. Biologically degenerate, they could contribute little to the task of upgrading the mestizo "race."[3] Attitudes toward Jews in modern times are complex, ambiguous, and partially determined by the ethnic makeup of the specific republic under consideration. Not surprisingly, however, the ancient doctrine of limpieza de sangre resonates through modern racist theories. As in the case of those other New Christians, the Native Americans, the status of contemporary Jews is closely linked to the Conquest period.[4]

Sources of Jewish Immigration—Why They Migrated

Jewish migration to the Western Hemisphere in modern times originated in nineteenth-century Europe. It was part of that great river of humanity which flowed from east to west impelled by the three titanic forces let loose by the Napoleonic wars: nationalism, industrialism, and democracy. This migratory movement was by far the most encompassing mankind had experienced to that date. It was motivated by an unparalleled increase in population, the advance of industrial capitalism, and ethnic rivalries intensified by economic competition. These forces caused millions of persons to abandon irrevocably their homes in Europe or the Near East, taking their families and their possessions with them as they left the Old World in search of a new.

Among these immigrants, the Jews—advance scouts of urbanization and industrialization and among the first casualties of the new social arrangements these forces engendered—figured in numbers far greater than their proportion to the general population. Jacob Lestschinsky has documented the intensity of Jewish migration:

> Of sixty-five million people who emigrated from Europe in a century and a half, about four million were Jews. This represents about 6 percent of the entire emigration from Europe. The percentage of Jews in Europe at the beginning of the nineteenth century was not more than 1½, never more than 2. The intensity of Jewish emigration was, therefore, three to four times as great as that of the general emigration from Europe. If we consider only those sections of Europe from which Jews emigrated, i.e., middle, eastern and southern Europe, the intensity of Jewish emigration is not three to four times, but six to seven times as great as that of the general emigration.[5]

High birth rates and declining death rates caused Jewish, as other, populations to increase despite the export of large numbers to the New World. Within the time span 1881 to 1939, Arthur Ruppin estimates that as many as five million Jews took part in international migrations, compared with the estimated world Jewish population of 7,650,000 at the beginning of this period. From two to three hundred thousand of these migrants were Sephardim who originated in the Middle East and North Africa. Mass migration converted Jews from a European to an American people. Whereas 72 percent of world Jewry had lived in East Europe in 1850, the ratio of Jews in East Europe to world Jewry was diminished by 1939 to 44.9 percent. Transit in and out of western and central Europe left those areas possessed of a constant 14 percent of world Jewry. But the 1.5 percent who lived in the Americas in 1850 had increased to 33.4 percent of the total by 1939.[6]

The impetus for large-scale migration was the lag between industrialization and the increase in population: people were increasing faster than the capacity of industry to absorb them. This process, which impelled Jews and non-Jews out of Europe in unprecedented numbers, worked itself out differently for the two groups. Among Gentiles, agricultural laborers and unskilled workers who could not be absorbed into the cities predominated. Among Jews, those who emigrated were mostly urbanized and engaged in urban or semiurban occupations as a consequence of having been forbidden to own land. With the rise of new semiurban elements, efforts were made to expel Jews from their urban occupations through the use of terror, much of it government-sponsored. Jewish migration had a dual motivation: economic necessity and the need to find new homes where their fundamental human rights would be secure.

Jewish intercontinental migration exhibited extremely complex patterns. The annual migratory flow waxed with the pressures placed upon Jews in their homelands and waned with the barriers placed in the way of their admittance to other countries. But Jewish migration may be divided, in rough and ready terms, into three periods.[7] These refer not only to dates but to the countries of origin of the immigrants. There is overlap, as well as gaps, between categories. Any periodization tailored to the larger Ashkenazic immigration will not totally suit the Sephardic. Nevertheless, the periods reflect not only changes in the origins of the immigrants, but meaningful periods in the history of the Latin American republics. Some notice of these periods will enable the reader to relate Jewish migration to Latin America with events taking place on that continent and worldwide.

The first European migratory wave (1830s–80s) consisted of German and French Jews. The ending of the Napoleonic wars had engendered a reactionary political current in Europe, reversing the trend toward greater civil rights for Jews that had been a product of the French Revolution. Hundreds of Jews took flight to ports in Holland, from which they embarked for the New World. Most headed for the United States, but some went to England and France. Still others took ship for ports in Brazil, Argentina, Colombia, Mexico, and Santo Domingo.[8] The pace of this emigration quickened after 1830, when industrial revolution and agrarian crisis brought starvation and dislocation to peasants and artisans, stimulating mass general emigration from Germany. Among the rest, some fifty thousand Jews (chiefly from the regions of Bavaria, Bohemia, and Posen) left Germany between the years 1830 and 1870. Only a small fraction of these headed for Latin America. Moroccan Jews, displaced by the Spanish-Moroccan wars of 1859–60, found their way to Brazil and Argentina in the following decades. Native speakers of Spanish, many had been educated in the French-language schools of the Alliance Israélite Universelle (AIU), where they imbibed a progressive spirit that may have fortified their interest in leaving their tradition-bound societies to try their luck in the New World.[9]

These migratory movements took place in the early decades of Latin American independence (nominally won between 1810 and 1824). Throughout the middle decades of the century, the new republics struggled to define their boundaries and their identities. To a certain extent, the debate over immigration policy catalyzed attitudes toward the condition of being Latin American. Acceptance or rejection of immigrants, or of certain categories of them, would become indicators of society's capacity to absorb them. Policies developed during the debates would set the stage for the reception of immigrants at least up until World War I.

Numerically, Jewish immigration during this period was scant; but its importance was not negligible. These were the immigrants who tested the conditions for Jewish life on the continent and who ascertained that there was a possibility—at times precarious—for the settlement of Jews in larger numbers. Furthermore, individual Jews played a role in the early economic development of Argentina, Chile, Mexico, Brazil, Peru, and Guatemala.

Where They Went

Argentina

During the first decades of Argentine independence, immigration was a point of contention between men of the Enlightenment and those who continued to function within a Spanish Catholic culture that did not agree to the proposition that other religions might be equally authentic. The forces for modernization, which favored lifting religious restrictions so as to facilitate immigration, won legal decisions that were not always put into practice because of the resistance offered by elements within Argentine society that were still tied morally and mentally to the old regime.

As an example of this discrepancy between word and deed, brought about by a real incapacity of these divergent forces to agree, a decree of the revolutionary government of 1810 may be cited: "English, Portuguese, and other foreigners who are not at war with us, can move to this country and will enjoy all rights of citizenship; and those who dedicate themselves to crafts and the cultivation of the countryside will be protected by the government."[10] At the time of this proclamation, the Inquisition still sat in Buenos Aires. Even after it was dissolved, in March 1813, its orders continued to be published from Madrid or Lima.

Many Argentines were comfortable with an inquisitorial mindset. In 1825, a treaty between the federal government of Argentina and the British government provided for, inter alia, freedom of religion for British subjects. The treaty failed of ratification in all the Argentine provinces, which at that date exercised considerable autonomy. Only in the province of Buenos Aires, where most British residents were concentrated, was enabling legislation passed. The right of religious dissidents to marry was won only after a long struggle. An 1814 law had provided that "authorities would give special consideration in marriage to increase the population," but it remained virtually impossible for a non-Catholic to marry save in a Catholic ceremony. After 1825, the right of dissidents to marry could be pressed under provisions of the treaty with Great Britain, but only in the province of Buenos Aires.[11] In short, few fundamental changes in the closed Spanish system were introduced during the first decades of independence. Cultural exclusivism and xenophobia characterized the country through the Rosas period (1835–52).

Following the battle of Monte Caseros, which brought down the dictatorship of Juan Manuel de Rosas, the policy of religious and national exclusivism that had tied the country to Spanish colonialism was discontinued. Immigration became a function of the Argentine state as a result of a conscious effort on the part of some sectors of the elite to replace the old inherited social structure with a model inspired by more modernized societies. Many of their ideas derived from the writings of Juan Bautista Alberdi (1810–84), who believed that Argentina would make no progress in the modern world as long as her interior provinces remained unpeopled. Popularized by the slogan *gobernar es poblar* (to govern is to populate), Alberdi's policy stressed the need "to make inviolable the mixed marriages which are the means for natural formation of the family in our America, called to populate itself with foreigners."[12]

Although Alberdi no doubt had Protestant immigration in mind, certain constitutional clauses that resulted laid the legal basis for the immigration of Jews. The constitution gave support to Roman Catholicism, but did not establish it: Article 19 stated that "private actions of men which do not offend order and public morality nor prejudice a third party, are reserved to God and are beyond authority of magistrates." There was not, however, a complete separation of church and state: Article 76 provided that the president and vice-president had to be communicants of the Roman Catholic Church. This provision was not removed from the constitution until 1994.

These constitutional provisions, which represent a compromise between traditional and enlightened views, did not completely resolve the issue of religious liberty. Approval of a system of state education in 1884 and of a civil register for marriage in 1888 led to a break with the Vatican. Meanwhile, until the coming into force of the latter legislation, the basic civil liberties of non-Catholics relating to birth, marriage, and death continued to be governed by laws formulated during the reactionary era of Rosas.[13]

Liberal economics provided the substructure for proimmigration views. Many members of the ruling elite believed that prosperity depended on the free movement worldwide of manpower, goods, and capital. It was particularly important that large numbers of foreign workers be brought in. "Increased population, economists . . . repeated, would stimulate expansion of the export industries, whose growth was often made synonymous with economic development."[14]

The specific economic interests that supported liberal immigration policies included most prominently the landed elite, who, according to Solberg, "were convinced that prosperity and growth required a steady flow of cheap labor. They expected, moreover, the European laborers to form a large, servile working class that would augment upper-class wealth but would not challenge the prevailing social hierarchy or distribution of economic power."[15]

Argentine expectations concerning immigrants focused upon the need for *brazos*—"arms," or farm and ranch hands. An instrumental view of the immigrants' utility to the Argentine economy pervades debates and polemics throughout the nineteenth century. Writing as late as 1909, the Argentine director of immigration recommends excluding would-be immigrants who are missing their right arm.[16] In context, this injunction clarifies the relationship between "immigrant" and "brazo."

Although the Argentine government paternalistically provided temporary housing and free transport to work areas for all "honest immigrants," they made no move to accommodate the whole human being. Specifically, no legislation was passed to alter patterns of land tenure so as to satisfy the brazos' inevitable demand for land of their own. In fact, in the very same year the basic immigration legislation was passed, 1876, there was also passed the first law of lands and colonies, which permitted land to be sold in lots of eighty thousand hectares. The result was to increase the concentration of land ownership and make it more difficult than before for a poor family to buy land of their own.

In addition to the liberal economic views that prompted many Argentines to support free immigration, there was the motive of "regenerating the race."

In this phrase, Argentine *pensador,* educator, and statesman D. F. Sarmiento (1911–84) summed up his opinion of Argentina's gaucho population and his expectations of the immigrants. Sarmiento hoped to eradicate the violent and nonproductive lifestyle of the gaucho by inundating the pampas with European immigrants. The latter, with their settled habits of work and modern technology, would soon turn the "desert" into productive fields. Not only would the immigrants foment economic development, but they would also spread modern European civilization throughout Argentina. Many intellectuals prior to 1905 were reacting against what they regarded as the superstition and fanaticism of the Spanish church and state, which had held sway in Argentina for three centuries. The only way to extirpate these traits from the national character was to introduce masses of Europeans who would bring with them the sweet reason of contemporary civilization.[17]

Despite the contemporary view of this policy as cosmopolitan, it was in essence racist, premised as it was upon the inferiority of people of mixed blood (and failure to recognize that centuries of warfare and reciprocal invasion had mixed Europeans' "blood" as well). Pseudoscientific racial theories that classified nonwhites as biologically inferior met a sympathetic response from the criollo upper classes, who had come into their privileged position by defeating the Indian on the battlefield and in the church. Such hopeless human material could only be improved through mass interbreeding with European immigrants, preferably those drawn from northern Europe, Spain, or Italy, homes of virile "races" of supposedly unmixed blood.

It would be interesting to speculate on the origins of this race hatred. Did it represent a displacement of the contempt peninsular Spaniards had long directed toward criollos? Were criollos objectifying in the gaucho the mestizo element in their own heredity that had caused them to be so depreciated? Or did concepts of limpieza de sangre, elaborated upon at such length with respect to Jews and Moors, provide a model for the treatment of other "races" whose ancestors had not been Christians? Whatever the psychological mechanism, the fact is that racial and economic rationales became intertwined.

Argentina in fact attracted enormous numbers of immigrants. The total has been calculated at 6,500,000 for the years 1857–1965, counting returnees; or 4,379,000 if only those are counted who remained.[18] These were poured over a base population of 1,200,000. For decades, foreigners made up almost 70 percent of the population of Buenos Aires (where up to a third of the entire population was concentrated). At the same time, almost half of the population of the provinces of greatest economic and demographic weight was also composed of the foreign-born.

These foreigners came not from northern Europe, as the enlightened faction had hoped, but from southern and eastern Europe, where the impact of the industrial revolution was just beginning to be felt. Northerners, already conditioned to industry, tended to choose the United States, both because of its higher level of industrialization and because there were elements of cultural affiliation dating back to the colonial period. During the mass exodus of northern Europeans, Argentina had been closed to immigration. Now the southern Europeans were being displaced by the industrialization process and accompanying population growth. Their linguistic and cultural affinity, as well as the long colonial relationship, encouraged them to choose Argentina.[19] In the century following the fall of Rosas, almost half the immigrants to Argentina were Italian; one-third were Spanish; about one-fifth consisted of Poles, Russians, French, and Germans, with Jews among the latter grouping.[20]

It is apparent that the first half-century of independence did not produce a climate favorable to Jewish immigration. In the absence of legal provisions for marriage or burial within their faith, few Jewish families were susceptible to the lure of Argentina. Various single men are known to have migrated, and these exercised the options of bachelorhood, remigration to Europe, or marriage to local women in Catholic ceremonies, followed by the raising of their children as Catholics. Some of these men rejoined the synagogue on the death of their wives. Case histories of all these patterns have been documented.[21]

The record of the birth of a child in Buenos Aires in the year 1835, to a Jewish father whose family stemmed from the province of Lorraine, provides the first—and characteristically ambiguous—trace of Argentine Jewry. Because it is not known whether the child's mother was a Jew, the child's own Jewish status is in doubt under prevailing religious standards. Sometime before 1844, one Henry Hart, an English Jew, migrated to Buenos Aires, where he entered trade and joined the organization that later came to be the Club de Residentes Extranjeros, a group whose membership included foreign merchants, stockbrokers, and persons involved in the development of Argentine railroads and the meat-packing industry. In the decade of the fifties, other Jews from England, France, Germany, and Alsace arrived in Argentina, where they entered various commercial activities.

In 1860, the first two Jewish weddings were authorized by Argentine authorities, and this date may be set for the origins of a Jewish community. Interestingly, the lawyer who pleaded the case on behalf of the prospective brides and grooms was a conservative Catholic who opposed civil marriage and believed that extending the right of religious marriage to dissidents was necessary in order to stave off the greater evil. Records of the wedding of the two Levy sisters reveal an extended kinship grouping with links to the areas of Lyon, Alsace, and the Rhineland. These connections define the most significant body of Jewish immigrants to Argentina before 1889.[22] The origins of early Jewish immigrants are confirmed by records of the Congregación Israelita, the earliest of which date from 1873. Sixteen of the Congregación's twenty founding members have been identified. They include persons born in Germany, England, Alsace, and Romania. Only one was a Sephardi, belonging to a Portuguese family that had settled in Hamburg.[23] In the seventies and eighties, several Moroccan Jews joined the Congregación; but by 1891, unable to agree on ritual matters and preferring to socialize among their own, they formed the Congregación Israelita Latina, adopting the Spanish and Portuguese rite.[24]

In the last decades of the nineteenth century, Moroccan Jews began to arrive, mostly from Tetuán, as well as Sephardim from Gibraltar. These merchants relocated frequently between Brazil and Argentina, depending on the business climate. Unlike the European Jews who favored the large cities, Sephardim were more likely to settle in the interior; in 1905, the director of a JCA (Jewish Colonization Association) school counted 3,000 Sephardim in Argentina, only 750 of whom lived in Buenos Aires. In this same period, Aleppine Jews were settling the Once district of Buenos Aires, while Jews from Damascus clustered in Boca and Barracas, predominantly Genoese areas of the city.[25]

Eighty-five percent of Buenos Aires Jews in this period were engaged in retail merchandising, as they had been in their native cities. They owned small shops that sold European imports; or they represented European firms, sometimes owned by relatives; or they established an Argentine branch of a London or Paris shop. They concentrated in jewelry, books, clothing, and household items, particularly china and porcelain. A few were high financiers and real estate brokers, and some owned real estate in the central core of the capital or in provincial centers. Although the professions were crowded with foreigners in mid-nineteenth century, Argentina's Jews seem to have figured among them in numbers less than their proportion to the general population.

A singularly romantic figure of the 1880s was Julio Popper, Bucharest-born adventurer, explorer, and publicist, who undertook a number of explorations through Tierra del Fuego. A mining engineer by profession, Popper prospected for gold but had uneven luck with the eighty thousand hectares of land and eighteen mines he owned at his death. Though he was lionized by Buenos Aires society, his reputation outran his luck; his debts outweighed his assets when death (possibly with the assistance of some mortal hand) took him at age thirty-six.[26] Popper was born a Jew but took no part in the affairs of the Buenos Aires Jewish community, which was being organized during his active years. His brother Max, who for a while supervised the Popper operation in Tierra del Fuego and who died there of tuberculosis at the age of twenty-six, was a member of the Congregación.

Though the rhetoric of the immigration debate had emphasized the need for large numbers of immigrants, foreigners continued to be the object of nativist suspicion. These fears created great social tension, as one-quarter of the persons in the country in 1895 (1,004,527 out of 3,954,911) were foreign-born. Among these were just 6,085 israelitas. Ethnocentrism manifested itself in the slow pace at which the Catholic monopoly of civil matters dissipated, despite legislation intended to accord religious toleration. Even the provincial government of Buenos Aires, the most progressive of the provinces, never activated provisions of an 1833 law providing for the registration of births, deaths, and marriages in non-Catholic families. As late as 1877, a Jew brought a case before the Superior Tribunal de Justicia in an effort to force the registration of the birth of his children, without baptism. Only after the victory of secularist forces in 1888 was the way cleared for mass Jewish immigration into

Argentina. Even so, the motive power of czarist oppression was required to get many Jews to settle in Argentina.

Chile

Many of the forces propelling Chile toward a proimmigration policy were similar to those at work in Argentina: the need for a larger work force; the belief that the European was genetically superior to the mestizo; and the theory that prosperity was a function of the free flow of capital and labor across international boundaries. There were two outstanding differences in the respective situations of the two countries. Chile's greater distance from world trade routes resulted in a smaller and tardier flow of immigrants. In the year 1895, Chile received just 665 immigrants to Argentina's 44,169, and in that year the proportion of foreign-born living in Chile was just 2.9 percent as compared with Argentina's 25.4 percent.[27] Furthermore, Chile industrialized at a faster pace than did Argentina. Large landowners were not as powerful a class in Chile as they were in the neighboring country, and the primary impetus for recruitment of immigrant labor came not from *hacendados* and *rancheros* but from industrialists and mining entrepreneurs. But Chileans looked down upon the *inquilino* (mestizo peon) with the same disdain with which Argentines viewed the gaucho. And the solution was the same as that sought by the Argentines: import a European work force that was already educated, habituated to industrial labor, and racially superior to the mestizo.

The first Jew, or descendant of Jews, who can be identified in nineteenth-century Chile is Stefan Goldsack, an engineer who was engaged in England by the diplomatic agent of Lord Cochrane, naval hero of the Chilean war of independence. Goldsack had worked in Woolwich with the inventor of a rocket that was put to use by the British navy in its wars against the French; he was charged with transferring the technique to the Chilean navy, which he did with little success, possibly owing to the Chilean government's having employed Spanish prisoners of war in its manufacture.[28]

Arrivals in Chile increased during the California gold rush, when traffic along the west coast of the two continents generally increased. The Jewish immigrants of the fifties and sixties came mostly from Germany and France, and they settled in a range of towns from Copiapó, capital of the northern mining district of Atacama, to Traiguen in the south. Some Jews established themselves in the German colonies that took root in the south of Chile; others were attracted to the mining industry of the north. Most, however, settled in Valparaíso, which had the largest foreign colony of any city in Chile.

Sephardim came to Chile in family groups from Smyrna, Istanbul, Monastir, and Salonika, extruded from their ancient homes by a combination of economic and discriminatory measures. Most settled in Valparaíso, where they were joined by individuals from Jerusalem, Damascus, Beirut, and islands of the Aegean. Although they organized their own institutions at first, their small numbers led quickly to intermarriage with Ashkenazim and the formation of unified houses of worship.[29]

The presence of Ashkenazim can be traced through records of the various German clubs that sprang up all over Chile, the first of which was the Club Alemán de Valparaíso, founded in 1838 by a group of German expatriates including both Christians and Jews, as well as in the records of the companies of volunteer firemen, the first of which was founded in Valparaíso in 1850, after fire had destroyed a part of that city. The records of the customs house, combined with advertisements in Valparaíso newspapers, reveal the presence of increasing numbers of Jewish retail store owners, particularly in ready-to-wear clothing.

An interesting figure of this period is Manuel de Lima y Sola, born in 1818 in Curaçao. Following the Curaçaoan pattern of bachelor migration, de Lima settled first in Caracas, then in Hamburg, and ultimately in Valparaíso, where he and several partners opened an import house. In Valparaíso, de Lima joined an already existing lodge of French Masons that met under the name Etoile du Pacifique. Becoming conscious of the need for a lodge where no language barrier hindered the admittance of Chileans, he initiated efforts that resulted in the founding of the first Chilean lodge, Union Fraternal, in 1853.[30]

The large foreign community of Valparaíso provided an atmosphere of comparative religious toleration in the mid-nineteenth century. Not so Santiago. A German traveler to that city during Holy Week of the year 1860 reported seeing numerous dummies, elegantly dressed and labeled "Judas Iscariot," being garrotted in front of homes where Jews were known to be living. Nevertheless, intolerable conditions in Europe impelled some Jews to settle there. Dr. Pedro Herzl, for example, stymied by the difficulties Jews had in obtaining medical diplomas from the University of Vienna prior to the revolution of 1848, settled in Santiago and became the first Austrian-trained physician to practice there.

In 1852, a confrontation between church and state occurred when the archbishop of Santiago, Rafael Valentin Valdivieso, ordered communicants to denounce persons suspected of heresy. The impact was immediate in the city of Copiapó, where it became known that a list of Protestants and Jews was being prepared. With masses of miners due to arrive in town for the celebration of Christmas, it was feared that riots would follow. The temper of the times is llustrated by the fact that, following publication of the bishop's proclamation, the citizens rallied in defense of religious liberty and against a return of the Inquisition to Chile.

Church and state were not legally separated until 1925. Cultural isolation led many individual Jews to convert to Catholicism, either to conform voluntarily to prevailing social norms or more specifically to marry, a rite that was sometimes celebrated on the groom's deathbed. A civil register for marriages, births, and deaths was established in 1885, and all except two of the Jewish families known to have emigrated to Chile during this period assimilated into the general population.

Mexico

In no country of Latin America was the struggle between church and state as prolonged and as bitter as in Mexico. The war waged for over a century by these titanic forces shaped the Mexican nation from its inception to the present day. As a consequence of the entrenched position of the Catholic Church, Mexican liberals acquired a different stamp from liberals in other countries. They became identified not with the cause of religious liberty but with the extirpation of church power, even though that be at the expense of religious liberty.

The first federal constitution of 1824, following overthrow of the upstart Emperor Agustín de Iturbide, declared that "the religion of the Mexican nation is and shall perpetually be the Roman Catholic Apostolic." No provision was made for the observance of other religions, and the ancient ecclesiastical privileges were guaranteed.[31] Despite the unpromising legal setting and the extremely unsettled conditions in the countryside, a few Jewish adventurers and itinerant peddlers made their way to Mexico in the early years of independence. They were able to become citizens only after 1843, when President Antonio López de Santa Ana repealed the law that limited citizenship to Roman Catholics and prohibited Mexican women from marrying outside the church. In the following decade, the names of ten persons who may have been Jewish can be discerned in Mexican naturalization records. Of these individuals, five came from Germany, three from France, one from Poland, and one from Turkey. Three settled in Zacatecas, two in Vera Cruz, and one each in San Luis Potosí, Tamaulipas, Santiago, and Mexico City. They gave their occupation as *comerciante* and were probably itinerant peddlers.[32] What religious life they led had to be clandestine because the holding of non-Catholic religious services was illegal. American soldiers serving in the Mexican-American War came upon isolated Jewish families, including one that was observing Yom Kippur. Among their company was one man who had come from a distant town disguised as a friar.

The fall of Santa Ana paved the way for the Reforma and the opening of immigration to non-Catholics. The Ley Juárez (1855), which attacked ecclesiastical and military privileges, and the Ley Lerdo (1856), which attempted to destroy the church's political power by divesting it of its property, came to be embodied in the liberal constitution of 1857. In its final form, the constitution omitted mention both of the Roman Catholic religion and of religious rights.

Although individual Jews settled in such towns as Aguas Calientes, Jalapa, Jalisco, Durango, Vera Cruz, Oaxaca, and Mexico City and in Baja California, this liberal period brought neither stability to the Mexican government nor relaxation to Jewish apprehensions, which were shaped more by popular attitudes than by the legal context. The church generally and the Inquisition specifically were more determinative of Jewish behavior than any relaxation of the law. Consequently, when German Jews entered Mexico as a result of the European upheavals of 1848, either they followed no Jewish forms or they did so clandestinely. And the religiously neutral constitution did not make all that much difference: letters written in 1862 show that Jewish immigrants still found it necessary to appear to be Catholic.

During these years, the capital city exhibited relatively greater tolerance than the countryside. In 1861, a group of over one hundred Jewish men organized in Mexico City and were holding regular meetings to collect funds for charitable and religious purposes. Under the guise of holding an annual meeting of a Masonic Grand Council, they met in a Masonic lodge to celebrate the High Holy Days. The development of this community was cut short by the turmoil of the French intervention.

Although the Liberals favored immigration, during the first decade of the restored republic (under Benito Juárez,1867–77), only a handful of Jews are found in naturalization files. Fear rather than law continued to govern Jewish behavior, and evidence of Jewish communal activity disappears from the records. Jews living in the federal capital had planned to build a synagogue, but this project was quietly dropped and no organized community came into existence at this time.

The reason for such pronounced self-effacement was the change that had occurred in the Mexican political climate. The liberalism of the Reforma had been tolerant of religious differences; the liberalism of the restored republic was antireligious. The years of foreign invasion, civil war, and chaos had taught Juárez and those who surrounded him the dangers of excessive liberalism. They moved over intellectually to positivism, with its exaltation of material progress and its denigration of spiritual values. Empiricism having replaced mysticism, there was no room left in official ideology for individual religious belief. The evolution from official toleration of religious differences to official disapproval of all religions made overt expressions by Jews quite impossible, for they were caught between the hammer of governmental anticlericalism and the anvil of intense Catholicism among the people.

When Porfirio Díaz rose to power in 1877, positivism proved congenial to his style. His dictatorial rule (the *porfiriato*), lasting thirty-four years, imposed a regime of law and order upon Mexico in the interests of foreign investors and the small Mexican elite. "Liberty, Order, and Progress" was the watchword, with the emphasis on order to the detriment of the liberties of the great mass of people. Because economic wisdom required opening the country to foreigners from industrialized countries who had capital and entrepreneurial skills, an atmosphere of religious toleration was made to prevail within the precincts of Mexico City. Thus, from 1879 onward, the number of Jewish residents began to increase. Most prominent among these were Alsatians, and almost without exception they considered themselves to be French. For them, religion was an accident of birth, a defect educated men should overcome, though a certain religious sentiment was not inappropriate for women and the lower classes. Many of these immigrants married Catholic wives, fathered Catholic children, and returned to France in their old age. These Alsatian Jews had no interest in organizing a community life, which might have attracted the disdain of elite circles and the hostility of the Catholic faithful, still capable of being aroused to frenzy by the church. They adopted a collective low profile that remained the dominant characteristic of the Mexican Jewish community for the next hundred years.

Under these conditions, their Jewish birth did not prevent individuals from making their way successfully in Mexican society; some gained positions of power unmatched by Jews in any other Latin American republic until late in the twentieth century. Most notable among this group was José Yves Limantour, the financial genius of the Díaz regime. Limantour achieved power second only to that of Díaz himself and might have been named successor to the dictator, had he not been disqualified by his parents' foreign birth. He was largely responsible for the fiscal soundness of the Mexican government in the period prior to World War I, a condition that contrasted brilliantly with the financial chaos that preceded it. Limantour put Mexico on the gold standard, abolished the sales tax (*alcabala*) that had trammeled domestic commerce since colonial days, and consolidated the Mexican railroads into one national system. His identification with Díaz brought about his own resignation along with that of the dictator when the Revolution erupted in 1910.

Eduardo Noetzlin and his associates, contemporaries of Limantour's, were members of a French banking firm with assets in Holland and Switzerland. Noetzlin founded the Banco Nacional de México, which served as an arm of the Treasury Department. Jean Baptiste Jecker, a Swiss adventurer and entrepreneur, entered Mexican history in a less favorable light as negotiator of the loan to the government of General Miguel Miramon that, repudiated by Juárez, became a cause of the French intervention. The Englishman Ernst Cassel became involved in Mexican industrialization as financier of the railroads. He was a friend of Baron Maurice de Hirsch and of Jacob Schiff, president of Kuhn, Loeb and Co., which participated, along with Speyer Brothers—another Jewish firm—in the reorganization of the Mexican railroads in the 1890s.[33]

By that time, Jews were involved in Mexican mining and railroads, the Banco Occidental of Mazatlán, and numerous family businesses. Jewish immigrants were owners of jewelry stores and department stores, purveyors of crystal and glassware, and owners and managers of hotels and restaurants. A number of patents issued to Jews in 1895—for the production of photographic paper, a trouser belt, a printing press, an apparatus for drying cement—show that Jewish immigrants had entered manufacturing. There were also intellectuals in this immigrant group, including the editor of *El Financiero Mexicano*, the publisher of *L'Écho Français*, the director of the Lycée Française, the director of the Normal School at Jalapa, and the statistician, cartographer, and social reformer Isidoro Epstein.

Despite the proimmigration policies of the Díaz government, Mexico attracted only a fraction of the 22 millions of immigrants abroad in the world between 1885 and 1910. In 1900, the percentage of foreigners in the country was 0.42; ten years later they comprised just 0.77 percent.[34] Nor did the country become a destination for the masses of Russian Jews compelled to emigrate in 1891. That year, the financier Jacob Schiff and railway magnate Baron Maurice de Hirsch studied the possibility of settling Russian Jews in Mexico, but agreed that the labor market was not conducive to such a project.

Jewish immigration remained individual, idiosyncratic, and focused in small trade. Sephardic and Arabic Jews had been entering Mexico in small numbers since the earliest years of independence. In 1900 they were organized into four congregations in Mexico City, without their ever having come to the attention of the fashionable French and Alsatian Jews of the capital. These *turcos* lived as virtual pariahs, plying their trade as peddlers in isolated areas where popular conceptions of the Jew had not progressed much beyond medieval diabolization. They had compacted the Jewish historical experience into a highly ritualized attachment to religious form. The establishment of their synagogues did not require the hiring of a rabbi, as most of the men were capable of leading the group in prayer. Between this low-status community with its attachment to religious norms and the high-status French and Alsatian community of the capital, characterized by its disconnection from Jewish life, there was no contact at all. A general Sephardic synagogue came into existence around World War I, with members from the Balkans, Syria, North Africa, and the Ottoman Empire, but over the course of time, the various ethnic groups spun off into their own separate institutions. This is the situation that prevails today.

Interestingly, at a time when European Jews declined to identify with their religious community for fear of calling down calumny, there was an indigenous movement to restore to public life the descendants of crypto-Jews. Francisco Rivas Puigcerver, born in Campeche, Yucatán, in 1850, was a baptized Roman Catholic who claimed to be heir to the Marrano tradition. In a magazine that he began publishing in 1889 called *El Sábado Secreto,* Rivas argued against the integrationist position and in favor of recognition of the diverse ethnic and religious elements that went into the making of Mexico. He urged the crypto-Jews of Mexico to declare themselves and to live openly as Jews. He also corresponded with publicists in Turkey in an effort to stimulate Jewish emigration from that empire to Mexico.[35] His efforts met with resonance among the Jews of Aleppo, who were living in poverty and without access to secular education. Letters from relatives who had already emigrated to Mexico persuaded many that their lives would improve once they crossed the ocean.[36]

Most immigrants to Mexico did not immediately apply for citizenship; and among those who did, it is not always possible to distinguish Jews. Possibly one hundred Jews became naturalized Mexicans over the course of the generation 1862–99. Of these individuals, forty-five came from Germany, ten from the United States, nine from France, and six from Austria. To these must be added those Jews who tended not to take out citizenship because they intended to return to Europe, as well as the Arabic speakers, whose poverty and lack of education or career held them back from attempting to participate in civic life. The Mexican census of 1895 found just .1 percent of the population to be non-Catholic, of whom .13 percent were israelitas.[37]

Brazil

European immigration to Brazil in modern times began with the flight of the House of Bragança from Lisbon to Rio de Janeiro during the Napoleonic wars. In 1808, the prince regent opened the ports of Brazil to direct trade with foreign countries, and the country remained open to European immigrants through the reign of his son, Pedro I. Brazil began her national existence as a monarchy, and church and state remained united under royal patronage following independence. But in this country of Catholicism "with the bones removed," in Gilberto Freyre's felicitous phrase, there was greater freedom of religion than in the Spanish republics of the same period. The Imperial Constitution of 1824 (under which Brazil was governed until 1889) recognized Roman Catholicism as the official religion, but guaranteed the right to exercise other religions in private. In Brazil, the church gave its consent to mixed marriages so that Protestant immigration could be encouraged. This concession was not granted in any of the Spanish American republics.

Brazilian interest in immigration sprang from several motives, not all of which were reconcilable one with another: the desire to create a class of small farmers who would engage in diversified agriculture and thus supply the consumer demand for food that large-scale monoculture neglected; an interest in whitening the existing population through miscegenation with Europeans;[38] and the provision of a pool of cheap manpower to perform the manual labor of the coffee, cotton, and sugar plantations as the end of the system of slavery drew near. But despite systematic recruiting of agricultural workers and subsidies for their transportation, immigration to Brazil lagged behind that of other countries of the Western Hemisphere, no doubt because of the perceived difficulties for immigrants in competing with the system of large estates and the heritage of black slavery. In consequence, immigration to Brazil remained a mere trickle until 1888, the year of abolition, when the number of immigrants jumped abruptly to 133,000.

Jews began to emigrate from Morocco to Amazonia shortly after independence was declared. These were probably Spanish-speaking Sephardim whose ancestors had settled in North Africa following the Expulsion from Spain. It is curious that they should have settled in Portuguese-speaking Brazil just when the Portuguese Jews of Curaçao were moving over to Spanish-speaking Venezuela and Colombia. The Moroccans seem to have adapted easily to their new environment, founding a synagogue, Porta do Céu (Gates of Heaven) in Belém do Pará in 1828.[39] Staking out likely sites along the river, Moroccan traders played a role in the development of the commerce of the region. Living at ease among their Christian neighbors, they flourished economically, broadening their activities into export and import (particularly of textiles) and also into navigation of the Amazon and exploration of riparian lands. They entered local politics and held municipal office. With the arrival of additional Sephardim from Africa, Syria, and Arabia, other congregations were formed in Bahia, Manaus, Ceará, and Rio de Janeiro, yielding a contemporary fourth generation of Brazilian Jews.

Dom Pedro II, second emperor of Brazil (1841–89), was an ardent supporter of immigration as a means of populating the country with modernizing elements and was particularly interested in attracting Germans to Brazil. A polymath who had a working knowledge of a dozen languages, he was a lifelong scholar of the Bible, which he studied in the original Hebrew. No doubt interesting conversations passed between the emperor and the French envoy, Count Joseph Arthur de Gobineau. The latter regarded the Brazilian population as "corrupted in body and soul, ugly to a terrifying degree," as a result of miscegenation.[40] The emperor, who carried on an intense intellectual friendship with the ambassador, is alleged to have told him that the latter's racial theories, according to which all achievements of civilization could be ascribed to the Aryan race, were "not suited to our climate."[41] At the royal palace, the emperor received a multitude of artists, including the American composer Louis Moreau Gottschalk and the actress Sarah Bernhardt, and had contact with a number of Brazilian Jews, ranging from the electrician who wired his palace to Lt. Col. Francisco Leão Cohn, who commanded a troop of the national guard on the frontier with Uruguay. After going into exile in France, Dom Pedro continued his studies under the guidance of Benjamin Mossé, rabbi of Avignon. In the year of his death, Dom Pedro's translation into French of liturgical poetry (piyutim) originally written in Hebrew/Provençal appeared under the title *Poesis Hebraico-Provençales du rituel Israélite contadin—traduites et transcrites par S. M. Don Pedro II d'Alcantara, empereur du Brésil.*[42]

West European Jews began entering Brazil during the latter part of Dom Pedro's long reign. The most significant number came from Alsace and Lorraine.[43] A group of Jewish immigrants founded the town of Espírito Santo do Pinhal, in the state of São Paulo, and from the 1850s onward they are found as proprietors of coffee plantations. They took an active part in the political and administrative life of the municipalities in which they lived, and some joined the Brazilian army. In the capital city of Rio de Janeiro, Alsatian Jews dominated the commerce in gems from 1856; they were also importers of pharmaceuticals, domestic articles, and luxury goods, including wines, liqueurs, and jams. By the seventies, German Jews were also engaged in sericulture, the manufacture of telephone parts, and the construction of hydraulic works. A member of this migration was Bertholdo Goldschmidt, born in Posen in 1817, who acquired Brazilian citizenship in 1857 and assumed a post as professor of German at the Imperio Colegio Pedro II. Goldschmidt, together with a colleague, edited the first German-language journal in Brazil (*Der Deutsche Beobachter*) and translated the dramas of Schiller into Portuguese. On his death in 1893, he was buried in the cemetery of São Francisco Xavier.[44]

The defeat of France in the Franco-Prussian War and the annexation of Alsace-Lorraine by Germany propelled more French Jews to Brazil, and particularly to São Paulo, which from 1881 was taking up more than her share of immigrants. Some individuals settled in cities such as Pôrto Alegre, Passo Fundo, and Santa Maria; but the Jewish colony in São Paulo City itself, which came to number several hundred, was the largest and liveliest, with strong representation in the liberal professions. French Jews were university professors, dentists, engineers, and artists. In São Paulo in the second half of the nineteenth century were to be found the composer Alexandre Levy, the painter

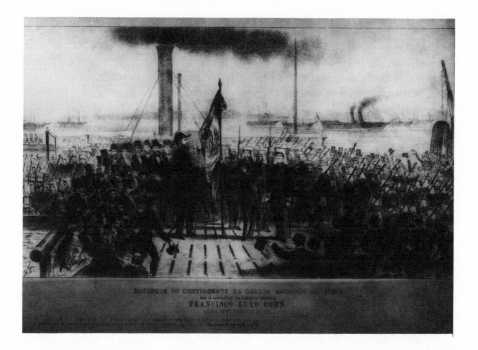

Since the days of empire, Brazil has offered Jews the possibility of advancement through command ranks of the armed forces. This engraving commemorates the embarkation of a contingent of the National Guard under command of Lt. Col. Francisco Leão Cohn in 1885.

Berta Worms, and the biologist André Dreyfus. This French colony assimilated to Brazilian society and ceased to be Jewish.[45]

Curiously, there also arrived at this time Jews from Portugal—not conversos or cristãos novos, but persons who had survived as avowed Jews. Some came directly from Portugal, others by way of the north, where they had been trading in vanilla beans, rubber, and those exotic feathers esteemed by Parisian women of *la belle époque*. All were drawn southward by the increasing economic dynamism of São Paulo.

The assimilation of Jews into Brazilian society was facilitated by the variety of positivism that flourished in Brazil during this period. Brazilian positivists were modernizers who sought to improve educational opportunity in order to create a technocratic elite. Emphasizing material prosperity, positivists wanted to foment conditions favorable to the growth of capitalism.[46] At the same time, and for corresponding reasons, the movement was anti-Catholic in its thrust. The liberality of Dom Pedro's regime was congenial to the spread of this new "religion" that denied the existence of a personal god and took "humanity, the

Great Being, as the object of its veneration."[47] The Positivist Church itself attracted only a few members; but the large number of people influenced by positivist thought leavened the intellectual ambience of the great cities of the Brazilian littoral, preparing, incidentally, a milieu that was much more receptive to Jews than was that of such tradition-bound areas as Peru.

As Dom Pedro aged, the imminent ascension to the throne of the pious Princess Isabella became a precipitant in formation of elements hostile to a continuation of the monarchy. Following the emperor's abdication, positivist and other progressive influences in the drafting of the republican constitution brought about the separation of church and state and the guarantee of religious freedom.

Peru

"That the Catholic Church is the State ecclesiastical establishment of Peru admits of no question, for, indeed, the system of interdependence of State and Church is one of the most comprehensive and absolute in Latin America. Furthermore, this ecclesiastical policy has been maintained with little or no change through the years."[48] In this way, J. Lloyd Mecham described the situation in Peru in 1966. The countries that formed the old viceroyalty of Peru were not active seekers of immigrants in the nineteenth century, their elite class preferring a status quo fortified by the church to modernization and the hazards of change. Until 1915, religious toleration could not legally exist, the public exercise of any religion but the Catholic being forbidden by the constitution. A law providing for civil marriage was passed in 1897; before that date, marriage was a religious sacrament that could be performed only in a church. In the matter of cemeteries, a dent was made earlier in the Catholic monopoly over civil affairs, as a result of the need to provide a respectable burial for foreigners sojourning in the country—foreigners who were Peru's main link with international trade.[49]

The political, social, and economic upheavals in Europe in 1848, and again in 1870, propelled some immigrants to Peru even though government was not recruiting them. Among these immigrants were Jews, mostly from Germany, but including a few from France, England, and Russia. German Jews were among the founders of the club Germania; some also joined the Jewish beneficent society when that was formed some years later.[50] Among these migrants were industrialists, bankers, diamond merchants, jewelers, engineers, merchants, and employees of these firms. Also included among them were representatives of European firms, such as the House of Rothschild, whose agents, the Jacoby brothers, established the first exchange bank in Lima. Other agents became involved in buying and selling Peruvian wool and cotton, as well as in mining ventures. The ties of these firms ran back to England and France.[51]

The Cementerio Israelita de Baquíjano was inaugurated in 1875 on property offered as a donation by Henry Meiggs, the American engineer who designed and supervised construction of the Callao, Lima, and Oroya Railroad, at that time the highest track in the world and one that "broke the back of the Andes."

The Sociedad Hebrea de Beneficencia de Lima, recalling the response of the patriarch Abraham to a similar offer, insisted on paying for the land.[52] It lies not far from the city's first racetrack, and the names of ten individuals and firms appear among the founders of both. Apparently, Jews were members of the Sociedad de Carreras, which later metamorphosed into the Jockey Club of Peru. The inference is that one could be openly Jewish and belong to this oligarchic redoubt. Social intercourse led to intermarriage. Although members of this migration founded the burial society that would later become the cornerstone of organized Jewish life in Peru, all of its original members assimilated into the Peruvian population and disappeared from Jewish ranks within three generations.

Very different from this Central European migration was that of Jews from North Africa—probably Spanish-speaking Moroccans from Tetuán and Tangier—who came to Peru in the mid-nineteenth century, attracted by Amazonia's rubber boom.[53] The initiation of commercial steamboat service made it possible for adventurers to penetrate the interior by way of the river, and people of all nationalities trooped to the area to enrich themselves or to die unchronicled in the jungle. Jews were among their number. They lived in the region of Iquitos till about 1910, when the development of East Indian rubber plantations ended the Brazilian boom. Of the 150 Jews known to have been in the province of Amazonas at that time, possibly 90 left the area. Many of the men who stayed had formed families with local women. There are therefore people living in Amazonas today with Sephardic names such as Benzaquen, Levy, Israel, or Abenzur who preserve attentuated memories of their Jewish origins.

Guatemala

Despite the very different conditions of Guatemalan life, the debate over European immigration took place in terms so similar to those which engaged the Argentines and Chileans that we are led inescapably to the conclusion that the context of immigration policy was molded by the same intellectual forces all over the continent.

Debate over the merits of immigration began while Guatemala was a member of the Federation of Central America, a union with El Salvador, Honduras, Nicaragua, and Costa Rica that coalesced after the fall of Iturbide of Mexico in 1823 and lasted only until 1838. Most articulate elements in the new republic were concerned with "improving" (read, Europeanizing) the quality of life. On the method, direction, and tempo of change, opinion diverged. Liberals generally were convinced that certain elements essential to development were not obtainable from domestic sources, and they looked abroad for help. Consequently, they framed laws that they hoped would attract immigrants and capital to the country to aid in the development of the economy and alter existing cultural patterns. Disestablishment of the Catholic Church and the proclamation of religious toleration in 1833 opened the way for admission of non-Catholics. Public lands were made available to private buyers, with one-third reserved for distribution free of charge to immigrant families or to the founders of new settlements.[54]

Legislation in support of immigration was spurred by a vision of prospective European settlers as active agents of social change, who would serve as models of entrepreneurial activity while teaching native citizens the virtues of civic responsibility. In addition to their material contributions, they were expected to alter existing culture patterns so that the modernization of Guatemala could begin. Generally, the majority Native American population, inheritors of the ancient Maya civilization, got short shrift. Although at first there was some Enlightenment sentiment that all men, even *indios*, were perfectible, there was an increasing tendency during the nineteenth century to view the indigenous inhabitants as a stumbling block to economic development. The large land grants being offered to foreign developers as often as not belonged to Native Americans, by usage if not by law. The cheap labor offered the colonists was theirs also, for the Maya had been freed from the onerous labor laws of colonial days only to be bound over under laws of vagrancy. It was considered a favor to the Indian population to Europeanize it, and this could even be done humanely: a European immigrant who married a Native American woman thereby qualified for a double portion of land.

Conservatives feared that a mass influx of foreigners might destabilize society or even lead to the alienation of national territory, as had happened in Mexico. But when they came to power they did not close off immigration entirely. Rather, they reduced the scope of institutional accommodations they were prepared to offer. Specifically, Conservatives reestablished the church and ceased support for sponsored programs of mass colonization. They retained incentives for individual settlers who conformed to existing social norms. Both Liberals and Conservatives anticipated an immigration composed almost entirely of agricultural workers. Liberals would have recruited these en masse, whereas Conservatives considered it more prudent to attract desirable immigrants individually. But neither approach succeeded. Changes in law were ineffectual in altering the nativist attitude of Guatemaltecos, and in the absence of any strong economic attraction, the immigrants simply did not come.[55]

When the Liberal party disestablished the church and proclaimed religious toleration in 1833, the way was legally clear for Jewish as well as for non-Jewish immigrants. Of the few who came, the majority were German; among the Germans were Jews. The first for whom there is any record came from Posen in 1848.[56] In that city, the civil status of Jews had long been at hazard, some of them qualifying for Prussian citizenship and some not. The full emancipation glimpsed as a result of the revolution of 1848 turned out to be a chimera, and the reactionary wave that followed compelled many Jews to emigrate.

In 1870, a congregation of German Jews formed in Guatemala City. This was an industrial and commercial community, occupying itself in textile manufacture, the curing of hides, and export-import trade. One of its number, Luis Schlesinger (1820–1900), may be considered an industrial precursor for Guatemala as a whole. Restrictions were placed by government on the commercial activities of foreigners, however (in 1952, the Guatemalan government still withheld citizenship from German Jews), and so the country never became an attractive place of settlement for large numbers of Jews. Religious toleration was a sine qua non, but not in itself sufficient, especially where so vast a gulf separated Jews from the native inhabitants.

The Jewish Population of Latin America in 1889

By 1889, only a few thousand Jews were to be found in all Latin America. Any enumeration risks the omission of individuals; however, the identifiable groups included the Portuguese Sephardim of Curaçao, who had by now dispersed to adjacent lands of the Caribbean basin; West European Ashkenazim from France, Germany, Alsace, Lorraine, Switzerland, and England, who were scattered in the metropolitan cities of Argentina, Chile, Guatemala, Mexico, Brazil, and Peru; Spanish-speaking Sephardim from North Africa adventuring in the Amazon region of Brazil and Peru; and Arabic-speaking Sephardim in provincial towns of Argentina and Mexico and along the Amazon.

These groups differed from one another in language, social mores, and religious practices. While early arrivals may have banded together for purposes of prayer, in most instances different interpretations of ritual, derived from their very different historic trajectories, led these ethnic groups to create their own separate synagogues, schools, and social clubs. Despite this lack of cohesion, all usually were perceived by the majority population simply as Jews.

Portuguese Sephardim fitted into mercantile societies on the fringe of the Spanish-speaking world. Appointed to key government positions in the Dominican Republic, they utilized their overseas connections to extend the republic's slim resources, in one instance arranging for a Dutch bank to consolidate the Dominican debt. As the Sephardim of Santo Domingo assimilated to the highest social strata, they gave up their economic ethos, adopting instead the mentality of those who prefer to invest their wealth in houses and land. They chose for their sons the traditional academic preparation for physician or lawyer, in preference to business. These families did not seek to conceal their Jewish origins; on the contrary, they tended to boast of them, possibly because Jewish descent implied they were white, a matter of importance to Dominicans in light of their long occupation by black Haitians.[57] The number of Sephardic families in the Dominican Republic had dwindled to twenty by the first quarter of the nineteenth century; the last survivor died an old man in the 1950s.

Ashkenazim were strangers to the Spanish-speaking world, but they proved almost as malleable as the Sephardim in the social setting in which they now found themselves. These western Jews came from societies that had been plowed and harrowed by the great wars of religion, rising nationalism, and the Industrial Revolution. They were imbued with the ideal of emancipation, of liberation from medieval restrictions, and of acceptance by the family of man. In accord with Enlightenment thought, they had freed themselves from the bonds of established religion in order to make themselves acceptable for citizenship on an equal footing with Christians. Indeed, a specifically Jewish Enlightenment (*haskalah*) had taken place, preaching that Jews should divest themselves of attributes that made them unacceptable to Christians in order to qualify themselves for emancipation. "Be a Jew at home, a man on the street," counseled the *maskillim* (enlighteners), the implication being that the world would accept as a human being the same individual it rejected as a Jew.

In the context of the European historical process, westernized Jews came to equate emancipation with acceptance by the Christian majority. If that acceptance required the rejection of Jewish tradition, so be it. Hans Kohn, the eminent historian of nationalism, described the phenomenon: "During the first half of the nineteenth century, assimilation swept through Jewish life like a veritable hurricane; originating in Western Europe, it moved eastward, wiping out with it practically all the upper strata of Jewish society. One purpose seemed to animate Jewish life: to escape from Judaism, to become like the gentiles."[58] This dream of emancipation alternately bloomed and withered in the revolutions of 1830 and 1848. The desire to escape from Judaism may have been a factor in rendering West European Jews available for immigration to Latin America, a continent that had no history of Jewish settlement, and therefore no ready-made structures for the legal isolation of Jews.

In the major metropolitan centers of the Latin American continent to which these German, French, English, and Swiss Jews came, they found an elite class that was more attuned to the cultural emanations of Europe—particularly France—than to the rhythms of their autochthonous societies. Social circles that were receptive to Masonry and to positivism formed a milieu into which these secularized Jews could comfortably assimilate. Although the social structures of these countries were still patrimonial and clerical, those sectors of the creole elites who wished to break with the past welcomed immigrants with modernizing skills. Their nonadherence to the Catholic Church made them welcome allies of the anticlerical elites. Jewish immigrants of 1830, 1848, and 1870 included engineers, financiers, doctors, linguists, scientists, and entrepreneurs—all skills the continent gravely lacked. Possession of such skills facilitated the entry of the immigrants into the upper reaches of the middle class, where their mobility was enhanced by the fact that many were estranged from their religion and eager to be accepted socially. Many Jewish immigrants continued to regard themselves as Jews while paying little attention to religious ritual. Having been partially assimilated into the gentile environment of Europe, they formed religious congregations in the New World but continued their assimilatory trend by marrying Catholic wives, sometimes in Protestant ceremonies. The opening of social circles to accommodate the newcomers was simplified by the readiness of both parties to relegate religion to secondary status. Intermarriage, the result of social acceptance, accomplished one of the major goals the proimmigration forces had set themselves.

The expectation that immigrants would supply the Latin economies with cheap labor went unsatisfied by this migration. Few in number, Jewish immigrants were completely irrelevant to the demand for agricultural labor since they included, as far as can be determined, no farmers at all (with the exception of the landowning German coffee planters of São Paulo). On the other hand, these immigrants did provide entrepreneurial skills that many Latin Americans, particularly the positivists, wanted to recruit to give impetus to industrialization. In the process, some Jewish immigrants achieved great personal success, unhampered by their origins or religious affiliation.

Of the Jewish immigrants from Arab regions of this period far less is known. They proceeded from Muslim areas that had not been reached by the intellectual currents that shaped post-Napoleonic Europe. For the most part, they retained a pious worldview that shaped their outlook and their mode of address toward the peoples among whom they lived. Nationalism, secularization, emancipation were to remain alien concepts for a generation or more, and intermarriage was vehemently rejected as an agent of erosion of Jewish life.[59] As pariahs who were alternately harassed and patronized by their Muslim overlords, the Jews had occupied extremely low status in their countries of origin.[60] They transferred their occupations, their outlook, and their status to the countries of their adoption. There is no known instance of these communities seeking to link up with the higher-status Ashkenazim of the great cities. They may not even have recognized one another as Jews.

Religious toleration was not a decisive consideration for non-Jewish immigrants to Latin America. Most came from Spain or Italy, with religious beliefs so similar to those of their hosts that no alteration in ecclesiastical structures was necessary in order to accommodate them. The real impact of the introduction of religious toleration was to encourage a diversified flow of immigrants, largely of Protestants, who of course far outnumbered Jews. Once immigrants entered a country en masse, as in Argentina, their very number and heterogeneity wrought unpredictable and irreversible changes in society, including the creation of tolerable conditions for Jewish life. Mass immigration in fact occurred only where religious toleration combined with economic opportunity. The experience of Guatemala shows that legal toleration alone was not enough to attract immigrants, Jews or non-Jews. But if the economic possibilities seemed attractive enough, immigrants came even where there were barriers to their absorption.

For Jews, religious toleration was crucial. True, Jewish individuals found their way to the most unlikely areas when the economic stakes seemed high enough (or, in later periods, when the need for refuge overwhelmed caution). But for the mass of people, the absence of a legal base for their existence—for marriage, burial, registration of the birth of a child, secular education—did not create an alluring prospect. Without religious toleration, no Jewish immigration of any magnitude took place, whatever the idiosyncratic choices of individual Jews.

Thus, formation of the contemporary Jewish communities was a function of religious toleration and economic incentive on the one hand, and of the massive immigration of heterogeneous peoples on the other. The combined activities of the newcomers did in fact commence the industrialization of the continent so devoutly anticipated by positivists and others, while at the same time upsetting the former balance of political and social forces, as the traditionalists had feared. In this way were the expectations of liberal and conservative alike brought to reality.

CHAPTER 3

Mass Immigration, 1889 to World War I

We came third class because there was no fourth.

—Pinie Wald

THE CONTEMPORARY JEWISH communities of Latin America were formed between 1889 and World War I, largely by East European Ashkenazim. The extremely high migration figures for this period (see Table 1) reflect the intense pressures that were being exerted upon Jews within their countries of origin, at a time when international travel was relatively cheap and most countries of the Western Hemisphere followed unrestricted immigration policies.

Most migrants of this period originated in the Russian Empire, Poland, and Romania, where a dual policy toward Jews was being exercised by governments of the late nineteenth century. Toleration for the Jewish commercial and industrial bourgeoisie that was engaged in modernization of the economy was accompanied by ruthless oppression and deprivation of the majority, a policy aimed at driving impoverished Jews to emigrate. The pressure was particularly severe in Russia, where the czarist government sought to divert attention from economic upheaval and social and political struggle by encouraging a brutal wave of pogroms.

In 1881, the assassination of Czar Alexander II was made the occasion for a series of government-sponsored pogroms. The May Laws of the following year forced confinement of Russian Jews to certain towns and townships, driving them from the rural villages where many had lived. As a result of officially countenanced mass destruction, Jews by the thousand—dispossessed, bewildered, and the responsibility of no one—fled over the border into Germany. From there many made their way, with the help of Jewish relief organizations, to the New World. These East European Ashkenazim, in their pell-mell flight westward, formed the bulk of the Jewish communities of the United States, Canada, and Latin America, in the process shifting the balance of the world Jewish population from Europe to the Western Hemisphere. In the twenty years from 1880 to 1900, half a million Jews entered the United States. But

TABLE I

Jewish Migrants from Europe according to Countries of Immigration, 1840–1942
(Absolute Numbers)

Years	United States	Canada	Argentina	Brazil	Uruguay	Other Countries of America	South Africa	Palestine	All Other Countries	Total
1840–1880	200,000	1,600	2,000	500		1,000	4,000	10,000	2,000	221,100
1881–1900	675,000	10,500	25,000	1,000		1,000	23,000	25,000	4,000	764,500
1901–1914	1,346,400	95,300	87,614	8,750		3,000	21,377	30,000	10,000	1,602,441
1915–1920	76,450	10,450	3,503	2,000	1,000	5,000	907	−15,000	5,000	89,310
1921–1925	280,283	14,400	39,713	7,139	3,000	7,000	4,630	60,765	10,000	426,930
1926–1930	54,998	15,300	33,721	22,296	6,370	10,000	10,044	10,179	10,000	172,908
1931–1935	17,986	4,200	12,700	13,075	3,280	15,000	4,507	147,502	20,000	238,250
1936–1939	79,819	900	14,789	10,600	7,677	15,000	5,300	75,510	60,000	269,595
1940–1942	70,954	800	4,500	6,000	1,000	2,000	2,000	35,000	10,000	132,354
1840–1942	2,801,890	153,450	223,540	71,360	22,327	59,000	75,765	378,956	131,000	3,917,388

Source: Jacob Lestchinsky, "Jewish Migrations, 1840–1956," p. 1554.

these numbers were to be eclipsed during the next fourteen years. Among the million and a half Europeans who fled their homes annually in the years 1900–14, fully one-tenth were Jewish. The vast majority of these entered the United States, with its reputation for religious toleration and economic opportunity.

But the desperate need for a haven forced Jews into areas they had not previously regarded as hospitable. By the last decade of the nineteenth century, some regions of Latin America had entered a period of economic growth, sparked by foreign investment in raw materials and in the infrastructure required for their extraction and shipment abroad. Ashkenazim now settled in all the Western Hemisphere republics, building substantial communities in Argentina and Brazil. Accommodating themselves to their new environment, Ashkenazim soon outnumbered the West Europeans and Sephardim who had preceded them, stamping Latin American Jewish communities with the East European orientation they retain to this day.*

Sephardic immigration also increased during this period, though at a lower level numerically than Ashkenazim because they were drawing from a smaller population reservoir. Emigration of Jews from the Ottoman Empire escalated after 1880. The years 1900–14 saw substantial Sephardic emigration from the Balkans, spurred by natural calamities and deteriorating economic conditions. How many Sephardim entered Latin American countries during these years is not known, but Arabic- and Ladino-speaking congregations were organized in both Mexico and Cuba, countries that had not as yet attracted East European Jews.[1]

The majority of immigrants gravitated to those countries that, out of a desire to encourage immigration, separated church and state. Individual Jews, however, settled for idiosyncratic reasons in every one of the republics, including those with the most limited vision of religious freedom.

Argentina

In 1876, Nicolás Avellaneda, third president of Argentina, sponsored an Immigration and Colonization Law designed to resolve "the problem of European immigration" by offering inducements to immigrants who may have been more inclined to go to the United States. The law provided for five days' bed and board at an immigrant hostel, assistance in finding a job, and transportation anywhere in the republic, all without cost. Especially desirable immigrants, such as European farmers and mechanics, were granted additional benefits.[2] More than any other country of Latin America, Argentina seemed to offer an optimal combination of religious toleration, strong government support for immigration, industrial employment, and land for farming. So great was the attraction that one-quarter of a million immigrants, mostly Italian and Spanish, were admitted to the country in the five-year period 1881–85, and this number

---

*The accuracy of Lestchinsky's calculations in Table 1 may be gauged by reference to figures for Brazil, calculated nearly fifty years later. Lesser identified 23,455 Jewish immigrants to Brazil in the years 1931–39, compared with Lestchinsky's 23,675 (*Welcoming the Undesireables*, p. 183).

was more than doubled in the following quinquennium.[3] Yet the number of Jews admitted to Argentina from 1881 to 1889 was probably no greater than 350.[4] At the beginning of this period, the Argentine government had authorized its agent in Milan to look into the situation of Jews in czarist Russia with a view to inducing them to migrate to Argentina. His efforts were unsuccessful, probably for two reasons: the underdevelopment of the Argentine economy, as compared with that of the United States; and fear that the religious toleration offered by the Constitution of 1853 might lack substance.

The modest effort to attract Jewish immigrants was met by opposing forces. The French language newspaper *L'Union Française* deplored the move, referring to Jews as "noxious insects and powerful parasites." *La Nación*, the prestigious paper founded by Bartolomé Mitre (president of the republic from 1862 to 1868), was more moderate. Recognizing the plight of Russian Jews, *La Nación* posed no objection to their individual, spontaneous migration to Argentina. But active recruitment was opposed: Jews were the least assimilable people in the world. In 1890, the same newspaper serialized *La Bolsa*, an anti-Semitic novel still widely circulated and read in Argentina.

The question of Jewish immigration to Argentina remained moot for the better part of a decade. The earliest mention of Argentina as a possible haven that can be found in the Jewish press of eastern Europe occurred in *Hatsefira* of Warsaw in June 1884.[5] By that date, the first group of Jewish settlers bound for Argentina had already been organized. In August 1889, this group of 824 Jews sailed from Bremen on the ship *Weser* with the object of taking up farming on a plot of land they had bought from an agent of the Argentine government. They were at first denied entry at Buenos Aires as "harmful elements," having been expelled from their home country. This on-the-spot decision by the port inspector was reversed, and the immigrants were admitted. Argentine immigration officials had more power over the admission of immigrants than was the case in other countries, and the commissioner's own orientation was a potent factor in determining admissibility. It is therefore fortunate, from the point of view of Jewish applicants, that the initially hostile attitude of Juan Alsina, commissioner in the crucial first decade of the century, softened sufficiently to enable him to comply with the law.[6]

In Argentina's great century of immigration, almost half the immigrants were Italian and another third Spanish. Jews would be counted among the remainder. The national census of 1895 enumerated 6,085 israelitas, a figure considered by one scholar to be a "serious underestimate."[7] The majority of these israelitas, 5,890, were foreign-born. Only 753 of them were living in Buenos Aires; the rest were trying their luck as farmers under the patronage of the Jewish Colonization Association (JCA) in the provinces of Entre Ríos, Santa Fe, and Buenos Aires.[8] By 1909, when JCA[9] conducted a census, 19,361 Jews were living in the agricultural colonies, 16,589 in the capital, and about 13,000 more in the cities of Rosario, Santa Fe, Carlos Casares, La Plata, Córdoba, Mendoza, and Tucumán, bringing the total of Jews in Argentina to just under 50,000.[10]

The number of israelitas in Buenos Aires and their neighborhood settlement pattern coincided closely with the number of Russian-born persons in the city. This identification was quickly made, and Jews came to be known as *rusos*.[11] Though some 85 percent of Jews did indeed come from Russia, another 15 percent were classified by JCA as Turks or Moroccans, reflecting the independent migration of peddlers into the interior. There were only a sprinkling of French, German, English, Italian, Austrian, and Romanian Jews. These ethnic divisions became an element in occupational choice, as may be seen from observations in the JCA report: "The Russians are generally engaged in the furniture trade, the Turks in haberdashery, the Moroccans in cloth and ready-made clothing, the French, Germans, Dutch, etc., in jewelry. Some of them are extremely rich but most of them are only small tradesmen."

The East Europeans felt themselves to be distinct from the Sephardim and "Orientals" (Arabic-speaking Jews), as well as from the West Europeans who had preceded them and whom they sometimes took to be descendants of Marranos, so attenuated was their Jewish cultural life. A view across the gulf that separated "easterners" from "westerners" has been provided by Pinie Wald, a sheet-metal worker and socialist activist who migrated from Lodz to Buenos Aires in 1906. "Originally, these people [the western Europeans] were separated by distance from us *Jewish* Jews; from up close, nothing changed. We don't fight one another, God forbid! We live at peace with one another. But we live as separate nations."[12]

Feverish worldwide migration characterized the years 1910–14. Possibly 41,000 more Jews entered Argentina during these years, bringing the Jewish community past the 100,000 mark on the eve of World War I. About one-quarter of this population was now in the JCA farm colonies and another one-quarter in provincial towns. (Among the latter, as many as 40 percent may have been engaged at least part-time in farming.) But Argentine Jewry was becoming increasingly concentrated in the capital. The numbers of colonists continued to grow, but the urban population grew still faster, so that over half of Argentine Jews—65,000 of 110,000—were living in Buenos Aires by World War I.[13]

Among these Jews, JCA identified only one hundred who were in the liberal professions in 1909. But unlike the more numerous Italians and Spaniards, who were for the most part peasants, the Jews included a high proportion of skilled workers.[14] The fate of this Jewish proletariat would be determined by the skills and ideologies the immigrants brought with them, by Argentine beliefs regarding immigrants, and by the capacity of the economy to absorb them into productive occupations. A description of the Jewish working class has been left by Pinie Wald: "The Jewish immigration was proletarian and arrived third class, since there was no fourth class. We were no different than the general run of people coming in, except that all the Jews came with the intention of staying. . . . The entire Jewish migration was proletarian, from the '90s of the previous century to the '50s of the present century."[15] Russian, Romanian, and (Austrian) Galician Jews had not been able to work in factories in the countries of their birth. In Argentina, according to Wald, they were hired without discrimination. Bosses treated them well, "not as Jews but as deaf and dumb and suffering immigrants."

By the 1890s, immigrant workers were organizing themselves into unions, a tradition already well established in Europe but still alien to Argentina. With no labor code to satisfy the legitimate aspirations of workers and no representation in government, unions oriented themselves toward the forcible seizure of power and liquidation of the state as an instrument of oppression. The earliest stage of labor organization in Argentina, as elsewhere in Latin America, was dominated by anarchists, making it appear to the propertied class that the organization of labor posed a direct threat to the continuance of civilized society. Jewish workers, driven by a thirst for autoemancipation that was nourished by classist interpretations of history, joined the most militant socialist and communist factions of the workers' movement. The salience of foreign-born labor leaders, in turn, provoked a chauvinist response, making the repression of industrial ferment appear to be not only enlightened but patriotic. The consequence was a series of violent strikes violently suppressed and the identification of Jews specifically as agents of social turbulence.[16]

In fact, Jewish workers were dispersed over a range of proletarian ideologies. Some turned their eyes to Zion, joining the labor wing of the Zionist movement; others gravitated to the Bund, the Jewish branch of evolutionary socialism and the favored workers' organization in their European homelands, which linked them with the general labor movement while allowing them to retain their cultural autonomy and specifically the use of Yiddish. Those who militated in the Socialist and Communist parties tended to drop their ties to the organized Jewish community in their desire to integrate completely into Argentine society. The clash of political ideologies was reflected within the Jewish community: the Communists became alienated from the leadership of the community, condemning the latter as petite bourgeois. The radical assimilators were condemned by the "respectable" members of the community as traitors to the Jewish people.

The Centro Obrero Israelita (Jewish Workers' Center), founded in 1897, included both workers and bosses. By 1905, Jewish tailors, carpenters, capmakers, and bakers all had organized. The first two groups joined the socialist-dominated Union General de Trabajadores, while others such as the bakers, who from all accounts suffered the most exploitative conditions, joined the anarchist-dominated Federación Obrera Regional Argentina (FORA). In the years surrounding World War I, Jews were active in all branches of the workers' movement.[17] In 1908, the anarchists started publishing one page of their newspaper, *La Protesta*, in Yiddish. Buenos Aires Jewish unions carried on the same heated debates as those which erupted in New York Jewish unions over the relative merits of organizing into separate Jewish locals (so business could be conducted in Yiddish) or merging with the general membership in each trade union. This debate ran deeper in Argentina than in the United States because Argentine society did not legitimize ethnic-based organizations. To persist in identifying Jewishly, as opposed to merging seamlessly into the immigrant mass, meant to condemn oneself to permanent marginalization. Most of these early Jewish unions failed to survive wartime layoffs and the police repression of 1919.

For a while, Jewish immigrants to Argentina were active in the national political arena. Among the founders of the Argentine Socialist party in 1896 were numerous immigrants and sons of immigrants, including Dr. Enrique Dickmann, son of Russian Jews who had migrated to the agricultural colonies. Other Jews who had been affiliated with the socialist movement in Europe through its Jewish sector, the Bund, retained their ideology after arrival in Argentina. Opposed to revolutionary solutions, in 1907 the Bundists founded *Avangard,* whose purpose was to promote evolutionary socialism among the Jewish working class through the medium of Yiddish.

Jews were represented in all branches of the workers' movement, but most heavily in the Socialist party. The three daughters of Moisés Chertkoff, who migrated from Odessa to Clara, Entre Ríos, in 1894, became, like their father, activists in the Socialist party. Participating on an equal footing with the mostly male membership, they broke the mold of contemporary patterns of female behavior, determined at that date by Catholic traditions of female submissiveness. Fenia, who arrived in Argentina with her teaching certificate already in hand, founded the library of colony Clara soon after her arrival; in 1902, she founded the first Centro Socialista Femenino, and later worked on behalf of immigrants. She wrote for *La Vanguardia* and founded the Asociación de Recreos y Bibliotecas Infantiles. All the sisters married men who went on to leave their mark on Argentine politics: Fenia married Nicolás Repetto, Adela married Adolfo Dickmann, and Mariana married Juan B. Justo. Carrying the tradition into the next generation, Victoria Gucovsky, daughter of Fenia, married Antonio de Tomaso.[18]

The Argentine anarcho-communist movement (FORA del V Congreso) had a Jewish component known as Arbeter Freynt; so did its syndicalist spin-off, FORA del IX Congreso.[19] Together these "progressives" founded the Algemeiner Yiddisher Arbeter Farband in 1909 in Buenos Aires that took part in the May Day parade that year during which several demonstrators were killed by the police. A short while later, a Jewish anarchist named Simon Radowitzky assassinated the Buenos Aires chief of police in revenge for these slayings. Antianarchist feeling erupted in the sacking of the offices of *La Vanguardia* and *La Protesta,* the Bundist and anarchist newspapers, as well as the Biblioteca Rusa, the Jewish workers' library. In the police crackdown and state of siege that followed, many revolutionaries fled the country or were deported. The socialist wing of the Zionist party (Poalei Zion), founded in Buenos Aires four years earlier, virtually collapsed at this time following deportation of its leaders. A general reaction against immigrants now set in. As in the United States, labor unrest, urban crime, and declining morality all were blamed on the immigrant. Demands that immigration be curbed began to come from previously proimmigration forces.

In 1909, Ricardo Rojas began the remythologizing of the gaucho that heralded the birth of cultural nationalism. Argentina, he wrote, threatened by invasion of foreign influence and ideas, must develop a collective consciousness based on native traditions. Immigrants were tolerable as long as they could be assimilated, and Argentina was generous. But resistance to assimilation was serious. The feeling of racial superiority, originally enlisted in the war against gauchismo, now adopted gauchesque virtues in the struggle to naturalize the immigrants.

For that purpose, Rojas undertook to reinterpret Sarmiento, the apostle of population growth. Sarmiento, Rojas wrote, was "a partisan of immigration conceived as a procedure for creating a fatherland in consortium with humanity, and not as a factory without historical destiny, formed by individuals without flag, or collectivities without ideals. . . . Sarmiento wanted immigration in order to populate the desert, refine the race, stimulate wealth, elevate culture, correct political customs; but all this under the aegis of a nationalist ideal, without which Argentina would run the risk of moral dissolution."[20] The way was being paved for the closing off of immigration.

In light of the onslaught of criticism of the immigrant as un-Argentine, publication of *Los gauchos judíos* in 1910, Argentina's centennial year, takes on importance. Its author, Alberto Gerchunoff, was born in Poland in 1884 and brought to Argentina, where he grew up in the Jewish agricultural colony of Rajil. Migrating to Buenos Aires at age seventeen, he became a reporter for *La Nación* and eventually its editor in chief. His best-known work, translated as *Jewish Gauchos of the Pampas*, achieved considerable success in Argentina among both Jews and non-Jews. In fact, he was not so much a Jewish writer as a writer who interpreted Jewish life to the Gentiles. In this role, he played a considerable part in the rooting of the Jewish community in Argentina. His novel represents the Jewish claim on Argentine history, a claim backed up by the expenditure of blood, sweat, and love in the agricultural colonies.[21]

Gerchunoff proposed that Jewish life in Argentina represented a continuation of the Jews' Spanish tradition, interrupted but not ended by the Expulsion of 1492. By settling in Argentina, Jews were simply recovering what was already theirs; they even learned Spanish easily, he averred, because they already possessed a Spanish spirit. To develop this line of thought, Gerchunoff had to ignore the disparate historical experience of Sephardim and Ashkenazim: the latter were never in Spain and were never expelled from there. But his effort to anchor the Jews within Argentine tradition was rewarded by the admiration of numerous critics, one of whom wrote concerning him, "que por ser judío, tenía mucho de español" (being Jewish, he had much of the Spaniard in him).[22] He was also rewarded by the veneration of thousands of Argentine Jews, for whom he spoke at a level of psychological, if not factual, truth.[23]

Gerchunoff was just one among many major contributors to Argentine culture whose origins lay in Eastern Europe. Samuel Eichelbaum, born to Russian Jewish parents in the town of Dominguez, has been described as "the preeminent Spanish-speaking playwright."[24] Joseph Kessel, born in Villa Clara to a physician who was among the first Jewish settlers in Entre Ríos, was received into the French Academy of History for his literary and historical works.[25] Abraham Rosenwasser, born 1896 in Colonia Mauricio, earned a distinguished reputation worldwide as an Egyptologist, and participated in salvaging the monuments swamped by the Aswan dam.[26] Cesar Tiempo (born Israel Zeitlin in 1906 in the Ukraine) lived a lively literary life in Buenos Aires as journalist, playwright, poet, and editor of the literary review *Columna.*[27] Other Argentine literary figures stemming from this migration include Enrique Espinoza (né Samuel Glusberg), founder of the intellectual journal *Babel;* Carlos Grünberg, novelist and poet; and Max Dickman, influential Buenos Aires writer.[28] Enrique Dickmann, who was elected to Congress on the Socialist ticket, likewise stemmed from this migration. Dickmann grew up in the Jewish agricultural colonies but became a physician, one of those many of whom it was said, "We planted wheat, and grew doctors." The roster of Jewish intellectuals, scientists, actors, and artists who were accepted into the Argentine pantheon bespeaks a high degree of integration of this immigrant stream in the early decades of the twentieth century. The hesitation among Jewish religious leaders to support immigration to Argentina, and their choice not to go there themselves, seemed to have been invalidated by the opportunities available to Jews in their new land.

Chile

Despite early liberal immigration policy, Chile attracted very few immigrants in the nineteenth century. The country remained difficult of access. Prior to the opening of the Panama Canal, the options were a hazardous voyage through the Straits of Magellan or an arduous crossing of the Andes by foot or muleback (the trans-Andean railroad was not opened until 1910). There was no attempt to organize mass Jewish immigration, such as occurred in Argentina. The result was that there were scarcely enough Jews for a *minyan* (prayer unit of ten men) in Santiago in 1906, when an earthquake impressed upon the residents there the need for supernatural support.

One extraordinary personality of the period was the mining engineer Mauricio (Moritz) Hochschild. Born near Frankfurt to a middle-class Jewish family, Hochschild decided to try his luck in Chile, arriving there in 1911. Backed by a substantial letter of credit, he began buying copper for export and soon prospered. Bringing his brother over from Germany to run the business in Chile, he himself moved on to Bolivia, eventually becoming one of the "big three" of the tin industry and a sponsor of efforts to resettle German Jewish refugees in that country.[29]

Most of the East European Jews who came to Chile in the years just prior to World War I were moving on from Argentina, where they had not been able to sink roots. They arrived partially acculturated, with some knowledge of Spanish and, says one author, a fear of appearing to be Jewish that they had learned in Buenos Aires. These early settlers seem to have lived in fear of the surrounding population, whom they saw as "consumed by drunkenness and dominated by religious fanaticism" (an observation contained in the Yiddish text, but not in the Spanish translation).[30] An effigy of Judas, looking suspiciously like the medieval caricature of a Jew, was still being taken out and garrotted each Holy Week. Consequently, many Jews feared to identify themselves publicly as Jews, and a social club organized in 1911 opened under the unlikely name Filarmónica Rusa.

The Chilean Jewish community gained recruits with the flight of political activists from Argentina following the police repression of 1909.[31] Some Jewish businessmen also left Argentina during World War I for Chile, where the economy was more buoyant because of worldwide demand for copper and nitrates. But central European Jews continued to predominate, and these were still scattered in foreign colonies for the most part. A small number of German-speaking Jews had become highly successful in banking and export-import houses in the major cities.[32] To the south, various Sephardic families settled in Temuco, capital of Araucania, in 1914. They came from Monastir, in Yugoslavia, and they called their first club Centro Macedonia; only later was the word *israelita* added. Other Sephardim, impelled by shattered economies and religious wars, left their ancient communities in Istanbul, Smyrna, and Salonika and emigrated to Chile, founding new communities in Santiago and Valparaíso.[33]

Chilean intellectual support for immigration reversed field around 1905, when the accumulation of economic power by foreigners and their consequent rise to middle-class status presented an unexpected challenge to existing interests. This reaction must have set in without much stimulus from Jews. The newly arrived East Europeans were mostly peddlers who had not yet had time to establish themselves or to draw substantial quantities of business away from established merchants. And, although under the circumstances precise numbers cannot be known, there were only from two hundred to five hundred Jews in all of Chile in 1914.[34]

Mexico

The dictatorial rule of Porfirio Díaz, who controlled the destiny of Mexico from 1876 to 1911, spanned the period during which the need for resettlement of the Jews of Europe was expanding exponentially. A determined modernizer, Díaz welcomed European immigration, and as a consequence, all Jewish aid organizations looked into the possibilities for Jewish settlement in that country.[35] In 1891, financial moguls Jacob Schiff and Baron Maurice de Hirsch discarded the idea after examining wage levels in the country; two decades later, North American rabbi Martin Zielonka was touting the advantages of Mexico as a home for the Jews. Periodically, the possibility was floated of creating a Jewish homeland in Baja California.[36] The outbreak of the Revolution of 1910 and the decades of chaos which followed, put an end to all such speculation.

Curiously, the minimal number of Jews who had meanwhile immigrated from Damascus, Aleppo, and the Turkish empire, and who had started out as peddlers, may have been pushed up into the petite bourgeoisie by revolutionary events. The destruction of infrastructure and disruption of existing trade channels permitted them to establish small enterprises to fill local gaps in the economy.[37] During the first two decades of the twentieth century increasing numbers of Syrian, Turkish, and Lebanese Jews were matched by increments from the Balkans, expelled by the wars of that period. In 1917, an unknown number of Russian Jewish men who had migrated to the United States crossed into Mexico to avoid being drafted to fight a war they feared would include an invasion of Russia.[38]

Mexico was not attractive to immigrants generally, and very few Jews found their way there during this period. Many who did attempted to obscure their identity, either out of a sense of alienation from the Jewish people or from fear that the Inquisition mentality had taken permanent root in the deeply religious countryside. In the absence of community organization, mythology takes over, and estimates of the Jewish population of Mexico in 1905–10 vary from seventy-five to fifteen thousand.[39] The *American Jewish Year Book* figure of 8,972 is plausible, but the number could not have been known with certainty.

Brazil

In the last decade of the nineteenth century, Jewish immigration to Brazil increased in numbers while becoming more disparate in origin. Immigrants continued to come from North Africa and western Europe, but to these were added Jews from countries of the eastern Mediterranean (Greece, Turkey, Syria, Lebanon, Palestine) as well as from Russia and adjacent countries of eastern Europe. These immigrants organized themselves into *landsmannschaften* on the basis of country of origin; the synagogues and mutual aid societies grew up without reference to one another. Nevertheless, they established a skeletal infrastructure for Jewish life that would ease the entry into Brazil of future waves of immigrants.[40] In this respect, Mexico and Brazil stand in contrast to one another, highlighting the far more relaxed religious atmosphere of Brazil.

Most of these immigrants settled in Rio de Janeiro, São Paulo, or the state of Minas Gerais; but smaller numbers dispersed to other provinces. The Brazilian national census of 1900 located 1,021 Jews in the country. During the years 1900–10, East European Jewish immigration increased. Many arrived in Brazil under shepherding of immigration agents, who had acquired the ships' tickets gratis from the Brazilian government upon representing that they were recruiting labor for the coffee, tobacco, and sugar plantations. The immigrants quickly sought escape from the debt slavery of the plantations, and most metamorphosed into peddlers. Rio also served as a staging area for the introduction of Jewish young women into the white slave trade during periods when the Argentine police cracked down on prostitution in that country.[41]

Some Ashkenazim came to Brazil under the auspices of the JCA, which founded Colonia Filipson in the state of Rio Grande do Sul in 1903, beginning with forty-eight families totaling two hundred persons, most of them children.

Unaccustomed to the soil and climate, the immigrants abandoned this colony within a single generation, turning to peddling and petty commerce in Pôrto Alegre, capital of the state.[42] The colony Quatro Irmãos, founded in 1910, suffered a most difficult fate. Caught up in the rebellion of 1922 that racked the state of Rio Grande do Sul, the colony was alternately occupied, taxed, and terrorized by opposing forces, leading to the impoverishment and departure of almost all of the settlers.

> ". . . I was standing in the door of my father's store. I was born in 1921: the revolution was in 1923. I won't forget him because the guy was my namesake. . . . He said, Jacob, I'm gonna lasso me a *chimango* at the barricade. He went out, caught one and was shot in the forehead and died. But he caught one, did his service to the gaúchos. . . . 1 remember when they had that revolution, the *chimangos* against the *maragatos*. The *maragatos* took out about twenty meters of track, to derail a train that was carrying 312 *chimangos*, which are the army of the Military Brigade. They killed almost all the brigaders—what a revolution."[43]

"The good intentions of the Jewish Colonization Association . . . never translated into a better life for the colonists," concludes their historian.[44] Instead of the agricultural colonies acting as magnets to attract new immigrants to the underpopulated parts of the country, as the government had hoped, urban areas filled up with refugees from the countryside—and not from the Jewish colonies alone.

On the eve of World War I, the most important Jewish communities in Brazil were still the Sephardim of the north. There were small communities in Itacoatiara and Parintins and a large one in Manaus that was not organized. The largest community was that of Belém do Pará, which possibly numbered eight hundred. Its local influence was reflected in the establishment of a chair in the Hebrew language at the Colegio Pará e Amazonas. Rio likewise had an organized Sephardic community at that date.[45]

In all, there may have been 5,000 Jews in Brazil in 1917, compared with Argentina's 112,000, according to a survey commissioned by the American Jewish Committee.[46] By that date, many Sephardim who had originally settled in the small riverine towns of Amazonia as traders and rubber brokers had moved on to Rio, São Paulo, Caracas, and other large cities in the wake of the fall in rubber prices.[47] The scant number of Jewish immigrants into the country in this period, when pressures for exodus from eastern Europe were great, corresponds to what is known about the relative unattractiveness of the country to immigrants at the turn of the century. As whites, immigrants arriving from Europe had an advantage in the labor market over black, recently freed slaves. Nevertheless, the predominantly rural and regimented nature of plantation labor was no attraction for immigrants who hoped that, by coming to the New World, they could improve the quality of their lives.

Peru

Between 1910 and 1915, numerous family groups of Sephardim emigrated to Peru. At first, they joined the existing society of German Jews—their acceptance by earlier settlers shown by the election of Sephardi individuals to office in the Sociedad de Beneficencia Israelita. They did, however, go off on their own within the decade, adding "Sefaradi" to the organization's title. Although a few East European Jews entered Peru from Poland and Russia in the closing years of the nineteenth century, the Ashkenazi migration did not really begin until about 1912, when identifiable family groups took up residence in the Lima barrio of Chirimoyo.[48] In the Cementerio Israelita de Bellavista, the places of birth inscribed on 875 tombstones mark the dimensions of the Peruvian gathering of exiles. Fifty of the deceased were born in Romania, 240 in Bessarabia, 7 in Bucovina, 52 in Russia (half these in Ukraine), 141 in Poland, 25 in Hungary, with a scattering of individuals from Czechoslovakia, Chile, Brazil, Colombia, Argentina, France, England, Yugoslavia, Switzerland, United States, Belgium, and Ecuador. So much for Yiddish speakers. German speakers totaled 178, most from Germany itself, with 23 from Austria. Sephardim comprised 154 persons or 18 percent of the total. They had been born in Turkey, Greece, Morrocco, and Egypt.[49] While most of these Jews settled in Lima, individuals have been identified in towns from Tumbes to Huancavelica, Cuzco to Arequipa. Overall numbers, however, were very small, numbering in the hundreds only. Most of these immigrants began as peddlers, returning home to the *shtetl* (provincial Jewish towns of eastern Europe) when they had put aside some money. But the rise of anti-Semitism in Europe after World War I put an end to their peregrinations, and those who had been able to establish an economic base in Peru settled there on a permanent basis.[50] Most of these stayed in Lima, but some opened stores and cafés in provincial towns, where advertisements for "Casa Bessarabia" could still be seen in the 1960s.

Panama

Sephardic immigrants had settled in Panama while the area was still a province of Gran Colombia. These were descendants of Portuguese New Christians who moved to British territory such as Jamaica and St. Thomas and there reverted to Judaism. The destruction of St. Thomas by hurricane in 1867 drove numbers of these Sephardim to relocate in Panama.[51] More Sephardim of the Antilles entered Panama when the French began construction of the canal. The assumption of the canal project by the United States initiated a commercial boom that attracted, among others, Jews from every part of the world. Partly because of the presence of the United States in the Canal Zone, and partly as a result of the mixture of nations in the infant republic, Panama developed a relatively liberal religous policy. Catholicism was recognized as the predominant religion, but freedom of conscience was also guaranteed, and the government was forbidden to interfere in religious practices. As a result, there was no practical or legal bar to the immigration of non-Catholics.[52]

In 1917, a well-defined occupational hierarchy was observed among Panamanian Jews. The "native" Jews (descendants of émigrés from Curaçao) comprised a quarter of the Jewish population of five hundred. Owners of commission houses and of large holdings in the public utilities, these Sephardim mingled with the highest strata of society rather more than with their coreligionists. About 15 percent of Jews were Syrians, a class of middle-sized merchants in dry goods, notions, and the like. Turkish and Egyptian Jews were peddlers and small shopkeepers, occupying a considerably lower social level than previously named groups. American and central European Jews had invested heavily in hotels, movie theatres, and furniture and clothing stores and had done particularly well since the arrival of the American canal builders. A few Jewish ranchers, farmers, dentists, lawyers, and opticians rounded out the occupational picture.

Uruguay

Although church and state were not legally separated until 1919, all Jewish observers attest to the religious toleration that prevailed in the republic in the twentieth century. Uruguay appears to be the only Latin American republic eager to acknowledge the cultural role of immigrants, even erecting a monument to them in a major public park. Or, as one immigrant put it, "that faceless seeker after happiness whom fate cast upon the Uruguayan shore . . . turned out to be a pioneer and founder of the modern national economy."[53]

Sephardim found their way to Uruguay in the early 1900s. They came, declassed and impoverished, from Lebanon, Syria, and Turkey. Although they arrived without resources, their knowledge of Ladino eased their entry into the Uruguayan economy. Most became peddlers, and their integration was facilitated by the absence of xenophobia. There was greater willingness on the left bank of the Plata than on the right to accept the immigrant innovator without concern for his religion. Immigrants received equal rights on arrival; all they had to do was obey the law. In this atmosphere, the Sephardim metamorphosed within a decade into merchants, handcraftsmen, and even small industrialists. Additional Sephardim arrived after the First Balkan War (1912–13). These were economically better off than their predecessors, and they laid the foundations of the present Montevideo Jewish community. By 1917, there were seventeen hundred Jews in Uruguay, three-fourths of them Sephardim. About fifteen hundred of the total lived in Montevideo, and almost all were middle or working class. A few extremely wealthy merchants had left their Jewish origins behind. About 10 percent of this population was in agricultural colonies, either established by JCA or initiated independently. Numbers of second-generation youth were attending the university, and about ten Jews held low-ranking positions in government.[54]

Paraguay

Paraguay has never appeared in a favorable light as a place of settlement for immigrants, despite efforts by successive governments to attract Europeans and Americans. The disastrous war of the Triple Alliance left Paraguay with a population of just 231,000; in a bid to repopulate the country, the constitution of 1870 provided for freedom of religion and offered numerous benefits to immigrants, including ease of naturalization. No large number of Jews took advantage of the invitation, probably dissuaded by the vision of a society polarized between a Spanish creole elite and a subjugated Indian mass, intensely Catholic, with little breathing space for non-Catholics.

Most immigrants were either Italian or Argentine—both Latin and Catholic. Exceptionally, two colonies of Protestant farmers—Mennonites and Methodist Episcopals—did establish themselves, but no mass settlement of Jews was attempted comparable to the efforts by JCA in neighboring Argentina and Uruguay. In Asunción itself, where Positivists and Freemasons engaged in open combat with the Catholic Church, the few Jews living there intermarried and gave up their Jewish legacy.[55] Seiferheld identified several individuals of Jewish descent who served their country as foreign emissaries in London and Paris.

The second half of the nineteenth century saw the arrival in Paraguay of a small number of Sephardim, including the anthropologist Moisés Santiago Bertoni and his son Guillermo Tell Bertoni, the latter a botanist and lawyer, who became active in Paraguayan politics.[56] Small numbers of Ashkenazim from Poland and Russia settled in Paraguay in the first decade of the twentieth century. In 1917, the director-general of statistics was a Jew. Additional arrivals from central Europe and the Balkans brought the community to six hundred by World War I.[57] The continuing pattern until the period of Nazism was of isolated individual Jews choosing Paraguay for reasons best known to themselves.

Bolivia

Bolivia, old Upper Peru, was one of the last bastions of the loyalist Spanish church during the wars for independence, and her first constitution amply reflected that fact: "The Roman Catholic Apostolic religion is the religion of the Republic to the exclusion of all other public cults." Half a century later, in 1871, this article was slightly revised in an effort to accommodate foreign immigration: the practice of non-Catholic cults was to be permitted "in colonies where it is tolerated." By 1905, this right had been extended throughout the republic, and over the next five years, the rights of civil marriage and of civil burial were instituted. Nevertheless, economic and social conditions were not deemed inviting by any large number of immigrants. The grant of religious toleration served to facilitate the entrance of Protestant missionaries to the country, but not of many non-Christians.

In 1904, several Russian Jewish families found their way to Bolivia. (The expression used by the Yiddish-language historian is *farblondzhet,* which carries the implication that these people had gotten lost and wandered into Bolivia by mistake.)[58] Twenty-five families were counted in that country by the representative of the American Jewish Committee in 1917. All were either owners of businesses or employees of these same firms. Bolivia, with its majority Aymara and Quechua populations continuing to live their age-old ways of life based on agriculture and transhumance rearing of flocks, was not Uruguay or even Argentina, where European-descended populations offered immigrants an opportunity for linking to the majority society. Peddlers did not tackle lightly this mountainous terrain whose inhabitants showed little desire for the products of the industrialized world.

Cuba

Cuba, which remained under Spanish control far longer than the other republics, is the single one in which Jews participated in the wars of independence. Filibustering raids against this last of the Spanish colonies in the New World were mounted—prematurely, as it turned out—from Gran Colombia in 1832 and from New Orleans in 1852. These included a number of Jews, who earned themselves a place in Cuban history. Of particular interest is the career of Luis Schlesinger, a Hungarian Jew who had fought in the revolution of 1848 and who subsequently fled to the United States. There he was recruited by Cuban General Narciso López, who persuaded him to lead a raid upon the island. The expedition took off from New Orleans and reached El Morrillo, Pinar del Río, on 12 August 1851. Captured by the Spanish and imprisoned in Ceuta, Schlesinger escaped and lived to write his memoirs.[59] Akiva Rolland, a Ukrainian Jewish adventurer, entered Cuban history as General Carlos Roloff and became the first finance minister of the independent republic. Substantial numbers of Jews, chiefly of Spanish origin, fought in the final war of independence in 1898. The American expeditionary force that served in that war included a number of Jewish soldiers who decided to remain on the island when the war was over. At its conclusion, some Romanian Jewish immigrants (referred to as "Americans" in Cuban Jewish literature because they had been naturalized on the mainland) took up residence in Cuba and opened businesses there under the concessions wrought by the U.S. military government. By 1900, there were about three hundred Jewish families in Cuba.[60]

The years 1902–14 witnessed intensive immigration to Cuba from Turkey and Syria (fifty-seven hundred persons, according to Cuban government figures). According to some historians, Cuba received more emigrants from Turkey than did any other part of Latin America, and most of these were Jews. Badly impacted by the reforms brought in by the Young Turk movement and by the chaos of the Balkan wars, they opted for Cuba because of the similarity of the language to their native Ladino.[61] This group was swollen by the arrival of refugees from the Mexican Revolution of 1910 and the counterrevolution of

1913 (following the murder of Francisco Madero). By 1916, there were four thousand Sephardim in Havana, but their numbers dwindled as the world war ended, some returning to Mexico and others proceeding to the United States.

East European Jews were slow to discover Cuba as a country of settlement. Close to four thousand East European Jews passed through the Cuban offices of various Jewish immigrant aid societies between 1910 and 1917, but the best estimate of the total Jewish population of Cuba in 1919 is just two thousand. As long as the United States and even Europe were viable options, Cuba was no more than a transit point for Ashkenazim.

Venezuela

As we have seen, Jewish life in Venezuela commenced with the migration of Sephardim from Curaçao and St. Thomas. A descendant of this group, David Lobo Senior, born in 1861 at Puerto Cabello, became rector of the Universidad Central of Venezuela and later chargé d'affaires of the Venezuelan embassy in Washington, D.C. Dr. Mario Capriles, born in 1872, served as president of the legislature of the state of Carabobo, then as deputy, senator, secretary, and finally president of the National Congress. Capriles was made a Caballero of the Royal Order of Isabella the Catholic, a suitable honor in light of the fact that his mother was a descendant of Abraham Senior, last Jewish minister of that queen.[62] Other noteworthy Venezuelan Sephardim in this period included a president of the Supreme Court, an official of the Bank of Venezuela, the man who introduced the telegraph into the country, and the founder of the Venezuelan Red Cross.

Over the course of time, increasing numbers of Sephardim contracted marriage with local families. Jewish communities at Tucacas (state of Falcón) and Barcelona (state of Anzoátegui) disappeared within the last century through assimilation. The longest-lived of the communities, and probably the oldest one on the continent, was situated at Coro, whose port is opposite the island of Curaçao. The cemetery at Coro was founded in 1832 by Josef Curiel for the burial of his infant daughter Iojevet. The stones there tell a story. In contrast to the cemetery of the mother community of Curaçao, where tombstones are engraved in Hebrew, those at Coro are in Spanish and sculpted with undeniably Catholic cherubs. Apparently, the Coro community originally lived as Jews but lacked the capacity to pass along their traditions. Gradually the community dissolved, bequeathing its descendants to the nation at large. Long neglected, the site was restored in 1970 under the direction of the Venezuelan minister of public works, José Curiel, a descendant of the family.[63]

The contemporary Jewish community of Venezuela originated with the migration of Jews from Morocco, Palestine, Syria, Lebanon, and Iran, beginning in 1900. Most started their new lives as itinerant peddlers, moving up within a generation or two into the ranks of merchants and bankers.[64] Most of the Moroccans were Spanish speakers from Tetuán. The frequency of movement between Morocco and Venezuela is shown by the fact that the principal shop in Tetuán in the 1920s was called La Caraqueña; the doctor of the Spanish legation in Caracas was a Moroccan Jew.

As far as can be ascertained, Russian Jews did not find their way to Venezuela during the period of czarist repression. The continual civil unrest to which Venezuela was subject in the nineteenth century was not conducive to immigration of any type. The intimate ties between church and state presented an additional problem. The temporal power of the church was contained in 1873, when the dictator Antonio Guzman Blanco broke the ecclesiastical monopoly over civil matters, including registration of births, marriages, and deaths and the administration of cemeteries. But the relationship between church and state remained symbiotic: religious liberty was guaranteed, but only under supervision of the state. The Venezuelan government continued to exercise the *patronato* (the right to appoint the church hierarchy) until 1964. In effect, the Catholic Church remained a state church.

Portuguese Sephardim had had long historic experience with this type of situation; the Spanish Sephardim who lived as *dhimmis* in Muslim lands, alternately protected and harassed by their overlords, may have found the atmosphere of Venezuela a relief. But Ashkenazim were well aware of the possibilities for full emancipation as introduced to Europe by Napoleon, and the promise of full citizenship held out by the evolution of democracy in the United States. Fleeing from czarist oppression and Catholic reaction in eastern Europe, they would have been most reluctant to step backward in time to enter a country where they would have had to subordinate their dreams to a monolithic Catholic regime.

The Jewish Population of Latin America in 1917

All countries of Latin America received Jewish immigrants during the period 1880–1914. The repression being experienced by Jews of eastern Europe was matched by the pressures exerted against Sephardim in the Balkans. Like the Ashkenazim, many Sephardim were forced to find new homes in areas that had never before attracted them. Just which Latin American republic an immigrant might choose appears to have been determined by historical circumstance, the idiosyncrasies of shipping agents, and the availability of financial support. As Haim Avni has shown for Argentina, the decision of JCA to sponsor agriculturists only, combined with JCA's limited organizational capacity, limited the overall number of Jewish immigrants they sponsored, at a time when the country would have been receptive to them.[65] Random choices of destination, made by immigrants whose knowledge of the continent was minimal, led to the appearance of new Jewish communities in every corner of the continent.

The survey commissioned by the American Jewish Committee in 1917 estimated at 150,000 the number of Jews then living in South and Central America and the Caribbean.[66] Of this number, from 110,000 to 113,000 were in Argentina. The influx of Russian and other East European Jews had by now reversed the balance between Sephardi and Ashkenazi, so that the latter now constituted about 80 percent of Latin American Jewry. The easterners were as unlike the central Europeans who had preceded them as both were unlike the Sephardim. The easterners arrived penniless and had perforce to fit themselves into the interstices of the host economies. There were no bankers or high financiers in this migration, no agents of the House of Rothschild. To the contrary, many were clients of Jewish philanthropies. Once arrived, they were under great pressure to make good. In addition, the easterners were more provincial than the German, French, and English Jews. Locked into the Russian Pale of Settlement, without access to national schools or national economies, Jews were not participants in the national life of Russia, Poland, or Romania in the sense in which Jews had participated in the national life of France, Germany, or England. Despite the influence of the haskalah, which encouraged secularization of Jewish life in preparation for emancipation, emancipation had never come. The Jews' capacity to come out into non-Jewish society depended on the willingness of society to permit them to do so; this had not come about in eastern Europe. Consequently, eastern Jews identified as Jews, rather than as citizens of the national societies within which they existed. They were still citizens of the shtetl, that small Jewish world, traditional, introverted, closed, which balanced uneasily upon the threshold of a hostile large world they could not enter.[67] Although religion per se may have been on the defensive in shtetl life as everywhere else in Europe, the grip of *Yiddishkeit* (Jewishness) was undiminished. Shtetl Jews arrived in Latin America with *Yiddishkeit* their chief cultural possession and no tradition whatever of free mingling with a gentile population. The easterners' attachment to the Yiddish language had no counterpart among the German, French, and Alsatian Jews, who had already translated their private lives into non-Jewish languages. East European Jews exhibited far greater need to continue their communal life together. They struggled to preserve their way of life through myriad communal organizations patterned after those which had served their needs in the old country and appeared to be equally necessary in the new. Schools, cultural centers, libraries, burial societies, mutual aid societies—all these organizational forms came to be synonymous in the minds of the East Europeans with the concept of a Jewish community. In turn, the existence of these communal organizations demarcated the Jewish populations more clearly than had been the case before the arrival of the East Europeans.

Among this group particularly, one senses a terror of Catholic lands, a rearousal of fears of the terrible pogroms still taking place in Russia and Poland, and beyond which lay memory of the grotesque massacres and forced conversions in Castile in 1391. Almost every immigrant memoir of this time begins or ends with intimations of a pogrom:

> With each passing second, Jacobo went deeper into regions peopled by barely recognizable silhouettes. Indefinite streets and houses waved in his mind as he relived events from his past. Sometimes he saw himself with a cane in his hand, walking down the streets of Chepén. Other times he was praying in a room with shuttered windows, or preaching

in the square in front of the church. He was publicly reproved by the priest. Guards took him from his house and dragged him through the streets. He was almost murdered by the people of Chepén. . . . On his first night in the hospital, Jacobo had had this same vision. Roused by his screams, two nuns had come into his room and found him crouching on the ground, his eyes tightly shut, shaking with fear. One of them had stayed by his side the rest of the night. The next morning, Jacobo asked her to remove the plaster crucifix from his room.[68]

A young, unnamed, Argentine Jewish narrator decides to write his biography. But he soon discovers that his project is in fact a *re*-writing, the rewriting of his father's European past. In order to inscribe himself, the narrator must inscribe the father. He has to repeat, retrace, and translate the facts and faces of a difficult past, a past whose tracks have been erased by the Holocaust but whose claim on the present is intensified by that very erasure.[69]

These survivors needed an act of will to entrust their lives to those whom they saw as descendants of their old tormentors. Ashkenazim had never been in Spain, of course, and neither had most Argentinians or most Mexicans. But who knew better than Jews how strong the grip of inherited tradition could be?

Some Latin American expectations of immigrants were being fulfilled. Twenty-six thousand Jewish farmers were on the land in Argentina in 1917, several thousand more in Uruguay and Brazil. But despite the tug of agrarian life in the "New Zion," the overwhelming majority of Jews, including three-quarters of the now substantial Jewish population of Argentina, lived in the cities.

Prior to World War I, Latin America's lack of industrialization and continued use of cities as religious and administrative centers rather than as centers for the production of goods meant that middle population sectors were small and elitist. Most Latin American cities remained limited in their functions and unintegrated by rail, canal, or road with their rural hinterlands; they exhibited little specialization of labor until the spurt of economic growth occasioned by the disruption of international trade during World War I. Buenos Aires and Montevideo were exceptions to this pattern, and these cities did become early recipients of large numbers of Jewish immigrants.

What area Jewish immigrants chose to settle in seems to have been controlled in part by the ethnic makeup and class structure of the host society. In the Andean republics and Central America, the ethnic gap appeared almost unbridgeable. In a country of landed aristocrats and landless peasants, they could be neither. Neither criollo nor autochthonous culture provided congenial space for insertion of a Jewish presence. The absence of a modernized middle class presented a serious obstacle for Jews. The mass of Italian immigrants to Argentina resolved their problem of social incongruence by migrating annually to harvest the wheat crop, returning home for the winter: the famous *golondrinas* (swallows). For Jews, there was no returning home. They needed places of permanent settlement. The need for a social context into which they could comfortably fit drew Jewish immigrants to countries with heavy European immigration. Thus, although there is no country of Latin America in which East European Jews did not settle, the largest cohorts headed for the southernmost republics, with their predominantly European populations, their nascent middle classes, and their social milieus that were favorable to industrialization. Modernizing economies meant employment, skilled and unskilled, for the laboring and middle classes. Secularizing values in Argentina, Uruguay, Panama, and the southern states of Brazil led to disestablishment of the Catholic Church and its relegation to secondary status. Such developments made it possible for Jews either to live as Jews or to intermarry comfortably.

Peasant societies, on the other hand, characterized by an Indian or mestizo mass and a Hispanic criollo elite, presented the immigrants—Jews and non-Jews alike—with the prospect of a mass society whose way of life they could only reject and an elite that rejected them. Such countries as Bolivia, Guatemala, Paraguay, and Peru were unable to attract much immigration no matter what legal frame they devised because there was no social setting into which immigrants could fit. For Jews, the matter was complicated by the prevailing religiosity of these societies, which made it difficult either to live as a Jew or to assimilate. Countries in this category did receive some Jewish immigrants in the period 1889–1917. But these individuals—preponderantly Sephardim and Arabic-speaking Jews—lived isolated as a merchant caste in a manner not dissimilar to the status of Jews in Europe of the Middle Ages. While they also migrated to the modernizing republics of the southern cone, Sephardim were strongly represented in countries such as Mexico and the Central American republics, which Ashkenazim regarded with dread.

By the end of this period, there were few who could trace their origins to the Portuguese Jews of Curaçao. These Sephardim—Jews, Catholics, Masons—had become well integrated into the upper classes of their respective national societies. They made meaningful careers for themselves in the national economy and government of Venezuela, Colombia, and the smaller Caribbean republics, enjoying a high degree of social integration in countries that retained an intense attachment to Hispanic Catholicism, countries that never seemed to East European immigrants to be viable options.

In addition to these groups there were estimated to be another fifty to sixty thousand persons in Latin America in 1917 who had been born Jews but who had severed themselves from Jewish life.[70] Their number is obscure, though not beyond conjecture. If the estimate of ethnic Jews not identifying with their religious community is anywhere near the mark, it indicates an assimilation rate of 25 percent within two generations of arrival on the continent. The mingled hope and fear of proimmigration forces that Jews would add to the biological mixture of "races" seems to have been warranted.

CHAPTER 4

Completion of the Contemporary Jewish Communities

No one is as hard on a Jew as an official who won't take a bribe.
—Sholom Aleichem

GLOBAL JEWISH MIGRATION was part of the great immigrant stream that coursed from east to west throughout the nineteenth century. Halted by World War I, the migrants resumed their westward flow once the guns grew silent—but in diminished numbers because barriers were now placed in their way. On the eve of World War II, these barriers became almost insuperable. The communities that are in place today are the product of interwar settlement patterns, as molded and reshaped by events since 1945.

The Migrants: What Moved Them?

The Jewish immigrants of post–World War I days were no longer *rusos.* Revolution in Russia held out the promise of equal rights to all sectors of the population and prohibited emigration equally to all. But to the west of Soviet borders, old attitudes of anti-Semitism were reinforced by the new ideology of fascism. As a result, increasing pressure was exerted on Jewish minorities. With national populations increasing faster than the capacity of economies to absorb them, the crisis of lack of land and lack of employment grew increasingly desperate in the interwar years. The surplus sons of peasants poured into the cities as unskilled labor. Their children, anxious to rise in the world, found that many positions in trade, industry, and the liberal professions were occupied by Jews, who had begun their modernizing role earlier. The very success of Jews in urbanizing themselves led to a nationalistic reaction against them.

Following the breakup of the Austrian and Ottoman empires and the fulfillment of the pledge of self-determination for small nations, national majorities gained access to the levers of power for the first time and were in a position to shape economic and political policies. Many of these were calculated to make life difficult for Jews, so that conditions throughout Central Europe became intolerable for Jews long before the rise of Hitler. Discriminatory taxes, boycotts, destruction of Jewish-owned property, and officially sponsored pogroms began the destruction of the Jewish communities that the Nazis were to finish. To many Jews in Poland, Romania, Hungary, Latvia, and Lithuania, emigration seemed the only way to survive.

Sephardim had been abandoning their homes in Turkey and the Balkans ever since the Young Turk rebellion of 1908 and the Balkan War of 1912–13. That conflict left the Jewish communities ravaged and thousands of impoverished refugees piled up in Salonika and Constantinople. Major Jewish communities in Monastir, Janina, Castoria, Kavala, and Adrianople were badly damaged, and their situation was worsened by World War I. The exchange of populations between Greece and Turkey (1923–28) destroyed the economic foundations of the Jewish community of Smyrna, sundered the ancient Sephardic community of Salonika, and propelled another wave of Ladino-speaking Jews toward the New World. Of the four million Jewish migrants in the period 1840–1956, two to three hundred thousand were Sephardic and Arabic Jews.

German-speaking Jews began appearing in numbers in Latin America in 1933, the year of Hitler's accession to power. But the rise of fascism in Europe coincided with the adoption of exclusionist immigration policies elsewhere. Draconian visa restrictions, initiated by the United States, rippled through the Western Hemisphere in the thirties, narrowing the options of the refugees. Jews who sought to escape the Nazi onslaught found it increasingly difficult to enter their preferred lands of destination and had to go wherever governments would let them in. The result was to increase the celebrated dispersion of the Jews to a greater degree than ever before in their history.

Immigration Patterns: Influence of the United States

If Jewish migration was a function of political events in Europe, the pattern this migration assumed was a function of United States immigration law. The United States had been the destination of choice of the vast majority of Jewish migrants, and under free market conditions this country absorbed 90 percent of them. By 1921, however, the United States had altered its perception of itself as haven of the world's "huddled masses, yearning to breathe free." In that year, the Immigration Quota Act established an annual quota of 3 percent of the total of foreign-born of each nationality resident in the United States, based on the census of 1910. One provision of the law allowed for the admission of immigrants from contiguous territory; this led some Jewish migrants to head for Mexico or Cuba in anticipation of entry into the promised land. However, that provision was canceled three years later. The Immigration Act of 1924 reduced these quotas further, to 2 percent of the foreign-born resident in the United States in 1890. As there were few eastern or southern Europeans in the United States in that year, the areas from which Jews now needed to emigrate were allocated extremely small quotas. Passage of such legislation caused the Jewish immigrant stream to be diverted elsewhere. Other countries—chiefly Palestine, Argentina, Canada, and South Africa—now experienced a rise, which actually made only a small dent in the number of Jews who needed to leave Europe and who were cut off from escape.

Latin America, as we have seen, had never absorbed more than a tiny fraction of Jewish emigrants. In the period 1926–30, the continent received 42 percent of them—but the flow was running at a diminished level (see Table 1, page 52). The number of European Jews able to find refuge in the various countries of Latin America during the thirties was drastically curtailed by restrictive legislation and unwritten policies that these nations adopted in emulation of the United States. From 1931 until the outbreak of World War II, an estimated 92,351 persons, or 18 percent of Jewish migrants, settled in Latin America. Of all the countries of the southern continent, Argentina had always received the largest number of Jewish immigrants. Over the course of a century, she absorbed 5 percent of the total European Jewish migration, ranking a distant third after the United States (71.5 percent) and Palestine/Israel (9.7 percent).

As the stream of Jewish migration was deflected from the United States, Argentina continued to absorb the lion's share within Latin America, admitting nearly 40,000 Jews in the period 1921–25 (twice as many as were admitted to all other Latin American countries combined) and nearly 34,000 in the following five years (about half as many as were admitted to all other Latin American countries). Rising xenophobia and the compelling example of the United States, however, caused Argentina also to curtail immigration, and 1923 was the last year in which a sizable number of Jews were legally admitted. During the thirteen years of the Nazi era, 1933–45, official Argentine records show that 24,488 immigrants declared themselves to be Jewish; to these must be added first-class passengers, Jews who failed to declare themselves, and those who entered the country illegally. As Haim Avni points out in presenting these figures, Jewish immigration must be understood in the context of general policy: Argentina wanted farmers, preferably northern European ones; urban migrants were barely tolerated, and refugees scarcely at all.[1] Jewish refugees from Nazism fit into none of the desired categories of immigrants. Uncertainty over the number of illegal immigrants who entered during this same period leads Senkman to offer a comparatively wide range for a possible total: between 28,129 and 38,160.[2] Newton believes that some 43,000 Jews entered Argentina between 1933 and the end of World War II, largely because the officials of neighboring countries "did a brisk and lucrative trade in visas and entry permits for persons desperate to escape the Nazi terror," and the Argentine government could not control its own borders.[3] After arrival in Bolivia or Paraguay, the comparative charm of Argentina drew many to the more developed country by whatever means possible. By any of these calculations, Argentina ended up

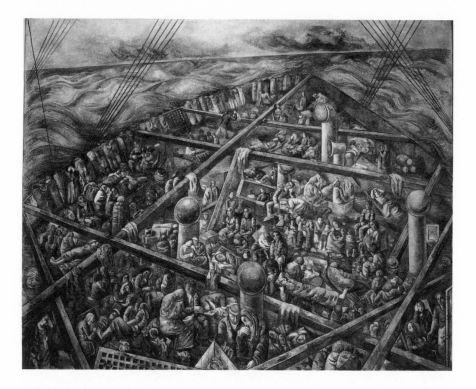

Conditions under which many immigrants came to America are imaginatively re-created in *Emigrant Ship,* an oil painting by the contemporary Brazilian Jewish painter Lazar Segall.

admitting more Jewish refugees from Nazism than any other country in the world except Palestine, and considerably more than other nations that had declared for the Allied side, as Argentina had not.[4]

The closing of Argentina to legal immigration swelled the immigrant stream to Brazil only slightly, due to a literal sea change in that country's attitude toward immigrants. Brazil admitted just 1,690 Jewish immigrants in 1925. Thenceforward, the number fluctuated between 1,000 and 5,000 per year until the outbreak of World War II, the largest recorded numbers entering in 1929 and 1939.[5] It is also likely that larger numbers of Jews arrived during this period without the formality of stating their religion. Only when the United States, followed by Argentina and Brazil, excluded mass immigration did new communities form in previously disfavored republics. Fragmentary communities came into existence in Paraguay, Bolivia, Venezuela, Colombia, the Dominican Republic, and Ecuador.

In the aftermath of World War II, about a million and a half more Jews migrated worldwide; 77.9 percent of these went to Palestine/Israel.[6] Latin America received about 37,000 persons from this migration. Some two-thirds of these were displaced persons who were admitted to various republics between 1945 and 1956. Largely kin of persons already admitted for permanent residence, their continent-wide distribution meant that they made little demographic impact.

Following the Suez crisis and the Hungarian uprising of 1956, some 8,300 Jews were resettled in Latin America, 70 percent of these in Brazil. Concentrated in the cities of São Paulo and Rio de Janeiro, these immigrants had a noticeable impact on the ethnic makeup of these communities.

All Latin American republics now have restrictive immigration laws, and the growth of contemporary Latin American Jewish communities has halted and even reversed. Over the course of the century 1840–1942, some 376,227 European Jews—fewer than 10 percent of the four million who migrated—entered Latin America. Plainly, for Ashkenazim, the largest sector of world Jewry, Latin America was not the first choice for settlement. It is conceivable that larger proportions of non-European Jews, for whom data are lacking, settled on the continent during this period; but their absolute numbers would be considerably lower because of their smaller population base. The disfavor with which Jews view Latin America as a permanent home was confirmed in the 1980s and 1990s when no one suggested diverting the mass migration of Ethiopian or Russian Jews to destinations in the southern Americas.

Nativist Reaction Against Immigration

Latin America of the post–World War I years presented immigrants with a different prospect than had earlier prevailed. In some countries, industrialization was creating new opportunities for employment in the expanding industrial sector, as well as broader scope for the deployment of entrepreneurial skills and capital. But the emergence of new social forces attendant on industrialization brought about an elitist reaction among those who viewed organized labor as socially disruptive. The rapid growth of cities and the development of an "alienated, restless, and increasingly militant proletariat" dismayed the creole elites, whose traditional notions concerning the natural servility of the laboring classes were being upset.[7] If they did not close off immigration immediately, it was because they still believed that immigration was essential for economic development.

By World War I, the naive faith in European immigrants as whiteners and enlighteners of inferior mestizo races had dissipated in the most modernized countries. Instead, a celebration of the native races had begun, intensified by rivalry with the immigrants, who were achieving greater economic success and swifter social ascent than seemed possible for any honest person. Carl Solberg interpreted this change:

> The gleaming image that European immigration had once enjoyed among Argentines and Chileans was tarnished by 1914. Only a quarter century earlier the elites of both republics had welcomed the foreign

influx with enthusiasm, but many of the changes wrought by immigration dismayed powerful segments of the population. Foreign-born business-men and professionals controlled ever greater shares of both nations' economies. Immigrant urban laborers organized, struck, and became continually more militant. The spectre of anarchism, and, some thought, of bloody social revolution, loomed. . . . After 1905 influential writers in both republics were rejecting the positivist and cosmopolitan-oriented ideologies invoked by the elites since the 1850s to justify liberal immigration policies. In place of cosmopolitanism, these intellectuals began to formulate nationalist ideologies that lauded traditional creole social and cultural values and stressed the belief that immigrants must adopt these values. Such a vindication of creole culture contrasted sharply with nineteenth-century Argentine and Chilean thought, which had disdained the Spanish and indigenous heritages as barbaric while regarding the immigrant as the very symbol of civilization.[8]

During the 1920s, it was still possible for Jews to emigrate to Argentina. Liberals who favored the admittance of immigrants, Jews included, as elements required for the industrialization and modernization of the country were still in control of immigration policy. But international Jewish organizations assisting the migrants viewed Argentina with skepticism. They were moreover focused on a different set of priorities: the need to force the British mandatory power to permit the entry of Jews en masse into Palestine. By 1930, as the need for emigration outlets intensified, the Argentine perception of immigrants became more problematic. The onset of the Great Depression, the perception that Jews and other immigrant groups were not melting directly into the *crisol de razas* (crucible of races) but persisted in holding on to elements of their cultural heritage, and, most specifically, the appointment of anti-Semitic individuals to directorial positions in the immigration service, all coalesced into a reordering of immigration policy.[9] In January 1933, just as Hitler came to power, Argentina once more tightened its immigration laws, virtually shutting its doors to legal immigration.

In October of that year, the League of Nations created the office of "High Commissioner for Refugees (Jewish and Other) Coming from Germany." The circumlocutory title reflects squeamishness over identifying just who the refugees were and why they had to "come" from Germany. Arriving in Argentina in his official capacity, High Commissioner James G. McDonald quickly concluded that he could not persuade the government to loosen its restrictive immigration laws. He therefore only requested a modification of regulations in order to permit 250 refugees a month. to enter the country as wards of the existing community. In this, too, he was unsuccessful.[10] Argentine policy remained immutably exclusionary during the war. A 1942 plan to rescue 1,000 French Jewish children, originally accepted by the Argentine president, was ground to bits by a Kafkaesque bureaucracy and came to nothing. The peculiar mirror world in which would-be rescuers had to function is revealed in a memo by the Foreign Ministry's Legal Office, which stated that the presidential decree authorizing admission of the orphans "would have brought about the entry of some 10,000 persons incapable of assimilating in our country, since the children's next-of-kin were likely to join them at a later date. Humanitarian considerations would certainly have prevented the turning down of their applications for immigration."[11] At the same time, it should be noted that neither the United States, Canada, nor Great Britain agreed to receive these children.

Exclusionist immigration policies were adopted almost universally in the years prior to the outbreak of World War II. Worldwide depression and commercial competition in dwindling markets prompted waves of anti-Jewish feeling in many sectors of the continent. In the face of a possible fascist victory in Europe, there was a desire to land on the winning side. As a result, the anti-Semitic broadcasts and publications of professional Nazi propagandists found resonance among classes of people who believed they were losing ground to the more aggressive economic style of the immigrants. Gradually an ambience developed that was less favorable to immigrants generally, and to Jews specifically. Anti-Semitic attitudes were in no instance as strong or as violent as those which swept Europe in the same period, but Jews experienced a general feeling of threat from the right: from nativists, from fascists, from German and Spanish immigrant colonies among whom Nazi-Fascist ideology took root, and from sectors of the unreconstructed church hierarchy. It was in this ambience that the present-day Jewish communities evolved.

The case of Brazil is instructive. Prior to 1938, several thousand Jews had been immigrating to that country each year, with no notable adverse reaction from the native population. The Brazilian Jewish communities had come into existence during the four decades from 1900 (when 300 were enumerated in the census) to 1940 (when 55,666 were counted).[12] Jews seem to have faced few barriers to entering society and the economy, contributing to the image of Brazil as a country singularly free of anti-Jewish sentiment—i.e., in the Latin American context, not racist. But in the 1930s, Jews seeking to enter the country were charged with being "simultaneously communists and capitalists whose degenerate life-styles were formed in putrid and poverty-stricken European ethnic enclaves."[13] "Brazil's Jewish Question," Jeffrey Lesser writes, "was really a struggle by Brazil's leaders to fit the bigoted images of Jews that filtered in from Europe with the reality that the overwhelming majority of Jewish immigrants were neither very rich nor very poor, were rarely active politically, and rapidly acculturated to Brazilian society . . . the imagined Jew, not the real one, was considered the danger."

Many of the most influential Brazilian statesmen of the interwar period were educated at prestigious law schools whose faculty were deeply influenced by the ideas of scientific racists such as Count Gobineau and Joseph Chamberlain. They transmitted to their students the need to improve the Brazilian "race," a goal to which immigration, properly handled, could contribute. This was a process in which Jews—perceived as a non-European "race"—logically could play no part. The impact on immigration policy was dramatic: in 1938, the number of Jews admitted sank to 530 as the result of a secret memo circulated to Brazilian consular officers by the Ministry of Foreign Relations prohibiting the granting of visas to persons of Semitic origin. The ban confirmed a policy that had already been in effect informally for two years and effectively reversed existing immigration policy. Whereas consuls had formerly been encouraged to recruit foreigners who were assumed able to assist in the modernization of the Brazilian economy, they now were instructed to defend Brazilian society from pernicious foreign influences. Interestingly, all this took place before establishment of the proto-fascist Estado Novo of Getúlio Vargas, and on the advice of policymakers such as João Carlos Muniz and Oswaldo Aranha, later to be lauded by Zionists the world over for their support of the United Nations' partition of Palestine.[14] Of equal interest is the fact that Jewish immigration bounced back the following year, hitting a decade high of 4,601, perhaps as a function of the famous Brazilian flexibility. Apparently, it was sometimes possible to manipulate racist preconceptions in order to parlay mythical Jewish power and aptitude for finance into real visas for refugees, and Jews continued entering Brazil despite official prohibitions. Whether mythology operated pro or contra Jews in any particular instance, the notion of Brazilian culture as devoid of racism is not supported by the record.[15]

Cuba was a logical destination for immigrants due to its proximity to European ports; the island was already home to Turkish, Romanian, U.S., and Polish Jews. Robert M. Levine, in his examination of this "tropical diaspora," concludes that Cuba had a better record of receiving refugees than did many other Latin American nations. But the door famously slammed shut on Jewish immigration with the rebuff of the German cruise ship *St. Louis* in June 1939. This vessel was turned away by Cuban authorities even though all the Jewish passengers aboard held landing certificates issued by the Cuban director-general of immigration; 734 of them also held visas for entry into the United States, with effective dates of from three months to three years of their arrival in Cuba.[16] The case was the subject of contemporary headlines, subsequent articles, and even a film; but some of the most odious elements in the case have come to light only recently. Unbeknownst to the passengers, their visas had been canceled by the Cuban authorities before the ship sailed, probably in an effort to channel the flow of graft to new appointees in the Cuban immigration authority. The Nazi authorities had been advised of the visa cancellation but permitted the ship to sail anyway, probably in order to demonstrate that no other country was willing to accept their human rejects, which indeed turned out to be the case. The repulse of the *St. Louis* and the refugees she carried was the result of a witches' brew of official corruption; mixed signals from the U.S. Department of State (on the one hand advising Cuba to admit more refugees so the United States would not be pressured to do so, and on the other, to hold down the number of refugees admitted so they would not create pressure on U.S. borders); and Nazi manipulation of the media (accomplished by allowing the ship to sail when the visas were already known to have been canceled and then hotting up the Havana press against the "Jewish invasion").[17] Efforts by American Jewish organizations failed to persuade the Cuban government to admit the immigrants. The only one to make it ashore was an attempted suicide who slashed his wrists and jumped overboard. Rescued, he was taken ashore; but his wife and daughter were not permitted to join him. Levine concludes,

> An enduring measure of the tragedy was that the deaths of 667 of the 907 *St. Louis* passengers who were returned to Europe and perished as part of Hitler's "final solution" could have been avoided by more skillful negotiation or by accepting [an] offer of the Panama Canal authorities to take the refugees. The *St. Louis* incident was all the more tragic because of the trajectory of its route—it came so close to shore that passengers standing on deck at night could see the lights of buildings and residences both in Miami Beach and Havana. . . . The atmosphere could fairly be described as sordid. All of the time in which the *St. Louis* sat at anchor at the far end of Havana harbor, the antisemitic fusillade continued, even in the Cuban Congress, where rival political factions speculated on how families of the hapless refugees could be made to pay millions of dollars for the right to land.[18]

From 1935 to 1938 there was a narrow window of opportunity when it would have been possible to resettle Jews in Latin America—not in the modernizing countries that Jews preferred and that had set their faces against their entry, but in smaller countries that had not previously been deemed suitable areas for their settlement. But in such countries resettlement was limited by multiple factors: underdeveloped economies, unbridged racial divisions, policies that favored agricultural laborers, the lack of funds to finance resettlement projects, the rising prestige of fascism, and—not a minor factor—the inability of German Jews to grasp the enormity of the danger they confronted and the corresponding need to seize any chance to escape.[19]

By 1938, when the Evian Conference on Refugees was convened at the initiative of President Franklin D. Roosevelt, the window of opportunity had closed. Only one small nation of extremely limited absorptive capacity—the Dominican Republic—volunteered to accept the refugees. But the need for refuge was so intense that a number of "errant vessels" headed for Latin American ports in the hope of landing Jewish passengers whose acceptability was extremely dubious. Their cases are too numerous to list here, but a history of the period recorded the dimensions of the problem and the chaotic pattern of refugee distribution that resulted.

> [In March of 1939] three boats: the Italian *Conte Grande* and the Hamburg-American *Cap Norte* and the *General Artigas* carried ninety-five refugees to Uruguay. Since their tourist visas were illegal, they were not allowed to land in Montevideo. But thanks to the efforts of HICEM, the Uruguayan authorities permitted them to disembark on condition that they proceed to Chile. In May, three boats with a hundred and fifty Jews on board embarked for Paraguay, via Uruguay. The HICEM committees in Buenos Aires, Montevideo and Asuncion then exerted their efforts to assure the arrival of the refugees in Paraguay.[20]

On a previous voyage three months earlier, the Uruguayan government had admitted 300 Jewish passengers from the *Conte Grande,* despite the fact that their visas for Paraguay had been annulled. This brought to 1,200 the number of German Jews permitted to settle in Uruguay over a four-month period, and gave rise to alarm in the local press over a "Jewish invasion." The government's response to the March arrival of the *Conte Grande* continued a relatively humane policy by agreeing to admit the refugees until arrangements could be made for their transfer to Chile.[21] At other times, bribery, swindles, and clandestine landings played a larger role than the beneficent actions of government officials. In May 1939, 3,000 Jewish refugees entered Bolivia with documents counterfeited in Europe and sold to them for $1,500 apiece. Two Bolivian consuls were dismissed as a result, and the outstanding visas were invalidated. Those refugees who were still in transit were stranded with worthless documents. Following intervention by HICEM, an agreement was worked out whereby the Jewish relief organization revalidated the visas (which implied a guarantee of support) and agreed to limit the number of such visas to four hundred per month.[22]

Bolivia became a destination for German Jews very late in the day. Bolivian Jewish community leaders estimated recently that some 5,000–7,000 Jews arrived in the country between 1939 and 1950, but a scholar whose own family lived through the difficult period of adjustment estimates Jewish arrivals at 12,000–15,000 just in the years 1938–40.[23] This number, which comprised a major addition to the country's non-Indian population, was made possible only through the entrepreneurial initiative of Bolivian consuls who sold visas illegally to the desperate refugees, who in some cases did not know just where Bolivia was located. What the newcomers knew in advance about Bolivia was what they could glean from encyclopedia articles or the "wild west" novels of a popular German author of adventure tales. Once they had arrived in the country, confusion was compounded. "Nothing is as one knows it, either in society or in nature," as one immigrant put it.[24] With the war in progress, and in the context of a possible German victory, the Bolivian Movimiento Nacional Revolucionario (MNR) adopted an anti-Semitic stance, possibly in a search for scapegoats who could be held responsible for the inflation that was pressing the middle class.[25] Though anti-Semitism may have been viewed by the MNR as no more than a tactical weapon, it appeared as a threat to the Jews who had so recently sought refuge in the country. Just as ominous was the propaganda being churned out by the German embassy and local Nazi officials. Observers do not believe that anti-Semitism ever became a popular stance; many Bolivians "forcefully attacked anti-Semitism and came to the defense of the immigrants," Spitzer writes, but neither was there an understanding of what and who Jews and Judaism might be. Though grateful for refuge, few among the thousands who transited Bolivia opted to remain there; for most, the gap between immigrant and native-born seemed impossible to span. Remigration began as soon as conditions permitted, and today Bolivian Jews number only in the hundreds. The remnant community has met the challenge of bridging cultural differences by establishing a beneficent public identity, sponsoring a public medical clinic, a school, a nursery, and donating an ambulance for use in rural areas.[26] These charitable deeds helped integrate those immigrants who had the desire and the flexibility to adapt to Bolivian society and make the country their permanent home.

Chile ceased admitting refugees from Nazi-dominated territories in December 1939. In April 1942, Mexico decreed that thenceforth only natives of the Western Hemisphere would be admitted as immigrants. Argentina, Bolivia, Chile, and Paraguay in effect barred entry to refugees from Germany and Axis-dominated countries by denying admittance to persons without passports signed or certified by the authorities of their countries of origin. Panama instituted similar restrictions. Only Ecuador and the Dominican Republic welcomed Jewish refugees throughout this period. In both these countries, however, the capacity of the economy to absorb new immigrants was severely limited. Under these pressures, a new class of conversos came into existence: Jews who submitted to baptism in order to gain entry into Colombia, Venezuela, and Brazil, countries that were admitting Catholics only.[27] In other instances, baptismal certificates were made available without religious formality. Some of these were authorized by Archbishop Angelo Roncalli, apostolic delegate to Turkey and Greece, later Pope John XXIII.

An unknown number of Sephardim from Greece and the Balkans entered Latin America on Spanish passports. In decrees of 1924 and 1932, the Spanish government had extended naturalization to selected descendants of Spanish Jews exiled in 1492, regardless of their current place of residence.[28] These visas were not, however, invitations to settle in Spain, where the constitution did not provide for the free exercise of religion. Sephardim who walked across the Pyrenees were allowed to transit the peninsula in order to reach Portuguese ports, but they were not issued visas until equal numbers of Sephardim had departed Spanish territory through the West.[29] Nevertheless, those bearing passports issued by Spain, a neutral nation, had some protection while traveling, or if captured by the Germans.

In such ways, thousands of Jews found themselves in countries where they had never considered settling and where very few European immigrants had ever settled. Under the circumstances, many refugees regarded their havens as temporary refuges until they could move on to places of known Jewish settlement in Argentina, Uruguay, Canada, Israel, or the United States. Many of those who moved on did so illegally: Jewish "expediters" who specialized in smuggling Jews from one country to another appeared in lightly populated areas such as the frontiers of Argentina with Uruguay, Paraguay, and Bolivia. Nevertheless, there remain in all the Latin American republics today Jewish families whose elders arrived in the stressful thirties and forties and who either chose to remain or were unable to leave.

In 1948, while Argentina was continuing to block the legal entry of Jewish immigrants, the status of as many as 10,000 illegal Jewish immigrants was regularized by the pragmatic Juan Perón. This was accomplished through legislation allowing illegal aliens to appear before authorities to be issued identity cards. The agency designated to administer the program was the OIA (Organización Israelita Argentina), which Perón had created as a partisan counterweight to the community's mainline organizations.[30] In this way, the president, a master of *Realpolitik*, achieved several goals at once: he placated the Jewish community, which had been lobbying for release of imprisoned illegals; he brought illegals into the national system of identity cards, thus making it easier to keep a watch on them; and he shone a light on his own supporters, the Jewish members of OIA.

Immigration of Nazis

The chronicle of Jewish immigration to Latin America would not be complete without mentioning also the immigration of Germans in flight from the destruction of the Third Reich. After the defeat of Germany, Argentina, like the United States and Canada, actively sought out German professionals who had been cut loose from their moorings by defeat in war and subsequent de-nazification procedures. As president, Juan Perón established offices in Switzerland and Denmark for the purpose of recruiting German scientists, technicians, engineers, and military instructors for emigration to Argentina. As these were "ex"-Nazis and Nazi followers, panels comprised of empathetic Argentine Nazis were established to interrogate them and validate those who seemed useful for free transportation to Argentina.[31] As Perón said, "What better business than for the Republic of Argentina to bring scientists and technicians here? All it cost us was air fare, while Germany invested millions of marks in their education."[32] The initiative bore fruit. During his two first presidencies, 1946–55, between 30,000 and 40,000 persons of German origin emigrated to Argentina, two-thirds of them from the Soviet occupied zones of Europe.

These postwar German immigrants did not come into a vacuum: a German community of some 250,000 already existed in Argentina, product of the same immigration laws that had allowed Jews to enter the country. German Argentines encompassed the range of possible political positions. There were Nazis and anti-Nazis, as well as others who remained politically unengaged. Nazi propaganda and Nazi money made substantial inroads among the latter, especially while it appeared that the Axis nations might win the war. Yet German Argentines ignored the suggestion of Nazi party officials that they return to their homeland in order to increase Germany's available manpower pool and also to prevent themselves from sinking to the level of despised *Mischlinge* (mestizos).[33]

The newly recruited German scientists and technicians were placed in significant military and academic positions; German scientists produced Argentina's first successful rocket launch as early as 1951. Other scientists were divided among various universities—in the 1950s, one third of the faculty of the Universidad Nacional de Tucumán was German. The researcher who interviewed members of this migration believes that most of the émigrés, impoverished and demoralized by defeat of the Third Reich, were more concerned with earning a living than with politics. But there were indeed some fifty war criminals among them, including Adolf Eichmann, Josef Mengele, Walter Kutschmann, Erich Preibke, Josef Schwammberger, and Klaus Barbie. The latter went on to perfect Paraguay's system of state terror under President Hugo Banzer. Some of these individuals were sought by the Allies, then by privately sponsored "Nazi hunters," for forty years before being extradited to Germany, France, or Italy for trial on charges of crimes against humanity. Meanwhile, they benefited from the lack of concern on the part of successive governments and the protective coloration offered them by their co-nationals. The existing German communities assisted the newcomers in finding employment, and lionized some, such as the marooned sailors of the *Graf Spee* (so useful for enhancing the local gene pool). Bariloche, the international ski resort, became known as a Nazi gathering place. Stories of a hoard of German gold secretly transferred to Argentine shores by submarine have never been verified. The two subs that are known to have landed were at sea when the war ended; their captains decided to make port in a country where they believed (correctly) they would not be interned. Meding's findings, which diminish both the physical and the financial importance of the Nazi presence in postwar Argentina, received the imprimatur of Argentine Jewish Nazi hunters through publication in a book edited by the same DAIA researchers who were analyzing the government's Nazi files.[34]

In continuation of its traditional policy of preferring Italians, Argentina resumed recruiting immigrants from that country after the war. But now the recruits included Ukrainians, Croats, and Yugoslavs who had taken refuge in Italy in order not to be repatriated to homelands that had fallen under the control of the Soviet Union. An alliance of ethnic organizations in Buenos Aires and the Vatican, plus intervention by the U.S. Department of State, resulted in the admission of some 5,000 of these displaced persons into Argentina. Under British pressure, anti-Communist Poles were also admitted.[35] Many ex-soldiers and partisans had collaborated with the Nazis; some, though hardly all, may have abandoned their anti-Semitic sentiments in mid-Atlantic. Meanwhile, despite the removal of an overtly anti-Semitic minister of immigration, and feints in the direction of authorizing family reunion, Argentina continued to limit drastically the admission of Jews. Only 600 Jews entered Argentina in 1947, a year in which official immigration totaled 116,095. Immigration doubled the following year, but only 680 Jewish entries were recorded, including persons in transit.[36]

Nazism and its hallmark, anti-Semitism, flourish in Argentina today. Its virulence is often ascribed to the presence in the country of Nazis. There is no doubt at all that Nazi political style has become the model for groups that, far from claiming ignorance of National Socialist "excesses," actually seek to emulate them. But Nazi anti-Semitism was able to naturalize itself in Argentina (a nation that has always been suspicious of foreign ideologies) because its message resonated within the nation's core institution. There is ample anecdotal evidence, but little documentary proof that the preconciliar church that lies at the heart of Argentine *nacionalismo* accommodated Nazism. To do so, it had to ignore the fact that the German party's origins were anti-Christian. The vector that transmitted the Nazi pathogen to Argentina was hatred of the Jews.

The Completed Communities

Barring another shift of opinion in favor of mass immigration (which appears unlikely in view of the nativist orientation of most polities) there will be no major accretions to the Jewish communities from outside in the foreseeable future. Although it remains possible for individuals to enter specific countries on payment of varying sums, the organized Jewish communities may be viewed as completed products of the age of immigration. That age being not far past, the Jewish communities are young. There are few "old families," and most Jews are close to their immigrant origins.

The majority of identifiable Jews arrived in Latin America in the years that bracket World War I. By 1960, 98 percent of Argentine Jewish children aged fourteen and under had been born in the country, by contrast with fewer than 3 percent of their parents and grandparents aged sixty-five and over.[37] By 1968, half the Jews of São Paulo were native-born. Of this number 21 percent had two Brazilian-born parents; only 3.9 percent had four Brazilian-born grandparents.[38] Clearly, with the advent of another generation since these surveys were made, and very little immigration in the interim, the vast majority of Latin American Jews are native-born.

The overwhelming majority of Latin American, as of United States and Canadian, Jews are of Ashkenazic origin. A survey of foreign-born Jews living in Argentina and in Canada in the 1930s showed that 80.9 percent of the former and 83.4 percent of the latter originated in areas defined by the researcher as Poland, Russia, and Romania.[39] During the period of mass migration, the major initiatives in Jewish life sprang from Ashkenazim, not Sephardim, and the former were being subjected to far more intense pressures than the latter. Consequently, Ashkenazim were far more likely than Sephardim to risk all on the frightening gamble of migration to the Western Hemisphere.[40] The exception is Brazil, which has always attracted a higher proportion of Sephardim. In the 1970s, so far as can be determined, Brazil admitted 177 Jewish immigrants from the Near East, as compared with just 24 from Europe.[41]

The national origins of Latin American Jews are remarkably varied. Most Latin American Jewish communities count individuals from a dozen or more different countries among their members. In fact, identifying the national origins of Latin American Jews was until recently a popular pastime. A journalist reported that the Jews of Guatemala and El Salvador are from Posen; Nicaragua is populated by Bessarabians and Hungarians; Costa Rica is Polish; and so on and so forth.[42] The cultural differences Jews brought with them to Latin America were emotionally laden for the individuals involved, and they quickly became institutionalized in Jewish life. Describing Mexican Jewry in 1972, Harriet

Lesser enumerated seven separate communities, each with its own lay and religious organizations. These included Arabic-speaking Sephardim from Damascus; Yiddish-speaking Ashkenazim from Russia, Poland, and Lithuania; Ladino speakers from Turkey, Greece, the Balkans, and Italy; Arabic speakers from Aleppo; German-speaking Ashkenazim from Germany, Austria, and Czechoslovakia; Hungarians; and English speakers from the United States.[43] Such institutionalized fragmentation was characteristic of Latin American Jewish life in its origins. The phenomenon, well known throughout Jewish history, has been explained by Rafael Patai:

> A certain degree of acculturation to the non-Jewish environment has taken place in every Jewish Diaspora. In view of these acculturative processes which have been very considerable, especially since the Jewish Enlightenment and emancipation, it is quite clear that the Jewish people as a whole cannot be termed an ethnic group. There are marked cultural differences among the Diasporas, and everywhere the traits in which one Diaspora differs from the others are the traits in respect of which it is similar to its non-Jewish environment. On the other hand, no Jewish Diaspora is culturally identical with its non-Jewish host people; or, to put it positively, every Diaspora differs from its gentile environment in several respects, of which Jewish religion and tradition and Jewish group identification are the most important. In relation to the gentile majority, the Jewish Diaspora of every country thus constitutes a different ethnic group, but the Jews as a whole constitute not one but several ethnic groups.[44]

Jews seeking new homelands exercised their options in ways not too different from non-Jewish immigrants. The United States was far and away the major recipient of all overseas immigrants, and probably three-quarters of all Jewish immigrants came here as well. The next largest recipient was Argentina, which accepted 11 percent of the 60 million Europeans who emigrated overseas between the years 1857 and 1965.[45] Among Jewish immigrants from Europe in the century that ended in 1942, 9.6 percent opted for some country of Latin America, and more than half of these chose Argentina. The largest number of Jewish migrants settled in countries that were receiving the largest contingents of European immigrants of all nationalities and religions. The smallest Jewish communities grew in countries that did not attract many Europeans. The evidence that roughly similar proportions among Jewish and non-Jewish immigrants chose Latin American destinations suggests that Jewish migration responded to the same elements of encouragement and discouragement as did non-Jewish immigration.

In societies to which entry was circumscribed by the ambit of Catholicism, landownership, and *abolengo* (good birth), industry and commerce offered entrée to the immigrant, whether as worker, entrepreneur, or lowly vendor of manufactured goods. Arriving as they did from modernized countries, the Ashkenazim in particular found opportunity for those with skills, education, capital, luck, or a combination of all these. At a time when industry was in its infancy, many Jewish immigrants were strategically placed to integrate them-selves into their new homes by way of the industrialization process. Economic expansion became the context for the burgeoning of new Jewish communities, and over the course of one generation or two, some individuals and some communities flourished economically to a degree that no one could have predicted.

For much of the immigration period, Latin American immigration policies were selective rather than open, largely because so much of the land had already been preempted before the age of immigration dawned. Reverence for the immigrant experience and the pioneering thrust westward, so prominent a feature of United States history, is largely absent, even (or most especially) in countries such as Argentina that were populated primarily by immigrants. Among the ambivalently received intruders, Jews were perceived as triple strangers: by religion, by ethnic origin, and by historical experience. Their arrival on the continent was almost in its entirety a product of modern forces: the advance of industrial capitalism from western, to central, to eastern Europe, and its impact upon populations living there. They had not passed through the Spanish crucible, and the autochthonous cultures were even more alien to them. The lives of the first and second generations were anchored, not in the historical or mythical past of their respective countries, but in the more recent past of their own countries of origin and in their collective consciousness of the Nazi holocaust and formation of the State of Israel. This incongruence between the mental frameworks of Jews and the Latin American societies into which they attempted to fit cannot be overstressed if we are to come to an understanding of the Jewish dimension of Latin American history.

The nineteenth-century tug of war between Catholic traditionalists and anticlericals created a middle ground where Jews could live comfortably as a secular minority. Many Jews who were in flight from the religiosity of the shtetl were prepared to move over to a secularized version of Judaism, provided they were not required to yield to another religion that had been historically hostile to them. In Latin America's metropolitan centers they found a comfort-ably secular milieu. Since World War I, however, Latin America generally has experienced a growth in nationalism that is characteristic of all developing areas. Though secular in nature, it is inevitably tinged by the Catholic heritage. Nationalism on the ascendant exerts pressure on all within its orbit to become part of a new, all-embracing nationality, be it Argentine, Brazilian, or any other. This pressure leaves little room for a minority group that conceives itself as related to a different tradition from that of the majority population and that maintains ties with its ancestral communities abroad. The result has been to increase the pressure on Jews to assimilate.

The late arrival of Jews to the continent takes on added importance in light of the fact that in the period between the wars, public feeling was turning against immigrants. The immigrant was a convenient scapegoat for the political and social turmoil that accompanied industrialization and urbanization. Anti-Semitism tends to emerge when anticipated social change fails to occur and the hopes of the poor or those excluded from power are dashed. At such times, the exclusive ideologies of the elite and the latent Jew-hatred of the mass reach a cathexis in politically convenient anti-Semitism. Intensification of hostilities in the Near East during the 1960s and 1970s introduced a new element in the form of anti-Zionism, which quickly attached itself to preexisting anti-Jewish feelings. The fruit of these poisonous animosities would ripen with deadly effect in the 1970s and 1980s.

The Parameters of Success: Cuba, Brazil, Argentina

Jewish communities developed rapidly in the interwar period in Cuba, Brazil, and Argentina. But they experienced an atmosphere far different from that of the nineteenth century. From the 1930s on, rising nationalism and accelerating rates of industrialization altered the expectations host societies placed on their immigrants, offering enhanced opportunity for economic and social advancement but increasing the pressures for homogenization. The controlling importance of conditions within the host societies is clearly illustrated by contrasting the destinies of the Jewish communities of Cuba and Brazil. Both originated in poverty and the struggle to survive; both began to appear viable in the forties and fifties. But one came to an abrupt end in 1959, whereas the other is currently the most buoyant on the continent. The trajectory of the Argentine Jewish community is not so easily summarized; alternately tolerated and repressed, the ultimate fate of Argentine Jews cannot be foreseen.

Cuba

Mass arrival of Jews in Cuba began in March 1921, when a change in American regulations enabled would-be immigrants to expedite their admission through a stopover in adjacent territory. Almost all Jewish immigrants who passed through "Akhsanie Kuba" (Hotel Cuba) during the next two years proceeded on to the United States.[46] A 1925 survey found that only one-fifth of the Jews then in Cuba had been on the island more than one year. This situation changed abruptly when their admission to the United States was barred by the change in legislation. From then on, immigrants had to adjust to Cuban society.

Adjustment proved difficult. The Jewish immigrants were for the most part poor and unskilled. They were thrown into an economy that was based on the large-scale cultivation of sugarcane; wage scales for field hands were far below the minimum requirement for a European lifestyle. Consequently, immigrants settled exclusively in the towns. There they found few of the factory jobs that would have enabled them to support themselves. A survey by the (United States) National Council of Jewish Women found that 90 percent of Jewish immigrants to Cuba were unemployed in 1924. Most of those regarded as employed were engaged in peddling, which is really a disguised form of unemployment.

The condition of these immigrants worsened when in 1933 the revolutionary government of Ramón Grau San Martín enacted the Law of 50 Percent, which stipulated that half of employees in any manufacturing plant must be Cuban citizens. Jews had not been able to become citizens during the previous decade, under the regime of the dictator General Gerardo Machado. When citizenship became available, the high fees and technical barriers prevented many from attaining it. Consequently, most Jews were noncitizens and barred from gainful employment. Those who had found jobs were mostly employed by other Jews; but Jewish employers now had to let go half of their work force. It is not to be wondered at that, of the twenty-five thousand Jews who entered Cuba between 1918 and 1947, fully half departed during that same period.

So large a number of migrants and transmigrants, most of them penniless, created a financial burden greater than the few established Cuban Jews could handle, and they were outside the concern of the Cuban government. In the years before the outbreak of war, anti-Semitic propaganda emanating from Nazi sources was leveled at the refugees, threatening the position of all Cuban Jews. Consequently, the Hebrew Immigrant Aid Society (HIAS) and the Joint Distribution Committee (commonly called "Joint" or JDC) stepped into the breach, providing interim aid in the form of loans, schooling, travel documents, and sponsors, all services the Cuban government did not offer and the immigrants could not provide for themselves. This "American intervention," reminiscent of United States government intervention in the larger polity, extended itself by the usual means to include interference in Cuban Jewish community affairs, which the local Jews were scarcely in a position to reject, even when, as in the case of the *St. Louis,* such intervention had disastrous consequences.

Jews who had been cast away on Cuba as a result of their efforts to reach the United States identified spontaneously with Robinson Crusoe. They were overwhelmed by fear and anxiety when they found themselves stranded on an island where they had no desire to be, inhabited by people whom they regarded as their cultural inferiors. The stories of Abraham Dubelman convey this culture shock as the immigrants struggled to Cubanize themselves. "The Balance Sheet" explores the dilemma of a Jewish peddler who has passed himself off as German and married a Cuban woman. He urges her to throw away her crucifix: "We must free ourselves of these useless things." His own unconcern for religion is a legacy of the haskalah, but he finds secularism insufficient as his children grow up in a Catholic world. Though he is successful in business—signified by his end-of-the-year balance sheet—when it comes to a final balance, all he wants is to be buried among Jews.

"But some, like Robinson Crusoe, felt Cuba had possibilities, though it was very primitive as compared to any European land that we had known,"[47] wrote the editor of the lively biweekly, *Havaner Lebn.* In the thirties, Jews came to realize they would have to "make their America in Cuba." With little commerce and less industry, Cuba obviously stood in need of an entrepreneurial class. Margalit Bejarano has charted the deproletarianization of Cuban Jewry. Legal and social opposition to the employment of foreigners squeezed Jews out of factory jobs at the very time that nascent industrialization gave promise of reward for entrepreneurs. Jewish workers, pressed to survive on wages kept low by an army of the unemployed, had before their eyes the model of Jewish bosses who were forging their way into the middle class. The transition from worker to boss was not easy; the move from wage earner to self-employed did not necessarily bring an immediate improvement in living standards. But as the Cuban economy grew, Jewish-owned factories prospered, propelling their owners out of the proletariat and into the middle class.[48] Those immigrants who accepted their fate and put their hands to the task prospered. As they improved their situation, they began to see Cuba not as a desert island but as a beautiful country worthy in itself. Cuba could be a desirable home, not just a way station en route to the real America. In 1934, the author of "Jewish Robinson Crusoes" exuded confidence.

The thirties witnessed the emergence of Cuban Jewish patriotism, expressed in a copious Yiddish literature of short stories, poetry, and novels, written by immigrants who had surprised themselves by falling in love with their tropical home. Dipping into the history of the Spanish conquest, Y. O. Pinis published an epic poem based on the resistance of an Indian chief against the invaders. Chief Hatuey is presented as a freedom fighter, spurning the hypocritical love offered by the Spanish priests as they advance with torches to perform their "act of faith."[49] *Clara*, a historical romance, commemorates the participation of descendants of conversos in the Cuban war of independence and their association with the Cuban hero Antonio Maceo.[50] Maceo himself was the subject of an epic poem by Eliezer Aronowsky, who won praise for this work from Don Federico Henriquez Carvajal, a companion of José Martí. *Maceo*, wrote Henriquez, "projects a red symbol on the horizon of Cuba."[51] Indeed.

Several pamphlets about the Liberator, José Martí, and his relations with Jews and Judaism were also published, among them "Martí y las discriminaciones raciales," "Martí y los hebreos," and "Temas hebreos en la obra de Martí."[52] Marco Pitchon's *José Martí y la comprensión humana* contains an essay on "Lo hebreo en el pensamiento de José Martí" that illustrates the fusion between Christian and Judaic thought in the mind of the Liberator.[53] The most arresting example is to be found in his statement that "Moisés no ha muerto, porque Moisés es el amor" (Moses has not died, for Moses is love). The fact that the founder of the Cuban nation identified with the Jews' earlier struggle against Spain eased the acculturation of the Jewish immigrants.

The economic advancement of those Jewish immigrants who remained in Cuba was spectacular. Moving perforce out of proletarian jobs into peddling or cottage industry, they became particularly important in the manufacture of furniture and shoes and in diamond cutting. By 1948, the majority of Cuba's twelve thousand Jews were reckoned as middle class; scarcely three hundred wage earners were left on the island. Jews were no longer represented in the labor unions, where they had been most active on first arrival.[54] Some of the German-speaking Jews had entered Cuban national life, including several university professors: Boris Goldenberg (sociology), Heinrich Friedlander (economics), and Desiderio Weiss (languages). Jewish lawyers, artists, and writers were all functioning in the forties.[55] Oscar Ganz, prime minister under Carlos Prío Socarrás, was the son of Jewish parents, and so was the person known as Fabio Grobart, a founder of the Cuban Communist party and by popular repute, the Comintern's man in Havana.

On the eve of the revolution, Cuba's population of over 6,000,000 included from 11,000 to 14,000 Jews, the majority of them by way of Eastern Europe, but with a substantial minority from Turkey. Most lived in Havana, with smaller communities in other cities of the island. A flawed community self-study found 75 percent of the working Jewish population to be engaged in petty trade, 15 percent owners of larger stores, and 10 percent producing consumer goods (apart from these loose groupings, other categories, such as professionals, were entirely omitted).[56] The community's buoyancy is demonstrated by the construction of an elegant community center, the Patronato de la Casa de la Comunidad Hebrea de Cuba, built at the then extremely high cost of three-quarters of a million dollars. The souvenir booklet published on the occasion of the dedication of the Patronato featured photographs and messages of congratulation to numerous young men and women who were completing the bachilerato or even graduate courses in medicine, engineering, architecture, and other liberal professions. Cuban Jews attained a level of self-confidence, acceptance, and comfort that was unusual in the Latin American context. Of course, Jews were not accepted into the best clubs or invited to occupy the highest positions of power, but anti-Semitism was not a part of daily life. There is every indication that Jews were settling in to enjoy the fruits of their labor, paid out over the difficult years of adjustment.

The Cuban Jewish community, however, came to an abrupt end as a function of the revolution of 1959. At first, Fidel Castro was warmly received by many Jews who had suffered along with everybody else from the caprices and injustices of earlier regimes. Measures to redress economic inequalities seem to have met with approval within the Jewish community, and there were Jewish activists among Fidel's early followers. Ricardo Subirana y Lobo was one of the financiers of the *Granma* expedition of 1956; later, he became Cuban ambassador to Israel. Enrique Oltuski Osachki, who served in the first revolutionary cabinet, was one among numerous Jews who held important roles in the government, in the Communist party, in scientific and cultural institutions. All were more or less disconnected from the Jewish community.[57] Fidel made special efforts to reassure Cuban Jews that no anti-Semitic policies would be adopted by, for example, making kosher meat available and arranging for matzo to be delivered at Passover (courtesy of the Canadian Jewish Congress). Jewish schools remained open long after church-sponsored schools had been closed. But the decision of the revolutionary government to restructure Cuba's economy on socialist lines led to the expropriation of capitalist enterprises, depriving Jews of the businesses they had founded when the Law of 50 Percent deprived them of their jobs. Former owners were left to live on compensation payments that could not equal the incomes they had been earning in free enterprise. Nationalization of the economy presented East European Jews with the same dilemma they or their parents had faced in Europe of the twenties and from which they had earlier fled. In addition, the close relationship between Cuban Jews and the United States seemed by 1962 to be a source of danger in the context of strained relations with the mainland.[58] As a result of such political and economic factors, the great majority of Jews, along with the majority of the Cuban middle class generally, abandoned the island. The community, which in the forties and fifties seemed well on its way to naturalization, never had time to coalesce. Although at all times there were Jews who stood by the revolution (and ceased to associate with the Jewish community), the community itself practically disappeared. By 1965, only 2,400 persons continued to identify as Jews; in 1980, fewer than a thousand. These continued to gather at the Patronato, now a splendid embodiment of the maxim *sic transit gloria mundi*.

Brazil

There were between 5,000 and 7,000 Jews in Brazil in 1917, with the Sephardim of the Amazon region still the most important community.[59] During the twenties, some 30,000 East European Jews entered the country, principally from Poland, the Ukraine, Bessarabia, and Lithuania. Most headed for the southern states, where industrialization was under way, seeded by the wealth generated by coffee exports. Between the years 1900 and 1939, the state of São Paulo alone absorbed 2,215,000 immigrants, and East European Jews comprised a part of this stream.[60] Arguably the most successful of these was Moshe Elkhanan Lafer, born in 1885 in a village near Kaunas (present-day Lithuania). Fleeing the Russian Empire, the twenty-five-year-old arrived in São Paulo, where he started as a worker in a print shop. Eventually, under the name Mauricio Klabin, he built an empire of his own, comprised of industrial, commercial, agricultural, and real estate interests. His adopted nephew, Wolf Klabin, founded the giant Indústrias Klabin do Paraná, manufacturers of cellulose and paper. Mauricio's daughter Mina married the architect Gregori Warchavchik, whose partner, Lucio Costa, worked with Oscar Niemayer in the building of Brasília. Daughter Jenny married the painter Lazar Segall. Daughter Luiza married Dr. Luiz Lorch, and together they founded B'nai B'rith of Brazil. So many Jewish institutions owe their existence to them that the Klabin-Lafer clan has been accused of "militant generosity." In the 1930s, descendants of the clan went into politics. Horácio Lafer was elected to Parliament three times, was finance minister under Getúlio Vargas, then foreign affairs minister under President Juscelino Kubitchek. His cousin, Celso Lafer, became foreign affairs minister under Collor de Mello in 1991, and Israel Klabin was elected mayor of Rio de Janeiro.[61]

Until 1922, Jewish immigration to Brazil was individual and sporadic. In that year, because of the increasing swell of immigrants in need of aid, JDC, HIAS, and HICEM all began operations in the country, providing temporary lodging and loans for the establishment of business and professional offices and settling a few families in the agricultural colonies that had been founded at the turn of the century. One-sixth of the present Jewish population of São Paulo stems from this migration. Most new arrivals settled in the district of Bom Retiro, and a description of their living conditions was sent home by an American social worker who had been commissioned to survey Jewish communities of Brazil and Argentina with a view to ascertaining welfare needs.

> São Paulo is divided into districts, and Bom Retiro is the district where the majority of the residents are Jews. Here they have reproduced the typical slum district, with overcrowding, poor housing, poverty, and so forth. It is the "east side" of São Paulo. A visit to some of the families under the care of the Damas Israelitas [Council of Jewish Women] disclosed that they live in sub-basements made up of concrete floors and walls, without windows and with poor sanitation—conditions which, in our larger cities, are looked after by well organized community agencies with trained social workers, who are totally absent in this Bom Retiro district. The minimal cost of living for a family in this district is $20.00 a month for a family of four. About 8,000 Jews live in this district, and 90 percent of them are very poor.[62] [There were 3,000 licensed and an estimated 1,500 unlicensed peddlers in the district at the time the memo was written.]

The Jewish community of Rio de Janeiro developed along similar lines. Immigration of East European Jews to that city began in 1903, with the arrival at the police hostel of "e mais quatro judeos da Bessarabia," as the police blotter has it. By 1914, there were probably two thousand Jews in Rio. After the war, Polish Jews began to arrive.

By 1933, the year Hitler came to power, there were forty thousand Jews in Brazil. In that year, German Jews began arriving. Some 27,500 entered Brazil 1931–42, by means legal and semilegal.[63] The exact number can never be verified, despite records kept by the Jewish immigrant aid societies, because some refugees entered with baptismal certificates. In addition, throughout most of this period, persons arriving as first-class passengers and able to show the sum of $20,000 for each family member could be admitted without regard to quota restrictions. An unknown number of Jews were admitted to Brazil on these terms.

The early years of the presidential administration of Getúlio Vargas (1930–45) confirmed the turnabout in Brazilian immigration policy. As the need for refuge increased, so did the difficulty experienced by Jews in obtaining visas for Brazil, as Claude Lévi-Strauss found when, after the capitulation of France, he sought shelter in the country where he had performed his distinguished ethnographic research.[64]

One-quarter of the Jewish population of São Paulo stems from immigration in the thirties. Many of these refugees from Nazism had been employed in industry, commerce, and the free professions. They brought with them their technical education and their work experience. Involved since birth in an industrialized society, they possessed skills that were at a premium in Brazil, then in the early stages of industrialization. Immigrants of all origins—German, Japanese, Polish—were already playing a substantial role in the country's industrialization process, and the German Jews were qualified to participate as well. The German Jews' relationship to their Judaism was markedly different from that of the East European Jews. Soon after arrival in São Paulo, the Germans formed the religiously liberal, politically non-Zionist Congregação Israelita Paulista (CIP), intended to assist new arrivals and further members' integration into Brazil. Their religious stance projected an assimilationist orientation, alienating the more traditional easterners and decreasing the amount of aid they were willing to extend to German refugees. The divisiveness that followed has been summarized in this way:

> Prior to migration, Eastern and Central European Jews were divided on the basis of national origin, class, and language, all the while being bound by a common religion often practiced in different ways. In São Paulo, where acculturative pressure was high and the laws of the Vargas government strictly enforced, conflict rarely took place between Jews as a group and non-Jewish society. Rather . . . old conflicts between Jews were recreated in the Paulista setting.[65]

The German immigrants, rich or poor, sought above all to dissociate themselves from the impoverished Poles, Lithuanians, and Bessarabians who were still immobilized in Bom Retiro. Even those without means settled far from the old Jewish ghetto, refused to avail themselves of existing social welfare agencies that had been set up for the Östjuden (a term the German Jews used with contempt), and no matter how hard pressed, refused to take up the schwarze Arbeit (black labor) that the Poles resorted to in order to feed their families.

The early years of the Vargas era witnessed the outbreak of anti-Semitic manifestations by Ação Integralista Brasileira, a party modeled on Italian fascism. Government policy was not specifically anti-Semitic, but Integralista attacks were tolerated as a way to appease right-wing supporters.[66] Although the Integralistas were suppressed in 1938, the Vargas regime progressively narrowed the area of civil liberties, and Jews were now confronted with a new threat. The Third Reich was making an aggressive attempt to turn Brazil's substantial German community into a fifth column. In the effort to abort this development, the Brazilian government promulgated a series of laws aimed at dissolving German, Italian, and Japanese cultural nuclei. Starting in 1938, all political activity by foreigners was interdicted. Only native Brazilians could teach in the elementary schools; curriculum had to focus on Brazilian history and geography. The following year, the military was called upon to enforce the denationalization of ethnic groups, and the foreign-language press was given a two-year ultimatum to convert to the Portuguese language.[67]

These Brazilianization measures, aimed at suppressing the Nazi initiative, struck at Jewish life as well, fracturing it along several fissures. Anti-German measures further alienated the Eastern from the Central European Jews, and at the same time brought Yiddish under the ban since police were unable to distinguish between the two languages.[68] Dispersed Jewish communities had re-created elements of shtetl life in their new surroundings, all in Yiddish, a language of German origin. As it became dangerous to speak German or any language but Portuguese in public, the Yiddish theatre, newspapers, libraries, and schools had to close, and the rich communal life of São Paulo's Bom Retiro and Pôrto Alegre's Bom Fim neighborhoods dried up. Jews who came direct from Germany were not speakers of Yiddish; in conformity with the haskalah tradition, they had established their principal religious congregation, Congregação Israelita Paulista, as a Portuguese-speaking body. As a religious institution, CIP suffered no interference from the Brazilian government. Individuals did, however, experience problems with the Brazilian police: designated non-Germans in Germany, in Brazil they were identified as Germans and treated as such.[69]

In the aftermath of formation of the State of Israel, repressive policies of the government of Egypt forced some 25,000 Sephardim to leave that country. The remaining Sephardim were deported following the Sinai war with Israel (November 1956). Some 20,000 Egyptian Jews wound up in Brazil, which reversed its formerly discriminatory policy by admitting them. These French-speaking Jews were singularly well equipped to integrate into Brazilian life. The linguistic affinity of French and Ladino to Portuguese enabled them to learn the language more rapidly than could speakers of Yiddish, Hungarian, or German. Those who formerly had been employed by multinational corporations in Egypt were snapped up by corporations such as Ford and Philips that were doing business in Brazil. Banks and industries large and small hired workers and managers from this labor pool. Some of the immigrants began working in paper or textile manufacture, achieving a comfortable living standard within a few years. Doctors, engineers, and pharmacists among the immigrants were allowed to revalidate their credentials.[70] Most Sephardim settled in São Paulo or its port city of Santos, where some achieved considerable wealth as bankers and owners of coffee estates. Two success stories involve international bankers: the brothers Joseph and Moise Safra, and Edmundo Safdie. The latter's investments (believed to be on a smaller scale than those of the Safras) were valued at $3.5 billion in 1991. Safdie is a member of the board of governors of Israel's Bar Ilan University, and is said to donate 10 percent of his accumulated profits each year to Jewish communities around the world.[71] Within a decade of their arrival in Brazil, Egyptian Jews had built their own synagogue, Mekor Haim, as well as a community center that offered religious, funerary, and social assistance and a religious school with more than 100 students.[72] Others ventured into the "interior," where their cultural affinity with Brazilian Arabs facilitated their integration into channels of trade and the politics of small towns.

The Brazilian census of 1970 located 120,000 israelitas in the country, an increase of 50,000 over the census of twenty years earlier. Community leaders offer estimates of 150,000 to 155,000 for the later date. At the lower extreme, professional demographers continue to estimate the Brazilian Jewish population at just 100,000, a figure that has remained on the books since 1960. But numbers do not reveal the Brazilian success story. By the late 1970s, a Brazilian social scientist concluded that the majority of Brazilian Jews belong to the elite 5 percent of the population who determine the economic and political contours of the nation. Individual Jews "have held prominent positions in government, as elected representatives to Congress, Senate, and state legislative bodies, as municipal counselors and secretaries to local governments, and even in the higher ranks of the armed forces."[73] Adolpho Bloch, who arrived in Brazil from Kiev in 1932, is the owner of *Manchete,* one of the most influential daily newspapers in Brazil, as well as of 25 magazines, 6 radio stations, and a television network.[74]

> The economic and social trajectory of Jews who migrated to Brazil beginning in the first decades of the twentieth century can be considered an outstanding success. Although most of them left their countries of origin without financial resources and under generally precarious conditions, within two generations they not only managed to acquire positions of wealth and prestige, but also succeeded in integrating with the cultural and political elites of the country. . . . [I]n Brazil Jews have situated themselves in the upper ranks of society in terms of income per capita, educational achievement, lifestyle, and political identification.[75]

Possibly owing to the legacy of Dom Pedro II, there are Judaic studies courses at the major Brazilian universities today. Brazilian Jewry has produced a widely respected generation of intellectuals, whose works appear in the bibliography at the end of this book. Taken together, they provide a foundation for writing the history of the Jewish community of Brazil, which does not as yet exist. Much of the yeoman's work in establishing a footing for Brazilian Jewish history was performed by the husband-and-wife research team of Egon and Frieda Wolff. Originally from Germany, the Wolffs came to São Paulo in 1936. Following a career in business, they dedicated themselves to collecting and publishing primary data on Jewish life in Brazil; the present count of their jointly published works totals forty-one.

Argentina

The Argentine Jewish community developed in the shadow of two human tragedies. The first and longest-running was the participation of Jews in the white slave trade. Among Jewish migrants, perhaps none suffered so traumatic a transfer to the New World as the women and girls who were trapped into white slavery.[76] Often these were village girls from impoverished families who were tricked into fraudulent marriages in Europe, then forced into bordellos on their arrival in Argentina. The Russian, Polish, and Romanian slavers, called *t'maim* (unclean ones) by the mainstream Jewish community, made their appearance in Buenos Aires in the 1880s, pandering to the hordes of immigrants, the vast majority of whom were single men. The danger to women was widely publicized in the Jewish world through such books as Sholom Aleichem's *A Mentsch fun Buenos Aires* and Sholom Asch's *Motke Ganiff.* The consequence was that Argentina acquired a bad reputation among Jews for years to come, and many families refused to allow their daughters to emigrate there.

The 1895 Argentine census turned up 61 Jewish prostitutes. In the following two decades, 3,243 Russian women registered with the authorities as prostitutes, and one may infer that many of these were Jews. In a survey conducted by the Argentine Department of Labor, 94 percent of the total group of prostitutes gave an economic motive for their actions.[77] Forty-four percent had no previous work experience. Among those who had previous work experience, most had followed the needle trades: 14.6 percent had been seamstresses, and from 6 to 7 percent had practiced the trade of milliner, presser, or tailor. An additional 6 percent had been servants, a role traditionally subject to sexual exploitation in Latin America. On into the 1920s, government statistics showed that some 20 percent of prostitutes were Jews.[78]

The existence of Jewish pimps, or *caftens,* created the opportunity for opponents of immigration to smear all Jews as panders and prostitutes. Despite the fact that a majority of the slavers were of other nationalities (pimps from every country of Europe, the Middle East, and neighboring Latin American states were importing women), in the prevailing atmosphere of the time, trade in women was touted as a peculiarly Jewish aberration. In fact, the infamous business enjoyed wide popular support, not only from the men who made use of it, but as a matter of public policy. Prostitution was accepted as a necessity by Argentines in order to protect criollo family values while satisfying the appetites of the hordes of temporary male workers who arrived in the country without their families. The trade was protected by the police and other government officials, who made a good living from it.

The Jewish community attacked the *t'maim* where it hurt: the slavers were Orthodox in their religious practice, but the synagogues excluded them from participation in services. The *t'maim* then formed their own congregations, *sifrei torah* (scrolls of the Law) and all. This aroused in respectable Jews the apprehension that Christians would be unable to distinguish between them and the slavers, tarring the reputation of all Jews. They began a years-long campaign to drive them out of business. Lacking any law enforcement capability, the community excommunicated anyone having business or personal relations with a *caften;* such persons were denied entry into any Jewish organization. Excommunication was carried to the extreme of prohibiting attendance at funerals of relatives of the *t'maim.* Jewish theatre owners were persuaded to post signs prohibiting *t'maim* from entering, which crippled the market, for theatre was where the procurers showed off their merchandise. Ezros Noschim, a Jewish organization dedicated to helping women and girls who had been seduced and trapped into prostitution, met unaccompanied women at the docks and steered them to safe homes. In a demarche on the Minister of Poland in Argentina, a delegation asked his government to refrain from issuing passports to single young women on the ground that the many *polacas* serving time in Buenos Aires brothels reflected badly on their homeland.

Still, legal steps against the trade might not have been taken but for the heroism of one Raquel Lieberman who, entrapped a second time after having once escaped her husband and keeper, at great risk to her life testified against the mob in court. One hundred eight members of Zwi Migdal, the association of *caftens,* were arrested on the basis of her testimony. None was convicted. There was no law against the traffic, nor had Argentina adhered to the Geneva Convention by which most civilized nations of the period condemned white slavery. Only when the constitution was suspended by a military coup and a provisional government installed in September 1930 did the Jewish community succeed in pressuring the government to deport the slavers from Argentina.[79] It is worth noting that the Jewish community was the only "foreign" community in Argentina to wage a war against their own countrymen in order to drive them out of business.

The second human tragedy that shadowed the early history of Argentine Jews occurred in 1919, at the height of the worldwide "red scare." The Argentine government had officially reversed its immigration policy, passing laws intended to bar the admission of "labor agitators." But channels for legitimate political participation did not appear. A perceptive political analyst commented that Argentine "labor leaders would naturally be left outside the prevailing system, since their coming to power through anarchist activities obviously implied the exclusion of all other sectors."[80] Despite the democratic rhetoric of the Argentine Socialist party, labor was not brought into the political process until the regime of Juan Perón in the 1930s.

Nacionalista reaction and economic grievances blended with classic anti-Semitism to climax in a pogrom during the so-called Semana Trágica (Tragic Week) of January 1919. Events began with a strike against an ironworks. Violence broke out, some workers were killed, and observers were quick to allege outside agitation by immigrants, especially Bolsheviks, Catalans, and Jews. The apprehensions of conservatives concerning the effect of immigration on the status quo were ignited by rumors of a plot by *rusos* to overturn the governments of Argentina and Uruguay and institute rule by workers' soviets. From the perspective of the oligarchy, immigration appeared to be changing Argentine society, and changing it for the worse. Admittedly, economic progress was taking place, but many felt the price was too high.

At the very time that the strike itself was being settled, the Jewish neighborhood of Buenos Aires came under murderous attack. "Now, reactionary mobs rather than angry workers roamed the streets shouting death to *rusos*—Russian Jews—who were somehow identified in the popular mind with anarchists and Bolsheviks."[81] The assault on Jews and Catalans was led by Rear Admiral Manuel Domecq García, who gave military instruction to the Guardia Blanca—volunteer squads of patriotic youth. Buenos Aires was compared with Petrograd two years earlier and "patriots" urged the volunteers to assault Russians and Catalans in their homes and neighborhoods.[82] This they did, destroying libraries, clubs, presses, and shops, as well as looting private homes and stores, while the police looked on. Pinie Wald was arrested as would-be dictator of a republic that was to be established, encompassing all of South America.

A Jewish deputation called on President Hipólito Yrigoyen to disassociate the mainstream community from the actions of hotheads and to request police protection for law-abiding citizens. Although the president declared that persecution of the Jews was "incompatible" with Argentine tradition and law, he nevertheless chided the deputation for having made its appeal in the name of the Jewish community rather than as individual Argentines, despite the fact that the community as a whole was under attack.[83] Nevertheless, the police were ordered to offer equal protection of the law to all and to put an end to attacks on Jews. In enforcing this order over the weekend following, 800 persons were arrested, 80 percent of them Russian. At the same time, 72 people were killed and 80 gravely wounded, another 800 receiving minor injuries, all in the Jewish quarter of the city. No exact accounting of the human toll was ever made, but estimates ranged between 850 and 1,000 dead, with 3,500 to 5,000 wounded.[84] There is no doubt that the Jews suffered most heavily: at one point, United States Ambassador Frederic J. Stimson reported that of 182 bodies collected, 150 were of Russian Jews.

As a condition that prepared the way for the attacks, Mirelman points to the "continuous antisemitic propaganda and education sponsored by some Catholic groups," as priests spoke on street corners and in churches against anarchists, socialists, and Jews.[85] But no evidence of a plot, Bolshevik or other, was ever uncovered. None of those arrested was ever brought to trial, for want of evidence. Wald himself was charged only with possession of a firearm, a charge that could have been brought against most porteños that week. Evidently, the "plot" was no more than a hoax cooked up by police and press to justify the attacks on Jews as a way of suppressing labor unrest. Montevideo police were also alerted to the existence of a "plot" by *rusos* to overthrow the government on the eastern bank. News of arrests in Montevideo encouraged Buenos Aires police to make more raids. Nothing, not even Bolshevism, is as contagious as panic.

"The Semana Trágica was only an isolated major antisemitic issue and thus did not constitute a strong enough incentive to the centralization of the Jewish community," concludes Mirelman.[86] It did not, for example, impel formation of an all-inclusive Jewish defense organization. Yet, while Argentine Jews themselves customarily downplay the events of of 1919, one cannot escape the feeling that a psychological process was set in train as Jews internalized the lesson of Tragic Week. Evidence is suggestive if not dispositive. Jews learned that political activity was more dangerous for them than for others and that the entire Jewish community could be attacked for the actions of anyone who had been born Jewish. This sense of collective destiny, the understanding that the entire community is hostage for the acts of individual Jews, remains strong among Argentine Jews. It surfaced during the military regime of 1976–83, when atrocities inflicted by the government on Jewish individuals met with a very guarded response from the organized Jewish community. The perception of the organized community as a hostage to government reprisal for the actions (or alleged actions) of individual Jews explains and aggravates the tendency of mainstream community leaders to reject radical political activity and radical Jewish activists as a danger to the majority of Jews.

Anti-Semitism had always been endemic among the Argentine upper class. As they reacted to labor unrest and the Great Depression, the elite deployed anti-Semitism in the service of nationalist reaction, to which Jews were especially vulnerable because they were nearly all foreign-born. In the years between the wars, elite fear of communism, freemasonry, and liberalism received additional support from fascist ideology. The allure of European fascism, with its concomitant anti-Semitism, struck a responsive note among many Argentines, who were particularly attracted by the ultramontanism of Charles Maurras (1868–1952), soon to become chief ideologist of the Vichy regime. Maurras turned the word *Jew* into an ideogram that stood for modernizing attitudes that immigrants were introducing into Argentina and that threatened the continuity of criollo values.[87] The ultimate libel was that the Jew was, and always would remain, an alien who did not belong to the Argentine nation. Unavailing was the fact that Jewish men responded together with non-Jews to the requirement of universal military service. Unavailing also was the evidence that Jewish Argentines acted in accord with their class interests, not in response to the atavistic call of imaginary bloodlines. The Liga Patriótica Argentina, a group dedicated to defending "Fatherland and Order" through the suppression of labor unrest, included Jewish members. Jewish property owners participated in an action against laborers (including Jews) in Villa Domínguez when the latter went out on strike against the threshing-machine owners. Although Jews fought on both sides of this labor dispute, newspapers (and some congressmen) portrayed the incident as a case of "Jewish revolutionaries" against "orderly Creoles."[88] Nor did the existence of Jewish agricultural colonies establish Jews as Argentines, for these, it was alleged, were no more than a plot to create Palestine in Argentina.

In the interwar period, the Catholic journal *Criterio* became a potent force in creating a hostile environment for Jewish life. Accusing Jews of deicide, it inculpated the current generation equally with their ancestors, because of their obstinacy in not accepting the Catholic faith. In articles on "the Jewish hatred of Jesus," and "Jewish persecution of the Christ," *Criterio* adumbrated its historical distortions with support for the accusations then being falsely leveled against Captain Alfred Dreyfus in France.[89] In a nation that was almost 100 percent Catholic, the views of the Catholic establishment could not but impress a distorted picture of the Jew on the minds of its communicants.

During these same years, a generational shift between immigrant and native Jews was leading to a profound cultural shift as well. Yiddish culture bound immigrants to their community of origin in Eastern Europe, while serving as a bond with fellow immigrants. The native-born generation, educated in Spanish, moved quickly into the mainstream of national concerns, and was progressively distanced from specifically Jewish matters that were still bound up in Yiddish. The secular weekly *Mundo Israelita* (Jewish World), founded in 1923 by León Kibrick and Salomón Resnick, aimed at educating this new Argentine Jewish generation and promoting native leadership of the community.[90] The editors encouraged the translation of Yiddish literature into Spanish and backed the formation of a *kehillah* (organized community; plural, *kehillot*). Meanwhile, several cultural associations merged to form the Sociedad Hebraica Argentina in 1926.[91] Within two years, SHA had a membership of 1,400; today, it is one of the premier cultural institutions of Buenos Aires. As authors and playwrights, Jews gained acceptability by identifying with Argentine rather than Jewish themes.

Despite social barriers, Jews adapted amazingly well to the conditions presented to them.[92] Barred from membership in the athletic clubs that are at the core of Latino society, Jews formed their own athletic associations. They named them "Macabi," after the Jewish resisters to Syrian rule in the second century B.C.E. Jewish sports teams and individual athletes were soon competing in boxing, rowing, basketball, soccer, and chess against other ethnically based clubs, for Italian, Syrian, and other immigrants were also adopting the local style. The strong urge toward assimilation causes Mirelman to claim that authentically Jewish values such as education, love of Zion, and *Yiddishkeit* were not being transmitted to the native generation, who grew up ignorant of Jewish culture.[93] The diagnosis is borne out by the testimony of an Argentine Jewish novelist in 1994, who said, "Being Jewish was a very conflictive thing in my childhood and adolescence. My mother said that if someone asked me 'what' I was, I had to answer, 'I am nothing.'"[94]

Technological advances opened up entirely new occupational fields for some newcomers. Max Glucksman (1875–1946) was producing, distributing, and exhibiting films in the early years of the century. Alberto Soifer, born on the agricultural colony Coronel Suárez, wrote tangos and other music for more than eighty movies. León Klimovsky, born in Buenos Aires in 1907, directed movies, and Luis Saslavsky (b. Santa Fe, 1908) wrote screenplays for Argentine and foreign films. Numerous Jewish actors and actresses, such as the Singerman sisters and Iza Kremer, gained fame, first by playing supporting roles in troupes imported from the United States, and then as artists in their own right.

A few individuals of incredible determination managed to work their way through the universities. Among professions they chose, the traditional one of medicine remained important, though matriculation at medical schools was fraught with anti-Semitic booby traps. Some of these are described by Mario Schteingard in his autobiography. Born in Vitebsk (Russia) in 1892, Schteingard earned his M.D. at the University of Córdoba in 1921 and later became the first Jewish member of the Academia Nacional de Medicina.[95] Margarita Zatzkin, born in Odessa circa 1885, earned her diploma in pharmacy in 1905 and her doctor of medicine degree in 1909, the first woman and first non-Catholic to earn degrees at the Universidad Nacional de Córdoba.[96] Paulina Weintraub de Itzigsohn, who earned her medical degree in Zurich, became physician to the colonists of Entre Ríos and La Pampa in 1911; her son José, likewise a physician, became director of the department of psychiatry at the University of Buenos Aires.[97] Psychoanalysis arrived in Argentina in the 1940s, introduced by a group of practitioners of whom two were Jewish: Arnaldo Rascovsky, a native Argentine, and Mary Glas de Langer, who came from an assimilated Viennese family. Psychiatrist Gregorio Bermann was among the founders of the World Health Organization and presided over the Asociación Psiquiátrica de América Latina in the 1960s. In Argentina, psychoanalysis has not escaped its reputation as "a Jewish science," one that has captivated wide strata of the population, who make no secret of their enlistment in Freudian or Lacanian ranks.

Immigrant pioneers paved the way for their children, who soon began entering the professions in significant numbers. The majority of immigrants, however, entered the Argentine economy as farmers or blue-collar workers.

PART THREE

AT HOME IN AMERICA

CHAPTER 5

Agricultural Colonies: The Burden of the Dream

> *We planted wheat and harvested doctors.*
>
> —A JCA colonist

THOUSANDS OF JEWISH immigrants established themselves as farmers in Argentina, Brazil, Uruguay, the Dominican Republic, and Bolivia. For the most part, they settled in groups, often under sponsorship of the Jewish Colonization Association (JCA). Only the colonies in Argentina lasted long enough to mold the character of Jewish migration to these countries and to leave an impress on the nation's history. Other colonies that were projected for areas as distinct as Baja California and Suriname never came into existence. Despite their evanescence, it is worth examining Jewish colonies in three different ecological settings as a means of furthering our understanding of the way Jewish immigrants could and could not adapt to Latin American society. The successes and the failures alike provide insight into the nature of the migration and the capacity of these societies to absorb European immigrants into their agricultural sectors.

Argentina

We have seen that Argentine expectations concerning immigrants focused persistently on their value as farmers. Despite high expectations, the social and legislative climate was never adapted to meet their needs. The accumulation of enormous tracts of land in the hands of a few families was already a permanent feature of the landscape by the time immigrants began to arrive. The large leased tracts characteristic of the early independence period were converted to permanent ownership under Rosas, and in 1876 the first law of lands and colonies permitted the sale of land in lots of eighty thousand hectares. This was the same year basic immigration legislation was passed, and successive governments never provided for the demand of immigrant farmers to buy

105

homesteads. Between 1882 and 1912, land values increased one hundredfold because of the subjugation of the Araucanians and the consequent expansion of the agricultural frontier. Newly opened land was sold at public auction, in tracts so large that the price was beyond the reach of ordinary farmers or immigrants, who lost out to speculators and investors.[1] As a result, the process by which *latifundista* families extended their domains actually intensified during the years when proimmigration forces were calling most vocally for recruitment of farmers.

Since land was not to be made available to individual immigrants, colonization became a corporate concern. Government allotted large tracts to foreign entrepreneurs, who in turn contracted with European firms to supply specified numbers of settlers. These were then allocated plots of land within the colony, together with the right to claim ownership after a given number of years. The entrepreneurs made their profit from shares in the harvest and by keeping a part of the land grant for themselves.

We may now ask why Jews should have decided to cast themselves in the role of agricultural pioneers in Argentina, a country that had not previously attracted their attention. The motivation was partly survival and partly ideology. The former is sufficient to account for Jews' emigrating to Argentina, but the latter is vital to an understanding of why they came as farmers.

The renewed outbreak of pogroms in Russia in 1881 forced Jewish intellectuals into a redefinition of their Jewishness that depended less upon amelioration of the gentile world's hatred of the Jew than upon alteration of the Jews' own state of consciousness, shaped ineluctably by objective reality. Several elements figured in what came to be called autoemancipation, after the title of a tract published in 1882 by Leon Pinsker. One was Zionism, which offered a political solution. Another was cultural nationalism, stressing the spiritual unity of scattered Jewish communities. The third was a return to nature and to productive labor on the land. These themes were to dominate Jewish life for the next ninety years and to result, inter alia, in creation of the State of Israel.

Apart from the nationalist mystique of Zion, there was nothing intrinsically attractive about Palestine, at that time a forsaken corner of the Ottoman Empire. The appearance on the scene of Argentina, with its offer of religious toleration and land for the farmer, presented the émigrés who were interested in "normalizing" the situation of the Jewish people with an alternative destination. Thus Argentina, because of its policy of recruiting European farm immigrants, became a link in the chain of migrations that was converting the Jews from a European to an American people.

In 1889, a group of Russian Jews arranged their own emigration aboard the steamship *Weser*. They found themselves stranded and penniless, however, when their contract for the purchase of farmland was not honored. Reduced to poverty, without food or housing, the immigrants hovered near the railway station, sustaining themselves with handouts from passengers. Many children died the first winter, and numbers of young women went off with white slavers. The entire enterprise would have died aborning had it not been for Dr. Wilhelm

Loewenthal, a Jewish sanitary engineer. Investigating on behalf of the Alliance Israelite Universelle, he brought the plight of the settlers to the attention of Baron Maurice de Hirsch. Thus began one of the most remarkable adventures in immigration the world had seen to that date.

Hirsch's intervention was prompted by a philanthropic urge whose manifestation in practical deeds earned him considerable status among Jews worldwide, for whom the giving of *tzdakah* (charity) is a meritorious act. His philanthropy had a practical bent. Although Hirsch sent money for the temporary relief of the impoverished Jews of Santa Fe, he went considerably farther and established the Jewish Colonization Association, an organization he envisaged as a way of restructuring the lives of diaspora Jewry. Ultimately, his investment in JCA exceeded the combined resources of all other contemporary Jewish philanthropies in Europe and the United States.[2] The guiding idea behind JCA was to accomplish the moral and physical regeneration of the Jews through agricultural labor. "What I desire to accomplish," wrote Hirsch, "what, after many failures has come to be the object of my life, and that for which I am ready to stake my wealth and my intellectual powers, is to give to a portion of my companions in faith the possibility of finding a new existence, primarily as farmers and also as handicraftsmen, in those lands where the laws and religious tolerance permit them to carry on the struggle for existence as noble and responsible subjects of a human government."[3]

The question is sometimes raised as to why the baron fixed on Argentina rather than on Palestine. Although, at a later date, the two destinations were to compete for immigrants, the dream of a renaissance of the Jewish people in the land of its birth had not yet found the man who could bring it to fruition. The one who was to do that, Theodor Herzl, was still fumbling to give shape to his inchoate ideas when he met with Baron de Hirsch at the latter's Paris home in June 1895. A week later, Herzl noted in his diary some arguments against Jewish settlement in Palestine: the proximity of Russia; the lack of opportunity for expansion; the climate.[4] The baron would no doubt have added the necessity of dealing with the Turks, with whom he had had scarifying experiences in the course of building the oriental railways that were the foundation of his fortune.

Hirsch was no visionary and had his own ideas about a Jewish renaissance. What was needed was to wean Jews away from urban occupations and get them back on the land. Herzl indeed faulted him for deprecating the finer qualities in Jewish life. But Hirsch was more than an imperious philanthropist. His style was to intervene in specific situations where he felt that money and organization could make the difference between success and failure of Jews to root themselves. He was a businessman, and the organization he created in his image operated on business principles, with contracts imposed upon the settlers as terms of their acceptance into the project. Hirsch was to initiate agricultural ventures in Canada, the United States, and Brazil, but he favored Argentina and determined to give that project every possibility of success. The presence of the stranded *Weser* immigrants in Santa Fe Province, on the edge of Argentina's wheat belt, provided the sort of opportunity he relished. There the lure of virgin land, which was attracting settlers in large numbers, meshed with the worldwide rise in the price of wheat to present prospects of a profit to be made through large-scale cultivation of grain. How better to combine philanthropy with good business practice than by transferring displaced Jews from Russia and settling them as farmers on land suitable for growing wheat? Thus Jews would become self-sufficient in the one occupation that, according to the baron's philosophy, could accomplish their "moral and physical regeneration." The refugees were about to acquire a manager.

JCA was founded 10 September 1891 as a British joint stock company, with an initial capital of $10 million (furnished by Hirsch, who later added another $30 million). On his death, Hirsch's shares were divided among the Jewish communities of Frankfurt-am-Main, Berlin, and Brussels, the Alliance Israelite Universelle (founded in 1860 at Paris as an educational and rehabilitation agency), and the Anglo-Jewish Association of London, which became the administrator. Article 6 of its charter prohibits the taking of any profit from the company; any surplus is to be dedicated to "facilitating the emigration of Jews from the countries . . . where they are persecuted . . . to other regions of the world where they may enjoy the rights inherent in mankind." In negotiations with the Russian government, Hirsch assumed responsibility for the transport of colonists from various European and Turkish ports. The Russians, for their part, agreed to issue passports to the refugees, which they had hitherto refused to do. These were one-way documents, invalid for return to Russia, but they facilitated the immigrants' entry into Argentina.

Previous colonizers had received their land free from the Argentine government; in many cases, they had also received funds for their maintenance during the first year of settlement, as well as seed and tools. On 21 May 1891, however, the alienation of public lands ceased. All the land that JCA came to control had to be purchased either from the government or from private owners. JCA organized and paid for the immigrants' transportation to Argentina; allocated land, tools, and farm animals; and provided shelter for the colonists during the transition years. It hired administrators to run the colonies and represented the colonists in their dealings with the Argentine government. What was demanded of the settlers was that they be "experienced farmers, with families large enough to provide sufficient manpower; they had to have some savings of their own and a willingness to forge the way in a new, pioneering endeavor."[5] JCA conformed both to Argentine law and to Jewish necessity by serving as colonizing agent for agrarian immigrants. Moreover, as Scobie notes, "the [Jewish Colonization] association introduced paternal protection and guidance totally lacking in private, company, or official immigration schemes."[6]

To start the project off, agents of Baron de Hirsch fanned out through the ports of Germany and Turkey, spreading word about the new land of promise, interviewing and selecting immigrants whom they considered fit for agricultural labor. One Constantinople contingent of two hundred families was organized into seventeen brigades, under captains who were responsible for the comportment of their charges. A *shokhet,* or ritual slaughterer, was shipped with the immigrants in order to allow them to observe Jewish dietary law, but the enlightened administrators urged their colonists to conform to public decorum on the boat, to see themselves as a self-conscious vanguard: "You are going in order to open a path for your brothers in captivity, accused of depreciating honest agricultural labor. Baron de Hirsch wishes to demonstrate to the world through your mediation that the accusation is false, and that Hebrews also can be good workers when they have the means to be so."[7] Thus, at the very start of the migration, the future relationship between administration and colonists was prefigured: the role of the administrators as big brother; the desire to transform the colonists' image; and the expectation that these migrants would prove a point that was very important in the ideology of the day: that Jews were capable of productive labor on the land.

Restrictions on Jews had prevented them from owning land in most countries of Europe; an exception was the southern region of the Pale of Settlement, most notably, the provinces of Kherson, Ekaterinoslav, and Bessarabia, where in 1898 some 150,000 Jews were working full- or part-time in agriculture.[8] It was from this region that many of the candidates came. But stevedores, blacksmiths, ironworkers, tailors, and shoemakers were also enlisted, if they were in good physical condition and had sons who might be expected to work alongside them. Many recruits were not farmers, but they were not city dwellers either. Most Russian and Polish Jews at that date lived in farming villages or rural towns (the shtetl), where they were intimately linked with the agricultural cycle.

The original plan was to resettle 25,000 Jews in Argentina during 1892, the first year of JCA's existence. In the course of twenty-five years, it was hoped that 3,250,000 Jews would escape from the Pale of Settlement to the Argentine pampas. In point of fact, just 2,500 Jews, one-tenth the projected number, were resettled the first year. In no year did total Jewish immigration into Argentina exceed 15,000, including those who went to the city as well as those who went to the farm. Although Argentina was the major destination for Jewish farmers under the JCA program, the colonies at their peak had only 33,000 Jewish farmers.[9]

The settlement scheme had to be scaled down as a result of the failure of the Argentine government to approve the sale of additional adjacent tracts of land and a dawning realization on Hirsch's part that the climate and soil in the areas where he was able to buy land were not totally suited to agriculture. Hirsch therefore shifted from his original project of one vast territory to one of scattered colonies that would not raise the apprehension of Argentines that a portion of their national territory might be alienated. This move also enabled JCA to try out agricultural conditions in other parts of the country. The accompanying map indicates the location, ultimate extent of land purchased, and date of installation of the first Jewish farmers in the Argentine JCA colonies. First to be settled were the remainder of the *Weser* group who still wished to go into farming after their rude initiation. Hirsch purchased a part of the tract on which they had settled under contract, and it was there that the first colony

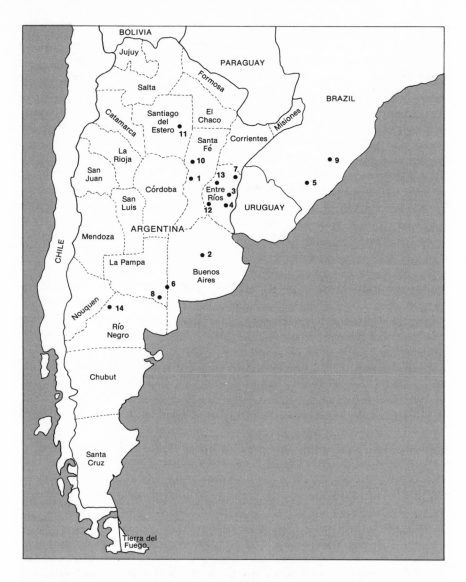

Jewish Colonization Association Colonies in Argentina and Brazil

Name	Settled	Hectares	Name	Settled	Hectares
1. Moisesville	1891	118,262	8. Narcisse Leven	1909	46,466
2. Mauricio	1892	43,485	9. Quatro Hermãos	1910	93,885
3. Clara	1892	102,671	10. Montefiore	1912	29,075
4. Lucienville	1894	40,630	11. Dora	1912	2,980
5. Philippson	1903	5,764	12. Cohen-Oungre	1925	23,074
6. Baron Hirsch	1905	110,866	13. Avigdor	1936	17,175
7. Santa Isabel	1908	47,804	14. San José (not colonized)		156

SOURCE: Adapted from Morton D. Winsberg, *Colonia Baron Hirsch*, p. 6.

of Moisesville was established in 1891. In succeeding years, five colonies were established in the province of Entre Ríos, another in Santa Fe, two in the province of Buenos Aires, and one each in the Chaco, La Pampa, and Río Negro. The early pace of settlement was rapid; four colonies were established in the 1890s and seven more before the outbreak of World War I.

Five years into its lifetime, in 1896 (the year of Baron Hirsch's death), the JCA project consisted of 302,736 hectares of land, settled by a Jewish population of 6,757. The years up to World War I witnessed JCA's greatest expansion; its area almost doubled while its population practically tripled. The largest population—20,382 Jewish farmers and their families, 13,000 Jewish artisans, businessmen, professionals, and their families, plus a non-Jewish population of about 5,000—was reached in 1925, following which the Jewish population began to diminish while the non-Jewish population continued to increase.[10] Although the population of the colonies appeared to be growing throughout the 1920s, the statistics obscure the turnover in personnel as disappointed settlers departed for the city and were replaced by new immigrants, not a few of whom settled on the farm because they were admitted to the country on agricultural visas. From 1936 to 1940, the colonies underwent a revival as JCA recruited German and Austrian Jewish refugees. Most of these persons, however, were middle-class professionals with no background of manual labor, and they tended to leave as soon as economic conditions permitted.

The total land area eventually acquired by JCA in Argentina came to 617,000 hectares, or a million and a half acres. This was transferred in settlement only in part; one-fourth was held in reserve for future immigrants or was not suitable for agriculture. The colonists were settled as family units. Although conditions varied somewhat from time to time and from place to place, the terms imposed upon settlers in Colonía Baron Hirsch were typical. Each colonist was awarded a lot varying in size from 75 to 150 hectares (185 to 370 acres), together with a house (two rooms and a kitchen), fencing, a well, a poultry run, ten to twenty cows, eight to ten horses, twenty-five to fifty fowl, a wagon, plow, harrow, harness, and miscellaneous farm implements, seeds, and maintenance for the first few months. In return, colonists signed a contract that obligated them to pay all land taxes and rent at the rate of 4 percent of the value of the land, 5 percent of the value of the buildings. The contract was to be reviewed after five years, and after eight, colonists would be given a definite title deed with a mortgage at 4 percent interest—if they had meanwhile succeeded in paying off 50 percent of the value of the land.

For a few years, the JCA colonies captured the imagination of the Jewish world, for they seemed to hold the promise that, here in the New World, the Jewish condition of rootlessness could be remedied. In fact, during the 1930s, a larger proportion of the Jewish working class was engaged in agriculture than was the case either in their countries of origin or in other major countries of destination. In the decade preceding World War II, the percentage of Jews gainfully employed who worked in agriculture was 4.3 percent for Poland and 4.2 percent for the USSR. The corresponding percentage for Jews of the United

States was 2.2 percent. But 5.8 percent of Argentine Jews gainfully employed
were in agriculture in 1935.[11] This certainly justified the baron's belief that
Jewish settlement on the land might succeed in Argentina.

Jewish agricultural colonies, however, were not to become a permanent
feature of Argentine life. Just 2,373 Jewish farmers (including independents)
were counted in the 1960 Argentine census, and the process of attrition has
continued since that date. To understand why the colonies failed, it is necessary
to examine both their internal life and the Argentine social structures into
which they had to fit.

The dominant theme of most memoirs of life in the JCA colonies is the
struggle between settlers and administrators. Administrators of the colonies,
mostly French and products of the haskalah, saw themselves as "always . . .
preoccupied with facilitating the assimilation of the people settled in their
colonies with the object of their becoming good agriculturists and patriotic
Argentinians, though conserving their religious faith."[12] Most diarists and historians among the East European colonists depict the administrators as anti-
Semites. Believing themselves culturally superior to the settlers whose affairs
they had been hired to administer, officials displayed a contempt for the mores
of the shtetl that was at all times galling and occasionally brutal. According to
one historian of the colonies, Hirsch's fundamental principle—that the project
not be handled as charity but be utilized to reconstruct Jewish life—was
perverted by the JCA administrators into a conviction that they must protect
the project against the settlers, who, as East Europeans, were lacking in culture
and not worthy of trust.[13] So for example, Hirsch's stricture that JCA help only
those who helped themselves emerged from the administrators' hands in the
form of a contract that many settlers had to sign by which JCA remained sole
owner of the land up to the very last payment.[14] JCA retained the right to expel
any farmer who was tardy in his current payment, without consideration for
sums paid up to that date. The right was often exercised. This philanthropic
feudalism turned the colonists into tenants rather than independent farmers.
In another extension of European mores, titles to land were given out to male
heads of families, although women worked alongside their husbands.

The tight bureaucratic mold, a product of the transfer of European attitudes
to Argentina, left no room for participation by the settlers in the determination
of their own affairs. With JCA legal owner of the land, farmers found they
could not get credit at the bank but were forced to borrow from JCA, a situation
that intensified their dependence. Gradually, Jewish tenants found themselves
being pushed into the same dependent relationship to their *patrón* as *minifundistas* all over Latin America. Jews, however, had arrived on the land with
financial and organizing skills; to evade this dependence, they founded cooperative credit associations. Originally organized with JCA support for the purpose
of buying seeds and supplies, the cooperatives turned into a weapon of struggle
against the JCA as the settlers endeavored to gain representation in the decision-
making process.[15]

JCA had reason to impede colonist participation in management. As a charitable organization, it was selling land at prices far below those charged by commercial companies. As the price of land rose steadily, colonists watched the value of their assigned property rise several-fold over the price at which they had agreed to buy it. Colonists who received title to their land before they had adjusted to rural life were tempted by its increased value to sell it, invest the money in other occupations, and establish themselves in the city. In fact, just such a fate overtook the colony of Mauricio, where victory of the colonists in a lawsuit claiming title to their land resulted in the exodus of nine-tenths of them between the years 1919 and 1930.[16] Such a development obviously ran counter to the philosophy of Baron de Hirsch and of the organization he had founded.

With hindsight, it is possible to relieve the JCA administrators of the charge of anti-Semitism without thereby declaring them to have been sensitive to the settlers' problems. Two of these were the source of continual friction: the pattern of settlement and the allocation of land to the second generation.

The pattern of settlement was crucial because Jewish life is communal in nature. The scattering of farmers on their land, combined with poor means of transport, would make it impossible to create the Jewish social institutions—synagogues, religious schools, libraries, facilities for slaughtering kosher meat, cemeteries—on which Jewish life depends. At first, JCA settled the immigrants in agricultural villages, a pattern typical of eastern Europe but not then in use in Argentina. Here the familiar old institutions were re-created—but at the price of agricultural efficiency because farmers spent a good deal of time getting to and from their land. Subsequently, JCA gave up the village pattern of settlement in favor of locating each family upon its own land. The increase in efficiency was then accompanied by atrophying of Jewish institutions as the isolation of the Argentine countryside closed down around Jewish, as around non-Jewish, farmers.[17]

The hostile eye of Arieh Tartakower emphasizes the latter development. In his view, JCA administrators, by scattering colonies over the Argentine map "as though for fear of the evil eye," deliberately inhibited the growth of Jewish cultural life, which they despised as inferior to their own and as an embarrassment before the Gentiles.[18]

Perhaps the most shortsighted aspect of JCA policy was the refusal to grant land from its reserves to the grown sons of established colonists. The policy was adhered to over a period of many years, despite considerable agitation on the part of those colonists who foresaw that stable settlement depended on making provision for the next generation. The JCA contended that it was concerned with settling new Jewish immigrants from abroad and that Argentine-born sons ought to strike out on their own. The difficulty was that, as we have seen, it was virtually impossible for an individual to buy farmland in small plots. This was true throughout the nation and for all immigrants. So little success did colonists enjoy in establishing themselves on the land that the very word *colono* came to be generally used as a synonym for *peon*, a term that has more the connotation of debt-serf than of freeholder. As a result of JCA policy, grown sons of colonists who wished to remain farmers had to become tenants of other latifundistas, accepting the same short-term leases then being offered other rural proletarians. Analysts of the Argentine economy generally point to these leases, which bore no assurance of renewal, as a major cause of rural poverty. With insecure tenure, the colonists had no incentive to make improvements to the land but tended to drift off toward the city.

Furthermore, as Avni has shown, despite all the difficulties the farmers experienced, JCA itself was turning a profit in the interwar period. At the same time, the "Yiko" or the "Jevish," as JCA was known locally, tightened the requirements for accepting candidates for settlement. Now, in addition to producing two grown sons to farm together with the paterfamilias, candidates had to pay their own fare, maintain themselves financially during a transition period, and contribute toward settlement costs. The Association was experiencing a great deal of difficulty in finding suitable candidates, and rejected two-thirds of those who applied under these terms. Finally, a settler who failed to perform to the satisfaction of JCA could be removed from the colony and declared no longer to be JCA's responsibility.[19] Even the rise of Nazism in Germany in the 1930s was not sufficient to galvanize JCA into developing plans for mass immigration: in January 1936, the Association brought over 46 settlers to their new colony of Avigdor; a year later, the grand total was 99.[20] JCA, whose role in Jewish agricultural settlement was crucial, never saw itself as a sponsor of large-scale immigration, but as a mechanism for settling highly selected, proven agriculturists on the land.

Although there is always a balance to be struck between the ability of immigrants to adapt and the environment to which they must adapt, it seems clear that the system of land tenure that characterized Argentina provided the context and determined the parameters of agricultural settlement. Of equal importance among external factors affecting the viability of the Jewish colonies was the marginal utility of the land JCA was able to buy:

> The JCA colonies were generally established in the less attractive agricultural regions of the country, because most of the best land in Argentina had entered the private domain years before, and either was not for sale or was too expensive. Taking advantage of a brief economic depression in 1890, the JCA began purchasing large tracts of land, in some cases entire ranches, on the outer margin of the fertile humid Pampa. Among the largest purchases were those made in the province of Entre Ríos. . . . The land purchased by the association has at best only marginal value for agriculture.[21]

Winsberg found the region of the Entre Ríos colonies to be better suited to cattle raising than to crop production. But the small size of the farms allotted to individual families precluded their use for ranches and forced the colonists to concentrate on agriculture even though they could not do so profitably. Similarly with Colonía Baron Hirsch, which is on the border between Buenos Aires and La Pampa provinces. The 150-hectare farms issued to the colonists were inadequate to sustain wheat production in this area's dry climate. Yet the colonists were constrained to grow just that crop because it was the only product that, if the harvest was satisfactory, would bring them a profit large enough to meet the payments on their farms, as well as provide for expenses. Paradoxically, the problem in this wheat-growing colony arose from the contemporary boom in the international market for wheat. By 1905, when Jews settled Colonía Baron Hirsch, Argentina was in the midst of an agricultural boom that saw her total crop acreage expand from 16 million to 50 million acres between 1899 and 1911. The high price of wheat on the international market had driven up the price of land, particularly any on which the valued commodity could be grown. Consequently, Colonía Baron Hirsch is situated beyond the climatic frontier of stable wheat production.

Increasingly, the JCA colonies became part of Argentina's persistent latifundia-minifundia complex of problems. An Argentine government agronomist had held that 500 hectares were the minimum necessary for economic self-sufficiency in agriculture, 5,000 hectares the minimum for efficient cattle production. The 75- to 150-hectare farms allotted to the colonists represented no more than one-fifth of the recommended minimum, "too little to live on, too much to die from" (tzum lebn tzu veinik, tzum shtarbn tzu fil). To complicate matters, the settlers were totally lacking in ecological orientation. Even those who had been farmers in their old homes were unfamiliar with the soil and climate of Argentina. The lands were virgin and difficult to cultivate by hand or with the old-fashioned machinery that some immigrants brought with them from Russia. In fact, this was precisely why the cattle barons left these lands to farmers—so they would break up the tough pampa grass and eventually plant the area to alfalfa for cattle. Under other conditions, the settlers might have benefited from the example of neighboring farmers. Agriculture in Argentina, however, was in a primitive state owing to the system of latifundia that did not require owners to cultivate efficiently in order to reap substantial returns. The absence of a class of family farmers left a social gap between the immigrants and the large landowners that could not be bridged from the immigrants' side. Consequently, the colonists' most intimate contact with native Argentines was with that "peon on horseback," the gaucho. It was the gaucho who taught Jewish immigrants how to ride, how to herd cattle, how to shelter against the elements, how to shoot. In the end, the gaucho taught the colonist his own primitive methods of agriculture—a rude twist to Argentine hopes that European immigrants would educate the gaucho to more advanced techniques. The legend of the Jewish gaucho emerged at the turn of the century: a person midway between the cultures of the ghetto and the pampa. The number of such Jews who existed is less important than the grip the image exerted upon people's minds: the Jewish gaucho symbolizes the settlers' physical and psychic investment in the upbuilding of the Argentine interior.[22] As for the impact Jews made on gauchos, some of them apparently learned Yiddish in order to communicate with their exotic neighbors.

The "Jewish gauchos" of song and story were really farmers, not cowboys. But they learned their survival skills from the seminomadic gauchos who roamed the Argentine pampas. The gauchos in turn picked up European skills from the settlers, including use of the Yiddish language.

The fact that the settlers' contact with the native Argentine population was restricted to the gaucho, who was still in the condition that led Sarmiento to expatiate on the conundrum of "barbarism" at the heart of Argentine seaboard "civilization," contributed to the colonists' conviction that they themselves stood at a far higher cultural level than the surrounding population and that their sons and daughters must be educated to be something better, even if this meant abandoning the farm that had represented in the first place the expectation of a new and better way of life. The problem of education generally, and Jewish education specifically, emerges as crucial to the Jewish agricultural experience.

Despite the avowed commitment of the Argentine government to free and universal public education, there were no schools in the areas settled by JCA. The Jewish settlers, still involved in an inherited tradition of learning, demanded that JCA establish schools for their children, and these in fact were set up at an early date. (Chapter 7 describes these schools.) Under the circumstances, however, neither the settlers nor JCA were able to provide quality higher education, and this limitation is cited by all informants as a prime reason for moving to the city. Scobie identifies isolation as a factor in driving all immigrants out of the countryside.

> In the countryside the immigrant could not form a cultural or social group with his countrymen as he had in the city. Most of the colonies were economic ventures and only occasionally, as with the early Santa Fe colonies or the Jewish Colonization Association, did they provide religious and cultural unity. Extensive tenant farming did not permit even accidental unity or contact. The very isolation and transiency of the agricultural immigrant's life retarded his assimilation into the national culture, not because he formed groups outside that culture but because he himself was so remote.[23]

Isolation was probably felt more acutely by Jews than by non-Jews because of their centuries-old attachment to education as a way of life. "There wasn't a book to read or a light to read it by," was the answer of one old colonist when asked why he had moved to the city. For Jews, education was a cultural imperative, overriding the territorial imperative of hanging onto the land that is so marked a feature of peasant life. The departure of young people was accelerated by the decision of JCA not to make land available to the second generation. But if the decision had been made to make such land available, one suspects that in the continuing absence of a national system of schools, departure from the countryside would only have been delayed by a generation.

Many forces antagonistic to all the agricultural colonies operated during the period under review, affecting Jewish settlement only because it was a part of the whole. The years 1895–97 saw exceedingly poor crops: these were the years when the first four Jewish colonies were started. After that, it became increasingly difficult for small farmers to get out of debt. One informant reported that his father, an original settler of Lucienville, died after forty-three years' labor on the land, still not the legal owner of it. By the turn of the century, the period when small owner-operated farms could produce wheat profitably was drawing to a close everywhere. From then on, only large-scale, mechanized producers could stay in business profitably. In drought years, marginal farmers were wiped out, and a succession of droughts in the 1930s forced farmers off the land in Entre Ríos as in Oklahoma. The worldwide depression of 1929–33 had its effect on all commodity producers. As the price of wheat on world markets dropped, colonists could no longer clear enough to make their farms pay. Often the sale or rental of their property provided a stake that enabled them to start a new life in the city, while the more successful farmers strengthened their position by adding to their own holdings. Following World War II, peronista economic planning, aimed at increasing industrial production, resulted in low farm prices and high tenant wages that again squeezed out small owners, leaving behind the familiar pattern of large-scale ownership of land by people who rarely farmed it and a class of tenant farmers lacking the political or economic power to acquire land.

The result of Argentine agrarian policy, despite the stated desire to conquer the interior, was to furnish hands to the city. Up to 1890, 70 percent of immigrants to the Argentine were peasants. Presumably, at least some of these retained an affinity for rural life despite their transatlantic transplantation. Over the years, however, decreasing proportions of immigrants actually engaged in agriculture. Maldistribution of land foreclosed on the possibility of populating the countryside with immigrants and sent those immigrants, willy-nilly, to the cities.[24] In 1914, native-born Argentines were distributed almost evenly between rural and urban areas, but 70 percent of the country's foreigners were living in cities, despite the asserted government policy of "internalizing" immigrants on the land and despite the fact that most immigrants were rural in origin.[25] The migration of Jewish farmers to the city must be seen in the context of the urbanization of both native and immigrant that is so prominent a feature of Argentine history.

Urbanization on such a scale indicates the presence of compelling economic and social forces that could not be resisted by that small segment of the migration which consisted of Jews. If they had succeeded in staying on the land, that would indeed have called for explanation. As it is, the partial and short-lived success of the JCA colonies reflects the ephemeral success of Argentine immigration policy, which was aimed at peopling the countryside with European farmers but was fatally limited by traditional social structures: the system of latifundia and the exclusion of the rural populace from national life through failure to provide an infrastructure of schools, hospitals, and highways.

A 1958 census of the 332 colonists who still owned farms in Colonía Baron Hirsch revealed the profile of the urbanizing movement among Jews. Of a total of 857 children, 571 were twenty years of age and over. Of these adult children, 55 percent were living outside the colony. Among the 316 adult children who had left their families, 207 or 66 percent were housewives, showing a high tendency among daughters to abandon farm life. Among sons gainfully employed, only 9 percent, having obtained land outside the colony, were engaged in agriculture.

Departure from the colony came most frequently between ages twenty and twenty-nine, with a resulting drop in the number of children under age ten in the colony. The diminishing Jewish population was replaced by Gentiles, who in 1960 comprised 67 percent of the colony's population.[26] From the point of view of the national economy, of course, it makes no difference whether the colonists are Jewish or non-Jewish. From the point of view of Jewish settlement, the urbanizing movement converted Argentine Jewry into an almost entirely urban element. In 1920, 22 percent of Argentine Jews were on the farm. During the next fifteen years, while the Jewish population of Argentina rose from 120,000 to 225,000–230,000, the proportion in the agricultural sector slipped to 11 percent. In 1960, just 2 percent of Argentine Jews declared themselves to be farmers.[27] The departing settlers moved not only to such major metropolitan areas as Buenos Aires, Córdoba, and Tucumán, but also to the small towns located within the borders of their colonies, especially

Moisesville and Basavilbaso, known fondly as Varsovia Pequeña (Little Warsaw).[28]

Although the JCA colonies did not produce a large and stable middle class of Jewish farmers, they did result in the rooting of Jewish Argentines in cities of the interior. Argentina is the only country in Latin America where considerable numbers of Jews settled elsewhere than in the national capital. The Argentine national census of 1960 found nearly fifteen thousand Jews living in Santa Fe and nearly nine thousand in Entre Ríos, provinces that were the site of seven of the colonies. Sixteen districts outside of Greater Buenos Aires had populations of one thousand Jews or more, and there was no district in the republic without its Jewish citizens.[29] Owing to demographic factors yet to be discussed, it is more than likely that these numbers have diminished in the decades since that census was taken.

The decay of the colonies, usually attributed to a stereotypical inability of Jews to relate to agricultural labor, can now be seen to have taken place within the context of a massive urbanizing movement that caught up the majority of immigrants and transformed Argentina from a rural to an urban nation. The primary factors in this movement were nationwide in scope and had nothing to do with Jews: the system of latifundia that squeezed small buyers out of the market; the steadily increasing efficiency of latifundia as machinery made possible economies of scale; the war between agriculturist and cattle baron, in which the latter used the former to open up new grazing lands.

Associated with the latifundia complex was the vital mediatory figure of the patrón. His presence humanized the system but also furnished a convenient target for the farmers' wrath, personifying as he did the whole system in which the small cultivator did not stand a chance. The JCA administration was, of course, the patrón. Without JCA there would have been no group Jewish settlement. But its wealth and the control over the lives of the settlers this wealth conferred made life intolerable for the colonists. They left with an attitude of resentment against JCA that persists to this day. It should be recognized, however, that at a time when, nationwide, farmers were being pushed into marginal areas by the aggressively expanding cattle industry, JCA could not successfully withstand pressures exerted from within and from without. In order to develop agricultural efficiency, the Association scattered the colonists' homesteads, thus inducing in the colonists a sense of isolation that most of them could not endure. For those second-generation families prepared to endure the isolation, JCA failed to provide land, conserving it instead for an expected onrush of new immigrants that never materialized. Thus, even those who would have preferred to stay on the land were driven to the city. The net result of JCA policy, as of government policy, was to stimulate the flow of immigrants from farm to city.

There can be no doubt that there was also a massive failure in human relations within the colonies and that this was important in the general failure to realize large-scale, permanent Jewish colonization. JCA had taken on the task of Argentinizing the settlers, a function they felt had to be performed if

Jews were to find a permanent home in that country. The settlers resisted the effort as an attempt to deprive them of their culture, which was all that remained to them of their former lives. The balance that was to be struck between assimilation to an Argentine standard and conservation of the Jewish heritage at once became a matter of bitter contention between colonists and administrators, who were at opposite ends of the haskalah experience. The emancipated Jews who set the standards imposed changes on the colonists in order to speed their acculturation. Had acculturation not taken place, collision with the larger society would have been inevitable.[30] But the colonists found the process exquisitely painful in the vacuum of the pampas, where they saw nothing of value to acculturate to. Absorption of the immigrants was retarded by the absence of social structures with the capacity to integrate them into the intellectual, economic, or patriotic life of the republic.

In retrospect, it can be seen that the Jewish agricultural colonies acted as cultural decompression chambers, where European Jews underwent transmogrification from European shtetl to Argentine city. In this sense, the JCA performed a function more properly exercised by government, but which the Argentine government had neglected to undertake. By the time the sons and daughters of the colonists emerged into city life, they were no longer frightened, insecure Jewish refugees who felt themselves to be at the mercy of assimilated administrators, murderous gauchos, and descendants of the Grand Inquisitor, but secure, acculturated Argentines of the Jewish persuasion. The generations of youngsters whom the colonists sent to the city appeared, not as exotic strangers, but as Spanish-speaking Argentines capable of participating in the national secular culture. The lodestone that brought the colonists—or, more pointedly, their children—to the city was the prospect of an education.

Though the colonies have almost been emptied of their Jewish inhabitants, the mythology they generated and the presence of their descendants in national life are visible reminders that Jews participated in the building of the nation. The relatively high degree of integration of Jews into Argentine life is due in part to the fact that the colonies satisfied both the Jewish and the Argentine belief that forging a nation is a job that must begin on the land. The colonies' major contribution to the Argentine nation was the colonists themselves.

Dominican Republic

Mass settlement of Jews in agriculture is an idea that has manifested itself twice in Dominican history: in 1881 and again in 1939. The earlier plan came to naught, but it probably prepared the way for the later project, which did meet with some success. The closing decades of the nineteenth century witnessed a debate in the Dominican Republic on the value of European immigration that took place in terms that are by now familiar to us. Proimmigration forces controlled the government when the exodus of Russian Jews began in 1881. The former president, General Gregorio Luperón, approached the Alliance Israelite Universelle and the Barons Gustave and Edmond de Rothschild with the proposition that some of them be resettled in the Dominican Republic. They would be received "with open arms. They will obtain land for farming purposes and secure citizenship."[31] While the Alliance delegated an agent to investigate the offer, the Dominican government prepared a list of Dominican personalities of Jewish descent who could inform the Alliance about conditions in that republic. The list is impressive, attesting to the acculturation of Sephardic settlers since the eighteenth century. It included the Dominican ambassadors in Paris and in the Low Countries; the consul general in Paris and in St. Thomas; the consul in Haiti; wealthy merchants in Paris and other European capitals.[32] Evidently, the death of the agent of the Alliance caused a break in negotiations, and the matter was dropped despite continued interest on the part of successive presidents of the Dominican Republic.

The second project for mass resettlement of Jews was broached at the Evian Conference on Refugees, which assembled during the week of 6–15 July 1938 at the initiative of Franklin D. Roosevelt. Only one government represented at the conference committed itself to admit Jewish refugees from Nazism. On behalf of General Rafael Trujillo, the representative of the Dominican Republic offered to admit one hundred thousand Jews to his country.[33]

In January 1940, an agreement was drawn up between the government of the Dominican Republic and the Dominican Republic Settlement Association of New York (DORSA). On land donated by El Benefactor himself, DORSA was to settle Jewish farmers whom it would select as suitable candidates. The expenses incurred were to be underwritten by voluntary (in practice, Jewish) agencies and to be repaid by the settlers. A bill of rights guaranteeing freedom of religion was included in the contract.[34]

The active partner in DORSA was Agro-Joint, a subsidiary of the Joint Distribution Committee. Founded in 1914, Joint was a relief and rehabilitation agency. It had no colonizing ideology (unlike JCA or the Zionist movement) but tried to help its clients overcome handicaps imposed by the objective conditions in which they found themselves. Where an agricultural solution was called for, Agro-Joint provided the social and technical framework for its realization. The organization and its administrator, Joseph E. Rosen, had cut their teeth in the Crimea, where they had offered technical assistance to Jews of the Soviet Union who were trying to establish themselves on the land.

Having been granted quasi-diplomatic privileges by the Dominican government, DORSA representatives were able to visit European refugee camps to select "suitable" persons for the project. Just how this was accomplished is a matter of some controversy. Some maintain that any refugee was free to sign up at an office that was opened for this purpose in Switzerland. That so few chose to do so was due to their refusal to believe in the reality of Hitler's final solution. There was nothing inherently attractive about going to farm some island in the tropics. Others maintain that DORSA recruiters knew that Switzerland's policy of barring most Jewish refugees from entering the country would automatically limit applicants, that they were indulging in social experimentation and were more eager for their project to succeed than they were interested in saving human lives. Their insistence on imposing high standards of health and capacity for physical labor resulted in the rejection of candidates at a time when rejection was tantamount to a death sentence. Wherever the truth lies, it is clear that the project early acquired an aura of social experimentation.

Eventually, several hundred suitable persons were selected and Dominican visas issued to them upon the posting of a $500 bond in New York against the likelihood of each one becoming a public charge. The first contingent of settlers was to consist of five hundred families, but the total population of the colony never reached that number. The first settlers reached the hacienda at Sosua two years after conclusion of the Evian Conference. They were mostly German and Austrian and included substantially more men than women. The majority were of urban background; their sound physiques and clear complexions had enabled them to gamble on another chance at life.

The settlers were endowed individually with two hectares of land apiece, a house, a horse or mule, two cows, furniture, tools, and $500 credit. This was all to be repaid on terms; as with JCA, the project was designed as rehabilitation,

German Jewish dairymen of Sosua introduced pasteurized milk and cheese to the Dominican Republic. Some of these dairies are still producing and marketing their products on the island.

not charity. Each settler was required to work his own farm: no Dominican labor was to be hired. As DORSA Director Rosen said: "We did not bring refugees here to add more white landowners to exploit the peons." This proletarian sentiment, imported by Rosen from his experience in the Crimea, condemned the settlers to life as minifundistas. In this status, they joined the approximately 85 percent of Dominican farmers who were in this same category.[35] The Jewish immigrants, however, unlike their Dominican neighbors, were not bound to the soil by ties of kinship, debt peonage, and all the other social arrangements that keep the peon in his place and make the latifundia-minifundia complex so difficult to break. The result was that most of the homesteaders drifted away from their farms to the cities, where they lived as clients of the Joint.

Disintegration of Sosua was accelerated by the rigid ideological strictures of the administrators. Quite early in the project, Rosen had decided to limit the total number of colonists to five hundred, since his experiment could be worked out on a small as well as on a large scale. Thus there were few arrivals to balance departures. The problem of settlement pattern that had plagued JCA was resolved in favor of scattering the farm plots to prevent urban clustering. This exacerbated the settlers' poignant sense of abandonment. Having just undergone traumatic experiences in Europe, they were not to have the solace of one another's company. Compounding the problem was the severe gender imbalance. Unmarried men preponderated among the settlers, and those who were unable to form families provided a continually destabilizing element; in 1942, Rosen evicted fifty "malcontents"—mostly young men in their productive years. The administration's mania for social experimentation extended to setting up cooperative work groups, each of which included one woman to do the laundry, but provision for marriage and the founding of families was beyond them.

Although the Yiddish press of New York was apprehensive over Sosua, dependent as it was on the beneficence of the dictator, Trujillo kept faith with the colony. To the closing years of his reign, El Benefactor continued making friendly gestures toward Jews. He donated $60,000 toward construction of a synagogue in the capital and issued a postage stamp honoring Sosua. It bore the legend "Sosua, R.D., Primera colonía de refugiados en América."

DORSA later claimed to have saved thousands of Jewish lives, but it is probable that no more than 800 refugees passed through the colony; perhaps another 3,000 obtained Dominican visas on the strength of the colony but never actually settled there. The largest number of settlers at any one time was to be found in 1943, when 476 Jews occupied Sosua. These mostly German and Austrian Jews had been well assimilated in their former homelands. In the Dominican countryside, however, there was no one for them to assimilate to. The landed aristocracy were beyond their reach, the campesinos close but trammeled by social and religious custom. Some Jewish settlers married local women, with conversions running both ways. The warm community life they continue to enjoy on the island has been captured on videotape.[36] But those who were primarily concerned with maintaining their Jewish identity left the island when the war ended. It is notable that persons who passed through the Sosua colony still recall the experience with nostalgia long after having emigrated to the United States. For many years they maintained a social club that held periodic reunions on the island.

Life at Sosua stabilized on an agricultural base after DORSA was dissolved. With the limit on the size of landholdings removed, the remaining families went into dairy farming. The Sosua cooperative markets milk and cheese throughout the island. Descendants of the Jewish farmers of Sousa bid fair to contribute to the republic's variegated ethnic makeup, along with descendants of the original Sephardim of Curaçao, long since assimilated.

Bolivia

Jewish agricultural settlement in Bolivia was an accident of World War II, unpremeditated by the Bolivian government, Jewish rescue organizations, or the immigrants themselves. As a measure to settle farmers on the land, it was a total failure. But several thousand refugees owe their lives to their willingness to pose as farmers and to the venality of Bolivian officials who sold them visas under this guise, bearing out Sholom Aleichem's wry observation concerning the beneficence of corruption.

In 1937, there were some 250 Russian, Polish, and Sephardic Jews in Bolivia. About 100 of these lived in La Paz, 50 or so in Sucre, and the rest were scattered in the vicinity of the tin mines. For the most part, they were merchants, fulfilling a function that highly stratified, not to say feudal, societies have traditionally proffered to Jews. In the ensuing years, possibly 5,000 German Jews entered Bolivia. Some estimates place the number of arrivals as high as 15,000, with the number of departures not far behind. In May of 1939 alone, with the lights going out all over Europe, 3,000 Jews entered Bolivia, most on counterfeit documents.

For the refugees, Bolivia was a transit stop on the way to Argentina, the United States, or any other country that would admit them. Many of those with documents had been issued agricultural visas, which carried the obligation to settle in that occupation. But lacking the means to buy land or the know-how to place it under cultivation, they were thrown on the charity of local Jews. Accumulating in the cities, the refugees attracted the critical attention of the press. Tension was heightened by the existence of considerable pro-Nazi sentiment within the Bolivian German community, all in the context of the contemporary possibility of a German victory in the war.

On 6 May 1940, the Bolivian government forbade issuance of visas to "persons of Semitic origin," thus bringing legal Jewish immigration to an end.[37] In the same month, the Sociedad Colonizadora de Bolivia (SOCOBO) was founded for the purpose of colonizing Bolivia on a nonsectarian basis. The initiative in this venture was taken by the tin magnate Mauricio Hochschild,

who subscribed half the capital of $200,000.[38] The remaining two quarters
were subscribed by the Refugee Economic Corporation and Agro-Joint.

The new Jewish agricultural colony was established at Buena Tierra, sixty-
two miles from La Paz in the province of North Yungas.[39] The site comprised
one thousand hectares, of which just four hundred could be cultivated, the
remainder being a water reserve. Located at an altitude of four thousand feet
in hilly terrain, the land could be worked only by relatively primitive methods.
Isolated by the treacherous condition of the roads, the journey to La Paz took
from three to nine hours, depending on the weather. Plans were made to grow
cocoa, coffee, peanuts, bananas, corn, sugarcane, oranges, tangerines, lemons,
limes, pineapples, and lumber. In 1940, a start was made in cutting timber
and dropping it by chute down the mountainside to the river. An observer
visiting the site believed that there could be from 75 to 100 colonists on the
land by the end of the year and that ultimately the colony could absorb 250
families permanently.

This evaluation proved overly enthusiastic. Three years later, the colony
reached its peak with just 42 families and a fluctuating number of single men.
At times, more than half the labor force (61 out of 112 adults aged 16 to 50)
were women unaccustomed to manual labor. With the help of an administrator
and local campesinos hired by socobo, the colonists brought 243.85 hectares
of land under cultivation and had another 95 hectares in reclamation projects
by 1944. In addition, they had built some fifty houses and a thirteen-kilometer
road connecting Buena Tierra with the town of Coroico. The same report
notes that Agro-Joint had expended a total of $338,150 on this project as of
June 1945. Despite the optimistic tone of the report, as of that date there
were just 50 persons remaining in the settlement. By the end of the following
year, all but a few had left, helped on their way by a bonus of $175 per family
paid out by Agro-Joint. The experiment had lasted just six years. The remaining
infrastructure and crops were turned over to the local population as a result
of the agrarian reform law of 1953.[40]

The obstacles to absorption of Jewish immigrants into Bolivia were the
small farms allotted them, the lack of roads and transportation, the difficulty
of acclimatizing to the weather and altitude, and a generalized feeling of
insecurity. Bolivia at this date was a prime example of the latifundia-minifundia
complex. In 1950, 59.3 percent of farmers owned just 0.2 percent of the
farmland; 3.8 percent of the population held 81.8 percent of farmland in
holdings of 2,500 hectares and more.[41] Joint's estimate that 250 Jewish families
could be settled on 400 arable hectares would become reality only if the
immigrants adopted the standard of living of the highland Indian, one of the
most depressed in the world.

In general, conditions within the country as a whole failed to satisfy the
needs that had driven the refugees there. The primary impulse had been flight
for survival, and the refugees selected Bolivia in preference to the concentration
camp. But they found the Bolivian political atmosphere less than reassuring.
In 1942, Congress debated an immigration bill that would have excluded

"Orientals, Negroes and Jews" from the country. In the course of congressional debate, Deputy Hernán Siles Suazo, representing the Movimiento Nacional Revolucionario (MNR), declared that Semitic immigrants "laugh at their obligations and are convinced of the impossibility of throwing them out because there is no country which would resign itself to support them."[42] The bill was never taken up in the Senate and so failed to become law. But its debate, together with the anti-Semitic tone of accompanying newspaper reports, had an impact on the immigrants, who had actually felt safer under the reactionary regime of Gualberto Villaroel. According to a Joint representative, "The explanation of this paradox is that the government of Villaroel had to justify before the world its democratic conditions, which is no need of the Herzog government, which originates in a union of left-wing parties." The same observer ascribed the desire of Jews to reemigrate to two reasons: the difficult climate and anti-Semitism. "[Recently] there was issued a decree by the Supreme Government ordering an investigation of the books of 'semitic' merchants who had entered the country since 1938. . . . It can also be noticed that there is an intensive anti-Semitic propaganda in the press and radio, without any attempts being made to curb it."[43]

The Bolivian revolution of 1952 brought to power the MNR, a radical grouping of mixed leftist and fascist components. Whatever the meaning of the MNR for the native-born, its hegemony could only intensify feelings of insecurity among the Jews in Bolivia, who identified it as the party that had sponsored the excluding legislation a decade earlier and countenanced anti-Semitic propaganda in its party press. In conditions of such uncertainty, it is not surprising that the pioneers of Buena Tierra did not feel the strong sense of identification with the country that would have sustained the necessarily long period of hardship required to root themselves in the land. In Bolivia, which is itself isolated from the rest of the world and where Jews were therefore in a very exposed position, the rural isolation that Argentine and Dominican settlers had found insufferable was intensified beyond endurance. The difficulties of relating to Argentine gauchos and Dominican campesinos were naught before the enigma presented to them by Aymara culture.

In the 1950s, Bolivians were beginning to confront the issue of their own ethnic identity. The majority Native American population, passive tenants of the countryside since the suppression of their rebellions in the colonial period, were emerging to make legitimate demands upon the national polity. The miners, foundation of the country's wealth, emerged as a political force; the tin mines were expropriated and nationalized. Social forces let loose by the revolution of 1952 swallowed up the minor conundrum posed by the acculturation and absorption of a tiny number of displaced urban European Jewish immigrants into the Bolivian agricultural sector. Bolivia had become involved with Jewish immigration only by chance, through the venality of its consular officials. Jews had come to Bolivia accidentally and because they had no alternative. Neither party was prepared to cope with the problems that resulted.

The departure of colonists to the city was followed by the departure of most from the country as a whole. In 1987, the Jewish community counted 480 Jews in Bolivia, a 50 percent reduction from the figure reported in 1975. Two-thirds of Bolivian Jews live in La Paz, with smaller numbers in Cochabamba, Santa Cruz, Tarija, and Sucre. Most are in commerce and trade, but some have entered the cultural life of the nation as musicians, artists, and promoters of athletic teams. These individuals have successfully acculturated, gaining acceptance from the larger society in ways that confute earlier fears of inbred anti-Semitism. La Paz–born violinist Jaime Laredo has been declared "a national treasure"; there has been a Jewish dean of the Faculty of Mining Engineering; and many participants in international conferences will have met the Bolivian publisher and book dealer Werner Guttentag, a major presence on the national cultural scene.[44]

An Appraisal of the Agricultural Colonies

All the Jewish colonization ventures had their origin in the calamitous uprooting of Jewish populations in Europe and North Africa, events that occurred far from Latin America and that were not the responsibility of any of the nations of that continent. Jewish farmers were well received in countries that welcomed heterogeneous immigration, but were trammeled by legislative and administrative rules and occasionally faced insuperable natural obstacles.

There was no prima facie reason for Jewish farmers to prefer Latin American countries of destination as opposed to such areas as Canada, the United States, or Palestine. Their involvement with the Latin American countryside was fortuitous in that these countries, at pivotal points in Jewish history, presented the prospect of available land combined with comparative religious toleration. But the ability to acquire land suitable for farming turned out to be circumscribed by existing patterns of landholding. Moreover, the advantage of the prospect was relative to other choices available and could not always be assessed accurately from a distance.

Those nations that became host to Jewish agriculturists did so because they had adopted as an element of national policy the recruiting of European farmers. Many of the Jewish colonists were trying to become farmers, either for reasons of idealism or to escape persecution, or both. Inevitably, the expectations of the parties failed to mesh, leaving the immigrants open to the charge that they had beguiled their hosts. Much, however, depended upon the flexibility of the host societies in accommodating immigrants. Negligent policies of the Argentine government allowed destruction of the agricultural sector and led most immigrants to relocate in the city; it is equally important to note that Argentine social and economic structures were flexible enough to accommodate immigrants within an urban setting. This was due to the fact that the country was absorbing so many immigrants of different races and nationalities that its nature inevitably had to change. In Bolivia, traditional social patterns and a wide ethnic gulf discouraged most European immigrants from trying to fit into national society.

The primary motivation of the colonists was physical security, or, more precisely, a desire to be exposed only to those hazards that are the common lot of humankind. They stayed on (whether as farmers or not) in countries where their physical survival as human beings and as Jews seemed assured (Argentina), but the majority abandoned places where they felt humanly insecure (Bolivia) or unable to continue living as Jews (the Dominican Republic).

All the agricultural experiments attempted to settle Jews on minifundia. This came about for a variety of reasons: the necessity to settle in groups under the aegis of a patron organization; limits on the finances of these organizations; preconceptions about the size of family farms drawn from experience in Europe; and an ideological bias against having Jews enter the Latin American agricultural scene as landlords. That the colonists were unable to produce efficiently as minifundistas should have come as no suprise, given previous experience concerning the disutility of small farms in Latin America. Today Jewish farmers, dairymen, and cattle ranchers exist in Argentina and the Dominican Republic. This development came about through the purchase by successful settlers of land belonging to colonists who failed and left for the city. The process was particularly notable among Germans, some of whom invested reparations payments from the West German government in land and equipment. Other estates have been bought by previously urban Jewish families for reasons of status. Jewish farmers and ranchers survive just as do non-Jewish latifundistas.

The roles of JCA, DORSA, and SOCOBO are traditionally the most controversial elements in accounts of Jewish agricultural settlement in Latin America. Many administrators were autocratic and heavy-handed, arousing the resentment of those who were struggling with the land. Yet even critics of these agencies concede that colonization could not have been attempted without them. Criticism of the agencies as inept, overly paternalistic, shortsighted, and so on are apt but beside the point. They filled a function that the local economic and social scenes required. These international Jewish rescue organizations became the patrón, that pivotal figure of the Latin American countryside, and criticism of the patrón might better be directed against the system that makes a patrón indispensable. The organizations loomed as large as they did in the lives of the Jewish immigrants because they provided essential services that were not available from any other source.

The accidental meeting of Jewish need with Latin American ambience found host governments unequipped to deal with ensuing problems in social welfare. Only Jewish organizations stood ready to fill the gap. These organizations were global in scope, nongovernmental in nature, Jewish in orientation, and not indigenous to the countries in which they operated. They were not responsive to foreign governments. In view of the oft-expressed fear that immigrants might import and retain their old national loyalties and mount a threat to the nationality of their host state, it may be said that Jews were the only immigrants to arrive in Latin America unburdened by ties of allegiance to a foreign government. But the agencies' lack of understanding of the local scene caused innumerable problems, which were widely aired in the press.

Although their sole concern was the integration of their charges into the country of their settlement, their motivation was not entirely clear. Avni concludes that the financial strength of the JCA was used, not to promote large-scale absorption of spontaneous Jewish immigration to Argentina, but to prevent the emergence of a rebellious urban proletariat liable to spoil the image of the colonization venture in the eyes of Argentine authorities.[45] He summarizes the ambiguous legacy of JCA in this way:

> From the outset, Jewish colonization had developed on the outskirts of the cultivated areas, redeeming many thousands of hectares of virgin land. The JCA, unlike the vast majority of settlement companies seeking to make a profit, devoted itself entirely to promoting small-scale farm-ing—just as the patricians had envisaged. In this respect, the JCA was much more consistent than was the Argentine government, which made no effort to prevent centralized landownership or the decline of produc-tion in the few colonies it had established in the early days of its immigration policy. Against the general backdrop of extensive, exploita-tive farming, the Jewish colonies stood out in their efforts to diversify, introduce new crops, and, above all, create an intensive, multi-branched enterprise in which breeding and dairy farming could be pursued along-side agriculture. This did not escape the notice of the government. Both the head of the Research and Statistics Department of the Ministry of Agriculture and an agronomist employed by the department depicted the Jewish colonies in Santa Fe as worthy of emulation. Provincial and federal leaders who visited the colonies publicly expressed their admiration; yet it was the infighting and scandals in the colonies, which reached the courts in Buenos Aires, that most caught the public eye. The JCA was presented as an oppressor, and its "foreign character" as a company managed by Jewish bankers overseas received greater cover-age than did its philanthropic and productive work.[46]

There were severe limitations on what the Jewish patrón organizations could accomplish. In no instance did appreciable numbers of Jewish farmers remain on the land. None of the organizations succeeded in attracting large numbers of immigrants relative to the number who were seeking an immigra-tion outlet; none succeeded in establishing permanent, viable Jewish colonies; and in the case of the Dominican Republic and Bolivia, the most they could do was to process immigrants in and out of the country in orderly fashion. Ideology appears not to have been a factor in success or failure. Colonies withered whether founded by idealists of the 1890s or refugees of the 1930s.

There were structural barriers to integration that immigrants, Jew or non-Jew, could not overcome without the active collaboration of governments. This collaboration, in the form of revision of patterns of land tenure, provision of schooling, and extension of the infrastructure through the countryside, was not forthcoming. Isolation made the Latin American agricultural sector no more promising for Jewish immigrants than it was for native-born Catholics, who likewise abandoned the countryside in droves. The passion of urban European

Jews to fling themselves upon the soil was misspent in resisting entanglement with conditions that antedated their arrival on the continent and over which they could exert no influence. These were, of course, the same entanglements that wasted the energies of native-born campesinos in their struggles with the landowners. To take the point a step further, they were the social arrangements that had created the campesino rather than the yeoman farmer.

The desire to normalize the Jewish condition by return to the soil can be seen in retrospect to have been romantic. The yearning for a life of rustic simplicity was a reaction against the brutalities meted out to Jews in the cities and towns of Europe. It was not a reasoned rejection of the modern world as a whole. The movement for autoemancipation through agricultural toil took hold in an age when all over the world the agricultural sector was yielding up its labor force to the demands and challenges of industrialization. Jewish farmers, in abandoning the land, were bringing to a close the epoch of belief in the possibility of autoemancipation through self-labor, an idea rooted in the age of Maxim Gorky and Leon Pinsker. This is why the shift of so small a number of persons out of farming and into city life—a shift that millions of people around the globe have made during the past hundred years—attracted so much attention from diagnosticians of the Jewish condition. It was the death of the dream, not the death of the colonies, that mattered. The impact of this death was felt the more directly as Jewish farmers of Latin America abandoned their farms within the context of societies whose rural and urban sectors are among the most polarized in the world. Thus, their abandonment of rural life was visible, abrupt, and irreversible.

The ending does not negate the beginning. As European Jewry entered the Holocaust Kingdom, each individual who found his or her way to the Dominican Republic or to Bolivia represented a triumph. Jewish farmers of Argentina (and the paradigm will serve Brazil and Uruguay as well) found not only secure homes, but also time and space in which to orient themselves to their new environment linguistically, ecologically, and behaviorally. They gained a breathing space before returning to the modern world or sending their children out into it. The colonies, which may at first have seemed impoverished replicas of European Jewish life, eventually nationalized the immigrants, turning them into citizens of the country of their adoption—where existing social systems were flexible enough to receive them. In this sense, they were a success even when—perhaps especially when—their inhabitants abandoned the farm for the city.

CHAPTER 6

The Economics of Jewish Life in Latin America

Doblemente cara al almuerzo la cuchara.
A spoon is twice as dear at lunchtime.

—Anon.

"HACER LA AMÉRICA" was the expression immigrants of all origins used to describe their struggle to force their new homelands to yield them the means of survival. Strategies the immigrants employed to "make America" varied from one country to the next and from one time period to another, but the reciprocal nature of their adaptation was crucial. What were the immigrants equipped to do? What gaps in the local economies permitted them to earn their living?

From the 1890s on, Jews entered the Latin American economies as peddlers, artisans, and workers in cottage industry. The peddler, typical figure at the turn of the century, was often perceived by local residents, together with his Syrian and Lebanese Christian and Muslim countrymen, as a *turco*.[1] Over the course of time, the peddler was increasingly supplemented by the artisan and, particularly after the arrival of German immigrants, by the owner-worker in cottage industry. The marginality of these occupations meant that breadwinners were frequently forced to shift from one to another, with displaced artisans becoming peddlers, peddlers saving up their money to buy machines to produce the goods they sold, and cottage workers peddling their products door-to-door.

Peddling

Packs on their backs and account books in their pockets, Jewish peddlers (*cuentaniks*) trudged the streets of major cities and provincial towns, selling small portable items of mass consumption such as matches, scissors, sandals, razor blades, religious articles, tableware, jewelry, and cloth. They sold their wares for a small down payment and an agreement that the customer pay weekly installments. Thereafter the peddler returned weekly to collect on his debts and to sell more goods. Because of the risk involved in extending credit without collateral, the peddlers took a high profit margin—probably 100 percent of the value of the goods. If they were lucky and the number of bad debts was small, they could save up enough money to establish themselves in a fixed place of business and perhaps hire newer immigrants to go out and peddle for them. If they were unlucky, they lost their investment. Initial parcels of goods for peddling were usually acquired on loan from some peddler who was already well enough established to be able to spare some. In addition, small loans were customarily made available without interest by the mutual aid societies that were among the first organizations to be established by the immigrants.

Successful cuentaniks graduated to the status of *clientelchiks,* spending their time on accounts collection and hiring more recent immigrants to serve as their *klappers,* or (door-) knockers. Klappers who worked their way up to become full-fledged cuentaniks often used this vantage point to buy a stall in the marketplace; from that point, the aspiration was to buy a respectable store.

Peddling is by its nature a solitary occupation. There was no central administration to keep records of what was going on, but contemporary writers observe that "90 percent of the Jews here are peddlers," or "most of the Jewish immigrants started as peddlers." An abundance of autobiographies, newspaper accounts, and novels and short stories persuade us that peddling was the accommodation Jewish immigrants typically made to the Latin American scene, at least between the years 1880 and 1939. Their choice of occupation was dictated by two sets of factors: one internal—the heritage of skills and attitudes the immigrants had brought with them; the other external—the economic and social structures they found in their new homelands. As one former peddler wrote:

> Perhaps a Colombian would want to ask how and why we entered national life the way we did. The truth is that we have arrived at being a very old people, enduring and experienced, because of our ability to orient ourselves in life; and that we have been forced by very difficult circumstances to invent ingeniously or else perish. . . . Our old activities, our property, our customs, had been left behind . . . [and so] we had to learn a new modus vivendi. We went out on God's streets, loaded down with merchandise, in an epoch when Colombia produced very little of her own; and we offered it on the installment plan, house by house, receiving in exchange, and by virtue of private contract, our daily bread.[2]

The internal factors that enabled Jews to enter peddling were their familiarity with commerce, their literacy (which made it possible to keep accounts), and their extreme poverty (which prepared them psychologically to undertake the most arduous work). The external factors were to be found in the gap between production and distribution of consumer goods that characterized the continent during the years of heaviest migration, the absence of consumer

The Jewish peddler and his young assistant became familiar figures in urban neighborhoods and in provincial towns. They sold on the installment plan anything that households needed, provided they could carry it.

credit, and the consequent exclusion of masses of people from the market for consumer goods.

The interaction of these factors can be observed in every country in Latin America. In Argentina, for example, the formation of economic policy was dominated by the interests of wheat and beef producers throughout the nineteenth century. In conjunction with the import-export houses and representatives of foreign firms, these interests favored low tariffs and a free field for the importation of foreign goods. These goods, because of their foreign origin and the lack of domestic competition, were priced at luxury levels that, in combination with the practice of Argentine merchants of dealing in small volume at high profit margins, resulted in extremely high prices. Because all sales were made in cash, many people simply could not buy ordinary consumer goods.

Jewish immigrants to Argentina, fresh from the cities and towns of Europe and already experienced in petty trade, were quick to perceive the opportunity that this uneven system of distribution left open for them. The introduction of credit was risky, as the poor had no collateral; but the immigrants were literate and market-wise and able to contain the risk. In the absence of other employment opportunities, large numbers of Jews entered peddling and petty trade.[3] The goal of every peddler was to accumulate enough savings to buy a fixed place of business and to get off the road. Some, with stamina, perspicacity, and luck, managed to do so. Their life stories generated a rags-to-riches mystique about the itinerant figure of the peddler. But success was by no means universal, and the peddlers were subjected to considerable personal harassment. Conditions in the 1920s were described in *Havaner Lebn:*

> When the situation in Poland forced Jews out into the world, Central America got her portion too. The Jews found there a great field for work and also the sympathy of the inhabitants. The latter spent their days in the bar and their nights with their mistresses, and they were astonished at these Jewish immigrants who were willing to undertake all kinds of work. Benefiting from their new social freedom, the Jews established nice communities in all five countries of Central America.
>
> But suddenly three years ago, things changed. The established merchant saw danger in the Jewish peddler who drew clients away from him. Patriots couldn't stand seeing Jews who had come here naked and barefoot and who were in a short time able to save money. The Jews of Guatemala got the first blow, when that country forbade peddling. Many Jews lost their money and had to leave the country, at a time when there was nowhere else to go.
>
> Even worse happened in El Salvador, where the mob was roused by charges that the Jews were Bolsheviks and had come to root out Christianity. Some Jews were killed, and the community went through tragic days.[4]

Sephardim and Ashkenazim alike began their new lives as peddlers, Ladino speakers being aided in their penetration of the market by their knowledge of the language. Turkish, Syrian, and Lebanese Jews entering Uruguay at the start of the century followed this trade, and so did the East Europeans who followed in the 1920s.[5] Jewish commerce imparted a foreign look to parts of cities. "Rua de Alfandega, the street of Jewish merchants in Rio de Janeiro, is full of narrow, crowded shops standing cheek by jowl, just as in Warsaw," writes a correspondent of *Havaner Lebn* in 1935.

> Most of these merchants came as shoemakers, tailors, or teachers; but arriving without means, they could not set themselves up in their trade. But one could begin as a klapper, with merchandise taken on credit. . . . You struggle to set up a territory with regular customers . . . the sun is fierce and sweat eats up your clothes . . . but the climate holds up the market for cloth.
>
> When the klapper has put together a few hundred customers, he becomes preoccupied with collecting installments on his captial, which is entirely tied up in the customers. He seldom goes out with his pack any more; now he is a clientelchik. Ninety percent of the Jewish

population of Brazil, and more than half of Jews in other South American countries, are occupied in this trade.[6]

"Peddling was the prototype of both Jewish and Syrian-Lebanese economic integration in Brazil," where the peddlers, known popularly as *mascates,* supplied household and dry goods to workers on the coffee plantations as well as to poor urban dwellers.[7]

Competitors for the worker's paycheck naturally complained. In Chile, as in many other areas, a high rate of alcoholism prevailed among the working class. The factory worker customarily stopped in at the tavern on his way home, often leaving a good part of his paycheck there. When the peddler caught the worker at the factory gate and wrested his money from him, he antagonized the tavern owners, who were quick to spread stories about Jewish usury. Peddlers were often accused by shopowners of robbing the poor, to which the peddler replied, "A lefl is tyer tsum essen" (a spoon is dear when it comes time to eat). No existing sector of the business community had previously provided items of common household use to the large mass of the population that had not enough cash to enter a real store. The peddler appeared at the housewife's door with the items she needed, when she needed them. The provision of credit meant that, for a few cents down, many a family could eat with table utensils for the first time in their lives.[8]

Two-thirds of the Jewish immigrants who entered Mexico during the peak immigration years 1924–29 and who had been gainfully employed in their countries of origin had been merchants and traders. These were Polish Jews who were being systematically extruded from their economic positions by the ethnic Poles, as well as declassed members of the Jewish petite bourgeoisie who took advantage of a temporary relaxation in the law to leave the Soviet Union. These merchants, small manufacturers, and independent artisans brought along their skills and experience; having been expropriated in their home countries, they arrived paupers. The B'nai B'rith Organization of the United States opened offices in Mexico City and Vera Cruz to supply such social services to the immigrants as finding jobs, housing, schooling, providing legal aid, teaching Spanish, and granting loans—all services the Mexican government itself took no interest in providing.[9]

In almost any terms in which the immigrants could be described—socially, psychologically, financially—they were not prepared to join the Mexican industrial scene as it then existed. Mexico's industry in the 1920s and 1930s was concentrated in oil wells and metal mining. To join the owning class required vast amounts of capital which the immigrants did not have. They could not join the industrial proletariat because as foreigners they were excluded from the labor unions, which were as much *cofradías* as unions; and most companies ran a closed shop. In existing small and medium-size industries of an urban type, such as textiles and clothing, workers were extremely ill paid and kept in a dependent relationship to both boss and labor leaders, which went down ill with these once-independent storekeepers and tradesmen.

To fit into his new homeland, the Jewish immigrant had to continue along the lines of his previous career as an independent businessman. For this, conditions in Mexico were propitious because the economy contained gaps the newcomers were qualified to fill. The same conditions that prevented formation of a Jewish proletariat encouraged formation of a Jewish merchant class.[10] But lacking capital to become a merchant, the Jew had first to become a peddler.

Most male immigrants to Peru were peddlers until government prohibited that activity in 1939. Even mountainous Bolivia was tackled by the intrepid peddler. In 1940, a Joint representative to Bolivia wrote:

> In Bolivia you see the Eastern Jew who does not attend courses to learn Spanish, but who speaks the dialect of the Indios. They appear in the most outlying villages, where hardly any Europeans have ever been, and manage to eke out an existence, sleeping in their wagons under the stars. Hardly a German immigrant has dared or would dare to do this. . . . Without wishing to be critical, but to complete the picture, I must say that the first care of each German is to get an apartment. As far as the German is concerned, an apartment must have a bath."[11]

Peddling was the chief means of support for newly arrived Jews in Havana until the police began arresting them for blocking traffic in 1928. The hostility of established shopkeepers, who continued to be comfortable with the privileges the crown had endowed them with four centuries earlier, resulted in the raising of the fee for a peddler's license from the equivalent of $6.25 to $125.00 per year. These peddlers seem to have been more militant than their coreligionists elsewhere, for they formed a Shutzfarain far Peddler (Peddlers' Protective League) and succeeded in having the sum reduced. But despite this success, the Farain soon dissolved because its members either bought fixed places of business or went into cottage industry.[12] A correspondent of *Havaner Lebn* recalls those days:

> When we first came to Cuba, we were mistaken for Germans, and since we didn't know the language well enough to explain, we kept that name. Besides, it might be better not to say we were Jews, or the grandchildren of the Grand Inquisitor would have our bones. Those were happy days, for we were on our way to America. Our career: writer (for relief). Those who had no one to write to for assistance became peddlers. . . . Every ship brought 600–800 Jews and they all became peddlers. We lived twenty or thirty families to a house, and candle-lighting on the Sabbath gave out that we were Jews. But where were our horns? Incredible! Then Eskimo Pie hit Cuba, and we all caried ice boxes around Havana resting on our stomachs, bound with a cord to our shoulders. Since the name "German" had by now worn out, the Cubans began calling us "Eskimo Pie."[13]

The change in status was jolting to many. Among the peddlers were men who had been skilled craftsmen but who, for lack of capital, were forced out onto the street. There were numbers of learned men from Polish religious academies, accustomed to a life in which the respect accorded them by the community compensated for their poverty. There was no demand whatever for their knowledge now, and they were particularly demoralized by the indignity of their new way of life. Severe personal disorientation was a common problem. The Cuban Yiddish press abounded in stories of Jewish peddlers enticed by fishermen and "taken for a ride" in the shark-infested waters surrounding the island. A story poignantly titled "Oif Nort" (In the North) portrays a young man arriving in Chile with a bundle of borrowed neckties to begin his career as a klapper. Freezing to death on that "northern" coast, he is terror-stricken by a display of *aurora australis.*[14] Disjoined from the ecology, ignorant of language and customs, isolated from all that was formerly familiar, the immigrant while still in a high state of confusion had to set about earning his living. This was the meaning of "making America."

Female peddlers and marketwomen were common enough to become the subject of newspaper caricatures and stories. But prostitution was the feminine counterpart of peddling, as women with no tangible resources supported themselves by selling the only product they had and that the public desired. These working-class women suffered the same downward pressures as men

"Passerby, if on our street one morning you should come across a very pale woman: it is my mother. . . ." Fragment of a poem by Isroel Ashendorf, b. 1909, Melnitze, Galitzia, d. 1956, Buenos Aires, Argentina.

and ended up on the streets or in brothels. Like peddling, prostitution came to an end in the 1930s, as governments ceased to tolerate it and as improved economic conditions presented women with better alternatives. No identifiable Jewish women prostitutes turned up in the 1960 census.

Artisans and Proletarians

In Argentina, whose Italian and Spanish immigrants came for the most part from agricultural backgrounds, proportionately more Jews than non-Jews arrived as skilled craftsmen. Jewish immigrants were qualified garment workers, carpenters, and furniture makers.[15] They were also tin and sheet-metal workers, jewelers, watchmakers, masons, coopers, shoemakers, capmakers, and bakers— all skills that could be utilized by an industrializing economy.

In addition to those who arrived with marketable skills, there were others whose skills were not so transferable. Clerks were hampered by their lack of knowledge of Spanish. Students excluded from Russian universities when quotas were imposed were not qualified for any kind of work. Underground conspirators against the czar, exiled in the bloody reaction that followed failure of the revolution of 1905, had no peacetime trade, but they had to learn one in short order. As Wald writes, "They had escaped from prison, from Siberia, or from the gallows. If they weren't proletarian before, they were now, either from need or from ideology. Their proletarianization took place in Argentina."[16] Buenos Aires of the period offered hundreds of jobs that were peripheral to the industrial process, such as tram conductor, hygiene inspector, and layer of electrical cable. Jewish immigrants found work with relative ease in the larger cities. Some went out as hired hands to the JCA colonies at harvest time or worked for Jewish furniture manufacturers in Córdoba, where their desire to work in a Jewish environment (thus, not required to work on the Sabbath) sometimes laid them open to grosser exploitation than in factories run by non-Jews.

In a study of Jewish males who joined the Khevra Kadisha (Burial Society, later Asociación Mutual Israelita Argentina, or AMIA) between the years 1895 and 1930, Sofer found that the garment industry employed more Jewish workers than any other: 64 percent of skilled workers in 1895, declining to 21 percent of the 1930 sample. The sweatshop, with its exploitative system of piecework in "inside" and "outside" shops, existed in Buenos Aires as it did in New York and London, with the difference that the cost of living was higher in Buenos Aires and that the country was so little developed that there was little demand for skilled labor outside the capital. Furniture workers and carpenters were the next largest category of skilled workers, their number starting at zero in the 1895 sample and rising to 23 percent toward the end of this period. Their upward mobility was more limited than that of the garment workers, possibly owing to the fact that it cost more for carpenters to buy themselves the needed machinery. Jewelers, who had the best working conditions of all, were less than 8 percent of any single sample.[17] The most common form of upward mobility was for a skilled worker to become a small shopkeeper. There was more lateral than upward movement, however, and substantial numbers of workers experienced downward mobility.

Workers who were able to accumulate capital set up workshops for the manufacture of consumer goods, husbands and wives working alongside their employees and often indistinguishable from them. Cottage industry, which absorbed so many Jewish urban dwellers, relied largely on the labor of women and children, the entrepreneur's own family. Unable to compete with imported luxury goods, household industries produced apparel and furniture for the mass market. Experience, grinding labor, and investment paid off for some: by 1940, thirty spinning and weaving mills had been founded by Jewish entrepreneurs, employing some four thousand Argentine workers. The pioneering role of Jewish immigrants in the knitwear industry is attested to by the existence, at the same date, of one hundred workshops, sixty medium-size factories, and three large factories for the production of underwear and sweaters.[18]

Androcentric methods of record-keeping (such as that maintained by the AMIA, on which Sofer based his analysis) for long obscured the work history of Jewish women. Reviewing available sources, Deutsch points out that women's economic activity began on the agricultural colonies, where many worked in the field alongside men, though few owned the land they tilled, because the European administrators of JCA habitually issued titles to males. Female participation in the work force, which has been repeatedly and pruriently summarized as a history of prostitution, in reality followed a trajectory that paralleled that of men: women engaged in marketing, cottage industry, and accelerating levels of professional activity.[19] Just keeping house, feeding and clothing their families in the filthy, overcrowded conventillos in which the immigrants were forced to live, required heroic labor.[20]

The picture of Argentina as a land of unlimited opportunity was as much a product of optimism as of reality. The Argentine economy was not sufficiently industrialized to generate opportunities for large-scale upward mobility. As immigration swelled, opportunities for advancement narrowed. During the thirty-five-year period 1895–1930, encompassing the bulk of the Jewish migration, 80 to 90 percent of Jewish workers remained in blue-collar occupations. Economic and political factors constrained those with ambition, elaborating structural difficulties they could not overcome.

> Inflation, the high cost of living, the lack of sufficiently protective tariffs, the reliance of domestic industry on foreign products, the high cost and frequent unavailability of raw materials, and the ever-present spectre of foreign competition, made the position of workers and petty proprietors precarious."[21]

The onset of industrialization led to displacement of skilled artisans, yet locally owned industry did not expand sufficiently to absorb all those who were displaced. Driven out by the operations of the machine, skilled craftsmen had two choices: to enter a factory or sweatshop, accepting the loss of status that entailed, or to go into business for themselves. The latter route resulted in less success than issued from similar developments in the United States. More Argentine Jewish entrepreneurs advanced and then slid back into the working class than advanced and stayed there. In spite of individual success stories, the bulk of those who began their lives in Argentina as workers and who had ended their careers by 1945 ended as workers.[22] It took Argentine Jews four generations to achieve the mobility that Jewish immigrants to the United States achieved in two. It was only in 1945, with the accession to power of Juan Perón, that major modifications in the social structure finally took place. At that time, Jews began to approach the mobility patterns of Jews in the United States.[23]

Cabinetry was the skill that predominated among Bessarabian Jews in Rio de Janeiro in 1910. The manufacture and sale of furniture became their principal means of support. Those who could not do carpentry could vend, and craftsmen or their relatives got their goods to market without submitting to the tyranny of wholesale houses. Also among the artisan-peddlers were dressmakers and shoemakers, as well as turners, producing common household utensils. In the days of no credit ratings, the peddlers sometimes drove a nail into the eaves of the home of a defaulter, as a warning to other klappers who might be tempted to extend credit.[24]

Polish Jews who arrived after World War I were watchmakers, dressmakers, and compounders of cosmetics. Their wares, too, went to market in the peddlers' packs. The work habits the immigrants had developed in Europe, where labor from sun to sun was a necessity in order to stay alive, sufficed in Brazil to generate comfortable incomes for the immigrants within a relatively short time. The German immigrants who reached Brazil in the years leading up to World War II included quite a few with transferable skills. Among these were tailors, shirtmakers, and hairdressers. Women often proved more employable than men, for with their language skills they found jobs as tutors, governesses, and salesclerks. Seamstresses able to interpret European styles for Brazilian taste found themselves in demand. The "craft" that suffered most from exclusionist legislation was medicine: doctors found obstacles placed in the way of their practicing in Brazil.[25]

Jewish immigrants to Cuba included locksmiths, watchmakers, mechanics, bakers, tailors, carpenters, painters, garment workers, and—most numerous—shoemakers.[26] Gaining employment in factories when they could, they sought admission to Cuban labor unions where these existed, or formed new ones in industries where there were none. Between 1929 and 1943, Cuban Jewish workers founded at least eight trade unions: shoemakers, peddlers, barbers, street photographers, tailors, seltzer-water vendors, merchants, and diamond workers.[27]

But union activity exacted a price: many immigrant labor leaders, including Jews, were arrested and deported by the Machado regime (1925–33). Under the revolutionary regime of Ramón Grau San Martín that followed, matters

For lack of capital, Jewish immigrants invested their sweat equity in cottage industries. Here a group of tailors poses on the threshold of Brazilian industrialization.

grew worse: new labor laws created a near-monopoly of jobs for the native-born, forcing Jewish workers either to reemigrate (if they could) or to become pieceworkers at home, outside the protection of the labor laws. In many cases, they moved from the domination of the foreman to the tyranny of the supplier of their raw materials. Specifically, the Law of 50 Percent, requiring that half of every employer's work force must be native-born, hit Jews with special force because they were almost all foreign-born and the employers who hired them tended also to hire other Jews. The result of the law was to deprive hundreds of immigrants of their jobs.

Many Jewish immigrants had belonged to unions in Poland and Russia, often affiliated with the Bund, the Jewish sector of the socialist movement. The exploitation to which they, along with all Cuban workers, were subjected, radicalized many, causing them to abandon the mild social democracy with which they had arrived and move closer to the communist position. Presciently, a Jewish sociologist who spent the war years on the island, wrote in 1944,

The Jewish workers in Cuba provided a ready ground for Socialist and Communist propaganda. They resented the exploitation to which they were exposed, and this feeling evoked in them a trend toward social rebellion and a longing for a better world. The colonial milieu, with a gulf dividing the rich from the poor, and the absence of skilled industrial workers, were not conducive to the emergence of a social-democratic movement. Social Democrats in Cuba have always been a small and uninfluential group. But the seeds of Communist propaganda have freely germinated among Cuban workers.

This circumstance favored the expansion of radical tendencies among the Jewish workers, too. The Bundists (members of the Jewish Social Democratic Party "Bund") played a negligible part. But the Jewish Communists succeeded in capturing the imagination of large Jewish strata. Their own organization was small. They gained influence, however, by availing themselves of neutral organizations.[28]

The Move to Industry

Other Jewish workers, with more luck and less ideology, became manufacturers of the goods they had formerly produced in other people's factories. They moved into industry by way of two paths: that of the peddler (often a displaced artisan to begin with), who began to produce the items he took for sale; and that of the practicing craftsman, who (by choice or force of circumstance) began to manufacture goods in his own home or workshop, using the sweated labor of his family.

Peddlers were under considerable pressure to change their occupation because of the difficult life it entailed, the marginality of the income it produced, and vulnerability to police and popular harassment. In Chile, the itinerant peddler was a casualty of the Great Depression. Chile was more advanced industrially than other Latin American countries, and more of its employment depended upon industry; so did weekly payments to the cuentanik. Most peddlers went bankrupt rather quickly. "A blessing in disguise" was the verdict of the *Chilener Yiddisher Wochenblatt.* In its issue of 12 January 1933, the editor wrote: "This is the time for Jews to go into industry. There are resources here, labor is cheap, and the industrial giants are only beginning to develop; so we can compete."

There had long been Jews in Chilean industry. As early as 1884, a skilled Jewish metallurgist who had migrated from Lithuania was asked by the government to open a metal foundry in the Santiago prison. Here he taught his skills to a succession of young men, one of whom became his son-in-law and head of a large steelworks. In 1901, the immigrant opened his own foundry, where he produced the first agricultural implements to be manufactured in Chile, using a technique he had invented himself.

Other firsts of Jewish immigrants in Chilean industry include factories for the manufacture of wagons (1906), mirrors (1908), leather clothing (1910), and gramophone records (1910). Jewish immigrants opened ready-to-wear clothing factories, plants for making furniture, hats, raincoats, and fur coats, and print shops. Chile's first plastics factory was opened in 1924 by Jewish immigrants. Ultimately, this plant manufactured over 1,500 parts, employed 350 workers, and had 30 salaried employees. In 1925, a mill for making thread was opened by Jewish immigrants.[29]

When the Depression finished off peddling, many more Jewish immigrants went into manufacturing, for which a good climate already existed. Lacking large amounts of capital, they began with cottage industry. Working as families—women, children, and men—in their own homes, they produced such common items of apparel as shirts, underwear, ties, socks, and suspenders, which at that time were not available on the mass market. The arrival of German-speaking Jews in the thirties added more entrepreneurs to the clothing industry. Read-to-wear, thread, patterns, elastic, and silk were some of the items produced. European Jews clothed the Chilean poor, and the *roto* (the "broken" man) disappeared from city streets. In 1956 it was estimated that Jewish-owned plants in the clothing industry employed between seventeen and eighteen thousand people.[30]

By the fifties, there were Jewish entrepreneurs in sugar refining, tobacco plantations, lumber, chemicals, patent medicines, olive oil, perfume, thermo-electric plants, packing plants, eyeglasses, zippers, air conditioning and heating, Bakelite, and glass utensils for laboratories. Jewish managers and engineers were employed in foundries, construction firms, and public works, carrying on a long tradition of Jewish technicians involved with Chile's development. A Jewish engineer, Adolfo Weiner, built Chile's national library as well as various streets in the capital. N. Rachitoff, a Jewish engineer, directed the construction of the main railroad stations in Santiago and Mapocho, and collaborated on the electrified line to Valparaíso. Engineer Akiva Pommerante built the railroad line to Curicó and later worked at Los Condes copper mine. Engineer León Levi worked on the naval base at Talcahuano.[31] Those Jewish industrialists and technicians figured in the growth of native Chilean industry, constructing infrastructure while providing employment to Chilean workers. As Chilean citizens, they had no need to repatriate profits to other countries in the style of foreign-owned firms. Participating as they did in the modernization of the country, Jewish immigrants integrated quickly into national life.

The phasing out of peddling among Jewish immigrants to Mexico came as a response to antiforeign agitation that made these isolated merchants feel too vulnerable to continue in their occupation. Xenophobia became apparent in Mexico in 1930 as the depression took hold. The price of silver dropped, thousands of Mexican workers were expelled from the United States, and economic pressures built up within Mexico that found an outlet in hatred of Chinese and Jews. Many newspapers, including the *Nacional Revolucionario* of the country's ruling Partido Nacional Revolucionario, published anti-Jewish articles. Merchants publicized such slogans as "Buy from Mexicans—boycott Jews."[32] In this context, a Jewish chamber of commerce (Cámara Israelita de Industria y Comercio) was organized for the purpose of resisting anti-Semitism and representing merchants' interests before the government. At its founding, its 298 members included 176 merchants and 92 manufacturers; 36 members lived in the province. By August of that year, membership had almost doubled.[33]

On 27 March 1931, the Mexican government published regulations that limited the location of market booths to certain areas and imposed onerous licensing requirements. Although the new requirements were met by the Jewish merchants, some 220 were nevertheless forcibly evicted from Lagunilla market the following month and their licenses revoked. Panic suffused the Mexican Jewish community, intensified by plans for a "Day of Commerce" parade that featured anti-Jewish slogans. The American Jewish Committee, a New York–based organization, sent an observer to Mexico in May of that year to investigate the situation. He found that the antagonism did not extend beyond the limits of the small peddler and market merchant. Only these were being called "judío," a standard Mexican term of opprobrium. Jewish professional men and representatives of foreign firms were not considered "judíos." Economic conflict among merchants was being taken advantage of by various government officials, the report continued, who exploit the opportunity to force people to buy more licenses. In the end, they evicted Jewish merchants to make room for their competitors. But "let it be said again that [the officials'] purpose was not so much discrimination against the Jews as the desire to mulct them, legally or illegally, and at the same time give greater opportunities and ample market space to native Mexicans."[34] Despite this benign report, it must be said that the two cars entered by Jewish manufacturers in the Day of Commerce parade were destroyed by hooligans of the infamous Camisas Doradas ("gilded shirts"). Ultimately, intervention by B'nai B'rith, and representations made through a former U.S. ambassador to Mexico, headed off the pogrom-in-the-making that the parade apparently portended.[35] Though the underlying anti-Semitism undoubtedly remained, hostile actions were prevented by the police, and tensions abated when President Ortiz Rubio declared that Jews were in the country legally and were free to pursue any occupation they chose.

The ousting of Jews from the marketplace appears to have benefited Jewish merchants in the long run, for it gave them a needed push to enter occupations in which they could succeed far better economically and, just as important, remove themselves from direct contact with religious fanaticism. Their market stalls destroyed, Jewish merchants invested in fixed places of business or in small manufacturing plants, where they began producing a variety of consumer goods that had previously been imported, such as paint, furniture, leather goods, plastics, pharmaceuticals, sweaters, stockings, underwear, film, and fishing gear. In 1946, a researcher assessed their economic impact in this way: "The Jews have since their settlement in Mexico a quarter of a century ago, brought into the uneven, unbalanced social structure of class-ridden, semi-feudal, industrially retarded Mexico, a pioneering spirit. With social, economic and political conditions entirely favorable toward industrial and commercial expansion, the relatively small Jewish community, with its accumulated experiences, skills and enterprises, can be said to have served as a catalytic agent in the economic life of Mexico."[36]

The number of Jewish ventures in import substitution increased at an accelerated pace during World War II, when overseas sources of supply were cut off. Backed by a communal bank (Banco Mercantil de Mejico), a credit union, and two small savings and loan associations, the Jewish immigrants continued their strong movement out of commerce and into industry and the free professions. By 1950, 12.6 percent of Mexican Jews who were gainfully employed were industrialists. Some were pioneering in industries such as tricotage that formerly had not existed at all in Mexico.[37]

Even when they succeeded in removing themselves from direct contact with masses of people in the marketplace, Jews did not always escape anti-Semitic manifestations. The classic entanglement between commercial rivalry and religious hatred surfaced in Ecuador in 1948 in the form of the medieval blood libel. The Jewish owner of a sausage factory was accused of intending to kidnap a Christian boy in order to use his flesh in making sausage. The case was publicized in a sensational manner by the local newspapers. A letter from the Joint representative in Quito reports the incident while the accused was still being held without bail and continues without transition:

> Applying for an import licence Jewish importers are required to produce preliminary invoices, samples, and sworn statements, provisions which are not mentioned in any decree and which are taken arbitrarily. . . . Mr. Apunte, sub-chief of the Commercial Department of the Foreign Ministry, stated that the *Jewish immigration had forced the country without transition from the patriarchal forms of life into the modern era,* and that the country should be cleaned as fast as possible of Jewish immigrants. (Emphasis supplied.)[38]

The abililty of Jewish immigrants to apply skills they had acquired in Europe to the production and sale of consumer goods was the key to their integration into local economies. For this to occur, the economic and social climate of the matrix society had to be receptive to immigrant entrepreneurial initiative. This was, for a short while, the situation in Cuba. Within a few years of passage of Cuba's Law of 50 Percent, 150 shoe factories owned by Jews were employing six to eight thousand workers and producing two million pairs of shoes annually. Eventually, Jewish firms accounted for 50 percent of all shoe manufacturing in Cuba, ending Cuban dependence on foreign suppliers.[39] Three hundred forty Jewish-owned factories can be identified during the period 1930–45. They produced woven fabrics, textiles, ready-made shirts, underwear, suits, pants, ties, shoes, and leather goods. Sixty-four such firms were advertising in 1933, 190 in 1934–39, and 189 in 1940–45; they were engaged in industry, wholesale and retail trade, and a variety of other economic activities.[40] Diamond cutting, the last industry to be imported to Cuba by Jews, was established in 1943 by Polish diamond workers and bosses arriving from Antwerp, resulting in the founding of twenty-four workshops employing twelve hundred persons.[41]

The Jewish proletariat, unable to survive in the social and legislative climate of Cuba, turned instead to cottage industry, leaving the proletariat (and, often, the Communist party) behind.

German immigrants to Brazil in the days just preceding the outbreak of World War II made a particularly good adjustment. Their careers illustrate most clearly the reciprocal nature of immigrant integration. Many German Jews arrived in Brazil with a lifetime of experience in the business and industrial world of the European continent. They came at a time when circumstances in Brazil were propitious for industrial takeoff and starting up a new plant required less capital than would have been needed in a fully developed economy. Habitual Brazilian tolerance made the Germans sought-after partners by the rising Brazilian middle class. Consequently, we find German Jews and their Brazilian partners investing in the fashion and textile industries, producing cotton, silk, and linen cloth, and ladies' ready-to-wear. Certain construction materials, electrical hardware, and locks were now manufactured in Brazil for the first time. The immigrants undertook for the first time the construction of houses of more than three stories in height, utilizing local materials. Elevators, porcelain plumbing fixtures, paper, and newsprint were first manufactured in Rio by Jewish immigrants. It was as though the industrial revolution had finally opened its cornucopia to Brazilians.

During World War II, Jewish immigrants started up a refrigeration industry that began the preservation of foodstuffs in this country that had hitherto been a net importer of food. Aluminum factories provided important stores of this metal to the Allied forces.[42] The firm of Klabin e Lafer built a diversified industrial empire on the base of their paper manufacturing plants, becoming the largest newsprint producer in Latin America. The two families, joined by marriage ties, are among the wealthiest in Brazil; their record of government service has already been mentioned.

Economic and Social Integration of the First Generation

Economic decisions by private individuals are not wholly open to investigation. Individuals participate in the economy as producers and consumers, not as Jews. But there does exist a theoretical framework for analysis of the economic structure and life of the Jews that may be used to organize and render coherent the vast amount of humanistic literature available on this subject for Latin America.

The perception of Jews as a minority in an economic as well as in the usual religious sense is a fruitful node with which to begin. The salient economic characteristic of Jewish communities is their minority status. These are permanent minorities: neither immigration nor the natural rate of increase will ever significantly raise the proportion of Jews to total population, given their initial tiny numbers. Certain economic consequences flow from permanent minority status. Such a minority cannot reproduce the full range of occupations. Their recency of arrival means that most sectors of the economy are already fully manned; immigrants therefore concentrate in the remaining sectors, where old residents will resent them less and where the selection of occupation is further limited by their own historical heritage. They arrive poor (having been pushed out elsewhere) and therefore start at a low level. Beginning at this lower level, although they suffer great poverty at first, they have more room to rise: when immigrants enter new areas with greater growth potential than the old, their economic rise may be of greater magnitude than that of the general population. As newcomers, they are more free of tradition and have more room to maneuver. But the immigrants' concentration on a narrow occupational range, plus the absolute increase in their numbers, leads to the apparent capture of some sectors of the economy, arousing a perception that they have become economically dominant over the natives.[43]

As applied to the Latin American scene, we may certainly agree that Jews represent a minority of such numerical insignificance that it would not be possible for them to man all sectors of an economy if that option were open to them. In point of fact, their late arrival excluded them from traditional sources of wealth—particularly ownership of land—and confronted them with basically urban options. Within urban parameters, immigrant Jews, like immigrants of other nations, tended to move into sectors that were less developed, for here they met less resistance from established folk. The Jewish migration, as we have seen, was propelled out of Europe by a series of convulsions whose source lay in the industrializing process. Jews, who had been factors in European industrialization and urbanization, were technically equipped and strategically placed to take part in the industrialization of Latin America.

In every country of the continent, Jewish entrepreneurs were among the first to see the potential for turning local commodities into salable merchandise, thus reversing the historic trend, which had been to export raw materials for manufacture abroad and subsequent resale at high prices on the Latin American market. This process of import substitution is generally regarded as having been the first step toward loosening the dependence of Latin America upon foreign markets. Having cut their ties to their countries of origin, Jewish immigrants had no need to export capital to pay off foreign investors, but were free to reinvest their earnings in the expansion of industrial plants. Many immigrants achieved success by competing within the commercial and industrial spaces they identified on their arrival. The result for some was a meteoric rise to affluence.

The neglect of commerce and industry has been so persistent throughout Latin American history that it has attracted the attention of sociologists seeking to link this economic aberration to cultural characteristics of the people. Yet economic development undeniably occurred. Whence did it come? The evidence is that much of it stemmed from the activities of immigrants. Not, of course, Jewish immigrants only; but immigrants generally, who in their overwhelming majority were not Jewish: "It was the immigrant population which provided most of the labor and entrepreneurship in the beginnings of industrial development."[44] The process began early and did not vary greatly

from country to country: immigrants took the lead in initiating the industrialization process prior to World War I. In 1895, 80 percent of Argentine commerce
and industry was already in the hands of the foreign-born. At that date, there
were barely seven thousand Jews in the country, and two-thirds of them were
in the agricultural colonies of Entre Ríos. The predominance of immigrants
and sons of immigrants in Argentine industry is documented through 1959,
when 45.5 percent of prestigious Argentine entrepreneurs were foreign-
born, while a goodly percentage of the rest were first-generation born in the
country.[45] A similar situation prevailed in Chile, where by 1914 immigrants
comprised a majority of owners of industry. Although they had been able to
buy little rural property, they had acquired large amounts of urban real estate.[46]
Many thousands of immigrants had already entered the Chilean middle class
by that date, when there appear to have been no more than five hundred Jews
in the country. Whatever commercial or industrial success Jews achieved in
Chile may well have been a function of their status as immigrants, rather than
as Jews.

In countries that were slower to industrialize, the picture is not greatly
different. A 1965 survey of sixty-one Bogotá executives of medium-to-large
firms revealed that although Colombia has had very little immigration, 41
percent of her entrepreneurs at that date were foreign-born. By way of comparison, the United States, with 10 percent foreign-born in the population at large,
exhibited a mere 5 percent of foreign-born in executive positions in medium-
to-large firms.[47]

In their effort to "make America," immigrants were able to make substantial
gains, in part because they were untrammeled by local tradition and desperate
to find means of subsistence. They rose economically with startling rapidity, a
mobility that was shared unevenly by Jews. The latter's late arrival, small
numbers, and concentration in a narrow occupational range led to the apparent
capture of some sectors of the economy at certain times and certain places,
calling down upon their heads ancestral antipathies that had remained embedded in Hispanic Catholicism. What in fact had happened was that
Jewish immigrants occupied niches in national economies for which they were
suited by experience. Adjusting themselves to local conditions, they became
peddlers or artisans, then, adjusting once more, moved into fixed commerce
and manufacturing, especially in new branches of industry that were just
developing under the impact of new technology. They thus became a part of
that much larger immigrant force that was beginning the modernization of
Latin America.

Economic advancement was not matched by social integration. Jews had
never developed linkages with non-Jewish campesinos; under the circumstances
outlined here, contact with the proletariat was broken. This is a startling fact,
considering that so large and so vocal a portion of Jewish immigrants arrived
with leftist and universalist ideals, determined to relieve workers of the world
of their chains. But the Jewish labor activists who so alarmed conservative
elites in the early decade of the century were ahead of their time. They met

little positive response from the masses, and severe political repression from the elite, both as activists and as Jews. In the 1930s, the Argentine proletariat, Jewish and non-Jewish, went over to Perón and have since remained in the party that he founded. In conformance with Sartre's dictum that a Jewish intellectual is a Jew, while a Jewish truckdriver is a truckdriver, many Jews who remained in the working class dropped their affiliation with the Jewish community. Meanwhile, economic and political forces converted the majority of the Jewish proletariat into a bourgeoisie. The combination of forces produced a community that, in statistical terms, is almost totally middle class. By the 1960s, when revolutionary ideologies ignited masses of dispossessed people from Cuba to Bolivia, from Chile to El Salvador, the advantaged position of the Jewish majority was no longer conducive to alignment with populist forces; for the most part, Bundism, communism, and the whole panoply of radical ideologies that arrived in the immigrants' baggage had been confined to the shadow play of communal elections.

Jewish links to the elite classes in Spanish-speaking countries were conspicuously weak from the start. Their exclusion originated in religious shibboleths reaching back hundreds of years. It also derived in part from identification with commerce. The extent to which the commercial and industrial occupations favored by Jewish immigrants excluded them from entry into the elite class was revealed in Sofer's analysis of 1939 and 1947 editions of *Quien es Quien en la Argentina* (Who's Who in Argentina). Ten Eastern European Jews appeared among almost 1,500 entries for 1939. Nine were men, and all lived in the federal capital. Their occupational patterns were "startlingly diffferent" from the community as a whole: six were writers, three were physicians, and one was an army colonel. Five were intermarried. By 1947, 31 Jews were included among 2,500 entries. There were two women, and two persons in trade or industry. The rest were doctors, attorneys, engineers, and authors. Of the 26 for whom marriage data appeared, 12 were intermarried.[48] Clearly, criteria for inclusion among the Who who were really Who's included distancing from Jewishly identified patterns of behavior, such as commerce and endogamy.

Depreciation of entrepreneurial pursuits has been remarked on for all Latin American societies, and entrepreneurial talent was from the start drawn from the foreign-born or the sons and daughters of immigrants. Of 119 high-level Argentine industrialists surveyed in 1959, only 11 were members of the criollo upper class.[49] This gap opened the economic opportunities for immigrants that have been discussed here, but also had a deleterious effect on the immigrants' social status. Immigrant entrepreneurs were at the root of modernization, but they lacked social prestige commensurate with their wealth. Within this depreciated group, Jews and Arabs found themselves on the bottom rungs of the social ladder, with a longer and harder climb to the top. The obstacles these "turcos" faced were more numerous and more intractable than those which confronted other parvenus.

The Second and Third Generations

Analysis of the 1960 Argentine national census produced a coherent picture of the occupational distribution of Jews in that country just past mid-century (see Table 2). In that year, 50 percent of Jewish males over age fourteen and 20 percent of Jewish females were in the work force. As compared with the total population of the country, this was a smaller percentage than average, probably because a larger proportion of Jewish youth were attending school. As compared to the general population of Buenos Aires (where school attendance was generally higher than in the countryside) the Jewish proportion of employed was larger because many Jews were self-employed and did not abandon their business interests at age sixty-five.[50]

Among Jewish men in the Argentine work force, 37 percent were in commerce, 22 percent were in industry, and 10 percent were executives and managers. For women, three groups each claimed about 20 percent of the employed: secretaries, commerce (primarily salesclerks), and the free professions. These percentages are all higher than for the general population.[51] In the younger age cohorts, fewer Jews were involved in commerce and more in the free professions and services. Most Argentine Jewish males were employers or self-employed. (The Argentine census defined "employer" as someone engaging at least one worker for pay.) Argentine Jewish women workers, on the other hand, were almost all employees. The younger the cohort, the fewer women were to be found in sales; a rising number of their Argentine-born daughters were engaged in the free professions.[52]

Schmelz and DellaPergola's analysis of the census data indicated clear differences between the Jewish and the general population. The number of farmers dwindled with younger age groups, and overall represented a smaller proportion of Jews than of the general population. Jews are concentrated in white-collar occupations; commerce is more significant among them; they tend to be employers or self-employed. These trends become more pronounced with younger age groups, except that, over time, there is a significant drop in commercial activity and a rise in members of the free professions.[53] The entry of Jews into professional ranks responds both to the patterns of Jewish history and to the developmental needs of their societies. As the latter became more persuasive than the former, traditional professions such as cantor, circumciser, ritual slaughterer, etc., were abandoned in favor of professions relating to modernization, such as engineering, business administration, accounting, and architecture. Jews still became doctors, but in the postwar years there was more deployment throughout the economy.

Not all Argentine Jews had made it into the middle class by 1960. The census turned up 10,000 Jews in the old immigrant occupation of peddler or selling from a market stall or kiosk; 1,500 persons, largely women, were servants in private homes. Twenty-four thousand production workers remained in the ranks of the Argentine proletariat.[54]

TABLE 2

Jewish Participation in the Argentine Work Force, by Sex, Assorted Occupations, 1960

OCCUPATION	WOMEN	MEN	TOTAL
Total	23,652	95,409	119,061
Free professions, including:	4,731	7,471	12,202
Architects, engineers	91	1,481	1,572
Chemists, pharmacists	452	934	1,386
Physicians, surgeons, dentists	615	2,583	3,198
Teachers	2,542	686	3,228
Artists, writers	368	656	1,024
Executives, including:	549	9,653	10,202
Managers, wholesale and retail stores	110	1,352	1,462
Owner-managers	405	7,851	8,256
Office employees, including:	5,721	8,641	14,362
Accountants	1,090	1,861	2,951
Clerks	4,246	5,410	9,656
Commerce, including:	5,155	35,415	40,570
Proprietors of stores	2,417	22,993	25,410
Peddlers, kiosk owners	2,510	5,784	8,294
Commercial agents	162	5,594	5,756
Market stalls, etc.	66	1,044	1,110
Farmers, hunters, fishermen, including:	54	2,297	2,351
Owners, managers of farms	24	1,902	1,926
Miners, stonecutters	4	49	53
Transportation and communication, including:	36	1,133	1,169
Drivers	24	1,041	1,065
Factory workers, including:	3,334	20,962	24,296
Textiles	479	2,695	3,174
Tailors, furriers	1,963	5,578	7,541
Shoemakers, tanners	179	1,652	1,831
Carpenters, woodworkers	26	1,888	1,914
Auto manufacture	69	1,180	1,249
Electricians (manufacture and repair)	27	991	1,018
Mechanics	35	1,516	1,551
Makers of precision instruments	75	1,569	1,644
Workers in service industries, including:	2,014	1,704	3,718
Cooks, servants in private homes	1,529	40	1,569
Others and not known	2,058	8,133	10,191

SOURCE: U. O. Schmelz and Sergio DellaPergola, *Hademografia shel hayehudim beargentina ube-artzot aherot shel America ha-Latinit*, pp. 119–20.

The dependence of immigrants upon prevailing economic and political conditions is well illustrated by contrasting the experience of Jewish immigrants in two other countries, Cuba and Brazil. We have seen that Jewish artisans in Cuba had great difficulty finding jobs in industry (because of the low level of industrialization) and even more difficulty hanging on to them (because of nativist labor legislation). The fact that they organized eight trade unions in the seven-year period 1929–36, in addition to joining existing unions, shows tremendous commitment to proletarian values, given the authoritarian nature of successive Cuban governments and the risks organizers ran of arrest and deportation. But all these unions shortly dissolved as their members were booted out of the proletariat and into the petite bourgeoisie. Their "upward mobility" was often more apparent than real in that many workers exchanged the regulated conditions of factory work for unregulated exploitation in outside shops.

The success of these unwilling entrepreneurs was quite spectacular. A contented Jewish bourgeoisie was in fact created. As a Cuban researcher has written, "At [the time of] the triumph of the Revolution, Jewish Cubans found themselves in the full flood of evolution toward superior forms of capitalism and social integration."[55] But a mere six years after having dedicated their elegant and costly community center, Jews found the rules of the game altered by the revolution of 1959. Restructuring the Cuban economy along socialist lines, Fidel Castro and Che Guevara incidentally ruined these new Jewish entrepreneurs. With the expropriation of their factories and shops, Jewish Cubans saw themselves reduced once more to the ranks of the proletariat, an event they perceived with a sense of déjà vu. Those whose dismay was not leavened by attachment to the socialist ideals of their youth fled the island together with the rest of the middle class.

The Brazilian economic "miracle," taking off from a coup by modernizing military officers in 1964, created a milieu favorable to capitalism. An exceptionally prosperous class of Jewish entrepreneurs developed. As of 1968, 41 percent of the members of the Jewish community of São Paulo were in the work force. The occupational breakdown for the 11,926 economically active individuals contacted by Rattner's survey showed that 27 percent were owners of firms and employers of a work force. Fifteen percent were directors and managers of business firms; another 15 percent were practicing one of the liberal professions; and 8.8 percent were self-employed artisans. Only 0.3 percent were manual workers.[56] By comparison, the Brazilian national census of 1960 showed 4.5 percent businessmen and managers in the general population, 1.5 percent in the liberal professions, and the vast majority in agriculture and manual labor. Although data are available for São Paulo only, it is likely that similar conclusions may be inferred for Jews elsewhere in Brazil. Rattner concludes, "On the evidence of data about the peculiar occupation structure of the Jewish community, corroborated by additional information about educational level, housing and land ownership in urban areas, travel overseas and general consumption patterns, we may assume that almost two-thirds of Brazilian Jews belong to the elite."[57] Brazilian conditions have been favorable to immigrants generally, and the Jews' heady success should be seen in context: immigrants make up nearly half of paulista entrepreneurs and another third are the sons and grandsons of immigrants. Financial success, however, did not preclude the fact that Jews, along with others, paid the price of political repression that was the other side of the coin of the economic miracle.

To 1960, the largest proportion (between 45 percent and 68 percent) of gainfully employed Jewish workers in Argentina, Brazil, and Mexico were in trade, a far larger share than among the total population. Most of these handled consumer goods at the retail level.[58] Over the succeeding years, some peddlers and storekeepers developed large-scale commercial enterprises. At the same time, this sector lost employment to industry and the professions. Manufacturing took up an increasing number of Jewish workers, rising most spectacularly in Mexico, from 15.6 percent of the Jewish work force in 1940 to 50 percent thirty years later. While the majority of non-Jewish industrial workers are employees of factories, Jews engaged in industry are more likely to be owners or self-employed. Almost no Jewish owners, however, can be discerned in capital-intensive industries such as utilities and transportation or in industries run by the military. In Mexico's sell-off of state-owned companies in 1990–92, no Jew can be identified among the successful bidders.

As in the rest of the modernizing world, the services sector in these three countries absorbs an increasing proportion of workers. About one-third of all workers were employed in services in the 1960–70 time span covered by Syrquin's research, most of these in underpaid and underemployed positions. The 15 to 17 percent of the Jewish work force employed in the service sector during this decade were almost totally in the professions.[59] Every community reporting to *Comunidades judías* in its biennial editions (1966–72) noted that a preponderance of its members were in trade and industry, with a rising percentage of the upcoming generation entering the liberal professions.

Entry into the Professions

As the numbers of Jews engaged in farming, peddling, and blue-collar manufacturing decreased, professional careers became more important among both male and female workers, whether immigrant or native-born. The entry of women into the professions began in the agricultural colonies, where the teaching staff in JCA schools, originally all male, converted rather quickly into a cadre of native-born female instructors. Women teachers, librarians, and physicians founded and staffed schools, libraries, and clinics in areas where previously there had been none.[60] In her biography of her father, a "pampista" who arrived in Argentina in 1891 to farm on an agricultural colony, Tuba Teresa Ropp relates that all three of the family's daughters earned advanced degrees, becoming a teacher, a midwife, and (the author herself) a physician.[61] Deutsch reports that as of the 1980s, 42 percent of the mothers of students in Argentine

Jewish schools worked outside the home, compared with 26.6 percent of all Argentine women.

Figures compiled by DellaPergola from several sources show that the 11.1 percent of employed Buenos Aires Jews in professional occupations in 1960 increased to 21.3 percent in 1974. The share of managers among the Jewish employed increased from 9.5 percent to 17.5 percent. During this period, the clothing industry, once heavily Jewish, was losing its Jewish workers. And interestingly, the long-term proclivity of Jewish entrepreneurs for self-employment had gone into reverse, as small businesses were absorbed by larger ones and their owners became salaried employees.This clearly denotes greater integration of Jewish with general economic activities.[62]

In 1959, Rattner identified 1,836 Jewish engineers, physicians, lawyers, administrators, university professors, journalists, and others, representing 16.4 percent of the Brazilian Jewish work force. The phenomenon of small business owners becoming salaried employees of larger corporations was most pronounced as São Paulo underwent rapid modernization.[63] In 1972, 26 percent of second-generation Jews of Cali, Medellín, and Barranquilla, taken as a group, were practicing in the free professions, primarily in medicine, architecture, and engineering.[64] In a 1994 study of the Jewish community of Mexico, 52.6 percent of employed Jews identified themselves as "directors, managers, or administrators," while another 26.7 percent identified themselves as "professionals."[65] The rate of upward social mobility was astonishing, considering that the community was barely 70 years old. Although data for Jewish professionals are incomplete, particularly as these relate to women, evidence of rapid mobility is supported by a survey of Pôrto Alegre (see Table 3, p. 156). Professionalization demarcates the occupational pattern of male and female Jewish workers from that of the majority populations.

Professionalization of Jewish immigrant careers proceeded quickly in Cuba as well, as successful entrepreneurs adapted to the local environment by preparing for careers in medicine, architecture, and the law. The 3 professional persons identified in the period 1902–27 were supplemented by 10 more in the generation 1928–45. During 1946–59, 266 persons, or 56.7 percent of Jews in service occupations, were working at a professional level.[66] "Many children of peddlers moved into the professions in the surprising space of just one generation. Jewish lawyers, doctors, dentists, engineers, pharmacists, architects, and public accountants filled the professional directories in the fifties, in proportions incommensurate with the size of the group (4 percent as opposed to 0.4 percent) in the general population. . . . The surprising and disproportionate move into the professions, in just one generation, signified the assimilation of values of the national elite and the gradual integration of this group into a new social status."[67]

Observation plus anecdotal evidence points to a strong representation of Jews in the liberal professions, but additional research is needed to clarify the extent of their presence and their influence. Their acceptability in academic life and the liberal professions is widespread and noticeable throughout Latin

America, a fact that has lowered barriers to intermarriage and partly erased the canard of Jewish financial power, since the most rabid anti-Semite could not claim that university professors are well paid. Education for the professions has enhanced Jewish social and economic integration in all the republics and created a cohort of persons qualified to take on public service in government and the universities.

Jews as a Middle Class

In countries with a large European-descended population, Jews occupy an intermediate space in the economy. Viewed as a statistical aggregation, they engage in middle-class occupations—buying and selling, manufacturing and distributing, teaching and administering, working in the cultural sphere. They earn intermediate levels of income, occupy adequate housing, enjoy long life expectancy, are able to have their children educated, and either pass their lifestyle on to their children or finance their emigration. As a middle class, they have functioned as a modernizing force within their societies; Jewish immigrants and their descendants contributed to the formation of an educated labor force and played an identifiable role in industrialization. If this population were to be treated as a separate entity on a chart delineating modernized characteristics, they would show up together with Argentina, Uruguay, Chile, the southern states of Brazil, and Mexico City as a modern country. Considering their geographic dispersal, they might better be referred to as a modernized archipelago.

There are important caveats. In Argentina, a number of Jews have remained stuck in the lowest income categories, and they have been joined in recent years by formerly middle-class families impoverished by inflation and economic stagnation. In 1990, the *Jerusalem Post* reported that about 5,000 Argentine Jewish families were living below the poverty level. In the context of economic crisis, some 2,000 people a day were emigrating; among them, unknown numbers of Jews. What was known was that 1,000 Argentines arrived in Israel in the first four months of 1990—a minority, according to informed observers, of all those Jews who were emigrating.[68] The national network of Jewish schools, clinics, and senior citizens' homes was in financial trouble. Social welfare assistance remained a primary mission of the AMIA, which ran an employment exchange on its premises; a free kitchen continued to function as in immigrant days. The Jewish poor exist alongside the non-Jewish poor; but they are less noticeable because they are taken care of within the community.

In countries whose national economies exhibit grave polarity between rich and poor, the long-lived and the doomed, with large masses of indigenous, black, or mestizo populations, Jews are, in economic terms at least, among the white elite. The Bogotá, São Paulo, Rio, Lima, and Mexico City communities are in this category. But sometimes, as in the case of Lima, the upper-class composition of the community is in part a result of the departure of the poorest families, who could neither strike it rich nor adapt to Andean levels of poverty,

TABLE 3

Professions of Heads of Families and Spouses, Pôrto Alegre, by Sex

PROFESSION	WOMEN	MEN	TOTAL
Housewife°	324 (22.3%)	—	324 (11.9%)
Commerce	184 (12.7%)	279 (22.1%)	463 (17.0%)
Teacher	257 (17.7%)	27 (2.1%)	284 (10.5%)
Physician	49 (3.4%)	189 (15.0%)	238 (8.8%)
Sales rep	35 (2.4%)	105 (8.3%)	140 (5.2%)
Civil engineer	8 (0.5%)	112 (8.9%)	120 (4.4%)
Lawyer/judge	44 (3.0%)	54 (4.3%)	98 (3.6%)
Architect/landscape	25 (1.7%)	47 (3.7%)	72 (2.6%)
Construction entrep.	22 (1.5%)	47 (3.7%)	70 (2.5%)
Public official	44 (3.0%)	20 (1.6%)	64 (2.4%)
Industrialist	13 (0.9%)	51 (4.0%)	64 (2.4%)
Dentist	23 (1.6%)	33 (2.6%)	56 (2.1%)
Psychol./psychoanal.	46 (3.2%)	6 (0.5%)	52 (1.9%)
Bus admin	13 (0.9%)	36 (2.9%)	49 (1.8%)
Bank employee	26 (1.8%)	22 (1.7%)	48 (1.8%)
University professor	27 (1.9%)	17 (1.4%)	44 (0.6%)
Accountant	12 (0.8%)	22 (1.7%)	34 (1.2%)
Engineer°°	3 (0.2%)	27 (2.1%)	30 (1.1%)

SOURCE: Anita Brumer, *Identidade em Mudança*, p. 94.
°In the age group 55 and over, 20.5 percent of women had never worked outside the home; among those a decade younger, only 5.3 percent had been housewives only; and in the age group below 40, just 2.1 percent.
°°Other occupations employing 1 percent or fewer of Jewish workers include economist, journalist, computer programmer, teacher of pedagogy, chemist, seamstress, artist, physiotherapist, historian, sociologist, nurse, librarian, archivist, police and military, forester, photographer, farmer, travel agent, nutritionist, and translator.

and so emigrated to Israel in search of better lives. Even so, 12 percent of the 3,430 Jews remaining in Lima received subsistence aid from the community in 1988, and 35 percent required scholarships in order to send their children to the Jewish school.[69]

For tourists unfamiliar with the prevailing ostentatious lifestyle of the wealthy, the expectation of Jewish wealth may appear to be borne out on first contact with mercantile and industrial entrepreneurs, especially in the Caribbean basin. There labor is cheap, and money will buy any amount of personal service. Luxury goods from Miami are just one vacation away. A life of comparable conspicuous consumption, were it to be translated into North American labor costs, would require a much higher income level. Actually, a princely lifestyle can be sustained in Peru, Colombia, Mexico, or Brazil quite cheaply, and a household with five or six servants may be only middle class in terms of the net financial worth of the head of household. Which is not to say there are no genuinely wealthy Jewish families, in commerce, manufacturing, and banking, only that very little research has been carried out concerning them individually or collectively.

In conformance with Simon Kuznets's analysis, Jewish immigrants were most successful when they entered newly emerging sectors of the economy that were not already being exploited by the native-born. Radio broadcasting, operating as it does in the public sphere, offers several prime examples. Jaime Yankelevich, who was born in Bulgaria but grew up on a farm in Entre Ríos, pioneered both radio and television broadcasting in Argentina, becoming a nationally known figure in the country's culture and politics. José Jerosolimski became virtually the official spokesman of the Uruguayan Jewish community through his popular radio program "Seminario Hebreo," broadcast from downtown Montevideo. In Mexico, Jacobo Zabludovsky developed radio programs whose increasing popularity became a factor in redefining *mexicanidad* to include immigrants as well as the native-born. Politicians, presidents included, befriended these men who became political players on their respective national scenes. Without detracting from their talent, it may be said that one reason these individuals with decidedly non-Hispanic names were able to succeed is that they arrived on an empty playing field.

In no country do Jews have access to the traditional dominant triumvirate of the church, the armed forces, and the landowning oligarchy. Their exclusion from the first and last is a foregone conclusion. Less comprehensible is that they should also be excluded from the army officer corps. Jewish men are conscripted along with everyone else where compulsory national service exists. But although thousands of Jewish conscripts transited the ranks before conscription was abolished by Argentina in 1995, just one Jewish army officer has been identified. Bernardo Wainstein was a classmate of Juan Perón at the military academy and participated in the revolution that brought the latter to power.[70] The possibility for other Jews to pursue a military career was foreclosed in the nationalistic thirties. Secret brotherhoods control access to crucial decision-making posts within the army, and during periods of military control, exclusivism becomes diffused to the national scene. In Chile and Brazil, the presence of several Jewish officers in the armed forces was continually alluded to by respondents as evidence that Jews are integrated in those countries. Jewish officers were not detected in other national armies. The assumption of respondents who were questioned on the matter was that a man who worked his way up through the military hierarchy would have to be one who had left his Jewish origins far behind. In Argentina, there was no way to put them far enough behind. In this as in other instances, not only law but prejudicial social attitudes determine the living space that Jews may occupy.

In the absence of political and social linkages, Jews came to be defined almost totally by their economic functions. Their character as an entrepreneurial community shows up in high relief against the background of a culture that traditionally looked down on the entrepreneur. But political isolation resulted in even greater emphasis on economic activity, because only wealth provides protection from disaster. Over the past decades, the size of Latin American Jewish communities has fluctuated with the rise and fall of governments favorable to the free enterprise system. Jews have been attracted to, and have remained in, nations that offered free scope to the entrepreneurial spirit and have abandoned republics whose social policies included the expropriation of their property. This has happened notwithstanding the fact that individual Jews have been among the initiators and proponents of such policies.

CHAPTER 7

"The Jewish Street"

. . . a permanent search for a balance point between Jewish existence and integration into the non-Jewish surrounding.

—David Schers and Hadassa Singer

OBSERVERS OF THE Jewish scene in Latin American cities often comment on its highly organized nature. Indeed, the centrality of the kehillah to Jewish life has more than once made it the object of paranoid fantasies about Jewish power or intrigue. But Latin American kehillot came into existence in response to the felt need for social services on the part of Jewish immigrants who were faced by a variety of needs that were met neither by government nor by that traditional agency of social welfare, the Catholic Church. In order to satisfy these needs, as well as to sustain their Jewish identity in alien lands, the immigrants founded communal organizations patterned on those they had left behind in Europe, Africa, or the Middle East. These organizations enabled Jews to extend mutual aid to one another and prevented the immigrants from becoming a burden on their host societies. Many kehillot originated in a legal struggle to obtain a permit to establish a Jewish cemetery.

Burial Societies

Commonly, the first need to impress itself upon the immigrants was for a place to bury the dead. A church monopoly of cemeteries existed in all parts of the continent when immigrants first arrived; access to them required not just death but baptism. At first, the Jewish dead were shipped to Curaçao or Jamaica for burial. Enlightened German and French Jews of the late nineteenth-century migration made local adjustments, particularly in Chile and Brazil. In the German colonies of southern Chile, for example, Jews were buried among their Christian fellows inasmuch as the religion of corpses was not regarded as an interesting matter.[1] A partial solution also was found in those areas where non-Catholic cemeteries were licensed as the result of treaty arrangements with Great Britain. None of these, however, provided specifically for burial in accord with Mosaic law.

With the arrival of the East European Ashkenazim, the problem grew more pressing. For this group, burial among their fellows was a strong compulsion. The continuity of tradition can be seen in the transfer of the rule book of the burial society of the Jewish community of Novo-Poltavka, in southern Russia, to the emigrants who were leaving for Basavilbaso (Lucienville) in Entre Ríos. There it survives to this day, long after destruction of the community that wrote it. In most of the republics, a bitter legal battle had to be fought to gain the right to bury the dead without the ministrations of the church. The traditional organization for provision of burial services among Jews is the Khevra Kadisha (Burial Society), and typically this was the first organization to make its appearance on "the Jewish street," that agglomeration of clubs, newspapers, shops, schools, and theatres that came to make up the Jewish lifestyle on the continent. At the start, the sole aim of these societies was to arrange for the burial of Jews according to Mosaic law. Gradually their functions expanded into other aspects of Jewish life, and a monopoly over burial remains at the heart of organized Jewish life on the continent today. This monopoly is the counterpart of the church monopoly that exists in society at large, and it gave to the Khevra Kadisha a power over people's lives that mimicked that of the church itself.

Charity

Charity was a discrete function for which the Jewish immigrants organized very early. When the Khevra Kadisha formed in Montevideo in 1915, there was already in existence a Sociedad de Damas de Beneficiencia Ezra, which contributed to the purchase of land for the cemetery. This women's organization provided material aid to the needy, founded a night school and library, and functioned as a savings and loan association. The one area in which it offered no services was religion, for the members were antireligious in orientation.[2] The founding of Jewish cemeteries often was not a function of religious feelings so much as it was a function of exclusion from Catholic cemeteries.

The founding of women's charitable organizations such as the Sociedad de Damas bespeaks a gendered perception of the roles of women and men in public life. The major social welfare associations, such as those mentioned below, were chartered and funded by men, and only men served on their boards of directors. In the dozens of photographs of "consejos directivos" assembled by Backal for her detailed history of the Ashkenazic community of Mexico, women appear in just two: in a group of teachers, and as members of a wedding party. This count omits the obligatory photograph of Golda Meier, prime minister of Israel, on a visit to Mexico. As recently as 1991, when a comprehensive self-study of the community was carried out, the twenty-two suggestions adopted for improving the services offered to the community did not include the recruitment of women into directorial positions.[3]

All the Jewish communities have either a volunteer Ezra (Assistance), a Gmilus Khassodim (known in the United States as the Hebrew Free Loan Association), or a Bikur Kholim (Calling on the Sick). In the early years of the century, when there was a perception of a communal responsibility for single women, Hakhnosset Kalah provided dowries for indigent brides. The Buenos Aires Ezra Society is now over eighty years old and maintains a major hospital in the city. In the seventies, half a million dollars were spent annually by the Jewish community of Buenos Aires on social welfare, including free medical aid, clothing, hot meals, and home care for the aged; summer camps for deprived children; and a free kitchen for the Jewish indigent. In 1986 2,000 people applied for direct relief to the AMIA, which budgeted $600,000 for social services. The actual numbers of Jewish poor were estimated to be much higher, but reticence held many back from applying for assistance. Economic crisis in Argentina, which was polarizing the population generally, also accentuated the gap between rich and poor Jews to the extent that it was becoming difficult for them to remain within the same institutions. While some Jewish families maintained their weekend cottages at country clubs, other families were no longer able to enroll their children in Jewish schools without financial aid.[4]

With the passage of time, social welfare became professionalized. The Jewish community of São Paulo, for example, maintains the following services, financed from within the community: a centralized hospital service to take responsibility for persons who need to be hospitalized for prolonged periods of time; social and economic assistance to new immigrants; a loan association; summer camp; Ezra Society, originally for assistance to the tubercular poor and now directed toward psychiatric care; homes for the aged; a polyclinic offering medical assistance at home, including an X-ray clinic, ambulance service, physiotherapy, dental care, and a pharmacy; a children's aid center, offering services for children with special needs; the Brazilian branch of National Council of Jewish Women, which subsidizes and trains workers in rehabilitation through productive work; a children's home for orphans and the maladjusted; and Alberto Einstein Hospital, whose facilities are open to the public. The professionals who staff these multivariate organizations are for the most part Jewish graduates of the Escola de Serviço Social da Pontifícia Universidade Católica de São Paulo.

Some charitable and social welfare efforts among Latin American Jews have been subsidized by international Jewish organizations. Their interventions during the immigration period have already been mentioned. Two additional instances may be cited as representative. Many impoverished Russian Jews, adrift in Mexico after 1924, attempted to enter the United States illegally. If caught, they were subject to deportation to their port of embarkation—in most cases, Russia. To prevent such an outcome, B'nai B'rith gave assurances to the United States secretary of labor that they would care for Jewish illegals if the border patrol would deport them only as far as Mexico.[5] Together with the Industrial Removal Organization (a spin-off of the Baron de Hirsch Fund, created in 1904 to spread Jewish immigrants out over the United States instead of permitting them to pile up in East Coast slums), B'nai B'rith then went to work to create "contented Jews," who would not be tempted to try crossing the border again. These organizations remained at work until 1931, when immigration into Mexico from non-Latin areas was phased out and there were no more new arrivals to rehabilitate.

Similar international concern has been shown for Jewish communities that dwindled in size, leaving behind a residue of persons unable to care for themselves. The end of World War II found seven hundred Jews in Cochabamba, Bolivia. Over the next twenty years, most of these left. Two hundred Jews remained in the city in 1965, 10 percent of them in the Jewish home for the aged. Six other Jewish institutions also existed in the city: a temple, a cemetery, a sports center, a community hall, a kindergarten, and a public dispensary that had been opened by the community as a philanthropic measure. The number and status of the Jews remaining in Cochabamba was inadequate to sustain all these institutions. Nevertheless, such social services were necessary to make life tolerable. The solution was for the Joint Distribution Committee to subsidize the community.

Such charitable interventions had a variety of outcomes. On the one hand, many individuals and families were sustained over extremely difficult periods in their lives. This was particularly important considering that there was no possibility of government aid and the immigrants did not qualify for assistance from the church. Under these circumstances, the attrition of Jewish communities was not permitted to result in the abandonment of the helpless and the nonproductive. For those capable of supporting themselves, agencies funded by United States Jews speeded their integration into their new environment and enabled them to become self-supporting (and taxpaying) citizens.

On the other hand, the cumulative impact of these "American interventions" was to identify the Jewish communities with the United States. This was a result of historical accident, in that a free Jewish population had survived intact in the United States and was financially able to help. Identification with the United States had specific consequences in Latin America, however, where intervention by the United States has often been viewed as sinister. The result of the postwar resettlement period, when United States Jewish charities were most influential, was to create a community of interest between some Jews in Latin America and official representatives of the United States government. For example, the program of nationalization and land reform initiated by the government of Bolivia toward the end of 1952 included the expropriation of all Hochschild properties. There were some indications that the Bolivian authorities might consider the SOCOBO agricultural settlements as part of the Hochschild patrimony as well, and therefore SOCOBO administrators contacted the United States embassy in La Paz to certify that the American Joint Distribution Committee was owner of the land. Although this did no more than register a preexisting fact, it had the effect of placing local Jews under United States, rather than Bolivian, protection.

Credit

Notoriously, credit in small amounts to people of no name has been nonexistent in Latin America. Provision of credit to the impoverished immigrants was a matter of immediate concern, and it was tackled at a variety of levels in all the areas of settlement.

The first successful agricultural credit cooperatives in Argentina were founded by Jewish farmers of the Baron de Hirsch colonies.[6] Founded at Lucienville in 1900, the Ershter Yiddisher Landwirtschaftlicher Farein started as a co-op for buying and selling produce and later became a representative organ for presenting the colonists' grievances to the JCA administration. In the following decade, co-ops were founded in Clara, Moisesville, and Baron de Hirsch colonies. Typically, they marketed farm produce, operated a general store, issued loans and insurance, and disseminated agricultural information. As the colonization process accelerated, a movement grew to unite the co-ops in order, as it was said, to provide the colonies with an address on the Jewish street. This accomplished, the movement chronicled its achievements in its own newspaper, *El Colono Cooperador,* published for over fifty years (1917–70).

Leadership in the co-op movement was taken by Miguel Sakharov, who is credited with uniting the Jewish colonists behind the idea of agrarian cooperation. Sakharov had led the unsuccessful negotiations with JCA over the provision of land for colonists' sons. The co-op leaders then tried to buy land on the open market, but were unable to do so. The co-ops spun off credit unions, hospitals, libraries, schools, sports clubs, and sick funds. They were prepared for political action when a strike of farm workers at Villaguay gave rise to a show of anti-Semitism in the Entre Ríos Chamber of Deputies in 1920. At that time, co-op leaders joined officers of JCA in presenting to the Chamber a memorandum listing the contributions of Jewish farmers to the province. In addition to providing a census of Jewish landholdings, schools, co-ops, and communal institutions, the memo reminded legislators that 220 Argentine-born Jews were serving in the armed forces or had already completed their national service.[7]

The Fraternidad Agraria, as it was known in its ultimate incarnation, served its members well during the agrarian crisis of the 1930s, when proportionately fewer Jewish than non-Jewish farmers were forced into bankruptcy, due to the availability of credit. In his assessment of Jewish agricultural colonization in Entre Ríos, Winsberg concludes that "the Jewish colonies in Argentina have made their greatest contribution to the rural economy through their leadership in agricultural cooperatives. . . . Lucienville's cooperative became the model not only for the cooperatives which were established in all the other Jewish colonies but for the entire Argentine cooperative movement."[8]

Another operation, typical for its time, was that of the Asociación Femenina Hebrea de Cuba, which started up a Caja de Préstamos (Loan Fund) in 1937. Its twenty-three founding members bought shares totaling $350, then sold additional shares to members of the community for a grand total of $900. Their

The farmers of Moisesville, in Santa Fe province of Argentina, founded consumer and producer cooperatives. Blending their financial experience with the needs of the pampas, they sparked development of a cooperative movement nationwide.

purpose was to aid the rehabilitation of small merchants, industrialists, widows and orphans by providing interest-free loans. Funds were lent to individuals to enable them to buy merchandise to peddle on the street so that, in the words of one informant, "our husbands could earn our daily bread and avoid becoming a burden on the public." In the first year of its existence, the Caja made forty-six interest-free loans ranging in size from $5 to $50, repayable in weekly installments. This type of homemade banking by women was characteristic of self-help measures during the peddling era.

A more sophisticated operation was the loan fund begun in La Paz on behalf of refugees through the agency of the American Joint Distribution Committee. When Leon Aronovici, the Joint representative, arrived in La Paz in 1940, he found already functioning a Hilfsverein—a relief organization for German Jewish refugees founded, funded, and staffed by officers of the Hochschild tin-mining company in association with other wealthy German Jews of the city. The Hilfsverein stood aloof from the East European Jews, some of whom could have contributed to the relief effort but who were not

approached because they were regarded as socially inferior. The East Europeans, for their part, did not rush to aid the new immigrants, who were Germans,
nor could they see themselves working with the Hochschild group, whom they
regarded as snobs. Aronovici realized that if he was to form a loan association
and help the immigrants become self-supporting, he would first have to bring
these warring groups together. This he was able to do (he regarded it as the
most important outcome of his mission), and the loan fund was established,
having on its board of directors both Germans and "Easterners." The fund
offered loans at 12 percent annually. That rate might seem high, Aronovici
conceded, but the prevailing interest rate in Bolivia for small loans was 4
percent monthly, or about 50 percent per year.

Having reported establishment of the fund, Aronovici looked into the future
to assess the possibilities for permanent settlement of Jews in Bolivia and found
these in the manufacture of needed goods from local raw materials: "Bolivia
lives from the mines, i.e., from the export of tin. The sacks for this are
imported. . . . There is no good vinegar, no decent ink, no bone buttons, no
cartons, paper, etc. These articles, which would require relatively small capital,
but proper expert knowledge, could provide a livelihood for many. Bolivia
imports all kinds of canned vegetables and fruits from the States, whereas
beautiful fruits grow in certain districts which are not made use of industrially."[9]
This expression is typical of those who became involved with the founding of
loan associations. Their object invariably went beyond charity or even temporary succor. They intended to enable individuals to become self-supporting
and to establish themselves economically in their new homes.

Credit for the small merchant or manufacturer lay at the heart of Jewish
economic strivings all over Latin America. Moreover, Jewish credit unions
provided the model and the impetus for formation of similar credit facilities
by non-Jewish groups: of the 242 credit unions functioning in Argentina in
1970, 124 were owned wholly or partially by Jews. But the success of the credit
union movement had its downside. Inflation and high interest rates afflicted
Argentina throughout the seventies and enriched the credit unions beyond the
capability of some directors to manage their funds prudently. Swollen coffers
attracted speculators, who operated on both sides of the law and invested too
heavily in construction. That industry collapsed in the context of a deteriorating
and increasingly panicked economy, and fraud in the management of the credit
unions led to their widespread bankruptcy. Their collapse took down with them
hundreds of thousands of small depositors. The harm done to individuals was
not recouped for years; community institutions suffered because the cooperatives had historically subsidized their budgets. Perhaps the worst damage was
the revival of ancient antipathies to Jewish "money changers."

Publishing

Cultural integration presented special problems for immigrants who arrived
without knowledge of Spanish and who therefore could not read the national

press. But Jewish immigrants had arrived in Latin America with a well-developed sense of the importance of the printed word, and their desire to stay informed and to express their own opinions led to the development of a vigorous press (in Yiddish or German for the Ashkenazim, Ladino or Spanish for the Sephardim). Most communal institutions began publishing newsletters and magazines as soon as they opened their doors. All ideological factions—anarchist, Bundist, Zionist, syndicalist, cooperativist, assimilationist, religious, secular—established their own periodicals and newspapers. Additionally, scores of creative writers, poets, and journalists found an outlet in the party press closest to their own orientation or created literary vehicles for self-expression. In Argentina alone, thirty-seven newspapers and periodicals can be counted that were published between 1898 and 1970 and that lasted more than six months or six issues.[10] Among the longest lived were *Di Folks Shtime* (1898–1914) and *Di Yidishe Zaitung* (1914–73). For half a century, the Jewish community of Buenos Aires boasted two Yiddish-language dailies, the *Zaitung* and *Di Presse*. Although the Yiddish language predominated at first, by the 1920s Spanish was emerging as the preferred language, especially for younger people. The spread of Spanish-language publishing beyond the bounds of the Sephardic community paralleled the passing of the immigrant generation and the narrowing of the cultural gap between Ashkenazim and their matrix societies. Increasing numbers of journalists crossed the frontier between the two.

Viewed externally, the most noteworthy feature of the Jewish press in Latin America is that it went unnoted in its heyday. Over the course of time, at least 250 Jewish periodicals were published in Buenos Aires alone, not to mention the dozens published in other cities and beyond Argentina.[11] Some were published over a period of fifty years and more. Yet no Jewish periodical, or any that can be identified as emanating from a Jewish source, was listed in the *Indice general de publicaciones periódicas latinoamericanas*, edited in the 1960s by the Pan American Union and the New York Public Library and occupying eight folio volumes. In the two-volume supplement, the judgment of the editors was expanded to include *Comentario* of Buenos Aires, but not the equally interesting *Comentario* of Rio de Janeiro. These two magazines (now defunct) were sister publications of the North American *Commentary*, which in its day was regarded as one of the most influential journals of opinion in the United States. Of the 250,000 entries in the *Indice*, some 50 are grouped under the subject heading "Jews of Latin America." These citations fall into two groups: articles about Jewish agricultural settlement in Argentina and Christological speculation on the Jewish religion. No references appear for any literature emanating from Jewish sources, nor are there references to Latin American political or social developments as these relate to Jews. This singular lapse (Japanese in Brazil, for example, are well reported in the *Indice*) bespeaks the invisibility of Jewish Latin America and the isolation—might one say, quarantine?—of Jews that prevailed at that time, both in the majority culture and among observers of that culture.

In its prime, the Jewish press was a vehicle for astute political observation and considerable literary creativity. Unfortunately, its scope and depth became impoverished over time. Probably the decisive factor was the self-censorship of editors, who were led to understand that the entire Jewish community might be held responsible for the political views expressed in their papers. The result was a contraction of the political horizon scanned by the Jewish press and a rigidifying of views among its dedicated readers. As late as 1978, the Buenos Aires community muzzled the crusading editor of *Nueva Presencia* during the Argentine military repression by cutting off his supply of newsprint. Currently, the avowed Jewish press concerns itself almost exclusively with two categories of information: the situation of Jews in other countries, particularly Israel; and internal Jewish affairs, such as community elections and social news. Jewish newspapers published in Lima, Caracas, or Santiago are interchangeable, except for the faces in photographs of local notables. Seldom do serious think pieces appear, or articles about the republic in which they are published. The communal newspapers published in the various republics resemble one another in editorial perspective as well. Their orientation is overwhelmingly Zionist (though two diehard Stalinist organs lingered for years in Buenos Aires and Montevideo). The disappearance of the numerous Yiddish newspapers that carried fiction and poetry as well as news, the wide-ranging political analyses that filled the pages of newspapers such as *Havaner Lebn,* either failed financially or were forced to contract the scope of their efforts. Their disappearance represents a net loss to both Jewish and Latin American belles lettres.

On the other hand, as Jewish readers gained access to the national press, they needed their own communal publications less. Journalists likewise no longer had to attach themselves to the Jewish media in order to gain a readership. Argentine Jewish journalists such as Jacobo Timerman reached a national audience as editor of *La Opinión* and an international readership with his denunciation of the military government, *Prisoner without a name, cell without a number.* Many Jewish creative writers have entered the national mainstream, some with, some without a specifically Jewish intellectual orientation.

The lengthy quarantine of Jewish intellectuals stands in contrast to the experience of their peers in the United States, who profoundly influenced contemporary American literature, contributing to it a distinctively Jewish component and in turn being adopted into the American literary canon. In searching for the causative factor, one cannot attribute the apartheid imposed on Jewish intellectual life in Latin America to any greater religiosity on the part of Latin American Jews that might have placed them voluntarily beyond the pale. To the contrary, all indications are that the majority of Jewish immigrants to Latin America were less observant than their cousins who migrated to the United States.

Religious Practice

The temperament of the immigrants and the nature of the societies to which they came go far to explain why religious congregations were not a priority item on the immigrants' agenda. Many of the early immigrants to Latin America were drawn from sectors of world Jewry that were already partially assimilated to the gentile world. Such was the case with the French, German, and Alsatian Jews of the 1870s and 1880s. Entering the profoundly Catholic environments in Mexico and Chile, they apparently viewed the founding of synagogues as a needless provocation.

Many East European Jews were more observant of religious practices, but here, too, the haskalah had made headway. The East European migration occurred at a time when religious and antireligious factions had the shtetl in turmoil. Even those who had been traditionalists at home were likely to discard many elements of ritual when they landed in the New World—indeed, escape from tradition was one force that propelled their emigration. Secularism was fortified by the intellectual atmosphere of the metropolitan centers of Argentina, Brazil, and Uruguay, where routinism had eroded the religious passions of the urban masses. As long as they were not forced into a defensive reaction by an overbearing church presence, many Jewish immigrants were content to adopt a secular orientation. Perhaps relieved at finding Catholic influence so nominal, they saw no need to agitate the religious question and generally remained apathetic toward it.

This is not to deny the existence of a religious impulse among any Jewish immigrants to Latin America. The East Europeans who settled the Entre Ríos agricultural colonies were observant; in their isolation, religious traditions continued of their own momentum until attenuated by time and the passing of the immigrant generation that had included religious personnel. But secularism and depopulation of the colonies determined the outcome: by 1959, there was no rabbi, circumciser, or ritual slaughterer in the entire province of Entre Ríos.[12]

Sephardim are better known for their faithful attachment to organized religion, usually associated with a traditional style of family life. Congregação Porta do Céu (Gates of Heaven) was founded by Sephardim from Africa, Syria, and Arabia in Belém do Pará at the turn of the century. There were four congregations of Syrian Jews in Mexico City in 1905, while the Alsatians still declined to declare themselves publicly. At the other end of the time scale, German Jews entering São Paulo just prior to World War II made it their first order of business to found their own synagogue, Congregação Israelita Paulista. The instantaneous adoption of a Portuguese rather than a Hebrew name conforms to the haskalah orientation of this group, for whom Judaism had become only a religion, not an ethnic identity.

There have been instances of an astonishing persistence of religious belief and practice. In Montevideo, communists supported their own cemetery and their own ritual slaughterer, who provided *linke shekhitah* (leftist ritual slaughter). And in São Paulo a religious congregation was formed by aged Jewish prostitutes, remnants of the white slave trade, and their offspring. (Known participants in the trade were not admitted to mainline congregations.) Other groups were more interested in merging with the majority populations than in establishing Jewish houses of worship.

Another circumstance that delayed the founding of synagogues was that observance of the Jewish religion does not depend upon an institutional structure; the presence of ten adult men (a minyan) is a sufficient condition for holding a religious service. This prayer unit can be brought together on an ad hoc basis to celebrate weddings and circumcisions, memorialize the dead, or observe the holidays, without any special framework. Indeed, the presence of a rabbi is not required. Therefore, in the early days when immigrants were few and far between and no sense of community united them, efforts to generate community participation were made only in times of personal crisis or during the High Holy Days (Rosh Hashanah and Yom Kippur, which occur in September or October). Thus we find the first minyan in Santiago gathering in a private home in 1906 to celebrate Rosh Hashanah. The following year, it was necessary to have a Jewish policeman released from duty in order to complete a quorum. The incident confirms a generalized lack of concern for religious as opposed to cultural activities: at the founding of the Sociedad Unión Israelita de Chile the year before, eighty-seven persons signed the charter; and two years later, fifty-four persons signed the charter of the Jewish social club Filarmónica Rusa.[13]

Overt organization of Jewish religious life in Mexico had to await the revolution of 1910, and then it occurred within an anticlerical context. The Constitution of 1917 vested ownership of churches and church property in the nation (Article 27); religious institutions could possess no juridical personality, and only persons born in Mexico might serve as priests or ministers of religion (Article 130). These individuals were deprived of political rights. The strictest enforcement of these constitutional provisions occurred during the presidency of Plutarco Calles (1924–29), whose administration coincided with the greatest influx of Jewish immigrants. These, coming to Mexico with an anti-Catholic perspective, would have been attracted at first to the radical anti-Catholic policies of Calles. At the same time, the very elements of that policy that non-Catholic settlers found attractive also operated to impede the organization of Jewish community life. There was, for example, no such thing as a native-born Jew (at least, none who spoke Yiddish) and therefore no possibility of recruiting a rabbi to serve Ashkenazic congregations. Measures taken by the Mexican government to decrease popular fanaticism were equally effective in blocking transmission of the Jewish heritage. In an environment that remained ineradicably Catholic, if unchurched, Jewish children would inevitably cease to be Jewish. In this situation lay the motivation for the formation of religious congregations by persons who were not religious. Secularism in Mexico did not block the establishment of synagogues as much as it permeated them, turning the synagogues into further expressions of Jewish secularism. The numerically small Mexican Jewish community divided itself into seven mutually exclusive sectors, each representing a different national origin and each barricaded behind the impenetrable fortress of its ancestral language. Alianza Monte Sinai, uniting Arabic-speaking Sephardim from Damascus, was the earliest congregation to be founded, in 1912. The later-arriving Yiddish-speaking Ashkenazim from Russia, Poland, and Lithuania originally worshiped together with the Sephardim, but a dispute over the proper reading of the Megillah of Esther (possibly fueled by the religious injunction to celebrate Purim by drinking a surfeit of wine) resulted in the founding of Nidje Israel in 1922. Two years later, Union Sefaradi came into existence, grouping Ladino-speaking Sephardim from Turkey, Greece, the Balkans, and Italy. Tsedaka U'marpe was founded by Arabic-speaking Sephardim from Aleppo in 1930. One hundred fifteen German-speaking Ashkenazic families from Germany, Austria, and Czechoslovakia founded Hatikva-Menora in 1939, Hungarian Jews founded Emuna in 1942, and English-speaking Jews (largely from the United States) founded the Beth Israel Community Center in 1953.[14] The range of countries of origin mentioned here clarifies the reasons separate congregations were desired: language, religious ritual, even dietary customs differed among these ethnic groups, and each felt more comfortable in a congregation that spoke their language. For the Americans, secularism was expressed more overtly by the formation of a community center rather than a house of worship.

As time passed and the immigrant generation passed on, first the German and the Hungarian congregations melted away, and then the historically distanced Damascene and Aleppine communities began to cooperate with one another. With the growth of religious identification occurring among United States Jews, the "American" community center evolved into a religious congregation. By 1994, all the ethnic communities were able to cooperate with the three major Mexican universities and the association for friends of Tel Aviv University in sponsoring a major research conference on Latin American Jewry.

The Jewish community of Buenos Aires is similarly characterized by a multitude of religious congregations based on ethnic origin. In 1954, a survey of Buenos Aires synagogues located from eighty to one hundred synagogues.[15] Two years later, another observer identified twelve Russian, five Romanian, fourteen Polish, two Galician, and five German congregations. He viewed these as being "geared to preserve particularist trends in Judaism rather than preserve Jewish life as a whole."[16] Old customs fade slowly: *Comunidades Judías* for 1971–72 claimed "about 50" synagogues for Buenos Aires, fewer than half of which had rabbis. At the same time, a North American rabbi serving a Buenos Aires congregation called Latin American Jewish life "the most secularized in the West."[17]

Compartmentalization by ethnic origin is the rule: the thousand Jews of La Paz formed three synagogues, one East European and two predominantly German. Guatemala City, with an estimated thirteen hundred Jews or less, likewise had three synagogues, Ashkenazi, German, and Sephardi—this in a population that is so secularized that it does not produce rabbinical students. Religious congregations seem to be part of a search for identity, rather than specifically religious institutions. The existence of a synagogue does not imply the presence of worshipers. "Santiago," commented one respondent, "has five synagogues and no minyan." Nor does the existence of a minyan imply the presence of a rabbi. The shortage of rabbis and other religious personnel mirrored the shortage of priests in the same area. At one point, the Rothschild Foundation imported a rabbi to provide religious services to the Jews of Entre Ríos and Santa Fe. In 1970, only forty-five rabbis were officiating on the entire continent. Many of these were elderly persons trained in a Europe that no longer existed. Others were Ladino-speaking Sephardim from vanished communities of North Africa. The Brazilian congregations were in a peculiarly difficult position inasmuch as there is no worldwide reservoir of Portuguese-speaking Jews from which their rabbis might be drawn.

The rabbis who came with the nineteenth-century immigration represented the Orthodox tradition. Congregación Kol Shearith Israel in Panama City was alone in retaining a rabbi of Reform tendencies. But neither Reform, nor the Conservative movement that attempts to bridge the two, made an impact on Latin America until the twilight years 1938–39. São Paulo's Congregação Israelita Paulista adopted Reform from the start and, in the 1970s, employed a North American Reform rabbi, Henry Sobel, who continues to occupy that position. Rio de Janeiro's Associação Religiosa Israelita, which stems from the same German migration, also adopted Reform and in the 1980s employed as rabbi a U.S.-trained Argentine, Roberto Graetz. When these congregations formed, movements for modernization of the Jewish religion had been well established in Europe and North America for over a hundred years. But despite some openings toward change, it would be fair to say that Jewish expectations of reform within the Catholic Church in conformance with decisions of Vatican II (the *aggiornamento,* or updating of teachings relating to the Jews) were not until recently matched by efforts toward reform within Judaism.

In the sixties and seventies, it appeared that Judaism might well die out on the southern continent. A 1966 survey of Jewish university youth in São Paulo revealed a strong tendency to abandon the patterns of traditional Judaism. Only 45 percent of a sample of Jewish students declared a belief in God, while 38 percent declared themselves to be atheists and 17 percent undecided. Synagogue attendance every Saturday was reported by only 4 percent of Jewish youth. Of all those who attended synagogue either occasionally or frequently, only 31 percent stated that they actually prayed; 66 percent declared they did not know how; and 3 percent that they knew how but were not motivated to pray. "In face of such results, it is inevitable to conclude that the young Jewish university student is abandoning religion. . . . [He] is not antireligious but simply unreligious. . . . His abandoning of religion does not occur due to an ideology contrary to religion, but simply due to indifference."[18] Nowhere did native sons come forward in any number to train for the rabbinate and spiritual leadership of their communities.

A start toward Jewish *aggiornamento* was made in 1954, when the few Conservative synagogues on the southern continent affiliated with the Conservative movement in the United States. This was followed a decade later by formation of a Seminario Rabínico in Buenos Aires under the leadership of Rabbi Marshall Meyer, a New England Yankee. The Seminario quickly began to fill the need for Spanish-speaking religious personnel educated in both religious and secular modes (seminary students also matriculate at a university). The Seminario opened a day school (elementary through high school), adult education courses, a teacher-training program, and the best library of Judaica and Hebraica on the continent and arranged for the translation of numerous religious works, including prayer books, from Hebrew into Spanish.[19]

The development of modern alternatives in Jewish spirituality has an importance beyond cultic competition. The early generations of Orthodox rabbis imported from abroad (England, Russia, Syria) regarded themselves as guardians of religious purity. They, and the ultra-Orthodox congregations over which they presided, resisted innovations such as the introduction of Spanish/Portuguese into the service, or the mixed-sex seating of men and women, and thereby forfeited the allegiance of generations of Jewish youth, who felt increasingly alienated from the only Judaism they knew. A particular barrier was the prohibition of conversion to Judaism in Argentina, even if proper Orthodox procedure were followed, instituted in the 1920s by both Sephardic and Ashkenazic rabbis. This prohibition, intended as a bar to intermarriage with non-Jews, became an impediment to the formation of Jewish families through conversion of the non-Jewish partner. The ban remained in force until the 1960s.[20]

The Seminario reversed the obsolescence of Jewish tradition as practiced in Latin America by training a generation of young women and men to assume leadership roles in their communities. Rabbi Meyer also instituted a conversion process similar to that available in the United States, thereby encouraging the formation of new Jewish families, and incidentally provoking the Orthodox to break with tradition and accept voluntary converts also. Without considering the respective merits of Orthodox and Conservative interpretations of Judaism, it is apparent to the observer that attendance at Orthodox synagogues is sparse and consists largely of old men, while the Conservative synagogues fill with large numbers of young married couples and their children. It is not uncommon to see boys and girls small enough to be seated two to a chair leading the congregation in prayer. Conservative and Reform congregations have also attracted adolescents, the age group most difficult to reach, a phenomenon observed by the author in Argentina, Mexico, and Cuba.

Education

The absorption of immigrants into Latin American societies was retarded by the absence of that most effective of acculturating institutions, the tax-supported public school. Whatever may have been the verbal dedication of successive governments to the cause of universal education, many areas of the *interior*—an evocative word—remained without schools during the nineteenth century. Pleas by educators that governments take cognizance of the poor and train their sons for productive labor—that they "colonize the country with its own inhabitants"—went unheeded. Education in Latin America was confined to a relative few and retained an elitist bias inherited from colonial days.

There is, by contrast, almost universal literacy among Jews. Entering Latin American societies at a very low socioeconomic level, their initial contact was with unschooled gauchos and campesinos, the "broken" men in transition from countryside to city, illiterate denizens of *villas miserias*. Confronted by the prodigious gap between themselves and the people they met, Jews worried lest their own children adopt a culture whose manifestations they regarded as inferior to their own. They had come to a new world to give their children a better chance in life than they had had, not to watch them sink to a level where they would remain marginal to society. The small, educated criollo elite comprised a sophisticated haute monde with which immigrants were most unlikely to come in contact. The schools they had created for their children were deemed untenable by Jewish families, for Catholic norms prevailed even where lay control had been established. Jewish parents dreaded having their children cast in the role of deicides. Even worse was the possibility that school would turn their children into their worst enemies. Interviews with Jewish families living in the Cuban countryside in 1933, published in *Havaner Lebn,* the Yiddish-language newspaper, shed light on the situation of immigrants living in isolation well into the twentieth century.

> "This Jewish family seized upon the visitor from Havana to ask about the availability of Jewish education in the capital. They are prepared to sacrifice everything in order to move their daughter out of her present ambience. Her friends attend a convent school, but tell this child she cannot go there because her parents killed Christ. Naturally, she cannot be allowed to become Christ's bride, as they shall all be. The daughter has begun to call her parents *judío* in the common pejorative way. And these parents—who are not even religious!—find the traditional hatreds imposed upon their child, turning her into their enemy."[21]

The need to provide education for Jewish children in a mode that would not traumatize families was the principal reason for the formation of Jewish communities, as contrasted to the settlement of individual families. Schools were needed in areas where existing schools were private and Catholic, admitting non-Catholic children either capriciously or not at all; these often purveyed an education that was unacceptable to Jewish parents. Schools were needed to provide basic education in areas where private and public schools were simply nonexistent.

The creation of schools was fundamental to the creation of Jewish communities because a critical mass of parents was required to start a school, which, once started, attracted to itself children from other families. Once brought together for a common cause, parents found other communal needs that could be satisfied through organized effort. Daniel Levy has brought attention to two parameters of Jewish educational autonomy. The first is the degree of freedom allowed by state and corporate bodies to create private schools. The second is the balance to be struck between maintaining Jewish identity (however defined) and enabling students to take their place within national societies.[22] To these, a third parameter may be added: which ideology was to control instruction?

Ladino speakers typically enrolled their children in existing state or private schools on arrival and arranged supplemental instruction for boys in sufficient Hebrew to enable them to say their prayers. German Jews arriving in the 1930s followed a similar course, having already accepted the idea of translating their lives into the language of the land. Furthermore, by the time they arrived, most nations had expanded and improved their school systems, particularly in locations favored by this migration, the urban areas of Brazil and Chile.

The problem of education was most intractable for East Europeans. There were few secular school systems in the years of heaviest Ashkenazic immigration; these immigrants did not know Spanish or Portuguese; they were unfamiliar with Catholic institutions and deeply fearful of them; and many were endowed with a strong sense of Jewish peoplehood that stimulated the desire to ensure Jewish survival in this alien environment. It was almost always the East Europeans who took the initiative in founding "integral" schools—all-day schools integrating secular and religious curricula. The trend to an integral education was also fortified by governments that legislated a Catholic curriculum. This was the case in Colombia and Peru, and also for a time in Argentina.

The need for schools became apparent immediately in the colonies of the Jewish Colonization Association. Despite the avowed desire of the Argentine government to provide free universal education, there were no government schools in the villages near which the colonies were situated. The original settlers, Yiddish-speaking Ashkenazim, if left to themselves, would probably have reconstructed the *heder* and *talmud torah* schools with which they were familiar (a system of combined religious and secular study, carried on in the Yiddish language and with emphasis on the teaching of Hebrew for the purpose of prayer). The JCA administrators, as we have seen, regarded themselves as emancipators who wanted to hasten in all possible ways the assimilation of the settlers into the Argentine countryside. When the colonists demanded schools, JCA set these up on the model of schools then being run by the Alliance Universelle Israelite in the Middle East and staffed by Spanish-speaking North Africans. Relations between teachers and parents were strained by their cultural differences, each group being firmly attached to its own version of Judaism. After considerable agitation, the colonists, who during the 1920s were footing an increasing percentage of the costs, acquired control over the curriculum, which reverted to a more Ashkenazic cast.

In 1904, the government of the province of Entre Ríos sent an inspector to visit the JCA schools. He found 850 children attending sixteen different schools,[23] supported with an annual budget of 33,200 pesos. The Argentine curriculum was being taught in Spanish, with courses in the "3 Rs," calligraphy, geography, history, and singing. The inspector applied to the children the Lockean stamp of approval: *mens sana in corpore sano*. "From the beginning," he added, "they learn three languages: Spanish, Hebrew, and their jargon" (Yiddish).[24] Nevertheless, it was these schools that in 1908 attracted the hostile attention of Argentine jingoes, who charged that they were un-Argentine in character and staffed by foreigners who despised Argentina.

The attacks were based on a report by the former director general of education in Entre Ríos, who had never visited the schools himself. They were given intellectual respectability by the Argentine intellectual Ricardo Rojas, who used the report to bolster his attack on the nation's liberal immigration policy in his 1909 book *La restauración nacionalista*.[25] Such charges continued to be launched over the years as part of the campaign to discredit immigration. But the idea that JCA schools were impeding the acculturation of Jewish children could have been refuted by reading the reports emanating from Jewish educators. It was clear from the start that the children would not learn Yiddish, the principal storehouse of immigrant culture. The atrophying of this language has now been documented by surveys conducted in the 1950s among Jews living in cities of the Argentine interior, who were largely descendants of settlers in the JCA colonies. At that date, Spanish had already become the universal language of the Argentine-born. Yiddish-speaking parents who used both languages when talking to their grown children used only Spanish with younger ones. In almost all cases, children who reported speaking Yiddish with their parents spoke Spanish with their siblings.[26] The general attractiveness of the Argentine landscape, the comparative malleability of society in face of the massive onslaught of immigrants, and the natural desire of second-generation immigrant children to be accepted by society at large were quite enough to start Jewish children speaking Spanish, even in the absence of state-supported schools. Yiddish-language instruction persisted much longer in the capital, however. The last Yiddish-based school in Buenos Aires, the Sholom Aleijem, closed its doors only in 1995. Thus a reservoir of speakers of elegant Yiddish survives in Argentina today. The editing and publication of a library of one hundred masterworks of Yiddish literature, *Musterverk fun der Idisher Literatur,* represented a major Argentine contribution to the world of letters.

Schools were also needed to transmit the Jewish religion. Sometimes these schools were handmade artifacts, as exemplified by a memoir from Mexico City.

> In the summer of 1923 a group of immigrants arrived, mostly from France, and among them were many orphans of school age. With the help of some acquaintances, I interested myself in them. Up on the roof, under an all-embracing sun, I cut a stencil, and then in a few hours a packet of circulars emerged from the mimeograph machine. The children divided them up for delivery to "the masses," inviting them to a meeting. The results justified the labor, because we then founded the first Talmud Torah (religious school), where I became the teacher.[27]

Ultimately, the Jewish school system of Mexico came to be regarded as the finest in the diaspora. The conditions for its creation were similar to those surrounding formation of the JCA schools in that an educational void existed at the time of the immigrants' arrival. Mexico had disestablished the church and prohibited clerical personnel from teaching. But the state did not suddenly develop the capacity to provide schooling for all children. Therefore, the various national groups in the federal district (Spaniards, French, Germans, and others) were encouraged to start their own schools. The Yiddishe Shule, or Colegio Israelita, was founded in 1924, the first year of large-scale Ashkenazic immigration. In keeping both with official Mexican secularism and with the worldly orientation of these immigrants, the Shule followed a secular curriculum. Families of the original twenty-six students "represented all ideological tendencies," a situation that, the essayist remarks, "could not last long."[28] An ideological struggle among Zionists, Communists, socialists, and dissident factions among these major tendencies smoldered within the school for years, ending with the exodus of the nonconforming groups. Ultimately, ten separate schools were established. In 1955, these schools enrolled a total of 3,200 children, and 84 percent of them were being taught in Yiddish. Fifteen years later, Jewish schools enrolled more children—5,475—but these represented a smaller percentage of the now larger Jewish population of the capital city. Only 10 percent of these were receiving instruction in Yiddish.[29] The decline of Yiddish as the medium of instruction cleared the way for Spanish and renewed encounter with the Sephardim. Its substitution by modern Hebrew, language of the State of Israel, signaled the victory of Zionism over other ideological factions and the relegation of diaspora culture to a past which many Zionists regarded as unworthy of the reborn Jewish people.[30]

The substitution of Spanish or Portuguese for other vernaculars is the dominant trend among the descendants of Jewish immigrants all over Latin America, as illustrated by a 1950s survey of the Jews of Valparaíso, Chile. Two-thirds of children under age eighteen reported knowing no Yiddish at all, a proportion that rose to 90 percent for children both of whose parents were born in Latin America.[31] A more recent survey of language spoken in the home among Jews of São Paulo showed an even more rapid adaptation. Fifty-eight percent of respondents gave Portuguese as their main language, while 33 percent named it as their second; Yiddish placed next, with 15 percent listing it first and 27 percent second.[32]

Following formation of the State of Israel, Yiddish was replaced by Hebrew in most Jewish schools, and Israel became the preferred locus for teacher training. Financial subsidies for Latin American schools were allocated by the World Zionist Organization and the Jewish Agency. Zionism conquered the schools on the way to conquering the communities as a whole. Leftist ideologies and the Yiddish schools, which sometimes were their vehicles, were discredited by Soviet anti-Semitism and decayed.

A correlation exists between the quality of national schools and the attractiveness of Jewish schools. The association was not often made by Jewish educators, who tended to attribute lagging enrollment to some moral failing in their pupils. But the fact of the matter is that these schools, founded at a time when there was an educational vacuum, no longer seemed so vital once that vacuum was filled. The test of this hypothesis lies in a comparison between

Jewish school systems in secularized societies with Jewish school systems in republics where the church has retained a controlling interest.

In relatively secularized Argentina, Jewish education has been the subject of a century of expenditure of funds and effort. Over the course of time, a central education committee succeeded in unifying school governance over a wide range of schools that differed in ideology and language of instruction. Eventually, leaders in the schools movement "captured" the leadership of the organized Jewish community as a whole, thus assuring the schools their financial support.[33] Yet, in the 1960s, fewer than 20 percent of Argentine-born Jews had received any Jewish education at all, and that mostly on a part-time basis. Interestingly, the proportion of Jewish children enrolled in Jewish schools tended to rise from one-half of children eligible for nursery school to a majority of first graders. Thereafter, there was a steady and unrelenting erosion of enrollment until completion of the secondary cycle: for 1,885 children entering first grade, only 126 graduated the twelfth, or 1 in 15.[34] These children were not leaving the educational process altogether, but transferring to government or other private schools.

As Jewish families entered the middle class, they shifted their children from communal schools at the elementary and secondary levels to prestigious secular schools in the private sector, most especially, those that are oriented to the United States. Increasingly, Mexican Jews enroll their children in the more prestigious private schools, especially those where English is the language of instruction. The majority of Jewish youth of São Paulo who are of ginásio or colegio age attend the great private schools of the city, those attended by the sons and daughters of the elite. There they not only learn their academic subjects but also make the professional and social contacts that will be invaluable to them in later life. The Jewish school, no matter how good academically—and some are very good indeed—cannot provide what is most desired: entry into general society and upward mobility within it.

In the 1970s and 1980s, primary enrollment fluctuated, with a steady diminution from 1983 to 1989; but secondary school enrollment in Buenos Aires nearly doubled, from 2,613 to 5,071 pupils.[35] While the educational researcher makes no attempt to correlate Jewish school enrollment with state policy, it is suggestive that enrollment of teenagers increased during the years of military repression when parents made great efforts to shelter their children from involvement in the civil war that gripped Argentina. According to another report, in the 1980s, 63 percent of Jewish children in Argentina aged three to seventeen attended Jewish educational institutions, most of them all-day schools.[36]

In Chile, where overtly secular norms prevail, fewer than 25 percent of Jewish children were reported to be attending Jewish schools of any kind in the early 1970s. Chilean Jews credit this fact to the high degree of acceptance their children find in national and private schools. For many years, Chile was the only country in Latin America, apart from Panama, where a Jew could legally become president. Lack of a religious bar to office is not unrelated to a secular educational system that accommodates Jews, making a parochial school system irrelevant. The story from another secular, industrializing country, Brazil, is interesting. Matriculation figures for Jewish integral schools in 1969 showed 50 percent of Jewish children enrolled in preprimary, kindergarten, and primary; 38.5 percent at the ginásio level; and 9 percent at the level of the colegio.[37] Jewish schools were funneling their students into the national schools of the republic. Twenty years later, 10,000 out of 22,000 Jewish children aged 3 to 18 attended Jewish schools, almost all of them all day. Most of those who did not attend Jewish schools were enrolled in other private schools.[38] Figures are lacking to indicate whether a similar pattern of increased enrollment in Jewish schools developed in Chile.

The situation in republics where the school system is dominated by the church is distinct. Peru's Jewish school system has continually enrolled 90 percent of Jewish school-age children in Lima.[39] In Colombia in the 1970s, where a Concordat governed relations between church and state, an overwhelming majority of Jewish children were enrolled in Jewish integral schools: 92 percent in Cali, 84 percent in Medellín, 68 percent in Barranquilla (in the latter city, Sephardim did not join the day-school movement).[40] Research has also established a direct relationship between the size of a Jewish community and the number of schools it maintains. Small communities overcome ideological and ethnic differences to support a single system. Once communities attain 30,000–40,000 members, these differences display themselves in a full range of schools that reflect the ideology or ethnic origins of their founders.[41]

The names of schools provide an interesting indication of their orientation. Schools using Yiddish as the language of instruction adopted the names of authors who wrote in that language, such as Sholom Aleichem, C. N. Bialik, or Y. L. Peretz. Zionist-oriented schools chose the names of Israel's national leaders such as Chaim Weizmann. The Cali school bears an ambiguous identity. It is named for Jorge Isaacs, a native son and author of *María*, an early Spanish American novel that was adopted into the literary canon. Isaac's father was a British Jew from Jamaica but his mother was Catholic, so technically the author was not Jewish under prevailing standards, though he is popularly regarded as such. Western Europeans seem to prefer the name of Max Nordau, a westernized Jew, while the Lima school is named for a converso whose grandfather was burned at the stake. The ambiguity of the identification that Jewish children of Lima are daily asked to make at Colegio León Pinelo is apparent. The Jewish colegio in Havana, nationalized by the government in 1961, underwent a name change from Theodor Herzl, the founder of political Zionism, to Albert Einstein. The world-famous scientist remained acceptable to Fidel Castro when his government broke relations with Israel, the state that grew out of Herzl's vision.

The controlling factor in the success of Jewish schools seems not to be the amount of effort and funds expended by parents or the moral fiber of their children, but rather the extent to which secular educational options exist. The highest enrollments in Jewish schools are to be found in small Jewish communities situated in countries where church and state are united or incompletely separated and that do not have large immigrant components in their populations (Peru, Colombia, even Mexico). In relatively secularized societies with large immigrant populations (Argentina, Chile, Brazil), the proportion of Jewish children enrolled in Jewish schools is low despite the expenditure of prodigious effort and substantial funds for the maintenance of communal schools. It is no exaggeration to say that the determining factor in success or failure of Jewish schools to retain their students has been the degree to which Jewish children have been able to attend national or private schools without undergoing protracted psychological trauma. It is in that light that we can regard Levy's calculation that, although Latin America's 65,050 children aged 6 to 17 years are only 5 percent of the total diaspora population of that age (excluding the former Soviet Union), they account for 18 percent of total day school enrollments. Furthermore, while an average 13 percent of children in the global diaspora are in day schools (as opposed to supplemental instruction), fully half the Latin American cohort are in day schools.[42] Generally regarded as a triumph for Jewish education, the figures may also be an index of the viability of national schools for Jewish children.

The Catholic Church and its enforcers in the military emerge as prime delimiters of Jewish identity. Restricted opportunity for Jews in ecclesiastically dominated societies results in the formation of protected reserves, within which Jewish parents attempt to preserve the dignity and identity of their children. Conversely, where society is relatively open, Jewish children enter the national educational mainstream as soon as they are old enough to vote with their feet and despite great efforts by their elders to slow them down. There is no evidence whatever that Jewish schools obstruct the acculturation of immigrants, as it was feared they would. To the contrary, Jewish educators despair that the schools have failed to forge a functional Jewish identity among second- and third-generation Latin American Jews, leading to considerable angst over the future of Jewry on the continent.

The real success of the Jewish educational system has been its record of integrating Jewish children into the mainstream of society. Jewish schools provided basic education at the elementary and colegio levels at times and in settings where governments failed to fulfill this function. Thus they enabled Jewish youths to qualify for admittance to the national universities, nearly all of which are open to applicants on the basis of merit. As the economic situation changed, the schools changed, too. In the 1990s, the opening of new technical training schools in Argentina and Chile provided a type of education not available from public institutions. ORT technical high school in Buenos Aires has a state-of-the-art electronics lab and offers its 2,000 students courses in industrial design, communications, computerized business administration, and photography.[43] Education has been the great escalator, lifting the children of immigrants into the professionally trained middle and upper strata of their national societies.

Institutionalizing Ethnicity

A pattern of intra-Jewish discord emerged as soon as Jews of different prove-
nance came in contact with one another.[44] The rivalry between Lithuanians
and Galicians, which is no more than a source of humor among North American
Jews, was set in concrete in the Latin American communities by their founding
separate institutions. The Russians, who claim to speak better Yiddish than
either, are patronizing of them both; all share a passionate dislike of Germans,
who "aren't even Jews."[45] For their part, Germans have a tendency to believe
all Jews would be better off if the East Europeans were just not so Jewish. Ethnic
rivalry permeates the Sephardic as well as the Ashkenazic camp. Antagonism
between Jews of Aleppo and of Damascus, rooted in Middle Eastern history,
prompted these groups to organize separately following their emigration to the
New World. Ladino-speaking Jews, who regard themselves as inhabiting a more
rarefied cultural plane than Arabic speakers, did not organize jointly with them,
though Ashkenazim lump them all together as Sephardim. So long as each group
insisted upon each jot and tittle of its religious liturgy, separate synagogues were
required. Despite prolonged negotiations, Sephardim and Ashkenazim often
could not agree to bury their dead in the same cemetery. The Yiddish-language
schools, pride of the Ashkenazim, by their nature excluded Sephardim. The
very active Yiddish literary world met no more appreciation among Spanish
Jews than among Spanish Catholics. Sephardim, with their roots in the Ottoman
Empire, refrained at first from supporting the Zionist movement, which they
perceived as an Ashkenazic enterprise that threatened the status of their relatives still living under Turkish rule. This attitude changed slowly over the years,
especially following the Six Day War in 1967, which caused an upwelling of
Jewish pride all over the world. Though diversity can be a source of strength,
one suspects that in the formative years of these communities, interethnic
hostility sapped the vitality of Jewish life.

A perceptive observer has explained ethnic antagonisms among Jews in the
following way:

> The difficulties of assimilation to the customs and language of the new
> home were already so great that it was unnecessary to create other
> problems in order to live with Jews who originated from different
> countries. Also, the Jewish immigrant from a Mediterranean country
> was as little familiar to the immigrant Jew of Western Europe as to other
> non-Jewish citizens of Brazil. Many factors contributed to the isolation
> of each group, among which [was]—why not say it?—prejudice.[46]

A secular nationalizing ideology might have absorbed the devotional energies of Jewish immigrants, overcoming their parochial loyalties. But during the
years of heaviest immigration, the Latin American republics failed to develop
an ideology capable of embracing non-Catholic immigrants. The most all-
embracing institution of the republics remained the Catholic Church. Immigrants who were Catholic could be received into it with relative ease, thus

relieving the trauma of the migratory process. For Jews, identification with the church was impossible. Thus many immigrants emphasized their Jewish tradition in order to provide themselves with needed social and psychological support and to provide their children with an identity capable of sustaining them in a milieu that was felt to be fundamentally hostile to them. This Jewish tradition, or better, these Jewish traditions, were then further narrowed to Russian-, Syrian-, Moroccan-Jewish and so on, because it was the only way that individuals knew to be Jewish. In re-creating the lifestyles they brought from home, they inadvertently walled themselves off from coreligionists whose customs differed from their own. These barriers endured in the absence of national traditions with which the immigrants could identify.

In all of this, one feels that a great opportunity was somehow missed. As the editor of *La Luz* put it in 1960: "Argentina was a new world for Sephardim: it returned us to the Spanish-speaking world, and at the same time brought us once more into contact with Ashkenazim."[47] Jewish migration to Latin America presented the possibility of a reunion between these two branches of the Jewish people who had lived apart for centuries. For some, it opened the vista of reunion with the Spanish world, abandoned in such sorrow 450 years earlier, and the dawn of a neo-Sephardic renaissance. This reunion did not occur, whether for lack of vision, overly rigid attachment to tradition, failure of nerve, or lack of leadership. The cultural affinities of Sephardim to the Latin American ambience were not utilized to ease the entry of Jews as a group into the matrix society. It took the shock of the Holocaust, the pride in achievement of a Jewish state, and the passing of the immigrant generation, to bring Latin American Jews to acceptance of a vision of themselves simply as Jews, without Old World modifiers. In the last third of the twentieth century, inherited national and linguistic barriers were wearing thin. The native-born generations were uninterested in the Old World quarrels that had divided their parents and grandparents, and were willing to unify their institutions, a reordering that was warranted in any case by the financial stress caused by dwindling membership in the old landsmannschaften. Easing of Ashkenazic/Sephardi relations has been signaled by increased cooperation at the organizational level and the election of officers across ethnic lines. In the mid-1990s, Ruben Baraja was elected president of the DAIA. Presumably, Baraja and Carlos Saúl Menem, president of Argentina, were able to find mutual ground in their common origins in Syria.

The Kehillah

All these institutions and activities—and more—are brought together in the kehillah, which evolved as the heart of each Latin American Jewish community. No precise English word exists to describe this institution; for that reason, the Hebrew term is employed here. The schools, sports clubs, synagogues, libraries, youth groups, social service agencies, and landsmannschaften described in this chapter eventually united under the kehillah umbrella in exchange for financial support and representation on its governing board. Social welfare agencies, and in some cases, the Jewish schools, became functions of the kehillah itself. The precise arrangements by which these varied activities were brought into coordination with one another vary with each community's particular history; but over the years, communities have become more and more centralized, and more and more financially dependent on their governing body. The principal source of funding—especially since the collapse of the credit unions—has been cemetery fees. However, in recent years, the contribution of various Israeli ministries to the Jewish educational effort has become preponderant.

The kehillah has a long history, predating Jewish settlement in Latin America. Until the nineteenth century, European, Near Eastern and African governments mandated the creation of kehillot, using them as a mechanism for imposing taxes on Jews collectively, to draft a quota of men for the army, and in general to deal with Jews as a discrete caste. In modern times, following the emancipation of the Jews, kehillot survive as voluntary associations because they supply needed services to their members. The kehillah as an institution exists in one form or another in most lands of the diaspora, adapting to local political conditions; in the United States, they are known as Jewish Welfare Boards or Jewish Community Councils. No American kehillah ever achieved the centrality or the universal membership of its historical prototype, because all are voluntary associations rather than impositions of government. However, they generally assume the role of principal spokesmen of their respective communities. As voluntary organizations, their importance, their relevance to Jews, and the political clout they wield on the national scene depend on what else is going on nationwide. For that reason, it is useful to trace the trajectory of some of these kehillot, and the obstacles they faced in achieving unity.

In the case of Mexico, as we have seen, ethnic and linguistic differences led to extreme fragmentation of community life.[48] In 1938, events in Europe impelled these communities to form a representative body in support of refugees and in order to represent Jewish interests before the Mexican government. Intended also to open channels of communication among the different ethnic communities of Jews, the Comité Central de la Comunidad Judía de México, as it was ultimately called, attracted 63 Jewish organizations by 1952. Ten of these were religious, nine communal, eight cultural, ten charitable, ten Zionist, ten juvenile, and six functional, such as the sports club and the communal newspaper. The Comité's board of directors was proportionally divided by ethnic group among sixteen Yiddish speakers (a majority), five Ladino speakers, three German Jews, two Hungarians, and two Sephardim from Damascus and two from Aleppo.[49] Ideologically viewed, Zionists were in the majority, with "progressives" proportionately represented.

At that date, Nidje Israel, the congregation of the Russians and Poles, was trying to convert itself into a kehillah, an effort that was being resisted by the other sectors. Like the others, it had already established a panoply of social services. Within the next few years, the Nidje Israel group was successful in forming a kehillah; Sephardim then formed their own. Ultimately, Mexico

City had no fewer than seven kehillot, each with its own schools, religious congregations, cultural activities, social welfare agencies, home for the aged, and ancillary financial and administrative services. In this situation, the kehillah, an organization that was intended to unify Jews, became instead a bulwark of disunion, fortifying the differences that separated Jews from one another. Only in the last decade of the twentieth century did the passage of time resolve some of these differences. With the aging of the immigrant generation, the smaller kehillot disappeared entirely and ancestral quarrels receded into the distance. The 1995 sample survey of Jewish Mexicans found that 34.5 percent identify as Ashkenazi, 26.5 percent as Sephardi, 3.2 percent as Hallebi (stemming from Aleppo), and 2.6 percent as Shami (stemming from Damascus). Those identifying as both Ashkenazi and Sephardi equaled 2.2 percent of the sample, while "simply Jewish" scored a resounding 29.7 percent.[50] The Comité Central now asserts greater importance, especially in managing the communities' relations with the government and the general public. It remains to be seen whether the Comité or any other body can achieve the flexibility that will be required effectively to convert itself into the sole kehillah for Mexico City.

Another obstacle to unity has been the diversity of political opinion. The intersection of ideological with ethnic fault lines created a complex field of (bloodless) battles, which often took place within the precincts of the Jewish schools.

> During the 1940s, Mexico City's Jewish schools became an ideological battlefield, the site for waging political warfare among the city's diverse Ashkenazi community. What began as a struggle to emphasize Zionist ideology in the ethnic school curriculum escalated into a fight to establish an ideological hegemony over the entire community's cultural and political life. By the end of this decade of conflict, Zionists had gained dominance over the community's largest school, giving them a strategic platform from which to promote their ethnic agenda and, at the same time, to diminish the effectiveness of other competing visions of diaspora Jewish identity—on occasion even excluding those they found too far out of line.[51]

Ideological disputes within Jewish institutions often reflect the class divisions that exist among Jews. At least 20 percent of the East European Jews who emigrated to Uruguay were factory workers and artisans who brought with them a working-class consciousness formed in Europe. Once in Uruguay, they continued to identify as socialists, Bundists, anarchists, social democrats, and social revolutionaries. Having given up their religious faith in favor of a universalist ideal, they felt they had little in common with the shopkeepers and tradesmen who made up the bulk of the Jewish migration. Following the Bolshevik Revolution, with its promise of Jewish emancipation, the various ideological trends crystallized among the Jews of Uruguay. In 1917, these left-wingers organized the Kultur Verein Morris Vintschevsky, dedicated to the spread of Yiddish culture, which it activated through the founding of Yiddish schools for children, a public library, and a dramatic troupe. (Drama, in the eyes of the Verein, was no entertainment for the idle rich, but a means of exciting the class consciousness of the workers.) In addition, the Kultur Verein operated a free soup kitchen for the unemployed and funded a free loan association. The Verein was affiliated with the Yevsektsia, the Yiddish-speaking sector of the Communist party of the Soviet Union. Also affiliated with Yevsektsia at this time was Avanguard, a Jewish workers' movement.[52]

The Jewish Left was radicalized by the events of January 1919, when Semana Trágica spilled over the Plata into Montevideo. Headquarters of several Jewish clubs were raided, about 80 percent of the Jewish population was under arrest at one moment or another, and a considerable but unknown number of Jews were deported. From that time forward, the Yevsektsia seems to have exerted greater influence over Jewish workers' organizations in Uruguay, possibly because they felt so exposed to government repression.

Poalei Zion (PZ, the socialist wing of the Zionist movement) also organized in Montevideo in 1917. When this party split into right and left factions worldwide, the Uruguayan Poalei Zion likewise split, each half remaining tied to its respective counterpart abroad. The Left PZ established an Immigrant Workers' Home and an Immigrant Workers' Kitchen in Montevideo during 1927–28. The Right PZ was more closely allied with the Uruguayan Socialist party, and its members were active in Uruguayan trade unions. Both factions cooperated with Histadrut (the organized labor movement in then Palestine); both factions published newspapers and opened schools.

In 1929, the Jewish Socialist party (Bund) organized in Uruguay. One of the founding elements of the Russian Social Democratic Labor party in 1898, the Bund believed in gradual evolution toward socialism. Following the Bolshevik Revolution, Bundists were alternately wooed and repressed by the Communist party, their leadership alternately promoted and imprisoned. In Uruguay, the Bund occupied itself with following from afar events within its sister organization in Poland; locally, it engaged in cultural work on the Jewish street. In addition to publishing a party newspaper, the Bund founded schools and concentrated on retention of Yiddish as the Jewish workers' language. These actions were in accord with Bund policy elsewhere, which was to create an enveloping social system within which Jewish workers could experience a full range of cultural and social events presumed to be helpful in forming a socialist mentality. The Bund in fact provided workers with a complete lifestyle, linked to the national labor movement, ineradicably Jewish, and apart from the traditional Jewish community.[53] Interviews with leftist Jewish women immigrants attest to the fact that, on arrival in Montevideo, they found themselves "at home" at Bundist gatherings. A generation of working mothers, their socialist consciousness was formed in Europe, but they contributed their ideas and their labor (as teachers, modistes, actresses, and door-to-door saleswomen) to the creation of a new society in Uruguay.[54]

Montevideo Jewish leftists divided between communist and Zionist camps, mutually antagonistic because communism opposed the development of a separate Jewish national entity, whereas Zionists, Marxist and non-Marxist alike, believed that the problems of the Jewish people could be resolved only within the framework of a Jewish national homeland. Rivalry between these "progressive" and "national" Jews prevented formation of a kehillah, since each faction jockeyed to dominate the organized community. Communists, opposed to Jewish "chauvinism," challenged the presence of Zionists on the governing board, while moderates and conservatives feared that, if a kehillah were formed, the communists with their superior organizing skills would dominate it.[55]

In 1931, an entity called the Yiddishe Kehillah fun Montevideo (Jewish Community of Montevideo) was brought into existence. Based on the existing burial society, its goals were to provide Jewish burial, represent the Jewish community of Montevideo, subsidize Jewish schools, create an orphanage and home for the aged, provide medical assistance to needy members, help the unemployed and the handicapped, and support Jewish agricultural colonization in Uruguay. This kehillah incorporated East European Jews only. Sephardim, German speakers, and Hungarians each maintained their own kehillot during the thirties, as well as two chief rabbis (an Ashkenazi and a Sephardi) and three separate school systems (religious, religious-Zionist, and secular-Zionist). All these organizations were sustained by a population of barely thirty thousand Jews. During the thirties, a struggle took place for control of the Yiddishe Kehillah. The progressives had developed one of several small free loan associations into the Banco de Goias and attempted to use it as an instrument for takeover of the kehillah. The bank was far more than a financial institution. With six thousand members and a capital of several million pesos, it was also a fundamental organ of the community. It offered credit, ran an ambulance service and pharmacy, sold health and life insurance, supported numerous cultural endeavors, and organized an agricultural colony.

Failing in their effort to take over the kehillah, the Moscow-oriented leadership of the bank set up a rival kehillah, offering membership at lower rates, another cemetery, and, as noted earlier, meat slaughtered according to both religious and communist writ. Tres Arboles, the agricultural colony, was patterned after a Soviet kolkhoz (collective farm). After three years of turmoil brought on by maladministration and strained feelings between the administration and the colonists, the colony collapsed and took the bank with it amid cries of malfeasance. Many depositors, progressive and otherwise, were wiped out by the bank's failure. The credit of Jewish merchants in Montevideo was harmed. And the fact that the government had to intervene to restore the situation was viewed as a humiliation by most members of the community.

In 1936, these warring sectors managed briefly to form a united front, the Council against Nazism and Anti-Semitism.[56] This front broke down with the withdrawal of support by the Yevsektsia, and the atmosphere of the Jewish community of Montevideo came close to civil war. Any attempt at neutrality was suspect to both sides. The leftists, having lost their representative institution and with it the hope of dominating the kehillah, apparently were forced out of Jewish communal affairs and subsequently merged into general society in Uruguay. For those who retained their Jewish identification, it was now possible to form a "roof" organization, which occurred in 1940, following mediation by officers of the World Jewish Congress. This Comité Central Israelita was recognized by the Uruguayan government as spokesman for the entire Jewish community. Having united all ethnic sectors and expelled the left, the kehillah now found itself governed by centrist forces. Zionism won out over the leftist line, and the Montevideo kehillah, like those of Mexico City and Buenos Aires, became invincibly Zionist.

In the 1930s, the Buenos Aires Khevra Kadisha modified its structure and its purposes, beginning a process of conversion from a burial society into a comprehensive service agency known at first as Asociación Mutual Israelita Argentina, and in more recent years as AMIA—Comunidad Judía de Buenos Aires.[57] AMIA, organized as a beneficent society, is prohibited by its constitution from undertaking political action. For the purpose of confronting anti-Semitism and racism, community leaders organized DAIA, the Delegación de Asociaciones Israelitas Argentinas, in 1934 as the community's political arm. Oppression of Jews in Europe was the issue that first brought 28 institutions from different ethnic communities together for united action. DAIA now has some 150 institutional members and continues to be the political spokesperson for Argentine Jews.

In the 1950s, Jews all over the world came to regard as imperative the expulsion of communists from the kehillot. The survival of Jews and the survival of the noncommunist "free world" seemed interdependent as Soviet anti-Semitism became more overt. Additionally, within Latin America, the activities of leftists had time and again endangered entire Jewish communities as radical activity by Jewish individuals drew down the wrath of the police and superpatriots on all Jews. The kehillot took upon themselves the task of cleaning up the Jewish street so that right-wing governments would not be tempted to do that job. In the short run, results were favorable, in that Jewish communities were able to survive under regimes that did not tolerate leftist movements, all of which the generals lumped together as communist and subversive.

Leftists who were expelled or voluntarily left the kehillah usually ceased identifying as Jews, constrained by two historical forces. One was the increasingly anti-Semitic nature of Soviet communism as revealed in such incidents as the Prague trials and the blood libel against Jewish doctors that occurred in the 1950s. To be a Jew and a communist were no longer perceived as compatible states. The other was the increasingly rigid line that the kehillot drew around the question of who was a Jew. The traditional taboo against conversion of spouses to Judaism was now joined by a political test: membership in a group that the government deemed subversive disqualified one from membership in a kehillah. From the point of view of organized community life, the departure of the radicals left the kehillot bereft of younger members and markedly conservative in its orientation. It also cut the ties of the kehillot to progressive European ideologies. This break was scarcely perceived by hostile observers, who continued to suspect the kehillot of harboring subversives.

The centralization of the Buenos Aires kehillah now proceeded apace, symbolized by the assembling of its administrative offices in a six-story building at 633 Pasteur, in the heart of the old Jewish district of Once. The building housed the offices of all the social welfare activities that have been described here: the Board of Education, Hebrew Immigrant Aid Society, Delegación de Asociaciones Israelitas Argentinas (DAIA), AMIA employees union, teachers' seminary, cemetery administration, charity, labor exchange, youth department, arbitration panel, Federación de Comunidades Israelitas Argentinas, publishing, scholarships and grants, legal assistance, and rabbi's office; cultural institutions such as the Center for Historical and Social Studies, press archive, Instituto Científico Judío (IWO) and its library, historical archives of the community, a museum, art gallery, theatre; and the offices necessary for the functioning of the institution, such as a telephone exchange, computing center, reception hall, security, and so forth. The agencies delivering these services—schools, social welfare organizations, landsmannschaften, etc.—are represented on the kehillah governing body and occupied offices in the same building.

The drive to rationalize and coordinate services and budget led to the creation of a strong bureaucracy. Over the years, AMIA came to be criticized for bureaucratic rigidity, political irrelevancy, and ethnic feuding, and its membership declined as native-born Jews came to perceive the kehillah as marginal in their lives. A 1970 survey found that 70 percent of AMIA members were over age fifty, 17 percent over seventy. Twenty percent of AMIA membership had no formal education or only a few grades of elementary, while another 32 percent graduated elementary but proceeded no farther with their education.[58] Forty-five percent of the membership sampled did not vote. The latter included a majority of the college-educated and those under fifty. AMIA had come to represent the elderly, the foreign-born, the Yiddish speakers. The young, the native-born, the better-educated, and the Spanish speakers were alienated from AMIA as a moribund institution.[59] Young, ambitious persons were not attracted by communal obligations or the lure of status obtained through officeholding in the community. The kehillah continued to back the Orthodox version of Judaism to which few Argentine Jews were attached; it retained Yiddish in the Jewish school system long after it was apparent that that language's lack of relevance to Argentina was keeping children away. The archaic forms of Jewish religious and cultural life offered to them by the kehillah compared poorly to the attractive secular world of the university that brought Jewish as well as non-Jewish youth into confrontation with issues of concern to them as Argentines.

Within AMIA, politics mirrored the politics of Israel. Members were elected to the board of directors by their constituent organizations according to a system of proportional representation that developed within the World Zionist Organization. The parties that put forward candidates on "lists" were replicas of Israeli political parties, and they mated, reproduced, and divorced along with their prototypes. Marxist parties competed (and did fairly well), but their ideology related to Israel, not to the politics of Argentina. This electoral pattern gave the kehillot a foreign appearance, and indeed their internal politics would not have been intelligible to a knowledgeable reporter on any of the great metropolitan newspapers. Monopoly over the cemetery enabled AMIA not only to finance kehillah services, but also to impose its interpretation of Judaism upon the community, and then to extend its ideas nationwide. In the 1950s, when representatives of thirty-six Jewish communities outside Buenos Aires agreed to form a federation to coordinate their activities, the old Khevra Kadisha retained its preponderant position.

Some of AMIA's rigidity stemmed from the fact that decision-making offices were occupied by the largest donors of funds, who tended to be businessmen interested in gaining social status by performing community work on a volunteer basis. The cohort of professional staff, such as teachers, religious counselors, and social workers, were by and large underpaid, lacking in status, and exercised little input into policy decisions. The lack of social esteem for professional workers extended to rabbis. All the chief organizations of the community being secular in character, a rabbi's influence was weaker in Argentina than in the United States. As in Israel, this fact did not alter the kehillah's unrelievedly Orthodox posture on questions pertaining to burial, marriage, dietary laws, and so forth. As the rate of intermarriage rose, no avenue of compromise opened: one had to be either inside the fold or outside it.[60] Expulsion of the radicals left their ideological heirs without ties to the Jewish community, free to join Third World groupings that claimed the allegiance of masses of university youth in the 1960s and '70s. As these movements became increasingly anti-Zionist, if not plainly anti-Semitic, cross-pressured Jewish university youth dropped their ties to the Jewish people in order to join the dominant political trends of their generation. Increasing numbers of Jewish youth simply opted out of Jewish life by entering into marriage by civil contract. They cared less where they would be buried than how they were to live their lives.

Salvation through Sports Alone

Institutionalized defense of the Jewish past may have been an adequate response in those republics and in those periods which were dominated by a monolithic church presence. It proved less adaptive in secular societies where religion was relegated to secondary status and upward mobility lay open, or partially open, to Jews. In these secular societies, Jewish youth of the 1950s and 1960s began abandoning the communal institutions they perceived as rigid, desiccated relics of an outworn age in favor of the exhilarating political and literary scenes of their national societies. Their assimilation was eased by the fact that, unlike the situation in the days of their parents and grandparents, they were no longer coming into contact with semibarbarous gauchos, marginalized slum dwellers, and the criminal underworld, but with middle- and upper-middle-class representatives of the most attractive elements in criollo culture. As they entered the broader society, some sought ways of identifying as Jews without paying dues to the United Jewish Appeal and the burial society.

In the 1920s, the Jewish community of Recife, Pernambuco, Brazil, fielded a soccer team, beginning a tradition that continues today of Jewish participation in the popular sport.

One institution proved able to supply Latin American Jews with a secular Jewish identity. This is the Jewish sports club. Variously called the Estadio, Centro Deportivo, or Hebraica, the sports club is a hybrid between Jewish and Latin American institutions. Sports clubs organized along national lines (the Italian Club, the Syrian Club, and so on) are to be found in all Latin American cities; sports are a central fact of Latin American life. Thus it is quite in order for the Jews to have their sports club, too, and every Jewish community surveyed has one. Typically these offer a library, auditorium, restaurant, nursery school, and offices of the Jewish social welfare agencies, in addition to athletic facilities for soccer, tennis, swimming, golf, and bowling. They are likely to offer such activities as continuing education for adults, dances, art exhibits, concerts, lectures, children's day camps, even psychological counseling. Jewish sports clubs compete in the countless local and international sports events that are a regular feature of Latin American civic life. They field teams for the Macabiad, the Jewish counterpart of the Olympic Games. Some clubs are located on choice real estate: Hebraica of Buenos Aires in the downtown business district, Estadio of Santiago on the outskirts of the city with a stupendous view of the Andes. The physical plant of the clubs tends to be impressive. Even more impressive is their record for attracting members. "There may be 7,000 people at the club on a fair Sunday," an Argentine social worker commented. "That is more than you will find at the Congregación on Yom Kippur."

The sports club became the first site for informal mingling among Jews of different ethnic communities. (The international fraternity, B'nai B'rith, was another locale where ethnic barriers eroded.) For the native-born generation, European and Levantine quarrels are irrelevant, and so are their languages. At the clubs that are their creation, the language spoken is Spanish or Portuguese. In assimilating to their national societies, they are also assimilating to one another. One result is an increasing incidence of what Latin American Jews call "intermarriage"—unions between Ashkenazim and Sephardim. The sports club seemed at mid-century Latin American Jewry's best hope for maintaining a Jewish presence on the continent. In keeping with the secular thrust of Jewish life since the arrival of the first Jewish immigrants, Latin American Jews placed their money on survival as a secular, rather than as a religious, entity. This picture would be significantly altered by arrival on the scene of the brutal military dictatorships of the seventies.

CHAPTER 8

Latin American–Jewish Demography

The hyphen is a useful commodity: It contributes a unifying feature where none would be expected to exist.

—Saúl Sosnowski

SOME 430,400 PERSONS who were identifiably Jewish were living in the Latin American republics in 1990, 208,000 of these in Argentina. Brazil, with 100,000, was home to the second largest contingent, Mexico ranking next with 40,800, and Uruguay fourth with 23,600 Jews.[1] In each of these republics, a modern urban setting was home to a European-descended, secularized population. In each, the transformation of economies from agrarian to industrial modes of production had begun by the time of World War I, the period when the largest number of immigrants was looking for new homes. Each of these republics had accomplished the separation of church and state, and each exhibited a nascent middle class, at least in a limited statistical sense of the term.

Venezuela and Colombia did not for the most part encourage immigration during the period of heaviest Jewish demand, nor did they separate church and state until recent years. But in the twentieth century, the process of industrialization attracted modernizing elements from abroad, and the size of Venezuela's Jewish community rose to 20,000 in the 1980s. Colombia's Jewry increased to 14,000 with that country's prosperity, but diminished to less than half as the drug wars intensified. In Chile, early industrialization and religious toleration brought into being a thriving community estimated in 1960 at 35,000; but this number dwindled to 15,000 as the nation was whipsawed by powerful competing forces of Left and Right. By 1995, the community had rebuilt its numbers to over 20,000.

Republics that today are the home of tiny Jewish communities are those which either failed to encourage, or actively discouraged, heterogeneous immigration. Nor have they for the most part committed themselves as yet to

191

economic and social modernization. In this group are countries with large indigenous or black populations, high rates of illiteracy, and grave polarization between elite and mass: Peru, Bolivia, Ecuador, Paraguay, the Dominican Republic, Haiti, and the Central American republics (see Table 4).

The geographic distribution of the Jews of Latin America is thus a function of immigration policies of the various nations, ethnicity of local populations, and level of industrialization. Without appropriate immigration policies, Jews could not legally enter or settle permanently in any country. Where indigenous populations predominated, European Jews had difficulty making homes for themselves, though Near Easterners and North Africans fared somewhat better. Over the long haul, only industrialized societies offered immigrants the employment or investment opportunities they needed in order to thrive. Finally, political violence and economic turbulence sometimes load the dice against immigrants who have not had time to grow permanent roots in their new homelands. The distribution of Jewish populations, calculated a decade ago, illustrates these factors. Sixty-one percent of Jews were living in the southern cone (Argentina, Uruguay, Chile, the southern states of Brazil) as against just 11 percent of the total population of Latin America. Against the 55 percent of the general population living in tropical South America, only 29 percent of Jews had settled in these regions.[2] The 9 percent of Jews who lived in Central America in the 1970s (as opposed to 26 percent of the general population) have diminished since that date due to the civil wars and interventions in Nicaragua, El Salvador, and Honduras.

Sources and Parameters for Jewish Population Studies

Fundamental to any enumeration of Jews is the determination of who is a Jew. According to Jewish religious law (*halakhah*), a Jew is a person born of a Jewish mother and who has not accepted conversion to another religion, or one who has converted to Judaism according to halakhic procedures. In practice, people are not necessarily guided by halakhah in determining their own identity. Many who qualify under halakhic definition choose to dissociate themselves from the Jewish people, while some persons born of Jewish fathers and non-Jewish mothers choose to regard themselves as Jews, a reinterpretation of halakhah put forth in recent years by Reform Judaism. Differences of opinion as to who should be regarded as Jewish account for substantially different estimates of the size of Jewish populations. Because of the existence of unaffiliated Jews who are difficult to identify in a census, the practice has arisen of adding to Jewish census data an estimate of the number of such persons likely to reside in areas known to be populated by Jews, thus potentially producing an error equal to that which would arise were no correction attempted. Reliance on estimates is, however, a necessity for all Jewish populations outside the State of Israel.

TABLE 4

Estimated Jewish Population Distribution in the Americas, End of 1994

COUNTRY	TOTAL POPULATION	JEWISH POPULATION	JEWS PER 1,000 POPULATION	ACCURACY RATING[B]
Canada	29,600,000	360,000	12.2	A 1991
United States	263,200,000	5,675,000	21.6	B 1990
Total North America[a]	293,000,000	6,035,000	20.6	
Bahamas	300,000	300	1.0	D
Costa Rica	3,300,000	2,500	0.8	C 1993
Cuba	11,200,000	700	0.1	C 1990
Dominican Republic	7,800,000	100	0.0	D
El Salvador	5,900,000	100	0.0	C 1993
Guatemala	10,600,000	1,000	0.1	B 1993
Jamaica	2,400,000	300	0.1	A 1995
Mexico	93,700,000	40,800	0.4	A 1991
Netherlands Antilles	240,000	300	1.3	A 1995 X
Panama	2,600,000	5,000	1.9	C 1990
Puerto Rico	3,700,000	1,500	0.4	C 1990
Virgin Islands	110,000	300	2.7	C 1986
Other	20,150,000	300	0.0	D
Total Central America	162,000,000	53,200	0.3	
Argentina	34,600,000	208,000	6.0	C 1990
Bolivia	7,400,000	700	0.1	B 1990
Brazil	157,800,000	100,000	0.6	C 1980
Chile	14,300,000	15,000	1.0	C 1988
Colombia	37,700,000	5,000	0.1	C 1993
Ecuador	11,500,000	900	0.1	C 1985
Paraguay	5,000,000	900	0.2	B 1995
Peru	24,000,000	2,900	0.1	C 1993
Suriname	450,000	200	0.4	B 1986
Uruguay	3,200,000	23,600	7.4	C 1993
Venezuela	21,800,000	20,000	0.9	C 1989
Total South America[A]	319,000,000	377,200	1.2	
Total	774,000,000	6,465,400	8.4	

[a] Including countries not listed separately.
SOURCE: Table compiled by U. O. Schmelz and Sergio DellaPergola, "World Jewish Population, 1994," in *American Jewish Year Book* 96 (1996): 434–63.

Accuracy ratings:
A=relatively reliable
B=recent but less accurate
C=unsatisfactory or partial coverage
D=essentially speculative
X=updated and revised

In countries that have separated church and state, the collection of information regarding religious preference is regarded as individious; in the United States, Jewish organizations have opposed inclusion of a religious question in the census. The reasons for this are rooted in history. Registration of Jews has in the past been used for purposes of discrimination; during the Nazi period, official records were used to identify Jews for transport to their deaths. Additionally, refugees who entered Latin American countries on fraudulent documents, such as visas purchased from corrupt officials or baptismal certificates issued to the unbaptized, are naturally unwilling to compromise their status for the sake of a census. Such life experiences combine with more remote memories of the Spanish Inquisition to limit the willingness of Latin American Jews to check the category "israelita" on a census form.

Despite the theoretical possibility of deriving information on Jewish communities from national censuses, these must be handled with extreme care. Two national censuses conducted in 1960 illustrate the pitfalls of relying on this resource without applying an adequate analysis. The Chilean census identified 11,700 Jews that year, or about one-third the number actually known to Jewish institutions at that date. Conversely, the Mexican census of the same year showed 100,750 Jews, a startling 470 percent increase over the 1950 census considering there had been no Jewish immigration in the interim. Only in recent years have demographers at the Hebrew University in Jerusalem developed the methodology required to break out of national censuses reasonable estimates for the numbers of Latin American Jews. Their methods are described in successive volumes of *American Jewish Year Book*.

There is no community-sponsored, centralized record-keeping of births, marriages, or deaths among Jews anywhere but the State of Israel. Communal records may be inflated due to failure to remove deceased persons from the registers and are in any event incomplete, because notification of births is not compulsory and because the unaffiliated are omitted. Gaps in data are difficult to fill because of uncertain political conditions that often make fieldwork impracticable. In practice, some efforts to fill lacunae in Jewish census data, if not objectively verifiable, are logically persuasive.

Prior to 1974, most of our understanding of the demographics of Latin Jewry came from studies prepared by Jewish community service organizations. The (U.S.-based) American Jewish Committee and the World Jewish Congress made periodic attempts to assess the size and viability of Latin American Jewish communities. Some of these studies, prepared by scholars and communal officials, are cited throughout this chapter, providing invaluable information for the projection of demographic trends through time. From 1966 through 1975, the series *Comunidades Judías* was compiled biannually by community leaders and social welfare professionals in each republic and edited by staff of the Comité Judía Latinoamericana in Buenos Aires. This useful work came to an end with the harassment and flight of staff during the military regime of 1976–83.

Since that time, several major demographic studies have been executed by qualified researchers. The demographic dimensions of the Jewish community of Argentina were defined by Israeli demographers U. O. Schmelz and Sergio DellaPergola through computer analysis of the national census of 1960.[3] Their work remains the foundation for study of the Jewish populations of Latin America. When first published, this census recorded 291,877 Jews, almost 100,000 fewer than the number believed by the Jewish establishment to be living in the country. The anomaly was taken up by Schmelz and DellaPergola, who analyzed the computer tape for "Jewish" and "without confession" responses. In a persuasive analysis, they determined that the published census total might be supplemented by 6 percent, based on the proportion of respondents living in Buenos Aires (the area where most Argentine Jews are concentrated) who were born Jewish and who answered "no religion" or "without confession" to the question on religion. Having considered the data on these respondents, the authors adopted a corrected total of 310,000 Jews in Argentina in 1960. This number became the most significant datum to emerge since establishment of Jewish settlement in Argentina, since it meant that one-quarter of the presumed Jewish population did not exist; that presumed rates of natural increase were inoperative; and that prophecies that the Jewish population would soon reach half a million were even farther from the mark. Furthermore, it called into question accepted population figures for Jews in other parts of Latin America. These had been rising *pari passu* with population estimates for Argentina and now had to be scaled down, from 324,000 to 240,000.

Publication of these estimates set off an uproar as community leaders sought to protect the higher numbers on which they relied to fortify the political position of the communities within their national societies. Reconsideration by the demographic team resulted, however, only in slight adjustments, and the communities were forced to accept the validity of the data, because, by the time a new analysis was published, the projected decline of the communities had visibly set in. As can be seen from Table 4, the Jewish population of Argentina is now down by one-third from the 1960 census.

São Paulo's Jewish population was surveyed in 1969 under the direction of sociologist Henrique Rattner.[4] A 1994 community census of Pôrto Alegre and its environs helps fill out our knowledge of Brazil.[5] In Mexico, a 1991 sample survey was carried out under the supervision of the aforenamed demographer from the Hebrew University.[6] In addition, smaller studies have been carried out in various communities. The data derived from these sources, when integrated with one another, present a consistent pattern. When this pattern in turn is compared with the demography of the matrix populations, the distinctive profile of Jewish populations appears in sharp relief against the profile of majority populations with which it is contrasted.

Demographic Profile of the Jewish Communities

Birth Rate

Data on the demographic characteristics of Latin American Jewry display an internal consistency that confirms the existence of a group that is quite distinct from the majority members of matrix populations. The gravest difference appears in contrasting birth rates. For whatever country we examine, the Jewish birth rate is just half that of the matrix population. In 1971–75, the crude birth rate for Argentina as a whole was 23.5 per 1,000; during the same period the Argentine Jewish birth rate was 10 per 1,000.[7] The number of Argentine Jews in each age cohort born since 1953 shows steady attrition. In 1960, there were 4,434 children aged eight, but only 3,662 aged four and 3,022 aged one. In the group below the age of four there were to be found only three-quarters of the number of children aged five to nine. The proportion of children dwindled faster than the number of Jewish women of childbearing age, not only because of a continuous drop in completed fertility, but also because of a continuous rise in the frequency of mixed marriages, in the majority of which children are not reared as Jews. The completed fertility rate of Argentine Jewish women in 1960 yielded a ratio of 947 daughters per 1,000 mothers, more than 5 percent short of the number required for replacement of the parent generation.

The São Paulo Jewish community was surveyed during the five-month period January to May 1969. The precise number of births, extrapolated over a one-year period, yielded a birth rate of 2.4 percent per year. This rate obtained during a period when the Brazilian population as a whole was experiencing a birth rate of 4.4 percent per year. Ninety-five percent of Jewish families have fewer members than the average Brazilian family. Moreover, there is a secular trend toward fewer children in Brazilian Jewish families.[8] In an earlier study carried out in 1965, Henrique Rattner found that Jewish university students in São Paulo belonged to families with an average 2.7 children, but that their parents' families had averaged 5 children per family. The Jewish population of Pôrto Alegre averages 2.4 children per married couple; a slighter higher number, 2.7, prevails among Jews living elsewhere in the state of Rio Grande do Sul. However, Brumer found a substantial proportion of unmarried Jews living alone, who apparently were not factored into the overall birth rate.[9] The Brazilian Jewish birth rate may be declining during a period when the country as a whole is experiencing accelerating population growth. A recent study suggests that the rate of Jewish population growth from 1940 to 1980 was 1.26 percent per year, in the context of overall Brazilian population growth of 2.69 percent.[10]

The 1991 survey of Mexico, where the average fertility rate is 3.2 children per woman, determined that Jewish women give birth to an average 2.7 children, down from 3.5 per woman in the preceding generation. These averages obscure substantial differences among the different ethnic sectors of the Jewish population. Jewish women aged over 65 and originating from Arab countries averaged over 6 live births, while elderly women among the non-affiliated (most of whom are Ashkenazim) had not borne enough children to replace themselves.[11] Overall, Arabic-speaking Jewish women bear 3.6 children; the American community in Mexico, 2.2, and the non-affiliated, just 1.3 children per woman for an overall average of 2.7. At present, uniquely in the Latin

American context, the community's birth rate is sufficient to maintain the size of the community for the next generation.[12] But this rate is dependent upon the maintenance of traditional patterns among Arabic-speaking Jews.

Low fertility rates characterize all Jewish populations of the diaspora except those originating in Asia and North Africa. Worldwide, the birth rate, and consequently the rate of natural increase, is lower among Jews than among the general population of their respective countries. Accordingly, and to the extent that Latin American Jewries in all the republics proceeded from a similar mix of ethnic strains, it is reasonable to infer similar rates for Jewish populations in those parts of Latin America for which there are no data. The inference is backed up by scattered available data on Jewish age structure in Brazil, Chile, and several small Central American communities. This phenomenon reflects modernized attitudes toward the family, the status of women, and child-rearing practices: Jews who imported low birth rates into their present countries of residence were converted only briefly to high levels of fertility by the Latin American experience, and that mostly in rural areas. Jews who arrived from Arabic countries with high levels of fertility experienced somewhat of a decline in their birth rate, as the Mexican survey indicates, but they still maintain a high enough birth rate to keep the entire Jewish community at a constant level.

Death Rate

A complete record of deaths among Ashkenazic Jews of Buenos Aires exists for the years 1953–63. It shows continuous increase, being 40 percent greater at the end of that period than at the beginning. In 1963, there were three and a half times more burials than marriages within the Ashkenazic community of Buenos Aires. This partially reflects increasing resort to marriage by civil contract. Nevertheless, a decline in the number of persons who identify as Jewish is undeniable.

The major cause of the rising death rate is the aging of the population. Schmelz and DellaPergola computed a rate of 10 deaths per 1,000 Jews of Greater Buenos Aires in 1963. The death rate for the general population of the city that year was lower, standing at 8.6 per 1,000. The composition of the two mortality rates was different. Infant mortality (death in the first year of life) was 9.3 per 1,000 among Jews, compared with 40 per 1,000 among the general population of Greater Buenos Aires in 1961 and 57 per 1,000 among the general population of Argentina in 1967.[13] The Jewish death rate continues low until age sixty, when mortality starts running higher than among the general population. Not only has the Argentine Jewish mortality rate surpassed that of the general population; it has also surpassed the Jewish birth rate. In 1971–75 there was a negative balance of deaths over births within the Jewish community, with 14 deaths and 10 births per 1,000 population per year, compared with 23.5 births and 8.9 deaths per 1,000 among the general Argentine population. As predicted, the period 1976–80 produced a negative balance of −4 per 1,000 in the rate of natural increase of Argentine Jews: more Jews were dying than were being born.[14] Surveys for the1990s in Buenos Aires and several provincial cities point to the continued aging of this population.[15]

The mortality rate among São Paulo Jews was calculated at 1.6 percent per year in 1968; the rate among the Brazilian population as a whole was 1.1 percent that year. The national figure includes a high rate of infant mortality: the hazards of infancy in Brazil were so great during that period that expectation of life at birth was calculated at forty-three years in 1950.[16] Although improvement in life chances have taken place in the intervening generation, mortality rates remain heavily weighted toward infants, while the majority of deaths of Jews occur after age sixty. In the 10,000-member Jewish community of Pôrto Alegre, search of cemetery records located one newborn death in the period 1991–93.[17]

In a humanistic analysis carried out in the 1940s, Tovye Meisel found the Mexican Jewish mortality rate to be 9 per 1,000 as compared to 15.5 per 1,000 among the general population. Both groups were growing in 1950: Jews at a rate of 1.4 percent per year, the majority population at 2.9 percent per year.[18] Over the next fifteen years, Mexican mortality dropped steeply as measures of public hygiene took hold. Mortality dropped by a third while the birth rate decreased only slightly, resulting in one of the highest rates of natural increase in the world. Among infants, the most vulnerable sector of the population, mortality continued high, with 61 infant deaths per 1,000 live births. However, there was no infant death among the approximately twenty thousand Ashkenazim of Mexico City during several years of the 1960s.

Infant mortality is at a very high level throughout Latin America. Considering only Argentina, Mexico, and Brazil, the location of a majority of Latin American Jews, recently calculated rates of infant mortality are 36 per 1,000, 50 per 1,000, and 70 per 1,000 respectively.[19] In these countries, the rate of infant deaths within the Jewish communities tends toward nil.

The global phenomenon of low infant mortality among Jews may be accounted for by a combination of reasons that are also persuasive within the Latin American setting: more intense urbanization among Jews over the past century and a half, when cities had better preventive facilities than did the countryside; earlier adoption of birth control among Jews, with the side effect of enabling parents to bestow better care upon each child; the low rate of illegitimacy; the comparatively high number of physicians among Jews; existence of Jewish religious observances that are supportive of good health. The Jewish demographic pattern extends to Latin America, where infant mortality rates resemble those on other continents rather than the rates that prevail among their fellow Latins.

Infant mortality rates are a commonly accepted index of modernization. The capacity to save infants from death caused by endemic disease is dependent upon relatively low levels of technology and a modest expenditure of funds. Inability or disinterest of governments in providing hygienic services is a salient characteristic of underdeveloped countries.[20] The contrast between high rates of infant mortality throughout Latin America and the low rate within Jewish communities throws into relief the modernized character of Jewish life as compared with the traditional pattern of human wastage that continues to prevail in society at large.

Longevity

The anticipated life span of Jews is almost the same as for non-Jews in the city of Buenos Aires, being 68.9 and 73.9 for Jewish males and females respectively, and 67.9 and 74.2 for non-Jewish males and females. Uruguay and Venezuela fall into the same long-lived category as Argentina. Outside the modernized sectors of the continent, life expectancy drops sharply for majority populations but remains high for Jews. For example, in 1968, 40 percent of São Paulo Jews were over age forty, 14 percent over age sixty. In the same year, only 25 percent of the general population of São Paulo was past forty, and just 6 percent was past sixty.[21] Jews achieved their pattern of longevity independent of their immediate environment. Among the general population of the city, those over forty gained 5.5 percentage points between 1950 and 1968, reflecting improved health conditions; but the Jewish age distribution showed no material change over this eighteen-year period. The average age at death among Pôrto Alegre Jews is now 76.5 for women, 72.2 for men.[22]

Since many of the health practices that eliminate infant mortality also work to prolong the life span, it is not arbitrary to conclude that life expectancy among Jews in areas for which no data exist approximates the modernized model shown for Buenos Aires more closely than it does the traditional rate still prevalent in most of Latin America.

Low fertility, low infant mortality, and extended life expectancy among Jewish populations contrast with high fertility, high infant mortality, and low life expectancy among non-Jewish populations (with the exception of Argentina). The result is a Jewish median age in the mid-thirties, in contrast to a median age in the mid-twenties for non-Jews (see Table 5). A longer life span, in addition to being its own reward, enables individuals to develop their skills to the utmost. The blighting of promising careers through early death is far less frequent among Jews than in the general population. Furthermore, survival into the sixties ensures that most parents are able to nurture their children to maturity. On a continent where throwaway children roam the streets in a battle for survival, within the Jewish community parentless children are rare.

Family Size

In countries that maintain traditionally high birth and death rates, the Jewish family stands out in sharp relief as having passed through a demographic transition: there are fewer wasted pregnancies, fewer children per family, and more of these children reach maturity. In Latin American nations that have passed as an entirety through the demographic transition from traditional to modern patterns of family life, Jewish populations are less clearly differentiated—except in the matter of infant mortality.

TABLE 5

Age Distributions of Selected Jewish Populations in Latin America, 1947–1980

COUNTRY OR LOCALITY	YEAR	TOTAL	0–14	15–29	30–44	45–64	65+	MEDIAN AGE JEWISH POPULATION	MEDIAN AGE GENERAL POPULATION
Argentina									
Total	1947[a]	100.0	24.6	24.8	25.6	19.7	5.3	31.4	25.0
"	1960[a]	100.0	20.5	22.0	22.2	27.5	7.8	34.7	27.0
"	1975[a]	100.0	15.4	18.1	21.2	28.6	16.7	41.6	47.9
Greater Buenos Aires	1960[b]	100.0	20.2	21.3	21.7	28.7	8.1	35.5	32.0
"	1973–74[c]	100.0	18.2	20.6	22.5	28.0	10.6	37.6	..
Tucumán	1960[b]	100.0	23.5	23.7	20.1	25.6	7.1	32.8	..
"	1974[c]	100.0	20.8	23.8	19.2	23.2	13.0	34.0	..
Bahia Blanca	1975[c]	100.0	21.9	19.3	18.7	29.8	10.3	36.0	..
Colonies	1960[b,d]	100.0	21.6	17.7	19.2	30.3	11.1	36.9	..
Brazil									
Total	1950[b]	100.0	23.8	25.5	22.0	23.3	5.4	30.5	18.9
" (Urban)	1980[b]	100.0	19.8	23.5	19.1	23.3	14.3	34.6	21.5
São Paulo (City)	1968–69[c]	100.0	21.6	24.8	17.1	24.9	9.3	33.2	27.2
São Paulo (State)	1980[b]	100.0	20.8	23.2	19.1	22.7	14.2	34.0	23.3
Rio de Janeiro (City)	1960[b]	100.0	23.1	21.1	21.3	27.5	6.9	33.3	20.8[c]
Rio de Janeiro (State)	1980[b]	100.0	17.1	22.6	19.3	24.9	16.1	37.9	24.3
Chile									
Total	1952[b]	100.0	22.8	18.8	22.2	27.7	8.5	36.3	23.5[f]
Panama									
Total	1960–61[c]	100.0	29.6	22.6	21.3	20.2	6.3	28.4	18.3
Colombia									
Bogotá	1977[c]	100.0	25.3	24.4	17.6	21.3	11.4	30.5	18.3[g]

[a] Reconstruction of Jewish population in Argentina, based on 1960 census data
[b] Population census
[c] Jewish survey
[d] Does not include all the relevant Jewish population
[e] State of Guanabara, urban population
[f] Province of Santiago
[g] Total country, urban population
SOURCE: *American Jewish Year Book* 85 (1985)

The average family size of AMIA members diminished from 4.53 to 4.14 between 1920 and 1930. There is evidence that this generation was practicing birth control: Jewish families were smaller in Argentina than in central Europe.[23] By 1960, Jewish families were smaller than non-Jewish families in Buenos Aires, with an average 2.2 children being born to Jewish married women, as compared with 2.7 for non-Jewish women.[24] Jewish households averaged a fraction under 4 persons each.

In all countries examined, Sephardic families are larger than Ashkenazic, as was seen in the case of Mexico. Modernization was a distinctively European phenomenon that Jews originating in Arabic or Balkan lands did not participate in as directly as did Jews of central, western, or even eastern Europe. Greater traditionalism in Sephardic life results in higher fertility rates and larger families. There is thus a consistent difference in family size between Ashkenazic and Sephardic families in all communities for which data exist, e.g., Quilmes (a district of Greater Buenos Aires), where in 1963 Ashkenazic families averaged 3.45 members compared to Sephardic families with 4.48 members.[25] Even when Ashkenazic and Sephardic families are averaged together, Jewish families are usually smaller than families in the population as a whole.

When Rattner conducted the São Paulo survey in 1968, 43 percent of the population of Brazil was below the age of fifteen. The corresponding figure for São Paulo City was 36 percent for the general population but just 21.32 percent for its Jewish population.[26] Urban families, whether Jewish or non-Jewish, tend to be smaller than rural families. But Jewish families are smaller than the São Paulo norm, and as a practical matter, since almost all Brazilian Jewish families are urban, Jewish families in Brazil are distinctly smaller than non-Jewish families.

The pattern of age distribution differs substantially for Jews and non-Jews. The Guatemalan Jewish community consisted of 1,030 persons in 1965, 26 percent of whom were under the age of fifteen.[27] In the Guatemalan population as a whole, 46 percent of the population was below that age. In 1960, 20 percent of Argentine Jews were under age fifteen, compared with 30 percent among the general population of the country.[28] An attempt to draw a Jewish "age pyramid" resulted in a boxlike graph, with each five-year cohort below age sixty containing an almost equal number of persons. Only two categories differed. The group that was aged fifty to fifty-four in 1960 contained larger numbers, men predominating, reflecting the migratory wave that peaked in the years just preceding World War I. The base of the pyramid narrowed drastically, reflecting the declining birth rate and the assimilation of infants into the general population via the intermarriage of their parents and non-affiliation with the community. Age pyramids for Mexican Jews differ notably by community of origin. But taken together, they reveal a younger population than characterizes Jews in other parts of Latin America: 24 percent of Mexican Jews are under age fifteen (compared with 39 percent for the general population of Mexico).

Part of the gestalt of underdevelopment is a high dependency ratio, exemplified by families which must provide for large numbers of children, many of whom do not survive to become themselves contributors to the family's welfare. Jewish families, with their reduced number of children, do not suffer this handicap, but neither do they have a population reservoir out of which future growth might occur.

Rate of Natural Increase

Many communities report insufficient numbers of births to compensate for deaths. Paraguay, for example, declined from 1,500 to 1,000 Jews during the 1960s.[29] The Bolivian community has been dwindling steadily. DellaPergola considers the Brazilian Jewish population "substantially stable" at about 100,000.[30] But as in the case of the Mexican Jewish community, which is maintaining itself at a stable level, Jews comprise a less significant proportion of each country's population today than a generation ago because of the more dynamic growth rate of the majority population.

Between 1960 and 1975, the Argentine Jewish birth rate went from a small positive balance of 200 (15,700 births to 15,500 deaths) to a negative balance of 5,000 (14,300 births to 19,300 deaths). Compounded by a high rate of emigration and a rising rate of intermarriage in which most children are not raised as Jews, the Jewish population shrank by 45,000 in that fifteen-year period (from 310,000 to 265,000),[31] dropping another 57,000 members by 1990 (some of these through emigration or through disappearance during the military dictatorship).

Jewish demography is of an entirely different nature from that of the Latin American populations among whom they live. The matrix peoples have high rates of natural increase (Argentina is the exception), preponderantly young populations, and a high growth potential capable of being unleashed by minimal expenditures on public hygiene. But Jews passed through the period of population expansion owing to better health care during the nineteenth century. They have already responded to the enhanced life chances of infants by limiting the number born. Thus, there is no scope for a Jewish "population explosion" based on better health care. With immigration foreclosed by most countries, the only source of population growth among Jews would be an increase in the birth rate; and such a trend was not observed in any country studied. To the contrary, Jewish populations are aging, and their mortality at present tends to run higher than among matrix populations. In this perspective, the probable fate of Latin American Jewry, already an insignificant numerical minority, is to become still less significant numerically in future.

Urbanization

The history of the Jews of Latin America is one of consolidation into metropolitan centers. Jews live in the cities, a majority in the great cities, and the largest number in the national capitals. In nations with just one major urban center, nearly the entire Jewish population of the country is to be found in it (Mexico, Costa Rica, El Salvador, Guatemala, Honduras, Nicaragua, Paraguay, Peru, Uruguay). Where a secondary city exists, the second largest Jewish community is located there (Bolivia, Panama, Venezuela). In those nations characterized by many urban centers (Argentina, Brazil, Colombia), Jews are found in all major cities and many minor ones.

Despite its rural bias at the beginning of the settlement period, Argentine Jewry today is almost totally urban. The 1895 Argentine census located 64 percent of israelitas in the rural province of Entre Ríos, and only 12 percent in the capital. By World War I, half of Argentine Jewry lived in Buenos Aires. The agricultural colonies waxed and waned on a diminishing curve as Jewish immigrants passed through the farms to provincial towns and thence to the capital. In 1952, there were identifiable groups of Jews in 836 Argentine towns.[32] Two decades later the *American Jewish Year Book* estimated that there were Jews in just 600 localities. In other words, the process of consolidation into towns and larger cities was continuing.

This consolidation begins in the provinces of the interior. A breakdown of the Jewish population of the province of Tucumán at two dates fifteen years apart shows the rural Jewish population declining by 21 percent while the Jewish population of the provincial capital increased by 19 percent.[33] The process is replicated nationwide. The 1960 census found 80 percent of Argentine Jews living in Greater Buenos Aires, compared with 33 percent of the general population who lived there.[34] The other substantial concentrations of Jews were in the cities of Rosario, Córdoba, Santa Fe, La Plata, Tucumán, Bahía Blanca, Mendoza, San Cristobal, and Paraná.

For Brazil, census returns of 1900, 1940, and 1950 show Jews residing in most states and territories over the past fifty years. But growth occurred only in major commercial centers and in cities that industrialized: spectacularly so in the case of Rio de Janeiro, the former federal district (where Jews came to constitute over 2 percent of the population), and São Paulo. By 1940, these two communities had eclipsed the smaller (and in some cases much older) Jewish communities of Pôrto Alegre, Belo Horizonte, Curitiba, Recife, Salvador, and Belém. The Jewish community, evenly divided between Rio and São Paulo in 1940, with 20,000–21,000 each, responded to the greater dynamism of the younger city. The 1980 census found 44,378 Jews in São Paulo, compared with Rio's 29,139. Together, the two cities accounted for 82 percent of the country's Jewish population.[35] Interestingly, the 17 percent of Jews now living in Pôrto Alegre who reported having been born in the "interior" came mostly from the areas of the old agricultural colonies of Col. Filipson, Erichim, and Quatro Irmãos.[36]

Surveying Mexico in 1948, Shatzky found that "apart from the city of Mexico there exist another 17 cities with Jewish communities. Little by little, Jews move from the small localities to the capital, in order to establish themselves among their coreligionists."[37] He was a prophet in his time: today, 93 percent of Mexican Jews live in the federal capital. In Uruguay, the great majority of Jews, like the majority of Uruguayos generally, live in the capital city of Montevideo. Communal officials in Costa Rica, Ecuador, Guatemala, Paraguay, and Peru, writing in successive volumes of *Comunidades Judías de Latinoamerica* during the 1960s and 1970s, reported that nearly all Jews living in their respective countries resided in the capital city.

The concentration of Jews in Latin American metropolitan centers derives from three historic roots: urbanization of Jews in their countries of origin, the massive urbanization that has taken place all over Latin America in the past decades, and the need of immigrants to integrate themselves into the economy.

"Jews massed into cities earlier than other population groups and at a faster tempo," writes Uriah Z. Engelman in his essay "Sources of Jewish Statistics." From the Middle Ages onward, this trend was observable in Europe, the movement being accelerated by laws that forbade Jews to settle in rural areas or to own land. "By 1925 more than a fourth of all Jews in Europe and America lived in the fourteen cities with a million population or more, while only 5.7 percent of the total population of the two continents lived in them."[38] Jewish immigrants, settling in the major cities of Latin America, were continuing urban lifestyles they had developed on other continents.

Most of Latin America has undergone an intense process of urbanization, without reference to Jews. In Argentina, for example, 70 percent of all immigrants, despite their almost exclusively rural backgrounds, had urbanized themselves by 1914. Jews, with a background in commerce and industry, were even more susceptible to the same pressures as those felt by Italian and Spanish immigrants. Seventy percent of Latin Americans now live in cities, up from 50 percent in 1960.[39] Had Jews resisted urbanization in order to remain interned in rural areas, this phenomenon would surely have called for explication. As it is, the intense concentration of Jews in cities conforms to economic and social processes within the matrix societies as well as to the thrust of Jewish history. An incidental by-product of their concentration in large cities is that Jews have a more visible (and possibly more influential) presence within their national societies than their small numbers would seem to warrant. As a consequence, and because of the hegemony which the metropolis has historically exercised over the countryside, it is not unusual for non-Jews to hold a grossly inflated notion of the number of Jews in the population.

Higher Education

Traditional emphasis on learning and the founding of schools in order to provide basic education for their children equipped Jewish immigrants to take advantage of the shift from traditional to modernizing attitudes in those countries where that occurred. In response to burgeoning opportunity, they shifted their attention away from specifically Jewish studies to career-oriented curricula geared to local economies. In the process of this changeover, education for the purpose of perpetuating Jewish identity came to be replaced by education as a means of integrating oneself into the economy of the adoptive society.

Among the immigrants themselves, university education was a rarity. Older sons of merchants and industrialists tended to enter their fathers' businesses;

most had no time to go to college. It was their younger siblings, and more generally, their children, who benefited from university admissions policies in increasing numbers. The younger the age group, the more Jewish university students are found within it. In 1963, a self-study of Jewish residents of the Quilmes district of Buenos Aires showed that 3 percent of those aged fifty and over held a university degree. The percentage of *universitarios* rose to 12 percent for persons aged thirty to forty-nine and 19 percent for those aged twelve to twenty-nine.[40] Obviously, a grouping that would bracket the usual university age more precisely would have yielded a higher percentage of students. This in fact emerged from the 1960 national census, which showed 40 percent of Jewish men and 21 percent of women aged twenty to twenty-four either attending college or with degree already in hand.[41]

A 1960 survey of the Jewish community of Valparaíso, Chile, that reached 90 percent of avowed members, or 1,050 individuals, showed that 27 percent of sons born in the country were attending university. Concomitantly, the proportion of merchants dropped from 63 percent in the fathers' generation to 32 percent in the sons'. "Here as elsewhere," concludes the researcher, "youth move from trade to the free professions."[42]

In São Paulo in 1968, nearly 66 percent of Jews aged twenty to twenty-four were enrolled at a university or higher technical school; an additional cohort of 24 percent of persons aged twenty-five to twenty-nine were so enrolled, as were 5 percent of persons aged thirty and over.[43] These figures contrasted spectacularly with the 3.3 percent of the general population of the city who were receiving higher education at that date. In the more recent Pôrto Alegre study, 33 percent of heads of families (both men and women) fifty-five years of age and older had completed university; that figure rose to 77 percent for those under age forty-one.[44]

The push for a university education and its use as a means of social ascent is by no means restricted to Jews. Nisei (ethnic Japanese born in Brazil) comprised 10 percent of all matriculated students in São Paulo at the same date. The figures do not enable us to determine to what extent university enrollment is the result of some specifically Jewish factor and how much results from the situation of Jews as immigrants. But two-thirds to three-quarters enrollment of youth of university age is a fact that must be considered in delineating the profile of Brazilian Jews, as well as in assessing their contribution to culture, politics, and the economy.

The concentration of Jewish students in the free professions is marked for every community studied. The careers most heavily represented among Jewish universitarios of Quilmes were medicine, 27 percent; engineering, 12 percent; economics, 10 percent; pharmacy and biochemistry, 9 percent.[45] Twenty-six percent of second-generation Jews of Cali, Medellín, and Barranquilla, taken as a group, were practicing in the free professions, primarily in medicine, architecture, and engineering.[46] The most popular course pursued by Jewish university students of São Paulo was engineering (25 percent), followed by medicine (13 percent), economics and business administration (11 percent), and the law (11 percent).[47] For Pôrto Alegre, the majority choices were medicine (21 percent), engineering (19 percent), and law (11 percent), followed closely by business administration (7.5 percent).[48] The pattern in Peru is similar: a decade of graduating classes from Colegio León Pinelo (1972–83) produced 19 percent engineers, 16 percent physicians, 13 percent psychologists, and 11 percent architects.[49] In no other country is the percentage of Jewish lawyers anywhere near the number found in Brazil. Without data to guide us, intuition asserts that the lawyer, the *hombre de confianza* (trusted person) is a role to which Jews have not been fully admitted in Spanish-speaking countries.

The data for São Paulo showed one-half of Jewish women aged twenty to twenty-four attending university, where they comprised two-fifths of Jewish students in the sixties. This is a continuation of the trend that appeared in earlier Argentine studies, which showed that in that country, 31 percent of Jewish students were women, as compared with 24 percent of women among university students generally (including the Jewish component).[50] The outcome of university education has been social mobility for women as well as for men. A survey of 125 Buenos Aires women engaged in stereotypically masculine professions found that a majority of the sample were daughters of immigrants; one-third of the cohort were Jews or daughters of Jews.[51]

The entry of Jews into the free professions in numbers far exceeding their proportion to the population conforms both to the patterns of Jewish history and to the developmental needs of their societies. That the latter is becoming more persuasive than the former is shown by the accelerating tendency to enter professions that relate to modernization, such as engineering, business administration, accounting, and architecture. Jews still become doctors, but there is more deployment throughout the economy. Rabbis, cantors, ritual slaughterers, and other personnel of religious life scarcely figure in the data; until recently, these officiants have had to be imported from abroad. An interesting facet of the statistics is the recent tendency of Jewish students to avoid humanistic studies, contrary to the Jewish experience in other countries. For example, during the 1981–82 academic year, a bare 1.77 percent of Jewish students matriculated at Venezuelan universities were enrolled in the humanities or arts and letters.[52] Pôrto Alegre enrollments drop to 2.8 percent for literature, 1.5 percent for history, and so forth. While the data are insufficient to support any conclusion, it is conceivable that avoidance of the humanities results from the psychological impact of the purges carried out against humanist intellectuals with such brutality in Argentina (1976–83) and Chile (mid-1970s).

It was earlier shown that Jewish economic mobility, where it occurred, was a function of the ability of immigrants to fill a gap in the production and distribution of needed consumer goods. An addendum to that observation is that Jewish social mobility is also due to the availability of educated Jewish personnel at times and in places where the demand for technically trained people was great enough to overcome traditional prejudice against them. Educational maintenance in community-sponsored schools during periods when governments were failing to educate their own people equipped Jews to partici-

The appearance of these Jewish youths on a Sunday outing in Mexico City in the 1920s bespeaks their families' rapid ascent to the Mexican middle class.

pate in the economic development of their countries when attitudes had shifted sufficiently to permit them to do so. Pursuing their own dream of personal advancement, Jews added materially to the reservoir of skilled manpower so ardently desired by modernizing forces.

Intermarriage

The Argentine census of 1960 showed that in the age group fifteen to forty-four, there were 930 Jewish men for every 1,000 Jewish women. Furthermore, more Jews married that year than could be accounted for in records of the Jewish community. Schmelz and DellaPergola concluded that more young and middle-aged males than females declined to identify themselves as Jews, that substantial numbers of Jews—more men than women—were intermarrying, and that most children of mixed marriages were not being raised as Jews.

In addition, the current generation of Jewish women is not replacing itself. Projection of the 1960 birth rate onto the known number of Jewish women aged fifteen to forty-nine in 1960 determined that there was a shortfall not of the anticipated 5 percent, but of 29 percent: 16,300 infants under the age of four in place of the expected 21,700. The difference represented infants born to Jewish mothers who had intermarried.[53] The high and rising rate of intermarriage among Argentine Jews has been noted since Jews settled in that country. Its extent had never before been charted. Its ultimate impact, unless the trend should be reversed, would be the assimilation of Argentine Jews into the general population, since intermarriage commonly is a prelude to the loss of Jewish identity. Consistent with their hopes for Jewish survival, the tendency of Jewish organizations had been to deplore the trend to assimilation while continuing to count the offspring of mixed marriages as Jews. Recent research, however, forces the observer to face facts. The Argentine Jewish community is steadily dwindling in size and faces a real question of viability. Based on partial data, DellaPergola conjectures that the rate of intermarriage in provincial Argentina may have been as high as 40 percent in the 1960s and has undoubtedly climbed higher by now.[54]

> The fundamental thrust of the projections, according to prevailing trends, is that the internal evolution of Jews in Latin America—especially in Argentina and typologically similar communities (e.g., Uruguay)—is set on a course of accelerating decreases. A negative balance of external migrations will intensify the demographic deficits, but even a hypothetical positive turn in the migratory balance would be no more than a palliative as long as the internal evolution adversely affects Jewish population size.[55]

In seeking to gain acceptance, many Jews opt to forgo their Jewish identity. This is a phenomenon common in the Western world since emancipation, but it appears to be more pronounced in Latin America, where conservatives reject cultural pluralism as a valid ideal and liberals who accept a Jewish presence insist on the Enlightenment principle that these strangers abandon their Jewishness. Abandonment of Judaism occurs most frequently during the university years; an anomaly of the situation is that so many Jewish students are studying under intellectuals of Jewish origin. The entry of increasing numbers of Jewish youth into university life has been coupled with a noticeable rise in the rate of intermarriage. The assimilationist course, which conforms to societal expectations, deprives Jewish communities of intellectual leadership at a time when their full acceptance as citizens is by no means assured. A study conducted among São Paulo Jews in the 1980s suggested that the frequency of intermarriage tends to be highest among native-born university graduates. In 69 of 80 mixed marriages, the Jewish partner had attended university, a higher educational level than prevailed among Jews who married endogamously.[56] The 1994 study of Pôrto Alegre provided a longer time line for intermarriage than other surveys had. Among respondents over 69 years of age and living in the city, 1 in 440 heads of family and 1 in 25 of their spouses (mostly, but not entirely women) descended from one or two parents who were not Jews. Among Jewish city dwellers between the ages of 21 and 30, the corresponding figures were 1 in 9 and 1 of 2.

Mexico provides an interesting variation on this picture. Intermarriage was found to be nonexistent (or unreported) among Arabic-speaking Jews living in that country. The 21.7 percent rate of intermarriage among members of the Ashkenazi Conservative congregation was doubled by intermarriage rates among the non-affiliated, who incidentally also had the highest rate of post-graduate degrees.[57] Obviously, other factors intervened as well, but still the data are suggestive. The differential rates of intermarriage point to the differences between modernized and traditional populations that became evident in the earlier discussion of birth rates. The speed at which assimilation occurs among the intermarried was graphically demonstrated by the finding that, while all non-affiliated males were circumcised, only 75 percent of their sons had undergone this fundamental Jewish rite.

Abandonment of the Jewish heritage is almost always couched in secular terms: there are few conversions to Catholicism. Evidence to this effect can be extracted from DellaPergola's findings for Mexico. Three percent of Jews contacted by the Mexican sample survey characterized themselves as nonaffiliated. Within this group, 18 percent of marriage partners had been born Catholic, but fewer than 1 percent of these spouses reported themselves to be Catholic at present. Meanwhile, the 72 percent of responding spouses who reported themselves to have been born Jewish dwindled to 58 percent who consider themselves Jewish at present. The number reporting themselves to be of no religion at all went from 8 percent at birth to 33 percent at present,[58] supporting the present author's earlier analysis that former Jews and their children tend to join the mass of the secular unchurched who populate Latin American urban centers. While Catholic spouses were leaving the church, Jewish spouses were abandoning Judaism. Anticlerical attitudes characteristic of this sector of the population target both the Catholic and the Jewish establishments (as irreligious as the latter may be), producing Jews who are willing to identify themselves as having been born Jewish, but who do not, or cannot, associate with the Jewish community. Where a secular option exists, Jews have shown themselves to be quite ready to assimilate.[59]

Intermarriage and assimilation to the majority culture are regarded as the primary threat to Jewish survival on the continent by Latin American Jewish leaders, who refer to the phenomenon as "the white pogrom." The rapid and increasing rate of assimilation is deplored and perceived by them as the most urgent item on the communal agenda, eclipsing in importance the problem of anti-Semitism which, as they correctly point out, exists all over the world. From the standpoint of the Latin American polities, assimilation vindicates proimmigration forces who welcomed Jews to their shores. Assimilation continues the process that appeared first in the Curaçaoan Jewish community, then in the Dominican Republic and Venezuela, a process at first confined to Sephardim. At first blush, Ashkenazim would appear to be more resistant to Hispanic and Portuguese cultures as well as to underlying indigenous and black elements.

But German and French Jews assimilated quite readily and so now are the East Europeans. In the course of no more than three generations, substantial proportions of Jews voluntarily abandoned their Jewish heritage in favor of an unalloyed national identity, despite the fact that there were few, if any, national institutions prepared to incorporate them together with their inherited culture. Persistent and diligent efforts on the part of other Jews to sustain and transmit their heritage on American soil failed to diminish the attraction Latin American cultures exercised over the immigrants.

Emigration

War, revolution, and economic chaos impel thousands of Latin Americans to leave their homes each year. Jewish Latin Americans are no exception. In times of political and economic stress, Jews, like other Latin Americans, emigrate if they have the financial means to do so. For those who have the need but not the means, international Jewish rescue organizations have come to their aid. Cuba's 12,000 Jews dwindled to fewer than 2,000 in the years immediately following the revolution of 1959. Uruguay, which reported 55,000 Jews in 1970, claimed only 48,000 two years later and 23,600 today, in the context of the large-scale flight of all population elements from that country. The Central American Jewish communities all but emptied out during the violent 1970s. Repression in Argentina and Chile in the 1970s caused the flight of thousands, among them, unknown numbers of Jews. The result of this emigration is to deprive Latin American economies of potential active elements, as well as to impoverish Jewish community life and challenge its ability to survive.

For Jews, emigration is also a response to the challenge of assimilation. Rather than see their children abandon their Jewish identity, some Latin American Jews prefer to raise their families in Israel or the United States, where their Jewish identity can be confirmed—though at the expense of their Latin identity. Out-migration has been proceeding during a period when in-migration could not occur. Colombia, which claimed 14,000 Jews in 1960, had half that number in 1982 and even fewer a decade later, by which time Colombians had become a noticeable presence in Miami, Houston, and New York. We have earlier seen how rural Jewish youth were drawn to the city by the prospect of higher education. This evacuation of the countryside by Jewish youth in quest of an education is replicated on a broader scale as young men and women leave such hinterland communities as Quito, Lima, La Paz, and Montevideo for New York, Hamburg, and Tel Aviv. Economic and political reasons propel many Latin Americans from their homeland, but for Jews, with a numerically small community to start with, departure of the college-bound reduces the number of potential mates so drastically that parents are encouraged to send abroad other children, particularly daughters, whom they would otherwise have kept at home, but whom they wish to see marry endogamously. While some of these students remain within Latin America, many depart for the United States or Israel with their parents' blessing to remain if possible.

No figures exist for Jewish emigration save in the case of Jews arriving in

Israel. Between 1948 (the year the state was founded) and 1986, 42,389 immigrants listed Argentina as their last place of residence, among a total 73,045 who emigrated from all of Latin America to the Jewish state.[60] (Between 1953 and 1969, no more than 350 Jews were *admitted* to Argentina in any one year.) In the 1970s, 13,000 Argentines emigrated to Israel, and 10,500 in the 1980s.[61] Whether or not these migrants remained in Israel, their departure went far toward emptying out the Argentine kehillah. Beyond Argentina, and controlling for population size, DellaPergola identifies Cuba, Bolivia, Uruguay, and Chile as the countries with the highest rates of immigration to Israel, conforming to his observation that "aliya peaks and troughs seem to reflect quite accurately some of the main political and economic events in Latin American societies."[62] Other exiles, for whom no figures exist, emigrated to the United States, Spain, Germany, and other Latin American countries. Mexico did receive Jewish immigrants during the decades of 1961–91; but almost all came from other Latin American countries and thus did not add to the size of the Jewish population overall.

Low birth rate, aging population, rising mortality rate, small family size, increasing rates of intermarriage, and fluctuating but continuous emigration characterize the Jewish populations of Latin America, causing them to diminish in size and to shrink to minuscule minorities. Urbanization intensifies all these trends. City life typically reinforces the desire to limit the size of one's family. Higher education paves the way for economic and social mobility, which in turn brings Jewish youth into contact with attractive non-Jewish mates, as well as with the potential for improved quality of life through emigration. Jews at both ends of the spectrum—those who intermarry and ignore their Jewish heritage and those who emigrate in order to lead fuller lives as Jews—contribute to the cultural homogeneity of the Latin American peoples, who are as yet undecided whether to accept cultural pluralism as a valid ideal.

PART FOUR

JEWS AND THEIR WORLDS

CHAPTER 9

Jews North and South

*In moments of disenchantment, Jaime realized the difficulties
inherent in going from any Jewish past to a Catholic present.*

—Mario Szichman, *At 8:25 Evita Became Immortal*

JEWISH LIFE IN the United States, so intensively researched, offers the
possibility of a useful comparison with Jewish life in Latin America. The
contrast between the two communities points up differences that stem only
in part from the immigrants (for they were roughly similar in their origins and
part of the same migratory waves) but also from the nature of the host societies
in which they settled.

Jews of the United States dwell within the boundaries of one of the world's
largest territorial sovereignties, characterized by secular norms, pacific alternation of governments, and a social milieu created by the immigrants themselves.
Jews of Latin America are scattered throughout twenty-one separate polities,
characterized by hierarchical religious norms, volatile politics, and a social
milieu that was created long before their arrival and to which they are expected
to conform. Examining the social structures of the two realms, one is struck
over and over again by the reluctance of Latin Americans to make the changes
necessary to integrate immigrants into their national societies. Despite demands
that immigrants assimilate, the latter's efforts to integrate themselves met with
suspicion, if not outright rejection. Although it scarcely can be said that the
United States was totally accommodating in this regard, comparison shows the
far more limited flexibility of Latin American institutions and their resistance
to the entry of Jews in particular into civic life.

The Jewish community of the United States came into existence within a
society that had been spun off from Europe in the Age of Enlightenment. The
Jewish communities of Latin America came into existence in societies that had
been founded and still were grounded in the pre-Enlightenment past. Jews
were emancipated by their arrival in the United States; Jews of the Latin
American republics have not been fully emancipated yet from the hateful
religious and political stigmata that followed them to the New World.

215

Spain in America was a fragment of medieval Europe that, once loosed from its European context, continued to evolve along the path determined by its heritage. Incorporating Indians and then blacks into the lower rungs of the corporate and patrimonial structure, Latin American societies took on an American coloration but retained their medieval orientation. In Louis Hartz's formulation, "the logic of feudal fragmentation" persisted, resulting in a "heart-breaking betrayal" of the Enlightenment.[1] The conquistadors were the last and the most successful of the crusaders, and if the latifundia that were settled upon their successors were not precisely feudal estates, clearly they owed more to the institution of feudalism than they did to either freehold tenure or industrial capitalism. Spanish and Portuguese statism, revived and strengthened by transplantation to virgin territory overseas, met no countervailing power strong enough to challenge it, and consequently life in the Indies quickly settled down on foundations long familiar to the peninsulars.

If Spain and Portugal were able, as they were, to resist the forces of Protestant and industrial revolutions, how much more resistant were the forces of tradition in these new nuclei of Iberia, whither only the orthodox could travel. Having destroyed the Amerindian civilizations, the conquerors grafted onto the ruins their own vision of the just society: Catholic, hierarchical, patrimonial. With certificates of clean blood they purchased posts in government and church, becoming the bureaucrats and managers of empire. The tone of Latin American society was set by royal pensioners and true believers, whose allegiance for the next three centuries was to remain immutably fixed to their royal master upon whom they depended for their wealth and status. They would never have left the kingdom had not the kingdom left them. When the French Revolution and Napoleon's invasion of Spain and Portugal cut the tie that bound, Enlightenment did not suddenly rush in. Rather, criollo elites took their nations out of the empire, generating "independence" revolutions that guaranteed that nothing would change. With the breath of liberty infused into them, medieval forms of life survived in Latin America long after their European originals had succumbed owing to their inadequacy in dealing with modernizing forces. These medieval forms included legal and social inhibitions upon Jews.

North America began receiving European settlers two hundred years later than South and Central America. During the intervening period, Europe exclusive of Iberia went through a great transformation. The Reformation and the wars of religion cracked forever the Catholic Church's pretensions to universality, paving the way for religious competition. A wave of rationalism began the rout of all religions, a process that was to bring to birth the Age of Enlightenment and lead eventually to the emancipation of the Jews from discriminatory laws and immurement in ghettoes. Industrial revolution transformed Europe's modes of production, while capitalism began to alter the relationship between employer and employed. By the eighteenth century, Europe was entering the modern age, and Jews were being freed of the age-old restrictions on residence, occupation, and family life that had trammeled them for centuries.

As a result of the difference in timing, the people who settled North America differed in mentality from those who had conquered the South. The eighteenth-century efflux of settlers out of England and northern Europe generally were the unlicensed and the unemployed, dissenters from old religions and cast-offs of the new industrialism, looking for land and work to set their hands to. Devotees of eccentric cults, they had reason to fear state churches and came more and more to view religion as beyond the grasp of government. Catholics, Lutherans, and others who in Europe had belonged to state churches were now in a minority and in time would have to tailor their beliefs to the new American reality. The rational revolution was beginning to make its impact; many were prepared to believe that the world was subject to natural laws, or at least to the laws of nature's God, and that an individual's relationship to this God was a purely personal affair.

In contrast to the image of the deicide, the devil, the usurer, the bawd, that confronted Jewish immigrants to Spanish- and Portuguese-speaking lands, Jewish immigrants to the English colonies found elements with which they could identify. South Carolina's charter had been drafted under the influence of John Locke, author of the first published appeal for emancipation of the Jews in the English-speaking world. The Puritans thought of themselves as Hebrews, "children of the covenant," who had been brought to New England's promised land by divine providence. Emphasis by fundamentalist sects upon the reading of the Bible led to the teaching of Hebrew in order that God's word could be heard in the original. Ancient Hebrew prophecy was one source of nourishment for the Enlightenment, and thus the climate of the colonies owed much to the Old Testament. Jews coming into colonies that honored the same tradition they did found a friendlier welcome than those who came to lands whose heritage—never fully repudiated—included the use of state power to eradicate it.

The nonconforming and dissenting colonists of the North rebelled against royal authority on very slight pretext, when it seemed as though Parliament was abandoning its laissez-faire manner of government. Placing power in the hands of the people, the colonists devised a constitution that limited the power that either government or church could wield over the citizen, by forbidding them to buttress one another. The anticlerical thrust of the Enlightenment made inevitable the separation of church and state, without the need to fight a war of religion on American soil. Emancipation of the Jews was thus achieved in the United States without bloodshed and without reference to Jews, for there were almost none in the country at the time. From the moment the republic was launched, Jews enjoyed civil, religious, and political equality. There were to be no religious tests for office, no bar to the marriage or burial of Jews, no limitations on place of residence or occupation. Furthermore, the terms of revolution from the mother country offered the promise that American society would continue to open outward, rather than collapse in upon itself as had happened so quickly in Spanish and Portuguese realms. The break with Europe allowed Jews to feel that they, too, had broken with the desolate past, that the United States would be a different kind of diaspora, one where Jews could live on equal terms with Gentiles because their values sprang from the same sources and were compatible with one another. This compatibility explains both the magnetism that the United States exerted for Jews and the common-place Latin American perception of the United States as entirely Jewish.

Lacking an established church, the United States attracted immigrants of every religious persuasion and of none. The diverse flow of peoples in turn confirmed the heterogeneous nature of American life. Immigrants arrived in such masses, into territory so nearly depopulated, that they created their own social norms, establishing as the national ideal the actuality of their own existence: the plural society. No one would deny that it was the dominant white, Protestant, Anglo-Saxon male who set the standards, but this dominance was not monolithic and did not totally exclude Jews. There was room for the Jewish as for the non-Jewish immigrant; a variety of identities could coexist. The social norm of cultural pluralism that developed in response to the immigrant experience was never completely accepted; curiously, it flourished side by side with the WASP ideal.

As a direct consequence, participation by Jews in the life of the United States has regularly been welcomed as a sign that they were becoming Ameri-canized. This process went so far that by the mid-twentieth century, Judaism was being accorded status as the third major religion in the country, despite the fact that Jews never accounted for more than 3.7 percent of the population and are today an even smaller proportion.

In total contrast, the Jews of Latin America have had great difficulty over-coming the perception of themselves as foreigners, unwelcome and illegitimate intruders into national life, and even as corrupters of the national spirit. Jewish immigrants to Latin America came to a continent already preempted by two powerful cultural traditions that either ignored or were hostile to them. The first of these, the autochthonous one, was not attractive to Jews. The vestiges of defeated Maya, Guaraní, or Inca civilizations seemed to have little to offer either Ashkenazi or Sephardi; nor did Jews have a place in the indigenous world, save in the role of devil to which the missionaries had consigned them.[2] Entry into their new societies had to depend on identification with the Spanish or the Portuguese.

The same was true for all immigrants: their common meeting ground was the church. But the church, which compassionately absorbed Indian and black, Italian and Pole, found Jews indigestible. The Jews were the one people whom the church had failed historically either to absorb or to destroy. In the unrecon-structed atmosphere of Latin Catholicism, where the line between church and state was blurred and overlapping jurisdiction persisted, Jews continued to be viewed as unassimilable. If they were outside the church, were they not also outside the state?

Until the present, national allegiances have continued to be filtered through

Catholic sensibilities. Most Latin American constitutions require that the president of the nation profess Roman Catholicism, a stipulation abandoned by Argentina only in 1994. The ubiquitous Christ figures displayed on mountaintops are a continual reminder of the Jews' inherited status as deicides. The more compassionate Catholic rendering of history, which reminds the faithful that Christ himself was a Jew, invites masochistic submission. The child in the classroom is daily asked to identify with either the crucified or the crucifiers. The choice of either role requires continual dissimulation and suppression. Jewish children must either pretend to be that which they are not or pretend not to be that which they are. Either choice results in utilizing only half their identity and the expenditure of considerable energy in suppressing the other half.

There are, of course, ecumenical efforts within the Latin American church, which wax and wane with the appointment of hierarchs with differing orientations. The number and influence of clerics working in the spirit of Vatican II varies by country. But the end toward which they strive—the reception of Jews into a common humanity formerly restricted to Christians—represents a difficult break with the past. This break, the all-important emancipation, occurred in the United States before the drafting of the Constitution.

On the part of the Jews, every attempt to identify with the majority culture brought them up against its essentially Catholic core, the centrality of the Inquisition mentality (displayed with such sadistic cruelty during the proceso), and their own role as victims. Despite the lapse of centuries and the historical discontinuity between Spain and the Spanish-speaking republics, echoes of the Expulsion reverberated in immigrant ears. The principal park of Mexico City, the Alameda, where children play and Diego Rivera painted, was known to Jews as the site of the auto-da-fé, where New Christian pioneers were reduced to ashes by their Old Christian compatriots. One of the main streets of Lima was still known as Matajudíos, Kill-the-Jews; Havana boasted streets named Inquisador and Picoto (gibbet). In colonial times, Jews had been pariahs. In modern times, omnipresent Catholic symbolism confirmed their status as outsiders, limited their access to education and to politics, and impeded their social acceptability.

We have seen that many Jewish immigrants to Latin America were alienated from religion and thus available for recruitment for life in lands where the survival of Judaism was not at all assured. Jewish immigrants who gave up their identity were free to intermarry, assimilate, and disappear as Jews, and that is even more true for their university-educated children and grandchildren. For those who wish to remain Jewish, life is more complex. Had the Latin American republics broken with the past, developing secular and modernizing national symbols, the way would have been paved for the acceptance of Jews into national life on the basis of equality. Hopeful immigrants at the turn of the century believed this was a possibility. There is a world of difference between merging with a secular population on equal terms and accepting a subordinate position on a Catholic standard. To the degree that the Latin republics choose to remain loyal to their Catholic core, Jews are closed out of dominant social institutions. Where no neutral ground appears between antagonistic Iberian and Jewish traditions, emergence of a Latin American Jewish identity is frustrated.

Pressure for conformity was felt by all immigrants, but a Jew had harder choices to make. One had to choose between continuing to feel a part of the Jewish people (which implied distance from one's fellow Bolivians or Argentinians) or starting anew as part (but not an integral part) of the Bolivian or Argentinian nation. The adjustment required was more demanding than that required of Catholic Italians and Spaniards. The terms in which the choice was presented were more urgent than the terms offered by societies that accept cultural diversity. Those Jews who continued to identify primarily as Jews ended by constructing for themselves their own private societies, within which everyone was known to everyone else and responsible for one another's behavior. This core society was then attacked: the building of AMIA, the Buenos Aires kehillah, was destroyed by bombs in 1994 (see pp. 265–68).

In the United States, numerous institutions evolved that took as their task the Americanization of the immigrant. Foremost among these was the universal, tax-supported public school. Notoriously, children were taught the pledge of allegiance to the flag before the alphabet. The primary interest of the state was in Americanizing the child; reading and writing could come later. A close adjunct to this process was the free night school for immigrants. It is not irrelevant that the prototype of such schools was opened in Baltimore in 1889 by Henrietta Szold, daughter of an immigrant Hungarian rabbi. Its first students were Russian Jews, and the subjects taught were American history and the English language. The assumption of responsibility for this school by the city of Baltimore represented a clear acceptance of the obligation to teach the newcomers English and prepare them for citizenship. Subsequently, the system of adult night school education became a permanent part of the American educational scene.

Universal military conscription into the citizen army of the United States during World War I was another homogenizing experience for immigrants. Work in the industrial plant, where labor, like machines, was viewed as interchangeable, though experienced at the time as dehumanizing, obliterated distinctions between white ethnic groups, whether immigrant or Yankee. Jews who flocked to the factories and sweatshops became subject to the homogenizing pressures of the industrial plant and, in the course of a generation and in the company of other immigrants, became "Americanized." Standardization of behavior patterns was speeded by the continent-wide network of transportation and communication, which made it possible for immigrants to blend to a national, rather than a merely regional, standard.

None of these nationalizing forces had free play in the Latin American republics. Burdened with some of the most difficult terrain in the world, Latin American communications and transportation responded to regional, not continental, exigencies. Industrialization did not really get under way until

World War I; abstention from that conflict meant that citizen armies—the great democratizing force ever since the French Revolution—never came into being. To the contrary, in the anomie that followed independence, soldiering degenerated into banditry. As for public education, it was the victim of the most profound apathy and prejudice on the part of legislators.

In the absence of nationalizing institutions, immigrants to Latin America were left largely on their own when it came to restructuring their lives to suit the conditions of their new homes. Inevitably, they tended to perpetuate the pattern of life of the old country, since it was the only one they knew. This process operated on all nationality groups and marginalized them from the political process. Its impact on Jewish immigrants was particularly severe because Jews were themselves divided into numerous ethnic groups characterized by differences in language, custom, and religious practice. In their search for mutually supportive relationships, Jews reproduced the varied institutions of their countries of origin. In the process, they unintentionally walled themselves off from one another as well as from the larger society. The result was that welter of interethnic rivalries which for many years incapacitated the communities for concerted action.

Since Jewish immigrants to the United States originated in roughly similar migrations, the same potential for divisiveness existed among them. Indeed, at the close of the colonial period, rivalry did develop between "aristocratic" Sephardim and "parvenu" Germans. Later, the aloof attitude of German Jews was to afflict the impoverished East Europeans. But despite episodes of conflict, these interethnic feuds did not become institutionalized as they did in Latin America. The representative and philanthropic bodies of active American Jewish life embrace Jews of every ethnic origin. In acculturating to a United States standard, Jews acculturated to one another.

The Americanization of immigrants was undertaken in religiously neutral terms. Development of secular public life in the United States and the consignment of religious belief to the private sphere enabled Jews to identify with the nation and to adopt its symbols and heroes without reservation. The religious affiliation of American presidents is not regarded as relevant in public school textbooks. Old Glory, Mount Rushmore, and Monticello are national, not religious, symbols. No schoolchild is required to learn what church, if any, Davy Crockett attended. Even the religious sensibilities of a Lincoln are transmuted into a nonsectarian faith that is as acceptable to Jewish as to Christian citizens. To be "religious" is a sufficient value in itself.

It is a truism of Jewish history that the elements wherein Jewish communities differ from one another are elements that have been taken over from their host societies. We have seen that the rigidities of Latin American Catholicism were early replicated within the Jewish communities of that continent. Monopoly over the cemetery gave the kehillah the same leverage as that exerted by the church. Rabbinical resistance to reform paralleled the opposition of Latin American prelates to the innovations of Vatican II. In the United States, Jewish congregations cast themselves in the Protestant mold, refashioning Jewish tradition and offering to the American Jew a variety of religious styles that parallels the range offered to Protestants. The Reform movement made a particularly swift and drastic adaptation to American life, reflecting the emancipation psychology of the movement's German founders. Conservatism threw a bridge between Reform and Orthodoxy, providing a way by which the East European migrants could grow into the role of "third major religion" America was offering. Later, Reconstructionism opened the way to continually changing interpretations of Judaism to keep it in touch with the evolution of American life. Eclectic religious practice in the United States contrasts strongly with the monopoly maintained until recently by the Catholic Church and by Orthodox Judaism in Latin America. The result is that third-generation American Jews are free to embrace their Jewish identification while assimilating to American life. There is no unbridgeable fracture between Protestantism and Judaism and ample meeting ground for the two traditions.

But it is in the area of economics that comparison of the Jewish situation in the North and in the South is most illuminating. The Jewish mode of entry into the North American economy included the same reliance on peddling that has been noted for Latin America. Following an initial period of itinerancy and forced savings, many peddlers moved into either fixed commerce or manufacturing (principally in textiles and the clothing industry). The immigrants' behavior patterns were similar, but the receptive molds of the two societies were distinctly different. Since industrialization began considerably earlier in the North, purchasing power was more widely diffused throughout the population. There was little of that contempt for commerce which was so notable a feature of the Latin South. Moneymaking, striving to get ahead, and competition for status were all qualities approved by the culture; indeed, success at these activities was widely regarded as a sign of grace. Although the individual Jewish entrepreneur may have been as disliked by his non-Jewish competitor as was his coreligionist in the South by his, nevertheless northern culture, suffused by the Protestant work ethic, supported his efforts to get ahead. Uncle Sam himself had been a merchant. He provided quite a different role model than did the plundering *hidalgo* of Iberian mythology. There existed in the United States no counterpart to the obloquy that Hispanic culture had heaped upon the entrepreneur since the thirteenth century, unless it were contempt for the man who depended on inherited wealth for status. Individuals with ingenuity and brains enough to turn potential into reality were admired—even if they were Jewish. With the recognition of entrepreneurial skills widespread through the population, there was nothing mysterious about the process of making money, and no legend of a Jewish conspiracy was needed to explain the financial success of individual Jews. Nor was it necessary to compose fictitious Jewish genealogies for non-Jews who showed business acumen.

Very few of the Latin American Jewish communities ever achieved the buoyancy that characterizes Jewish life in the United States. One might name Curaçao under Dutch rule, Panama during the building of the canal, Chile during World War I, contemporary Brazil (whose national motto is "Order and

Progress"). The factor common to each was the existence of an expanding free enterprise economy. Jews have attained status in societies that measured them by their achievements, and they have been kept in a subordinate position where status was ascribed by birth.

In addition to the petty merchants and craftsmen, there were Jewish proletarians in both migratory streams. The reciprocal nature of immigrant acculturation and structural assimilation emerges clearly in the field of labor organization. Jews were prime movers in the initiation of labor unions in the United States. Workers with their roots in the Bund organized unions that set standards for the entire labor movement with respect to collective bargaining, the forty-hour week, medical insurance, workers' pensions, and the arbitration of grievances. In fact, it could be said that during their time in the factory, Jewish workers revolutionized the condition of the American working man and woman.

Along with their fellow activists, Jewish labor leaders suffered police repression at the start, not because they were Jews but because they were labor leaders. But the most forceful among them—people like Sidney Hillman, Morris Hillquit, Alex Rose, Rose Schneiderman, David Dubinsky—ultimately came to wield considerable influence in state and national politics. Merely to name them confirms the salience of Jewish labor leaders and their emergence from a parochial to a national stage. Their daily activities as they struggled to earn a living in decent conditions opened up key institutions in American society.

Not so in Latin America. Early union activity by Jews was met not only by police repression but by goon squad action against Jewish neighborhoods and homes. The strike at Vasena ironworks in Buenos Aires in 1919 ended in a pogrom in the Jewish district of Once. Over the course of a generation, as it became clear that a Jewish contribution to national political life was not acceptable, the ideals of the Bund were compressed into the hothouse atmosphere of the kehillah, where they could have no practical effect save for casting votes in favor of a socialist version of Zionism. Jewish labor leaders never gained national acceptability for their ideas, a failure shared by their non-Jewish colleagues. Failure of the Radical party of Irigoyen in Argentina to act upon its principles is notorious. Socialism influenced the Latin American labor movement, but did not permeate the culture. In Argentina, socialism was swamped by *peronismo*, a personalist movement that manipulated the loyalties of workers while reducing their unions to dependency on the chief executive. Egalitarian ideologies found no resonance in society as a whole. In this hierarchical setting, Jews, as a subordinated minority, were permitted to occupy a well-defined niche in society, circumscribed in terms of commercial and financial services rendered. While Jewish individuals might be elected or appointed to public office, legitimacy was not accorded to any political interest of the Jewish collectivity.

In contrast to the political neutralization of Jews in Latin American politics, Jewish immigrants to the United States plunged into local politics as soon as they had mastered the English language. By the turn of the century, there were Jewish ward heelers, poll watchers, ballot clerks, and campaign orators in East Coast cities. Jews were admitted to Tammany councils and nominated to municipal office. They were appointed corporation counsels and assistant district attorneys; they sought election as assemblymen and aldermen, and many went on to judicial appointments. The "Jewish vote" was being sought in New York by 1905, and candidates campaigned vigorously in wards populated by Jews.[3] Political activism among Jews depended not only on their own proclivities (presumably shared by their cousins in Buenos Aires and Bogotá) but on what has been called the democratic mold. The political culture offered access at entry level to any group that could bring together sufficient votes to force attention to their needs.

The pluralist society of the United States incorporated immigrant Jews politically, as Latin American societies did not. The process was crucial not just for immigrants, or only for Jews, but for the entire working class, which was enabled to use the engines of major political parties to bring about vast improvements in living conditions and to achieve political status sufficient to guarantee that these gains would be permanent.

The level of political activity among American Jews has regularly been measured at higher levels than among American non-Jews. This involvement can be documented at every level from the college campus up to and including national elections. American Jews wield influence beyond the weight of their numbers in many areas related to politics, as journalists, party organizers, volunteers, and consultants. For long, the number of Jewish officeholders did not reflect the degree of their political activism; residual bars reduced the appeal of Jewish candidates. A 1974 study found that in the history of the United States, 108 Jews had been elected to high office—governor, senator, or congressman. Six-tenths of 1 percent of all senators elected to that date were Jewish. By that year, however, Jews were represented proportionately in high office: two were governors, three senators, twelve congressmen, or 2.9 percent of all the high elected officials in the nation.[4] The 103rd Congress, elected in 1992, included 33 Jewish representatives and 10 senators,[5] a demonstration of the growing acceptability of Jewish candidates over the intervening years.

Jewish individuals have not been permitted to play a commensurate political role in the Spanish-speaking republics. The few Jews who hold office are extremely susceptible to displacement by shifts in the balance of power between major contenders—as happened dramatically in Chile in the sixties and seventies. Both President Salvador Allende and General Augusto Pinochet, who overthrew his government, appointed Jews to high office. Their forced resignations mirror the departure of all officials from administrations that lose power; however, in the case of Jews, such a development leaves this minority totally unrepresented in government. Political access is never quite good enough. Political activity itself has come to be feared as exacting disproportionate penalties from the community as a whole, as it did in Chile. The electoral process, which has not functioned satisfactorily for the general population, has been even less satisfactory for Jews in terms of either representation or integration.

While American Jews can participate in elections and then sit back to watch their outcome with equanimity for their fate *as Jews,* Latin American Jews must constantly gauge the level of anti-Semitism among their governors. Jews are insufficient numerically to affect the outcome of elections, even if they were to vote as a unit (there is no evidence that they do) and even if elections were to be decided by a count of the ballots, which frequently they are not. There has been one notable effort to elicit Jewish support on the part of those whose duty it is to arrange elections. In 1943, in the face of anti-Semitic demonstrations and the fear that Argentina would be perceived as the last refuge of fascism, General Juan Perón created the Organización Israelita Argentina. This Argentine Jewish Organization was intended as a means of enrolling Jews in the peronista party, but the mainstream community was too suspicious of Perón to take advantage of this opening. The OIA never achieved the numbers or the political weight to challenge the DAIA, and eventually faded away.[6]

Inability to compete in local and national politics leaves Latin American Jews peculiarly vulnerable to shifting political ground in volatile polities whose legal norms do not provide for their entry into society on equal terms. Jewish vulnerability derives only in part from official ideology. Jews qua Jews fared well under the reactionary Trujillo of the Dominican Republic and the radical Fidel Castro of Cuba. The military junta of Argentina licensed the most revolting anti-Semitic acts; at the same time, the equally authoritarian military junta in neighboring Chile went to considerable lengths to reassure its Jewish community. The common element is expedience. It may suit one government or another to accommodate Jewish interests or to squeeze them; nowhere do legal and social norms provide for their treatment solely on the basis of their citizenship. The anti-Jewish stance of medieval Catholicism is available for recycling by *nacionalista* political parties with a paranoid vision of Jewish conspiracies or by Third World party-liners parroting anti-Israel slogans. Latin American Jews are dependent on the goodwill of the powers that be, rather than on legal norms and ingrained habits of toleration. In this situation, it is probably irrelevant whether a government is of the Right or of the Left—anti-Semitism is a weapon available to either, and the Jewish communities make what arrangements they can to safeguard their security.

The absorption of immigrants is a reciprocal process: immigrants must learn new forms of behavior, adopting the cultural patterns of their host society; and the host society must be willing to move over and accommodate the immigrants. Seven variables of the assimilation process have been identified, each subject to an infinite number of variations: acculturation, meaning that immigrants have changed their cultural patterns to those of the host society; structural assimilation, implying admission into cliques, clubs, and elite institutions; acceptability as marriage partners; a sense of peoplehood based exclusively on the host society; the existence of prejudice; overt discrimination; and civic assimilation, marked by agreement on values and the distribution of power.[7] If we attempt to fit Latin American Jewry into this schema, we find that Jewish immigrants to Latin America acculturated rapidly, translating themselves from Yiddish, Ladino, Arabic, and a host of other languages into Spanish or Portuguese in the course of a single generation. To a far greater degree than in the North, however, structural assimilation has been slow to occur. Societies have been reluctant to grant Jews access to important sectors of their national societies.

On the other hand, Latin American Jews enjoy greater acceptability as marital partners in the South than in the North. The revelation by demographers in 1974 that half the projected Argentine Jewish population simply did not exist testifies to the willingness of Jews to assimilate and the ease with which they may do so if they cease to regard themselves as Jews. Magnus Mörner long ago pointed out that Latin Americans tend to interpret acculturation in biological terms.[8] An astonishing variety of peoples have been digested through intermarriage and miscegenation, and Latin absorptive capacity includes Jews.

The rate of Jewish intermarriage is high not only in areas such as Argentina that are populated by Europeans, but likewise in countries such as Cuba and Brazil, whose populations are exotic to most Jews. "We fell in love with our children and married their mothers," as one early chronicler put it. The trend toward intermarriage accelerated as more Jews entered the universities and went on to the free professions. Modern urban lifestyles support abandonment of religious affiliation, and increasing numbers of intellectuals of Jewish descent stopped identifying with the Jewish people. This trend reached the point where increasing numbers of marriages between Jews take place by civil contract, in order to avoid any contact with religion. Since the offspring of such marriages are not Jews, there is a possibility that the East Europeans, on the surface the least digestible of Jewish immigrants to Latin America, will go the way of the Portuguese nation of Curaçao, the Alsatians of Mexico, and the Sephardim of the Amazon. The dissolution of the Jewish people would prepare the way for full-scale participation by the descendants of Jews in the peoplehood of each of the republics, the fourth stage of the schematic representation of the assimilatory process referred to above. For this to happen, social and political structures would have to open further, because of residual prejudice against the *descendants* of Jews.

The philo-Semite (and there are many in Latin America, even discounting the superstitious who wear a Star of David as a good luck charm) tries to destroy prejudice by naming heroes he wrongly believes to have been Jewish: Christopher Columbus; Bartolomé de Las Casas, apostle to the Indians; the poet-philosopher Sor Juana Inés de la Cruz; Antonio José Sucre, Liberator of Ecuador; Ferdinand the Catholic; Francisco Madera, revolutionary president of Mexico; not to mention all the inhabitants of Antioquia. It might be said that these claims and disclaimers muddy the waters even more, for they foster the myth of the hidden Jew. The reality of Jewish life on the continent is contained in the daily existence of Jews. The myth of the Jew is manifest in persistent "accusations" of Jewish ancestry against heroes and politicians; rumored plots by Jewish bankers to take over entire countries in cahoots with Jewish communists; newspaper reports of the imminent arrival of Israeli parachutists on their way to invade Patagonia; and the omnipresent Christs whose vivid sufferings ordain, if not the punishment of the Jews, at least their subjugation. Among surface manifestations, one may note that anti-Semitic tracts such as the notoriously fraudulent *Protocols of the Elders of Zion* are widely sold on Latin street corners, along with those other escapist fantasies of the disinherited, lottery tickets. Folk anti-Semitism feeds the jealousies and hatreds of people condemned to poverty by their own elites.

Henry Ford's scurrilous *International Jew* is among the anti-Semitic pamphlets widely sold at newspaper kiosks throughout Latin America.

Adherence to such a value system ordained the near total exclusion of Jews from civic life. Five hundred years ago, Jews—and even Christians descended from Jews—were barred from settling in the New World. With the advent of independence, Jews were admitted to the republics but continued to suffer legal disabilities. School systems were based on philosophical tenets that Jews rejected and that rejected Jews. By the end of the nineteenth century, most legal prohibitions had been removed and a more promising environment created for non-Latin immigrants. But major social and political institutions continued to rebuff Jews. This is amply demonstrated by the paucity of Jewish officeholders; the vulnerability of Jews in public life to anti-Semitic libels; the absence of Jews from high ranks in the military; and the continued acceptability of anti-Semitic graffiti and gross caricatures of Jews in the media.

The blockage of the entry of Jews into the core of national life represents, in a way, the compromise between proimmigration and anti–immigration forces: Jews were admitted to the Latin republics, but they were not granted the boon of civic assimilation. The process, which is so far advanced in the United States, has made a beginning in Brazil but is just getting under way in the Spanish-speaking republics. Jewish efforts to enter into the full responsibilities and rights of citizenship have consistently been blocked and their influence circumscribed, thus limiting the impact Jews individually or as a group can make upon society in any dimension other than the economic. Clearly, the chief limitation to the total assimilation of Latin American Jewry is the reluctance of society to admit Jews to membership.

If there was one area of the world where Sephardic immigrants would seem to have had an advantage over Ashkenazim, it was in the Spanish- and Portuguese-speaking American nations. In fact, at the turn of the century, it was proposed by Gerchunoff and others that the re-encounter among Jewish and Christian inheritors of the Iberian tradition would produce a Sephardic cultural renaissance. The exact form that this *neosefardismo* might assume was left quite vague: would it merely involve renewed interest in Sephardic poetry and cuisine, a refurbishing of the legends of the Golden Age of Spain? or would something new, something gloriously unforeseen, emerge synergistically out of the twentieth-century re-encounter between the winners and losers of 1492?

The prospects for *neosefardismo* were based on the return of Spanish-speaking Jews to a Spanish-speaking milieu. Sephardim had compacted their historic experience into their home language (known variously as Ladino, Judezmo, or Heketia) which, even after the lapse of centuries, remained mutually intelligible with Castilian Spanish. Once returned to a Spanish environment, might not the bright flame of Sephardic genius be reignited?[9]

But the most cursory comparison between the conditions under which Sephardim flourished in Iberia, and the conditions under which *neosefardismo* was anticipated to flourish in Latin America, shows decisive differences. Jews lived in Iberia from the third century of the Christian era until 1492 and were integral to the peninsula's history. Sephardim arrived in Latin America already stigmatized by the Expulsion of 1492, which stamped them as undesirable foreigners. Sephardic culture flourished in Iberia largely under the Muslims, who assigned a subordinate status to Jews but treated them as one of the "peoples of the book" whose religious sensibilities were superior to those of pagans. In the Spanish domains in the New World the Catholic Church anathematized both Muslims and Jews as heretics, to the point of accusing them as cannibals and idolators, accusations that could not have prevailed in

Spain itself, where Jews and Muslims were well known by their neighbors. Moreover, among the immigrants to Latin America who were known as Sephardim (under the broad definition customarily used by Ashkenazim), only a minority were actual inheritors of the Spanish legacy. Most were speakers of Arabic who had received the Sephardic tradition at the hands of the Spanish exiles centuries before. In combination with the hardship of the migratory process, these factors were enough to thwart, at least for now, the hopes for a neo-Sephardic renaissance.

Neosefardismo did find a home in Latin America, but not among its Jewish legatees. Its best-known exponent was the criollo Jorge Luis Borges (1899–1986), whose interest in kabalah animates his best-known works. The revival of this aspect of Sephardic tradition has passed on to a new generation of authors, some Jewish and some not. But Jewish authors working in a neo-Sephardic mode live in Spain, not Latin America.

Latin America Jews are orphans of history, balanced between brutal rejection and tentative acceptance, cultural marginalization and biologic absorption. They seem poised between permanence—vide their integration into cultural life—and dissolution, as marked most vividly by their high rate of emigration and declining population totals.

In the eyes of nacionalistas for whom hispanicism and Catholicism are the very core of nationality, Jews will never be able to overcome their image as conspirators against religion, state, and family. In the liberal mind, choice really lies with the Jews: to become wholly naturalized by dropping their Jewishness or perversely to continue marginalizing themselves behind the walls of their synagogues and sports clubs.

United States Jews passed through this existential identity crisis during the immigrant generation and have since succeeded in integrating themselves as Jews into the American psyche. Being Jewish and being American are not regarded as incompatible states. Skepticism concerning the permanence of this happy resolution is at the core of the Zionist thesis.

CHAPTER 10

Latin American Jewry and Israel

We tried to sell them holy water from the Jordan River,
but they weren't interested.

—Israeli embassy spokesperson

WHILE THEY WERE emigrating to the West, the hearts of thousands of Jewish immigrants were in the East. "Argentina or Palestine?" was a question that was earnestly posed at a time when few European Jews knew anything at all about Argentina, and rather too much about the ill-favored and neglected province of the Ottoman Empire. For a few years, there was genuine hesitation as to which country offered the best possibility for renewing Jewish life, worn down by the oppressions of Europe. The issue was debated between those who would draw the Jewish people toward Western civilization, and those for whom the millennial Jewish attachment to the land of the Bible was paramount. When the first Zionist congress convened in Basel, Switzerland in 1897, delegates from all over the world voted to resolve the problem of Jewish homelessness by sponsoring a return to Zion. The Basel Program stated that "Zionism seeks to establish a home for the Jewish people in Erez Israel secured under public law." It was welcomed by many, though assuredly not all, Jews in the Latin American diaspora. In Buenos Aires, where only a few thousand Jews lived at that date, a group immediately formed in support of the Zionist ideal. In Santiago de Chile in 1917, Jews who normally kept a low profile and did not even have a house of prayer publicly celebrated the Balfour Declaration in which the British mandatory power undertook to foster a Jewish homeland in Palestine. Jewish nationalism offered an emotional focus for immigrants who were having difficulty establishing themselves in their new societies, and an outlet for political activity on the part of people who were marginalized from the political processes of their adoptive homelands by the invincible Catholicism at their core. At the same time, Jewish attachment to the Zionist ideal raised apprehensions of dual loyalty in the minds of those inured by centuries of attachment to the monolithic standard of the apostolic Roman Catholic state.

In South and Central America, Zionism faced little competition for Jewish loyalties. The absence of guarantees of religious freedom made Latin America a speculative venture for Jews in the nineteenth century, and we have seen that far fewer were attracted to the southern continent than to the northern—possibly 376,000 compared with 2,800,000 over the century 1840–1942. Those who came were for the most part not the deeply religious, but the areligious and the antireligious, for whom the absence of the all-embracing Jewish organizations that already existed in the United States was not a disadvantage. Rabbis of the period were urging Jews not to settle in Latin America because of the danger of assimilation. In the cosmopolitan centers that attracted secular Jews, it was easy to intermarry and acculturate to their counterparts, the anticlerical Catholics who comprised an important sector of the population. Immigrants alienated from traditional religion found secular common ground in the liberal urban sectors of nineteenth-century Argentina, Uruguay, Chile, and the southern states of Brazil.

Since the rabbis who inveighed against Jewish migration to Latin America did not themselves emigrate there, a shortage of religious leaders prevailed from the start. Spanish-speaking rabbis had to be imported to the continent from North Africa and the Balkans. Traditionally, the most Orthodox of rabbis were hired by these fundamentally secular communities, in order that the thing be done right on behalf of people who often as not were totally secular in their way of life. Consequently, rabbis were viewed more as facilitators of ritual than as spiritual guides. Absent a religious core, Zionism became the Jewish religion, the glue that held together the diverse ethnic groups of people who identified as Jews.

Zionism supplied another need as well. In most of Latin America, formal citizenship was difficult to attain, and distinctions between criollos and immigrants rankled. As a result, immigrants of all ethnic origins tended to retain their identification with their former motherlands. But Jews, almost all of whom arrived in flight from their previous places of residence, had no motherland. This lack in itself aroused suspicion, activating the myth of the Wandering Jew. It came as a relief to have that lack supplied in 1948 through creation of the State of Israel, legitimating Jews as a people like any other. In fact, few Jewish immigrants had come to Latin America from Palestine/Israel, but the Jewish state was recognized and acknowledged to be their spiritual homeland—the *madre patria*. At first, it didn't seem to matter that a certain confusion arose over the meaning of the terms *israelita* (an alternative term for *judío*, or Jew) and *israelí* (a citizen of Israel).

Within the organized Jewish communities, Zionism, which had been present from the start, was reinforced by internal struggle against the Communists, who prior to 1948 followed the Kremlin line in opposing creation of a Jewish state. During the 1950s in Jewish communities worldwide, these struggles ended with the expulsion of Communists from all community agencies. In the authoritarian states of the southern and central Americas, communities also conducted sporadic purges of elements, such as anarchists and labor union leaders, who might offend the local power structure. Concerned that the activities of individual Jewish radicals would call down reprisal against the entire Jewish community (as happened in Buenos Aires in 1909 and on both sides of the Plata in 1919), the Jewish communities undertook the responsibility of policing their own. The ostracism of left-wing Jews from community life can be viewed from different perspectives. It was either a wise precaution on the part of a marginalized and highly insecure group lacking political power or it can be seen as a defensive measure by property owners to blunt the demands of the proletariat, with class interests outweighing religious and ethnic ties. The result either way was to move the rump communities perceptibly to the right. Zionists who belonged to left-wing parties remained within the community, but limited their efforts to designing a utopian society in Israel. Compartmentalizing their ideology, they took care not to apply their progressive beliefs to the local scene. Those Jewish radicals and Communists (the whole panoply of believers whom Yiddish speakers called *linke*, or lefties) for whom Marxist values outweighed Jewish ones, and who believed that Marxist ideology was applicable to society worldwide and should not be confined within national boundaries, joined non-Jews in left-wing political movements and cut their ties to the organized Jewish community.

Unable or unwilling to participate in national politics, the organized Jewish communities of Latin America withdrew into a privatized ethnic sphere to which entry is gained by purchase of a burial plot in the Jewish cemetery and payment of an annual contribution to the United Jewish Appeal (a worldwide fund-raising campaign whose principal beneficiary is the State of Israel). Psychologically, the communities became tied to Israel. Until recently, elections to the governing boards of the communities were carried out along Israeli party lines: voters in Buenos Aires had the same choices before them as voters in Tel Aviv, though what the functional relationship of these parties might be to the local scene was unclear. When a new party competed in the Buenos Aires kehillah elections in 1984 with a platform that called for greater attention to Argentine conditions, many referred to that party as "apolitical."

Latin American Jewish communities developed extremely high levels of dependence on the *madre patria*. Some transmit the bulk of the funds raised through annual campaigns directly to Israel, leaving inadequate financial support for the needs of their own institutions.[1] Owing to fluctuating economic conditions and the difficulty of raising additional money locally, the communities became increasingly dependent on outside support to maintain their school systems.[2] This came primarily from the Jewish Agency, a semiautonomous agency that preceded formation of the independent State of Israel and that oversees the resettlement of Jews in that country. As Zionism conquered all other ideological tendencies within the schools, Hebrew language instruction gained supremacy over Yiddish; as a consequence, the communities relied increasingly on Israeli teaching personnel, or on local youth trained in Israeli academies. Organized Jewish life came to revolve around Zionist activities: the sale of Israel bonds, celebration of Israel Independence Day, the training and hiring of Hebrew teachers, and so forth. Many Jews dwelling in small communities, such as Quito or Barranquilla, became accustomed to sending their children to Israel for their education or to look for mates. In times of uncertainty, Jews who feel endangered use the *madre patria* as a temporary sanctuary for themselves or their children. In the stressful year 1982, the Jewish Agency reported that one-fifth of the known number of Latin American Jews were in Israel; a large proportion of these were not immigrants but persons visiting Israel temporarily. In some countries, recruitment for immigration to Israel has been conducted at a pace and with an intensity that denies the validity of Jewish life in the Latin diaspora. The Zionist educational process in Latin America appears to be driven by the conviction that there is no future for Jews on that continent, and that the best Israel can do for the Latin diaspora is to expedite its removal, like the Ethiopians, to Israel.

Over time, Latin American Jewish communities came to supply elements of importance to Israel. In addition to collecting and transmitting funds designated for the absorption of immigrants, Latin America contributes the immigrants themselves. From 1948 to 1986, 73,045 persons "made aliyah" (emigrated) to Israel from Latin America, the largest number of these from Argentina (42,389); even Ecuador contributed 133 immigrants.[3] Although not all of these remained, by 1995, 47,900 Israeli citizens were known to have been born in some country of Latin America.[4] Jews living in Latin America are occasionally able to apply political leverage in support of the government of Israel. They offer well-paid employment to Israeli teachers and youth group leaders, according them status as important figures in kehillah life. The Israeli ambassador enjoys an exalted status and is frequently invited to honor a gathering with opening remarks or to bless the publication of a new book; he or she is also likely to be called upon to umpire internal disputes. The relationship is symbolized by jocular references to the Israeli ambassador as "the viceroy." The analogy is drawn from Latin America's own past, when the area was indeed ruled by a viceroy. Although many nacionalistas retain a lingering esteem for Spain as their *madre patria*, few express a wish to return to colonial status. Latin American Jews, however, seem to have converted themselves voluntarily into dependents of Israel. Like the colonists of old, they offer up taxes and young people to the *madre patria*, while relying on Israel for foreign policy leadership and defense.

The ease with which the terms *israelita* and *israelí* may be confused, and the close relationship between Latin American Jews and Israelis, sustain the suspicion among nacionalistas that Jews' extraterritorial loyalties exceed the bounds of patriotic propriety. The accusation of double loyalty dogged the communities from the start, and continues today. Even well-intentioned, well-educated persons, in speaking to Jews, are likely to refer to "your" ambassador, meaning the diplomatic representative of Israel. Ignoring their Jewish citizens' loyalty to their Latin homelands, some governments have been known to take advantage of the presumed intimate link between local Jewish citizens and the Israeli foreign ministry. A well-authenticated account has an official of a former Peruvian government calling in leaders of the Lima Jewish community to warn them that, should "their" government (i.e., Israel) fail to sell Peru the same Kfir fighter planes it had sold to Ecuador, the government could not be responsible for the enraged reaction of citizens. Through their ever-increasing identification with Israel, Latin American Jews became involved in international relations, although the degree of influence they are able to exercise is very unclear. On the other hand, the *perception* of Jewish influence over policies of the State of Israel can also be manipulated to enhance security.

The ambiguities inherent in Jewish attachment to Israel emerged when Israeli agents kidnapped the war criminal Adolf Eichmann from a street in Buenos Aires on 30 May 1960, touching off a wave of anti-Semitism.[5] The depiction of Israel as an imperialist state, prepared to violate the sovereignty of weaker states in order to gain its own ends, won credence throughout the Third World in the succeeding decade, starting a reversal of the previously favorable equation between *israelita* and *israelí*.

The incident did not lack its positive aspect. Observers who were in Buenos Aires at the time report that strangers approached Jews on the street to congratulate them. The same spontaneous admiration flowed from Israel's victory in the Six Day War (5–10 June 1967) and from news reports of Israel's dramatic rescue of hostages at Entebbe airport in July 1976. The perception of Israeli strength and audacity reflected favorably on Jews overseas. The perception that local Jews have influence on foreign governments—not just Israel but most particularly the United States—has on some occasions persuaded a government to rein in anti-Semitic proclivities among its followers. This appears to have been the case with Perón of Argentina and Pinochet of Chile. The perception also tinged the mentality of Brazilian foreign minister Oswaldo Aranha, whose "notion of Jewish world influence played an important part in [his] attempt to present Brazil in a more liberal international light."[6] As Lesser has shown, Brazilian Jews were able to manipulate this notion in order to wrest more visas for refugees from a reluctant foreign ministry.

Latin American–Israeli Relations

Prior to creation of the state in 1948 and during its early years, Israel's foreign policy objective in Latin America was to win and retain support at the United Nations and other international forums. Her major asset was the world's awareness of the Holocaust and consequent sympathy for Zionist aspirations. For some Latin Catholics, the belief that they themselves were descended from conversos may have played a role. Also to be factored in is the skill of pre-state and Israeli diplomats in strumming the chords of a common Judeo-Christian heritage, to which many Latin American diplomats responded altruistically. Others may have been more cynical: for every Jew who reached Palestine/Israel, one less would be applying for admission to their countries.[7]

Latin American governments were crucial to the establishment of the Jewish state. When, in 1947, Britain requested that the United Nations take up the Palestine problem, the 11-member committee (UNSCOP) formed to look into the matter included three Latin American countries: Guatemala, Uruguay, and Peru. Jorge García Granados and J. Rodríguez Fabregat, the representatives of the first two of these states, were principal supporters of the partition scheme that authorized Israeli statehood; the plan was likewise backed by the chair of the UN General Assembly, Oswaldo Aranha of Brazil. Thereafter, Latin American votes helped achieve the two-thirds majority needed to secure the plan's adoption. Thirteen of the 33 affirmative votes were Latin American (Bolivia, Brazil, Costa Rica, Dominican Republic, Ecuador, Guatemala, Haiti, Nicaragua, Panama, Paraguay, Peru, Uruguay, Venezuela); 6 countries of the region abstained (Argentina, Chile, Colombia, El Salvador, Honduras, Mexico); and only Cuba was opposed. In the war that followed, with Israel under a U.S. arms embargo, weapons reached the Jewish state principally through Czechoslovakia (then under Soviet domination), but also via several Latin American states, including the Nicaragua of General Somoza, who facilitated the work of Zionist emissaries by providing them with Nicaraguan passports. Twelve Latin American embassies were established in Jerusalem, despite UN and Vatican calls for the internationalization of that city and the United States' insistence on keeping its embassy in Tel Aviv. There was a greater margin of support for Israel among the Latin Americans than among the African or Asian member states, and for many years the former provided the necessary votes in support of Israel in the United Nations General Assembly.[8] In a portent of things to come, Israel's military victories in the round of wars with its neighbors enhanced Jewish status in Latin America as elsewhere—perhaps more than elsewhere, considering the centrality of the armed forces in the politics of the continent.

Hemmed in by the economic boycott imposed by the Arab world after her war of independence, Israel first sought to break out of her isolation by cultivating ties with Asia and Africa. But economic assistance and military support did not produce the hoped-for payoff: as a by-blow of Arab-Israeli wars, almost all the African and Asian states broke relations with Israel. This in turn led Israel to look to South and Central America for diplomatic support and trading partners.

In the sixties and early seventies, Israel entered into technical assistance agreements with every Latin American nation but Cuba.[9] Hundreds of Israeli technicians worked on community development projects ranging from well-digging to literacy campaigns to road building. In Nicaragua, to take the example of one country only, Israel assisted with planning and implementation of the Ato Grande Project for settlement of 155 families on the land as farmers and also collaborated in planning the Rigoberto Cabezas Project for the resettlement of another 2,000 families on 70,000 hectares. Technical assistance was provided by Israeli experts on-site in Latin America, and also by bringing Latin Americans to Israel for training. Official figures of the Department of International Cooperation of the Israel Foreign Ministry show that 7,726 Latin Americans were brought to Israel for technical training between the years 1958–82.[10] "The sentimentality which had prompted Latin America's initial support for Israel" waned a few years after independence, the director-general of Israel's Ministry for Foreign Affairs acknowledged, and Israel "found a way to fill this vacuum through its technical cooperation activities in Latin America."[11]

By 1976, Latin America had been engulfed by a militaristic tide; sixteen of twenty Latin American nations (all but Mexico, Colombia, Venezuela, and Costa Rica) were under military rule. Demand for Israeli weapons outstripped the demand for agricultural assistance, and Israel emerged on the world scene as a major arms supplier. Commercial success followed her victory in the Yom Kippur War (1973), and that year Latin America became the chief export market for Israel's arms industry.[12] But Israel's military and commercial successes did not endear her to people who were forced to live under military regimes in Argentina, Chile, and elsewhere. At the same time leftist nationalist governments in Cuba, Peru, and Nicaragua scorned Israel as an ally of the United States. In short order, Israel's role in selling arms to militarized governments erased her earlier favorable reputation among liberals and overwhelmed the goodwill generated through technical assistance programs and community development. Liberal opinion worldwide, formerly favorable to Israel, now turned against her.

At the same time, Latin American governments of all tendencies were declaring their independence from the United States, whose own interests had led to her assuming the role of Israel's major ally. America's automatic majority at the United Nations, a given in the early days when Latin American governments complacent to U.S. policy comprised 35 percent of the UN's membership, was dwindling. Membership increased far beyond expectation, and a coalition of 77 non-aligned states came together to dominate the world organization's various units and agencies. In what Charles de Gaulle called "that *apatride* talking machine on the Hudson," the logic of opposition to U.S. hegemony in Latin America called for rapprochement with Arab resisters to U.S. policy in the Near East, and joint opposition to U.S. allies—especially to Israel, whose own claim to national liberation was now denied.

Latin Americans, after all, had for centuries been only distant observers of the European scene. The saga of Jewish homelessness, persecution, and the Zionist response to the Holocaust took place far from their own continent and did not engage everyone's attention. Throughout the sixties, many Latin Americans found their passions increasingly engaged by a different global current: the rebellion of people who had been excluded from the bipolar equations of the Cold War, and their coalescing into a Third World made up of those living in non-nuclear, underdeveloped economies. Despite obvious differences in historical experience and level of economic development, and despite very tricky rationalizations regarding race (for the Latin Americans had been accustomed to seeing themselves as white while their new allies had adopted an identity as people of color), increasing numbers of Latin Americans during the sixties were identifying themselves as Third World peoples. The identification was eased by the fact that the United States, foremost defender of a status quo increasingly deemed intolerable, was leading the First World.

Enter the Palestine Liberation Organization

In a bid for leadership of the Third World, Cuba initiated fraternal relations with the Palestine Liberation Organization (PLO) at the First Conference of the Organization of Solidarity of the Peoples of Asia, Africa, and Latin America, held in Havana in 1966. Not for another seven years, in 1973, did Castro break relations with Israel and license the opening of a PLO office with diplomatic status in Havana.[13] Shortly thereafter, the Cuban government began training PLO military and intelligence cadres at camps in North Africa, Iraq, and the USSR. In a reciprocal mode, the PLO took Nicaraguan, Brazilian, and Argentine guerrillas for training at their camps in Lebanon, South Yemen, and Libya. Pressure by Arab states to abandon Latin Americans' long-term support for Israel and recognize the PLO gained strength in 1973–74 when oil prices quadrupled, putting the squeeze on Latin American economies. Representatives of the Arab League suggested that no underdeveloped country that backed the cause of the Arab world would suffer an energy shortage. Guyana had broken relations with Israel shortly after Cuba did so in 1973. By June 1980, the PLO had opened officially recognized offices in Mexico and Peru. Ecuador, Peru's rival, welcomed the PLO in 1982. By mid-1987, PLO embassies were functioning in La Paz, Managua (now under the Sandinistas), and Havana.[14]

On the nongovernmental side of the street, the Palestine Liberation Organization established links with revolutionary groupings such as the Montoneros in Argentina, the FDR-FMLN in El Salvador, the Guatemalan URNG, and the FSLN (Sandinista Front for National Liberation) in Nicaragua. In addition, the Popular Front for the Liberation of Palestine made fraternal contact with Chile's MIR and other revolutionary groups.[15] Perhaps even more important than actual linkages was the climate of approbation that grew up around the PLO and the cathexis achieved between Latin America's struggle against "U.S. imperialism" and the Arab world's struggle against "Israeli imperialism."

In this atmosphere, the UN General Assembly passed its Resolution 3379 equating Zionism with racism in 1977. Among Latin American governments, only Brazil, Cuba, and Mexico voted for this resolution, while eight (all small Caribbean and Central American states) voted against, with Argentina and others abstaining.[16] Passage of the resolution fixed the equation in the minds of many who had no historical grounding from which to evaluate Zionism as a movement of national liberation. Whereas formerly it had been an honor to be associated with Israel, by the late seventies, Zionism had become a suspect activity. Moreover, criticism of the Israeli government, legitimate as an element of political discourse, had in some quarters degenerated into anti-Semitism, the irrational hatred of an entire people because of their ancestry.

As status quo and revolutionary forces faced off across the hemisphere,

PLO gains were limited by the distrust of the respective military establishments, which feared the importation of terrorism into their own countries. An example of the tergiversation which this imposed is to be found in Brazil, whose military government recognized the PLO in June 1979 as "the sole legitimate representative of the Palestinian people," but refused to authorize the opening of a PLO office in Brasília. Recognition came during a visit to Brazil by the vice-president of Iraq. That country was at that date supplying 400,000 barrels of oil a day to Brazil, more than half her oil supply. Brazil was also selling armaments to Iraq, in quantities that dwarfed Israeli arms sales to Central America. In the decade 1974–84, Latin Americans compiled a trade deficit with the Arab world of more than $59 billion in U.S. dollars.[17] Although the governments supplying the oil were also principal backers of the PLO, the Brazilian military dictatorship supped with a long spoon. Having just finished eradicating a native guerrilla, the military could not have relished the prospect of importing terror from abroad. This attitude seems to have been shared by the other hardline military dictatorships of the period, such as Chile and Argentina.

Symbolic actions were something else again. In 1980, of 13 nations whose embassies were in Jerusalem, 12 were Latin American. Two years later, reacting to a Knesset (Israeli parliament) resolution legitimating the unilateral annexation of the city of Jerusalem, the Latin Americans had all moved to Tel Aviv, thereby withdrawing their acknowledgment of Jerusalem as the capital of Israel. (Costa Rica and El Salvador subsequently returned.)

Taking advantage of an increasing tilt in their direction, Arab representatives meeting in Tunis in 1979 decided to concentrate their efforts on Latin America in a bid to oust the Israelis from that region as they had previously ousted them from central and western Africa. Concurrently, they unleashed an anti-Semitic campaign designed to undermine the status of Jewish Latin Americans. The anti-Zionism that now became a rallying cry for Latin American leftists was increasingly couched in terms that were indistinguishable from anti-Semitism. The two hatreds coalesced in the summer of 1982, when the massacre of Palestinian Muslims by Lebanese Christians was made the occasion for armed attacks on Latin American Jews. The linkage between "freedom fighters" in Latin America and the Near East bore fruit in anti-Israel, anti-Jewish demonstrations that took place all over the continent in the summer of 1982 in the wake of the Sabra and Shattila blood libel. Newspapers formerly known for their pro-Israel stance began to question not only Israel's actions, but its right to exist. Phrases such as "Nazi-Zionism" and "the Palestinian holocaust" surfaced in Mexican and Brazilian newspapers. For certain sectors of Latin opinion there was no longer a distinction to be made between *israelí* and *israelita*. In Colombia, masked men invaded a synagogue in the city of Medellín and desecrated the sanctuary; in Barranquilla, demonstrators marched to the chant of "death to the Jews." In Venezuela, a gang broke into the Israeli embassy in Caracas and painted anti-Semitic slogans on the walls; a few weeks later, the Jewish Center in Maracaibo was attacked by university students. After the opening of the PLO office in Lima, Peru was flooded with anti-Semitic literature, and the main synagogue of that city was bombed. Even in Ecuador, a nation of notably equable temperament that has been hospitable to Jews, the situation deteriorated following arrival of the PLO. The Israeli embassy in that city was bombed, resulting in the deaths of two Ecuadoran policemen and the maiming of a passerby. And in Brazil, where public demonstrations had been outlawed for ten years, the first public protest march to be licensed was an anti-Israel demonstration.[18] These events were linked: Israel was targeted as the oppressor of subject peoples; Latin American Jews were identified with Israel; and the effort to delegitimate Jews as citizens of their own countries proceeded apace.

Nevertheless, the State of Israel increased her trade with Latin America during the seventies and eighties. After 1979, when the Iranian revolution cut off her principal source of petroleum, an alternate supplier was found in Mexico, which came to supply 40 percent of Israel's needs. Joint Mexican-Israeli investments in agriculture, electronics, solar energy, and construction followed. Israel's exports to Argentina rose from $16 million in 1974 to $51 million in 1983, while her imports from Argentina went from $4 million to $11 million and higher during the same period.[19] The number of branches of Israeli financial institutions in Latin America increased from three in 1977 to twenty-five in 1982. By 1984, the visitor to Uruguay would be met on her arrival by billboards advertising the services of no fewer than six Israeli banks. Other branches opened in Mexico, Panama, Brazil, Venezuela, Argentina, and Chile. Israeli agribusiness started up in several locations in the Caribbean, including commercial fish farming in the Dominican Republic, an enterprise that was born when some entrepreneurial young men saw photographs of Sosua, the agricultural colony founded in wartime by German Jewish refugees and abandoned by them at war's end. New Israeli technologies were licensed for shrimp pond breeding in Honduras and the Caribbean, and solar energy in Chile. So many Israeli students took to backpacking all over South America that the Israeli government opened hostels for them in major cities.

But the composition of Israel's trade with Latin America had changed. In the period 1974–85, Israel sold planes, missiles, helicopters, machine guns, and armored carriers to fifteen different Latin American governments, including that of Guatemala, one of the most repressive in the hemisphere.[20] "We tried to sell them holy water from the Jordan River," an Israel embassy spokesperson said, "but they weren't interested. What they wanted was weapons, and that's what we sold them." Israel also continued selling arms to the Argentine military junta while that government was prosecuting its "Dirty War" against its own citizens. Meanwhile, Argentina, Brazil, and Chile were selling planes, tanks, and armored cars to Iran, Iraq, Libya, and other Arab states committed to the destruction of Israel.[21]

As of spring 1987, arms and related supplies accounted for from 20 to 25 percent of Israel's industrial exports overall. Israel had more than 300 arms-sales agents around the world, operating under economic guidelines. There appeared to be no coherent mechanism for assessing the political, social, and diplomatic implications of weapons sales. An interministerial committee on arms sales existed, which examined selected sales, but only after the fact.[22] Trade in the weaponry generated by the Israeli economy on the basis of that country's security needs came to dominate Israel's relations with the Western Hemisphere. Only peripheral consideration was given to the way in which that trade would affect Jewish citizens of nations that were their trading partners.

Israel and the Jews of Latin America

More than most, Israeli policymakers are influenced by history. During the Nazi era, when an entire Jewish world faced extinction, no Jewish state existed and no sovereign entity considered that there was a moral imperative to rescue Jews. This fact became the driving force behind the ultimate realization of the Zionist dream: the founding of an independent Jewish state open to all the Jews of the world. One of the first acts of the independent State of Israel was to enact the Law of Return in 1950, giving any Jew the right to settle in Israel and to receive Israeli citizenship.

Since then, the issue of Israel's responsibility for Jews living beyond its borders, and who are citizens of other countries, has arisen many times. Each crisis has redefined the issue and required Israel to adjust its response according to circumstances. A prolonged diplomatic, economic, and public relations campaign in the 1970s, in which Israel had the support of the United States Congress, resulted in the granting of the right of exit to Soviet Jews who were suffering discrimination. By contrast, a single commando raid by the Israel Defense Forces on the airport at Entebbe freed 56 Jewish hostages being held by terrorists. In the 1980s, a long-term, secret diplomatic effort enabled Israel to extract almost the entire Jewish community from Ethiopia. Obviously, each of these situations differed from the others, and Israel's responses also differed. But the knowledge that Israel was capable of mounting such rescue operations probably increased the feeling of security experienced by vulnerable Jewish communities. At the same time, these same operations raised serious questions regarding the limits of sovereignty. The ways in which Israeli policy played out, and the result for Latin American Jewry, can be illustrated by examining events in two very different sets of circumstances: in Argentina during the so-called Dirty War, and in Nicaragua during that country's civil war between the Sandinistas and the *contras,* supporters of deposed President Anastasio Somoza.

The Argentine Dirty War

The coming to power in Argentina of a military junta in March 1976 and the initiation of the repressive Process of National Reorganization (the so-called *proceso*) confronted the Israeli embassy in Buenos Aires with a novel set of circumstances. As diplomats, they had to deal with whatever government was in power; as Israelis, they could not be indifferent to the condition of Argentine

Jews. What that might be was not clear but had to be deciphered from a welter of events, statements, and signals, all in the context of armed violence.

The first test of Israeli policy came in July 1976, when eight Jewish individuals were arrested in the city of Córdoba.[23] The status of these eight varied in ways that are significant in a diplomatic context: the embassy could properly be concerned to protect Israeli citizens, but had no standing vis-à-vis Argentine citizens. In this instance, three of those arrested were Argentine citizens; the other five were Israelis—four of these with dual Argentine and Israeli citizenship. The Israelis were representatives of the Jewish Agency, operating legally in Argentina on the basis of an agreement between the two governments for the purpose of fomenting immigration to Israel. The three Argentines were members of Hashomer Hatzair, a legally organized Zionist youth group with a socialist orientation.

Córdoba had for years been a focus of left-wing rebellion, and some members of Hashomer Hatzair, applying their ideology to the local situation, had integrated themselves into the Revolutionary Popular Army (ERP by its Spanish initials). The mission of the Jewish Agency representatives was to get them out of the ERP and back into Zionist ranks. The embassy might have ignored the plight of the three Argentines, since they were not Israeli citizens, and the subversive activity of which they were suspected was strictly an Argentine affair. But the arrest of the eight presented the danger that the Zionist movement as a whole would be compromised, bringing under suspicion the entire organized Jewish community. The danger was real, since many nacionalistas, particularly in the military, had a preconception of Zionism as a subversive ideology.

The Israeli embassy initiated diplomatic negotiations with a view to obtaining the release of all the prisoners. In the course of tense discussions, ambassador Ram Nirgad explained to the generals the goals of Zionism as relating entirely to the creation and maintenance of the State of Israel as a Jewish homeland; and assured them that Israel desired the continuation of the current regime in Argentina. All eight prisoners were released following thirteen days of detention, during which they were tortured and sexually molested. Thereafter, throughout the proceso, the junta did not disturb Zionist organizations or Jewish Agency representatives, a pronounced victory for the continuation of Jewish life in Argentina.

As reports of anti-Semitic atrocities in prisons and clandestine concentration camps leaked out of Argentina, discussions began worldwide regarding the feasibility, and the necessity, of evacuating the entire Jewish community from that country. Some condemned the posture of local community leaders as excessively passive and urged an all-out effort to extricate and evacuate Jews who were being targeted by the regime. Tension was racheted up several notches by the arrest in April 1977 of the journalist Jacobo Timerman, who was both an Israeli asset and a friend of one of the powerful generals; and the unraveling of the financial empire of one David Gravier, a financier whose apparent death in an airplane crash began the unraveling of an international scheme to launder the millions of dollars in ransom money in the guerrillas' treasury. There seemed to be real potential for the unleashing of a campaign of anti-Semitic attacks, based on the two myths so basic to Argentine nacionalistas' perception of Jews: that of divided loyalties and that of financial skulduggery.

In August 1977, Prime Minister Menachem Begin invited a group of Argentine community leaders to Israel to discuss their situation. Begin expressed his concern and suggested that the community plan for a massive emergency emigration.The Argentines agreed the situation was grave, but did not accept Begin's proposal, asking instead that Israel increase financial and pedagogical support for their schools.[24] A planned visit to Argentina by an Israeli parliamentary delegation to inquire into the fate of disappeared persons was postponed, evidently at the request of the Argentine Jewish community. The issue of Argentine Jewish prisoners and disappeared was discussed in Israeli Knesset committees, but not debated publicly in a plenary session of the Knesset until June 1983, by which time the individuals in question were dead or out of the country.

When in 1983 the Argentine junta resigned, the scale of its atrocities began to be revealed. The official commission appointed by incoming President Raúl Alfonsín documented nearly 9,000 fatalities among the civil population; human rights groups have always claimed that the number was closer to 30,000. Among the dead and disappeared were almost one thousand Jews, a proportion far in excess of their numbers in the population at large. There followed recriminations against anyone who it was believed could have influenced events. Families of Jewish victims reserved particular vitriol for the community's official leadership (the DAIA) and for the Israelis. What, in fact, had Israel attempted, and what had been accomplished?

No Israeli operation on the model of Mossad's evacuation of Jews from Algeria and Morocco was undertaken. Both the Israeli embassy and the DAIA handed up lists of names of the disappeared, but neither could win at the cynical shell game the junta played, releasing a few prisoners from time to time but claiming that they had no information on the majority of missing persons.The Jewish Agency was instructed to rescue Jews in distress, but as a civilian body, it lacked the training or the means for carrying out extralegal operations. At crucial times, just one officer was assigned to processing the applications of persons seeking protection. When the Agency acted, it did so within restricted guidelines set by the Israeli government: nothing was to be done that might compromise *legal* emigration to Israel (aliyah), which the Israelis expected would exceed the number of Jews who needed protection at any given moment.

So far as can be divined, Israeli diplomats gained their few successes by pursuing two lines of action. The first had to do with the so-called right of option. Argentine law allowed for the deportation of prisoners to a foreign country willing to accept them. Italy, Spain, and France made use of this law to extricate some of their own nationals. In October 1977, Minister of the Interior General Albano Jorge Harguindeguy recognized Israel as among the countries entitled to invoke the right of option, even for Argentines who were not Israeli citizens. Moreover, Israeli consuls were ceded the right to visit Jewish prisoners in jail in order to explain this right to them and assist in carrying out the formalities.[25] The right of visitation was in itself vitally important, even for those who refused to exercise their option of exile, because it made it more difficult for the government subsequently to "disappear" a prisoner.

The other approach was *milut,* or extrication, a project that assisted Jews who were being hunted by the authorities by smuggling them into Uruguay or Brazil, and then providing them with means to escape to Israel. (Fugitives were not safe in neighboring countries because of cooperation between security forces. When Reneé Epelbaum's son was abducted in Buenos Aires, she sent her two other children across the river to Mar del Plata, whence they were also "disappeared.") Operating outside the law, the Israelis nevertheless had their own rules. The Jewish Agency was instructed to try to save individuals who qualified under Israel's Law of Return and their mates regardless of religion, without regard to political orientation as long as they were not common criminals. An acknowledged terrorist could make aliyah on his own, but not with Jewish Agency assistance. Nothing was to be done that might jeopardize legal immigration or the good relations that existed between Israel and the Argentine government. The Jewish Agency official in charge of this operation was never molested by the Argentine government, though it was known what his duties consisted of. An estimated 200 persons were extricated in this way during the most dangerous years, 1976–78.[26]

Perhaps the greatest Israeli achievement is its claim to having prevented the escalation of anti-Semitism from the level of criminally sadistic treatment of individuals to officially sponsored acts against the Jewish community as a whole. At the time of the Córdoba crisis, Ambassador Nirgad was able to contain the damage locally, deflecting the junta response away from the Zionist movement, which would have inculpated the entire Jewish community as subversive. Later, the collapse of the Gravier financial empire held the potential for an all-out official attack on Jewish businessmen as agents of the guerrilla insurgency. That this did not happen is at least in part due to the Israeli presentation, which seems to have persuaded the generals that one Jewish businessman is not the equivalent of the entire Jewish community; and that the junta's reputation abroad—particularly in the United States—would be irreparably damaged if it licensed an officially anti-Semitic policy.

In sum, Israel's response to the problematic situation of Argentine Jews was conditioned by factors that operated within certain defined parameters. Uppermost among these was the limitation inherent in Israel's desire to maintain good relations with the Argentine government. In a world in which many states are overtly hostile to the State of Israel, Argentina's long-standing policy of neutrality between Israel and its enemies was perceived to have permanent value transcending the imperative of the moment. This neutrality had been severely compromised by Israel's infringement on Argentine sovereignty by the abduction of Eichmann; Israel went to great lengths to restore the preexisting balance.

A second parameter was the action of the DAIA in urging outsiders not to intervene in their affairs. The warning effectively confused observers (who were increasingly aware of anti-Jewish atrocities and had trouble understanding why the DAIA would deny the importance of these events) and hampered efforts to assist those in distress. The government of Israel, for good or ill, was guided by DAIA's evaluation that intervention would only make matters worse.

The desire to maintain good commercial relations, and especially to continue the sale of Israeli arms, marks a more blurred parameter. Israel continued selling armaments to Argentina during the Dirty War. Some Israeli weapons bought by the junta were undoubtedly used for repressing the civilian population, Jews and non-Jews alike. Critics (including Rabbi Marshall Meyer, a principal defender of human rights during the proceso) condemned Israel's readiness to sell weapons to morally indefensible regimes, and questioned why Israel evidently never used the threat of withholding weapons as a way to pressure the junta into relieving the situation of prisoners. Defenders of Israeli policy believe that the access to the top command that arms sales created positioned Israel to intervene in order to alleviate the suffering of some prisoners; whether or not this was done is all but impossible to prove or disprove on the basis of available evidence. Major sales did not take place until December 1978, when much of the damage had already been done.[27] But Israeli representatives claim that arms sales, and the good repute they garnered from the junta, prevented deterioration of the status of the community as a whole. Most civilians continued living normal lives throughout the years of the proceso.

Israel's arms sales should also be considered in the context of the global trade in weaponry. According to a report by the respected Stockholm International Peace Research Institute that monitors arms sales worldwide, between 1976 and 1981 Israel supplied 13 percent of the weapons imported by Argentina, an amount surpassed by the United States, which supplied 17 percent despite the embargo imposed by the Carter administration in 1978. West Germany, France, Britain, Switzerland, Belgium, Spain, and Austria were all selling arms to the junta without regard to human rights concerns or specifically to the plight of their own nationals caught up in the Dirty War. Manufacturers in any of these states would have been happy to reap the estimated 150 millions of dollars per year that Israel was earning, had the latter withdrawn from the trade. This equation conforms with diplomatic practice but evades the issue of whether Israeli diplomats were able to discuss weapons sales and human rights at one and the same time.[28]

The number of persons saved by Israeli action may total 500: 300 cases of "extrication" of hunted persons and 200 prisoners freed (the disappeared, by definition, could not reappear). A researcher generally critical of the Israeli record nevertheless finds that it compares favorably with that of Germany, which took no action at all to defend her nationals trapped by events in Argentina, and received very few exiles within her own borders.[29] All the nations surveyed gave priority to commercial relations over human rights.

Nicaragua and Iran-Contra[30]

Nicaragua was never home to many Jews—the population was estimated at twenty-seven families in 1975; in 1982, Sergio DellaPergola offered a combined estimate of 150 Jews for El Salvador, Honduras, Belize, and Nicaragua.[31] For our present analysis, the relevance of events there relates not to the fate of the Jewish families who were uprooted by a decade of civil war; but rather the illumination of the Nicaraguan scene and the Cold War mentality of the Reagan administration, which attempted to import into the United States the discredited technique of manufacturing anti-Semitic alarums in order to manipulate Jews.

Largely engaged in industry and commerce, Nicaraguan Jews prospered in the free market economy developed under dictator Anastasio Somoza García and his son and successor Anastasio Somoza Debayle, who ran Nicaragua as a commercial enterprise with themselves as the principal stockholders. The Somozas were supported economically and politically by the United States as part of a policy of defending the status quo that the United States has maintained almost without interruption since 1898. Nicaragua's dependence on the United States in turn was a factor in orienting the Somozas toward a favorable policy toward Israel; while other Third World nations were morphing into anti-Israel positions, Nicaragua continued voting in favor of Israel at the United Nations. Israel, for her part, searching for overseas markets and specifically for outlets for the surplus weapons produced in her endless struggle to maintain military superiority over her neighbors, continued to sell arms to the Nicaraguan government until the defeat of Somoza by the Sandinistas in 1979. This seems to have been strictly a business proposition: Israel never had a resident ambassador in Managua, and it is most unlikely that arms sales were prompted by gratitude for Somoza's support, which had been based on his own calculations of self-interest.[32]

The rebellion against the Somoza regime, led by the Sandinista Front for National Liberation (FSLN), had the fraternal support of the Palestine Liberation Organization from 1970 on. Sandinistas who received training under the PLO in Lebanon fought with the PLO against King Hussein of Jordan or participated in Al Fatah actions in Europe. A joint communiqué issued in 1978 by the FSLN and the Democratic Front for the Liberation of Palestine praised "the bonds of solidarity which exist between the two revolutionary organizations" and condemned the support of the United States for Israel and for Somoza's Nicaragua.[33]

The victory of Sandinista rebels over government forces in July 1979 prompted the departure from Nicaragua of those—Jews and non-Jews—who had supported the dictator, and the expropriation of their property. As in Cuba, individual Jews who had fought for the revolution remained and were integrated into the new society; some served in the new government. On 20 July 1980, at the celebration of the first annniversary of the revolution and with Yasir Arafat in attendance, the PLO was granted formal diplomatic recognition and authorized to open its office in Managua. Two years later, in August 1982, following Israel's invasion of Lebanon, the Sandinista government broke relations with Israel. By then, correspondents for major newspapers were reporting that, with President Reagan unable to supply all the weaponry he might have wanted to because of congressional restrictions, Israel was becoming the U.S. arms broker and proxy in Central America.[34]

It has been pointed out that the Nicaraguan civil war was internationalized to a greater degree than any previous Latin American conflict. In Nicaragua in the 1970s, the East-West confrontation between the United States and the Soviet Union intersected with the North-South confrontation between the United States and the Third World, turning a civil war into an international crisis.[35] Global communication made it possible for partisans of revolutionary factions as disparate as the Nicaraguan Sandinistas and the Palestine Liberation Organization to contract alliances with one another despite their inhabiting different hemispheres and different cultures. Once linkage was achieved, internal and external elements interacted, resulting in a synergistic explosion that engulfed parties apparently distant from both disputes. States once deemed too weak or too distant to intervene in Central America, such as Saudi Arabia, Libya, Cuba, Israel, and Brazil, became actively involved, drawn in by perceived ties of ideology, ethnicity, or the desire for economic gain.

The Sandinista Front won the war, but the war did not end; the ousted Somoza forces (the counterrevolutionaries, or Contras) launched a struggle to regain power. U.S. President Ronald Reagan, convinced that the Soviet Union was gaining a foothold on the isthmus by way of the Sandinistas, extended military assistance to the Contras. This policy was opposed by the U.S. Congress, where there was considerable sentiment that Nicaraguans were warranted in overthrowing an oppressive and unjust regime. In times past, the president of the United States might have imposed his fiat unilaterally. In this case, the president was prevented from doing so by the Congress. When Congress decreed (in the first Boland Amendment) that funding for the *somocistas* must stop by May 1984, the administration decided to act through allies and client states, a decision that was taken in secret and contrary to U.S. law. The White House established the "Enterprise," a supposedly private-sector initiative to raise unauthorized funds and utilize them for operations in Central America. CIA Director William Casey set up a "self-sustaining, off-the-shelf" operation led by Lt. Col. Oliver North, designed to keep the Contras in the war despite the specific congressional prohibition. In the words of Congress' final report, the Enterprise "served as the secret arm of the National Security Council staff, carrying out with private and non-appropriated money, and without the accountability or restrictions imposed by law on the CIA, a covert Contra aid program that Congress thought it had prohibited." A major contributor was Saudi Arabia, which immediately poured $32 million into the counterrevolutionaries operating in Nicaragua and Honduras.[36]

One operation set up jointly by the CIA and Pentagon, code-named Tipped Kettle, enlisted Israel to provide $10 million worth of munitions to the Contras from the cache of Soviet weapons captured from the PLO in Lebanon. Asked to take over the training and funding of the Contras, the Israelis at first declined the honor, but they sold more war booty to the Contras in the summer of 1984, after the Sandinista government had unilaterally broken relations with Israel.[37] By 1985, Israel was supplying arms (and possibly training as well) to neighboring Honduras and El Salvador, evidently in support of pro-Contra operations based in those countries.[38] These sales had undeniable advantages for the Israelis. Though they were not particularly interested in the region for its own sake, they were able to unload tons of Soviet equipment taken from defeated PLO forces in Lebanon. In the mid-1980s, armaments accounted for 20–25 percent of Israel's industrial exports and its defense industry employed more than 60,000 workers.[39]

> In order to understand the nature of Israel's military negotiations with Central America, one must realize that Israel would not refrain from selling arms to any regime, whatever the political orientation of that regime. Although Nicaragua, El Salvador, and Guatemala are often purposely singled out, one should not forget to mention Israeli military transactions with China, the nationalist reformist regime of General Velasco Alvarado in Peru and Allende's regime in Chile. The national principle is that Israel should make efforts to become less dependent of [sic] other powers. . . . There is more access if a non-restricted policy is observed.[40]

Furthermore, by obliging the United States president, Israel began to heal the breach in U.S.-Israeli relations provoked by other policies of the Likud government. Congruence in the two nations' policies led to the negotiation of a strategic accord in November 1983, which was of prime importance to Israel's position in the Middle East. But the accord that was so beneficial for Israel in the Middle East had a pernicious effect when exported to the Western Hemisphere. In reinforcing U.S. policy in Central America, Israel was adhering to a bankrupt policy of defending the status quo in the face of obvious and urgent need for change. As a U.S. ally, Israel inherited the hostilities that had accrued to the United States as the hegemonic power on the isthmus for over a century. American liberals flinched at the news that Israel was arming repressive regimes and counterrevolutionary forces in Central America (overlooking, perhaps, the fact that Costa Rica, neighbor to the conflict, remained friendly to Israel throughout the war). Owing to the internationalization of the crisis, Israel's actions triggered the hostility of progressive forces around the world, who (somewhat reflexively) backed the Sandinistas. This is the point at which the coupling of Arab with Latin American nationalism produced a crop of dragon's teeth. Driven by its own security needs and economic considerations, as well as by the freewheeling activities of arms dealers, Israel carried out (or permitted its private citizens to carry out) actions in Latin America without considering the local ramifications of such a policy. Entering the wars on the side of the deposed dictator may have afforded the Israeli government some satisfaction because of the Sandinistas' links with the PLO and other Arab organizations hostile to Israel. But that equation omitted the impact the U.S.-Israeli alliance was having upon Jews living in the area. Realistically, the interests of a handful of Nicaraguan Jews could not override security considerations for the State of Israel, but there is no evidence that their well-being was considered. Nobody seems to have asked them.

Whether anti-Israel sentiment, motivated by Israeli arms sales to the Contras, was spilling over into anti-Semitism directed against Jews now became a political issue in the United States. If anything could counter revulsion against the policy of supporting the discredited Contras, that would be evidence that anti-Semitism had been dragooned into the service of Third World unity. Given the vulnerability of Jewish communities in Latin America (the atrocities committed in Argentina were just coming to light) and considering also the Sandinistas' links with Arab groups committed to the destruction of Israel, it was not an unlikely story. In November 1983, President Reagan told a press conference that "The results of the self-proclaimed blood unity between the Sandinistas and the PLO are evidence for all the world to see and are an evil echo of history. Virtually the entire Jewish community of Nicaragua has been frightened into exile." The president urged his listeners to "please share the truth that Communism in Central America means not only the loss of political freedom but of religious freedom as well."

The basis for the charge was the expropriation of property owned by Nicaraguan Jews, including a building that had been used as a synagogue, now converted by the Sandinistas into a children's center. But sources familiar with events on the ground pointed out that all property owned by persons who had supported the government and who had left the country had been expropriated. It was possible for those returning to Nicaragua to reclaim their property through the courts. A delegation of American Jews affiliated with progressive organizations found "no body of credible evidence to suggest that the Sandinista government has pursued or is currently pursuing a policy of discrimination or coercion against Jews, or that Jewish people are not welcome to live and work in Nicaragua."[41] Subsequently, the Sandinistas offered to return the disputed building to local Jews (who, however, lacked funds for its maintenance).

Whether anti-Israel sentiment, motivated by Israeli arms sales to the *somocistas,* spilled over into anti-Semitism directed against local Jews, became a hot political issue in the United States, where it may indeed have influenced some American liberals not to oppose the Reagan policy of support for the Contras. However, ultimately, the administration could not make its charge stick. There was no credible evidence of anti-Semitic actions in Nicaragua, where the principal players were well able to distinguish between israelís and israelitas. Thus, the chief effect of the president's allegation was to introduce onto the American scene the ancient, discredited political technique of manipulating Jews by raising the specter of anti-Semitism. This indeed was "an evil echo of history."

Hostage Dilemma

When Israel entered the Latin American revolutionary and counterrevolutionary wars as an ally of the United States, she inherited overnight the contumely which the United States had taken a century to accumulate. This was a matter of small moment for Israelis, living half a world away with their backs up against the wall in a war in which the United States was their principal ally. But it was a matter of major importance to Jews living in the Spanish/ Portuguese-speaking world, because these communities are small and vulnerable, not totally accepted by the societies in which they live, and are identified with the State of Israel. In some contingencies they might be protected by the Jewish state; now it seemed they could be as easily destabilized. Either way, their ability to determine their own political orientation could be eroded. Furthermore, to the extent that the reputation of their *madre patria* was besmirched by her loss of moral standing, their own situation was undermined.

The initial insecurity of immigrant Jewish communities had encouraged their identification with Israel, a virtual *madre patria* that replaced their real motherlands which had rejected them. At first, both parties gained from the relationship: Jews enjoyed the reflected glory from Israel's military victories. Israel gained overseas supporters who contributed lives and money to the building of the new state. But much was lost, also. Jewish lives could be disrupted by forces at work in a country that was far from them geographically and empathetically, in which their interests were not the primary element taken into acount in formulating decisions. Although Israel takes an interest in the well-being of diaspora communities, that interest is inevitably Israel-centered and focused on the recruitment of immigrants, not on supporting Jewish life in other countries. Moreover, the welding of Jewish with Israeli interests confirms the paranoid suspicion rife in chauvinist societies that there exists a worldwide Jewish conspiracy devoted to projecting Israeli power over prostrate Christian nations. This mythology did not gain a grip in Nicaragua, whose leaders were perfectly capable of distinguishing between Israeli arms merchants and Jewish Nicaraguans; but it is a factor of consequence elsewhere, particularly in Argentina, where Israeli arms sales were justified by some Jews with the rationalization that these would attenuate the myth of Israeli predatory intentions.

Arguably, Latin American Jews allowed their focus on Israel to preempt realistic engagement with the conditions of their own lives. Every diaspora community is affected by actions of the State of Israel. Those that have established a sturdy presence in national politics are able to resist the impact. Latin American communities, being small and lacking access to the decision-making centers of their respective nations, are more powerfully affected by Israeli actions. This diminishes the influence they can bring to bear on the terms of their own lives. Furthermore, while they are likely to become identified with specific Israeli policies, they have no voice in their formulation. Nor can they expect that Israel, its foreign policy options limited, will allow itself to be constrained by the possibility of negative impact on the Jews of Ecuador or Bolivia, or even Argentina. Israel has a better track record at extricating Jews from difficult situations than at making local situations tenable for Jews who want to remain in them. From the Israeli point of view, anti-

Semitism confirms the Zionist thesis that ultimately, Jewish life in the diaspora is untenable.

With the turn to democracy that swept the Latin American republics in the 1980s came the partial taming of their military establishments, most notably in Argentina, where budget and ranks of the high command were both reduced by President Alfonsín. Improved relations among Argentina, Chile and Brazil enabled the reduction of competitive national armies and presaged the growth of regional security agreements. Worldwide, the market in armaments shrank throughout the decade 1983–93, with industries steadily reducing their production capacity. Israeli production and sales were likewise on a downward curve, reflecting not only decreased international demand but also the start of the peace process in the Middle East. In 1995, the Stockholm International Peace Research Institute published a list of the 100 largest arms-producing companies in the OECD and developing countries. Four Israeli firms made the list, at numbers 38, 75, 80, and 88 with respect to size. Together, these sold an aggregate $2.3 billion worth of arms internationally in 1993, comprising just 1.5 percent of global arms sales.[42] Both the absolute and the relative importance of Israeli arms sales were apparently destined to be of less importance in the future.

These events left their mark on the Jewish communities of the area. With the return of democratic regimes throughout much of Latin America, Jewish communities experienced a comparable *apertura,* or opening up, a process that inevitably led to reconsideration of the place of Zionism and of Israel in Jewish life.

CHAPTER 11

Jews and Non-Jews

"Buenos Aires, shtot mein liebe, Ich bin farlibt in dein tsebliter yugnt . . ."
(Buenos Aires, beloved city, I'm in love with your flowering youth . . .)

—Yiddish version of a Carlos Gardel tango

FOR MANY LATIN Americans, the reality of Jewish life is obscured by mythology. Only the dissipation of myth allows the reality of Jews and Judaism to appear. Apparently, this happens more readily at the personal than at the societal level. The acceptability of Jews as marriage partners is widespread, causing Jewish leaders to express more concern about assimilation than about anti-Semitism. Yet happy exogamous marriages exist side by side with murderous manifestations of race hatred.

Within Jewish spaces, behind the symbolic walls of the kehillah, highly organized Jewish communities regulate the behavior of their members by excluding the intermarried, the criminal, and the politically radical. The politically correct clubs and synagogues and beneficent societies that result present to non-Jews the appearance of a people unified in character and goals. But the suave facade of country club life masks the abandonment of Judaism by those who do not find ethnic allegiance compelling, as well as the emigration of others who desire to live a less circumscribed life as Jews. The number of Argentines who identify themselves as Jews has dropped by one-third in the past thirty years; across the continent, total numbers have decreased in this period from 550,000 to 377,000.

In public spaces, Latino Jewish entrepreneurs, academics, artists, and literati have experienced increasing success. As third and fourth generations acculturate, the social acceptability of Jews increases. In recent years, this has translated into wider acceptance of political participation by Jewish individuals. But acculturation has not diminished the hostility directed at Jews by sectors of the military and the church, which emerges in extreme forms when these sectors attain political dominance.

No wonder then that the texture of relations between Jews and non-Jews

251

in Latin America continues to puzzle observers. Dichotomies of attraction and repulsion, marginalization and integration, assimilation and particularism, anti-Semitism and philo-Semitism animate the literature on Latin American Jewry. Conclusions that may be valid for one country may rightly be challenged if applied to another. Argentina is not Brazil is not Nicaragua. This chapter attempts to interpret the nature of the relationship between Jews and non-Jews in Latin America. Because the largest Jewish population is to be found in Argentina and this community has been the most intensively studied, attention is first focused there.

Argentina: Attraction and Repulsion

The most obdurate anti-Semitism is that which derives from the conviction that Judaism is a worldwide conspiracy aimed at destroying Christianity and subjecting the world to domination by Jews.[1] This belief is central to Argentine *nacionalismo*, and it is practically impervious to reality-based evidence. At most, nationalists may harbor a difference of opinion as to whether the propensity to subversion is diluted by distance from the Jewish people and Judaism through intermarriage and assimilation. For *populistas*, assimilation renders Jews acceptable. For *integralistas*, however, once a Jew, always a Jew, even if formal conversion has taken place. Both brands of nationalists reject the liberal philosophy that brought non-Catholics and non-Latins to Argentine shores, and both reject the multicultural society that is emerging from the immigration period. Their ideal is an organic society overseen by a corporate state, and Jews, the ultimate nonconformists, are the special target of their hostility.[2] Despite the persistence of extreme anti-Semitic beliefs, it has been said that Argentina as a nation never adopted an anti-Semitic policy.

> It is clear that, with the exception of laws and policies concerning immigration, there has not been a systematic legislative effort to discriminate against Jews in Argentina. But it is also worth noting that there was often room in the interstices of legislation for the administrative expression of anti-Semitism. For much of the period discussed [1930–83] Jews were effectively excluded from certain areas of official life. For example, there was not a single Jew in the middle or upper officer ranks, although both Chile and Brazil had Jewish generals. The foreign service was also essentially closed to Jews. During the tenure of the military regime of 1943, many Jewish teachers were dismissed from their jobs. Under the military governments of 1966 and 1976 a great many Jews were removed from the civil service posts and university positions they had acquired when the [democratically elected] Radicals were in power.[3]

Avni argues that the closest Argentina has come to adoption of an anti-Semitic policy was when it refused to admit Jewish refugees from Nazism. Catholic religious instruction in the public schools has been another sensitive area; while not explicitly anti-Semitic, it has allowed for the transmission of anti-Semitic ideas. Local legislation outlawing kosher slaughter or restricting the public use of the Yiddish language also shaped the Argentine Jewish experience, although some of these measures were transitory.[4]

It may be that discrimination, like beauty, is in the eye of the beholder. Perhaps Argentine Jews, like Mao Zedong's allegorical fish who do not know what water is, are so acclimated to high levels of free-floating anti-Semitism that they accept it as the natural order of things. As individuals and as a group, they accept limitations and discriminations that appear outrageous to North Americans as the cost of living in a Catholic society that partially excludes them, yet exerts a sweet charm over them. The romanticized story of the agricultural colonies has rooted them in the very earth of Argentina. Those who came to the city were mostly able to attain a satisfactory way of life. Criollo ways—the close-knit family ties, the intense intellectual life of cafés and bookstores, the streets and restaurants filled with throngs of people until well past midnight—contrast delightfully with dark memories of the old country or more recent impressions of chilly northern climes. There seemed to be no reason why life should not continue to unfold pleasantly into the indefinite future.

This dream began to crumble in the fifties and sixties during the administrations of two democratically elected presidents. It is part of the Argentine paradox that the viability of Jewish life in that country was brought seriously into question during the constitutional administrations of Presidents Arturo Frondizi (1958–62) and Arturo Illía (1963–66).[5] Within the context of an ongoing economic crisis and tension between civilian and military forces, anti-Semitic verbal and physical attacks escalated. Anti-Jewish graffiti appeared on city walls and attacks on Jewish businesses and institutions were carried out by right-wing groups, without eliciting a police response or even official acknowledgment of the incidents. Out of a long catalogue of anti-Semitic actions, Senkman lists some examples from the period 1959–62.

Beginning in 1959, propaganda fliers and anti-Semitic graffiti scrawled on the walls of Jewish institutions in Buenos Aires encouraged violent attacks on Jews. In March, students at Colegio del Salvador, while protesting a change in the national constitution, incidentally took up an anti-Semitic chant. In April, the Sociedad Hebraica Argentina was violently attacked. In May, a gang confronted Jewish children in Villa Devoto on their way to a Zionist festival. Synagogues in the city of La Plata and the province of Córdoba were attacked. In July, a bomb exploded in front of Congregación Israelita de la República Argentina in the center of Buenos Aires. In August, armed men entered the Faculty of Law and Social Sciences at the University of Buenos Aires and destroyed stands that had been put up for an exhibition by Hebrew University. In August and September, additional attacks occurred against Jewish institutions: October witnessed attacks against Jewish youth centers in Córdoba, Paraná, and La Plata; and in December the patios of the Faculty of Economics at UBA were painted with swastikas and anti-Jewish slogans. Throughout

December and the following January, anti-Jewish inscriptions appeared all over the country, cemeteries were desecrated, and Jewish businesses were painted with swastikas, especially in La Plata and Córdoba. Threatening phone calls to members of the Jewish community heightened the tension. When school resumed, there were more attacks against Jewish students at Colegio Nacional Sarmiento.

In this atmosphere, the abduction of the Nazi war criminal Adolf Eichmann by Israeli agents triggered an organized campaign of attacks on Argentine Jews by the political faction Union Cívica Nacionalista and the neo-Nazi group Tacuara, on the pretext that national sovereignty was in danger. The pot boiled over with the national debate over the reintroduction of Catholic instruction in the schools. In this debate, the priest Julio Meinvielle found his metier, reissuing his anti-Semitic book, *El judío en el misterio de la historia* (The Jew in the Mystery of History). An uninterrupted fusillade of anti-Semitic attacks by UCN and Tacuara in anticipation of elections culminated in June 1962 with the kidnapping of a young Jewish woman, who was forcibly tatooed with a swastika on her breast. Neo-Nazis disrupted colleges and universities all over the country upon Israel's execution of Eichmann.[6]

Attacks on Jewish individuals and institutions met with no official objection and were carried out with impunity. In some instances, police refused to accept victims' complaints and denied to the press that any attack had taken place. Anti-Semitic acts were dismissed as staged events for the purpose of covering up "Jewish economic crimes." The DAIA, which made representations to the police and to presidential aides, was accused of falsifying incidents in order to foment a communist plot.

Meanwhile, the army, which held the civilian government in checkmate, "obsessed with radical or leftist conspiracies," confused working-class action, such as union-based or peronista politics, with its chief enemy, communism.[7] Senkman's explanation for the failure of these transitional democratic regimes to act (they were bracketed and displaced by military coups) is that both Frondizi and Illía were primarily interested in neutralizing social and political unrest. Because neo-Nazis and right-wing goons were battling the threat from the left, they chose to ignore their attacks on Jews. At the same time, these democratically elected presidents failed to assess the damage being done to the social fabric by the license being allowed to the right wing to carry out criminal acts against the civil population; the intensive focus of government and military on stopping the advance of peronism and communism conditioned them to excuse the "excesses" of gangs who included anti-Semitism in their anti-communist arsenal.[8] The strident propaganda pouring out of a variety of presses at this time, and the closing of Jewish leftist institutions while groups inspired by Nazi ideology continued to operate freely, prepared the public to believe in the existence of a "Jewish communist plot." Strong feelings of insecurity permeated the Jewish community, most of whose members had voted for the Radical party that now was presiding over their deteriorating position.

The leaders of DAIA nevertheless continued to support democratic forces.

They reasoned that anti-Semitism was being used as a political weapon by reactionary forces seeking to destabilize democracy in the interest of a return to authoritarian government, and that both Frondizi and Illía failed to see the danger because they shared the attackers' goals: to block the ascent of the left to power.[9] On the basis of this analysis, and knowing that a demonstration on behalf of Jewish rights would get nowhere, DAIA called for a protest strike by democratic sectors at all levels of society against terrorism by "Nazis" (meaning Nazi-influenced nativists). The theme was: "They'll begin with the Jews and end with democracy." The work stoppage, carried out on 28 June 1962 following the attack on Graciela Sirota, was a success, attracting considerable numbers of non-Jewish as well as Jewish participants. For their constituents, DAIA offered a defense of personal dignity as Jews and as Argentine citizens whose rights were being infringed.

The chaotic democracy that engulfed Argentina in the 1960s was brought to an end by General Juan Carlos Onganía (1966–70), who ousted Illía and initiated the destruction of Argentine intellectual life by pillaging the universities. Libraries burned books, plays were proscribed, intellectual and artistic life virtually shut down throughout the country, in a period argentinos describe as *mccartismo*, but which went a great deal further than McCarthyism in the United States. Repression of faculty and students and the closing of universities during this regime led to the flight into exile of a large number of Argentine intellectuals and artists, and came close to destroying the country's intellectual and artistic life. Not surprisingly, with nacionalistas in power, anti-Semitism became another instrument of policy. Under Onganía, all Jewish officials were removed from government posts, and assassinations and acts of hooliganism against Jews went unpunished.

At the same time, numerous fascist organizations were operating in Argentina, fueled by ideas scavenged from the wreckage of the Third Reich. It is not necessary to imagine sophisticated Nazis seducing naive Argentines into adopting their agenda: their message resonated sufficiently within local culture to make itself at home in criollo terms. Thirty years after the collapse of Nazism in Europe, its ideology was alive and thriving in Argentina, Peru, and Chile. In the latter country, Dignidad, an enclosed community of neo-Nazis, survived intact. Extreme right-wing newspapers and magazines such as *El Fortín, Cabildo, Restauración,* and *Patria Peronista* were peddling anti-Semitism with articles such as one that declaimed, "We confirm that the white slave trade and drug traffic are two instruments utilized by Zionist imperialism to corrupt our youth. This should be investigated as a conspiracy against our nation." Organizations such as Tacuara, Falange de Fe (Córdoba), Centuria Universitaria Nacionalista, Falange Restaurador Nacionalista, Centuria Nacionalista, Agrupación Nacionalista Argentina, and Partido Acción Nacionalista, all were propagating a line based on hatred of Jews as cosmopolitans who imported foreign ideas—communism and capitalism—that corrupt the body politic. In support of the charge of a Jewish plot to subjugate Argentines to "international bankers," a government-controlled television station broadcast in February 1975 a dramatization of *La Bolsa* (The Stock Exchange), the hoary anti-Semitic libel that newspapers had serialized three generations earlier. The "Andinia Plan," fabricated by the professional anti-Semite Walter Beveraggi Allende, popularized the paranoid delusion that there existed an international conspiracy to create a second Jewish state in the south of Argentina.

While coping with the threat from the right, Jews also came under attack from the left. Radical groups aligned with Middle Eastern guerrilla factions became overtly anti-Semitic in the seventies, drawing on racial prejudice to bolster their anti-Zionist agenda, not only in Argentina but all across Latin America. Revolutionary groups established contact with the Palestine Liberation Organization and Popular Front for the Liberation of Palestine, working toward an alliance of Third World revolutionaries whose principal target rapidly became Israel, and by extension, Jews anywhere in the world. In neighboring Brazil, the combination of dependence on Arab oil, a rapid transition from dictatorship to democracy, and agitation by professional anti-Semites among left-wing supporters of the Palestine Liberation Organization triggered vituperative attacks against Jews. Jews were attacked for having links with Israel, and Israel for having links with imperialist powers (the United States, Great Britain, the International Monetary Fund) that allegedly held the continent in a position of economic dependency.[10]

These radical groupings attracted Jewish as well as non-Jewish students. In the 1960s and 1970s, multitudes of university-educated Jewish youth were becoming as alienated from the Jewish establishment as non-Jewish youth were from the criollo establishment. By 1976, fewer than 10 percent of Buenos Aires Jewish youth (estimated at a total 90,000) belonged to any Jewish community institution. Among university students, the proportion of the affiliated was just 5.8 percent.[11] The revolutionary movements sweeping South and Central America caught up these unaffiliated Jewish youths. There were Jewish Montoneros in Argentina and Tupamaros in Uruguay, Jewish Cubans in the ranks of the revolutionaries of 1959, and Jewish Sandinistas in Nicaragua in the seventies. In the process of joining the revolution, they distanced themselves from other Jews and from Judaism, either as a matter of principle or in order to establish their credentials with their comrades in arms. The hostility of left-wing groups toward Israel exerted pressure on these young Jews to prove their exclusively national loyalties by dropping their ties to Jews and Judaism.[12] Having adopted the stance of the militant left, these Jews viewed Israel as an imperialist power, allied with the oppressor class they were rebelling against.

A full-scale civil war broke out in Argentina in 1970, with left-wing guerrillas organized in the Revolutionary Popular Army (ERP by its Spanish initials) and Montoneros (an offshoot of peronism) in armed rebellion against a series of corrupt and inefficient governments. Right-wing gangs, organized as the Argentine Anticommunist Alliance, or Triple A, began kidnapping and murdering leftists, apparently with the connivance of the police. Among other violent acts, attacks on Jewish institutions and individuals escalated. Buenos Aires became a center for the publication of anti-Semitic literature, handed out freely to pedestrians on La Florida and other shopping streets, some of which went so far as to incite pogroms ("save the fatherland—kill a Jew" ran one slogan). The administration of President Isabel Martínez de Perón, under the dominance of her adviser, the spiritualist José López Rega (who may have been the sponsor of the AAA), was using anti-Semitism as an instrument of terror. Given Argentina's history of oscillation between ungovernable democracy and brutal authoritarian rule, by 1976 many middle-class Argentines viewed a military junta pledged to restoring constitutional norms as the lesser among several evils. This judgment was concurred in by the organized Jewish community, as represented through the DAIA.

Dirty War

The military junta that took power in 1976 terminated the threat from the Left by means of a "Dirty War" aimed at physically exterminating subversion. Many Jews, like other middle class citizens, anticipated relief from the harassments, kidnappings, and politically motivated murders that had characterized the Left's assault on organized society. Unfortunately, in practice, the military were more violent than the guerrillas, better armed and organized, more anti-Semitic, and able to utilize the figleaf of legitimacy to act on their murderous ideology. As the then Chief of Buenos Aires Police, Colonel Ramón Camps, said at the time: "First, we will kill the guerrillas. Then we will kill the guerrillas' families. Then we will kill the friends of their families, and the friends of their friends, so that there will be no one left to remember who the guerrillas were."

The junta, organized as the Process of National Reorganization (called the *proceso*), acted on this premise by killing an estimated 10,000 to 30,000 civilians, many with no record of political activity of any kind. (The Commission appointed later to investigate the matter was able to document 8,800 cases, but many families were too frightened to come forward to report their losses.) As planned, disappearances occurred in chain reaction.

Aída Leonora Bruschtein was a single woman of twenty-four who taught literacy in the slums of Monte Chingolo, greater Buenos Aires. She was maltreated and shot, before witnesses, by uniformed personnel of Battalion 601 (Intelligence) of the Argentine army. She was identified through fingerprints taken from her hands, which were sent to her family in a jar. The Bruschtein family initiated a lawsuit against the army for homicide. While the matter was *sub judice,* a group of armed men, dressed in civilian clothes and backed by twenty carloads of soldiers, invaded the home of her parents in the center of the city in broad daylight. Aída Leonora's father, sixty years old and a biochemist, was in bed convalescing from a heart attack. The intruders, shouting, "How dare you charge the Argentine army with homicide, Jew son-of-a-bitch," dragged the invalid from his bed and carried him away with great brutality. The act was never acknowledged officially, and his body was never found.

Adrian Sidon, fiancé of Aída Leonora, was killed by the police on a public sidewalk. His body was never delivered to his father, a well-known lawyer and entrepreneur who demanded it persistently.

Patricia Villa, sister of a daughter-in-law of the Bruschteins, was detained while working in the office of Inter Press in Buenos Aires, before numerous witnesses. One week later, her family was notified by the navy that Patricia had died, but they did not indicate where she had been buried. The authorities demanded that the family keep the episode secret, or what had happened to other members of the family would happen to them also.

At six in the morning, in a joint operation of the federal police and the army, Irene Bruschtein de Ginsburg, sister of Aída Leonora, and her husband, Mario Ginsburg, were detained. She was an artist and he a master workman and student of architecture. Their children Victoria, not quite three years old, and Hugo Roberto, eighteen months, were abandoned at the door of the building where their parents were sequestered. They remain permanently disappeared.

One month earlier, Victor Rafael Bruschtein, seventeen, had been detained in the home where he resided with his mother, in Moron, province of Buenos Aires. He also disappeared.[13]

Edy Kaufman, a respected investigator of human rights abuses, estimates that Jews accounted for close to 10 percent of the disappeared, far exceeding the proportion of Jews in the population at large or even within those professions—university faculty, social workers, psychiatrists, union leaders, literacy teachers—that were specifically targeted.[14] Testimony of prisoners freed from some of the 304 detention centers maintained by the proceso confirms that Jewish prisoners were singled out for particularly abusive treatment, often to the accompaniment of verbal assaults that mimicked Nazi rhetoric. Of course, 90 percent of victims were Christian, mostly Catholic like their victimizers, and they included priests and nuns as well as lay religious leaders.

Strangely, it was difficult to discern immediately the orientation of the military junta toward Jews and the Jewish community. Mainline Jewish institutions were not attacked. Jewish parents were not slow to draw conclusions, enrolling their children in community schools, synagogues, and sports clubs where activities focused on strictly Jewish concerns (religion, Israel, Hebrew-centered education), soaking up the youngsters' time that might otherwise have been spent getting involved with suspect groups.

Censorship of the press, plus fear of speaking out, made it difficult to understand exactly what was going on, and some interviewees claimed that they were unaware of the repression until they made a trip abroad and were able to read about ongoing atrocities in the foreign press. The conflicting opinions of community leaders were reported by Israeli embassy officials and are just now being extracted from that government's archives.[15] On one side were those who believed the junta members themselves were not anti-Semitic;

they accepted the generals' statement that, in battling subversion, which threatened the very existence of the state, "excesses" (such as torture and summary execution of prisoners) could be expected to occur, that such acts were not sanctioned by the junta but were the work of gangs they were powerless to control. Those who believed the statements of the *moderados* (moderates) led by Gen. Jorge Rafael Videla concluded that the atrocities being committed against *detenidos* (those who were arrested and held in jail) and *desaparecidos* (those who had been snatched off the street or from their home and made to disappear without trace) occurred either because the victims had been involved in the subversion or because they were the unfortunate victims of unauthorized actions by militias operating independently of the junta. No doubt there were anti-Semites among the personnel who carried out these actions, but anti-Semitism was not a settled policy of the junta. People who accepted these assurances did so in part because they believed that behind the moderate faction waited the *duras*—hardliners who included in their ranks known anti-Semites whom the community had good reason to fear.

In May 1976, DAIA president Nehemias Resnitzky traveled to New York to press this point of view. He had been assured, he told representatives of North American Jewish organizations, that the junta would restore democracy after fixing the economy and that official anti-Semitism was out of the question because Argentina needed U.S. financial support. The extreme right of the Argentine political spectrum, however, was capable of using anti-Semitism to distract people from their real problems. He pleaded with U.S. organizations not to publicize crimes against Jews in order not to fall into what he described as a trap by leftist groups to discredit the junta with charges of anti-Semitism and thereby leave it vulnerable to a putsch by the *duras*.[16]

The other school of thought held that the scale of government repression far outweighed the danger posed initially by the ERP, Montoneros, and various Maoist groups. By May 1977 the armed subversion had been physically exterminated, but the repression ground on. Rumors of the existence of moderate and hardline factions were only a version of the "good cop, bad cop" routine familiar to every police interrogator. The specter of a putsch by hardliners was a ploy to get the gullible to go along with the junta, which really was in control of the actions of its "wild men" and was using state terror as an instrument of governance.

The sadistic behavior of camp guards and their commandants did not emerge from nowhere. The way had been prepared for it by years of racist articles and cartoons in literature and the press; sermons by Catholic priests whose anti-Semitism went unreprimanded by their bishops; rallies of nationalist organizations; anti-Semitic graffiti and vandalism at Jewish institutions; letters and telephone calls to community leaders threatening mayhem to themselves and their families; bombs placed in synagogues; kidnappings, and physical attacks on Jews.[17] Such actions, and popular as well as governmental acquiescence in them, laid the basis for the explosion of anti-Semitism that took place within the protected precincts of proceso prisons. Yet, as much as one year

SUBVERSION

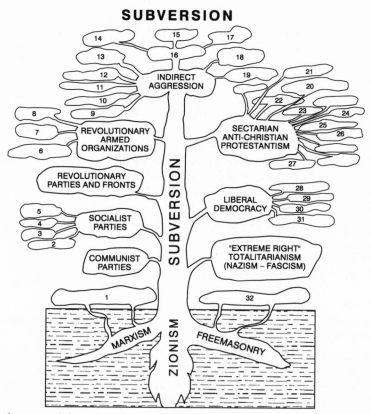

In this diagram of the Argentine military mind, the tree of subversion grows out of the tap root of Zionism and its collatorals, Marxism and Freemasonry. From these roots grow (1) societies and leagues for defense of human rights, women's rights, pacifism, non-aggression, disarmament, "etc." Communist parties spring directly from the trunk of subversion. Socialist parties sprout (2) national, (3) Argentine, (4) vanguard, and (5) democratic branches. Revolutionary armed organizations include the (7) Montoneros, (8) FAR (Revolutionary Armed Forces), and ERP (People's Revolutionary Army) in addition to the spectral (6) Other. Indirect aggression caps the tree of subversion, sprouting (9) union corruption, (10) secular education, (11) liberal economics, (12) liberal politics, (13) drug addiction, alcoholism, prostitution, and gambling, (14) the Third World, (15) postconciliar modernism, (16) progressive Catholicism, (17) liberal Christianity, (18) hippie-ism, pornography, homosexuality, and divorce, and (19) the mass media, including art, the press, radio, TV, cinema, magazines, and books. Sectarian anti-Christian Protestantism subverts society through (20) "American noblemen of fire," (21) evangelism, (22) Anael Lodge, (23) Mormonism, (24) Jehovah's Witnesses, (25) Modern school New Acropolis, (26) Hare Krishna, and (27) Siolismo–Youth Power. Liberal Democracy spawns (28) Radicals, (29) Christian Democracy, (30) Social Democracy, (31) Populist Demagogy. Surprisingly, the extreme right branch of totalitarianism (Nazism–Fascism) appears to have no off-shoots at all in Argentina; but Freemasonry leads directly to the threat of (32) Rotary Club, Lion's Club, and Junior Chamber. (*The original drawing, "La subversión," was obtained and translated by Edy Kaufman and is reproduced in "Jewish Victims of Repression in Argentina under Military Rule, 1976–1983."*)

after the coup, the Jewish community seemed unconcerned about anti-Semitic attacks by the junta. This may have occurred in part because they had grown inured to the level of free-floating anti-Semitism that had always surrounded them. But their apparent willful ignoring of reality also stemmed from the fact that the censored press misrepresented the deaths of prisoners who had been tortured and executed without trial as having resulted from armed confrontations between the armed forces and the guerrillas. This caused some observers to blame parents of the disappeared for not having brought up their children "correctly." It took years for many civilians to realize that the nacionalista forces had moved beyond random acts of terror to the systematic use of terror to cow them into submission. In coming to power, the military gained the capacity to activate its paranoid fantasies through the machinery of the state. The primitive notions of what or who a Jew might be were transcribed in dozens of prison interrogations and recorded in survivors' memoirs.[18] Their worldview is graphically displayed in the diagram "La Subversión" (see opposite page) included in a pamphlet found on the desk of the vice-director of the Escuela Superior de Guerra Aerea in 1980 and evidently intended for distribution to the officer cadets.[19] The barbarity of its conception is exceeded only by its lack of understanding of the real world.

The Dirty War was plainly directed against "subversives," but much depended on the definition of that term. For nacionalistas, activism on behalf of the poor *subverts* society, campaigns for women's rights *subvert* the family, and belief in a subconscious *subverts* Christianity. These were presented as specifically Jewish crimes, the culprits: Marx, Marcuse, and Freud (but not Jesus). Practitioners in these fields were especially targeted by the regime; and Jews were disproportionately numbered among them. Were they being disappeared and tortured for these suspect activities, or did being Jewish constitute a suspect category in itself?

Onganía's anti-intellectual campaign turned out to have been only a prelude to the large-scale winnowing of intellectuals and artists, community outreach workers, labor union leaders, social workers, psychologists, and psychiatrists undertaken by the generals of the Process of National Reorganization. Demonized as subverters of the social order and perverters of Christian family values, Jewish professionals fled to Mexico, Spain, Israel, and the United States. The extinction or exodus of the talented added a bitter epilogue to the history of immigration policy. Governments at the beginning of the twentieth century had preferred farmers to intellectuals. Two generations later, elites were still trying to prevent foreign ideas from contaminating criollo minds.

Argentina was not alone in adopting an authoritarian-bureaucratic style of governing in the 1970s. Contemporaneous Brazilian, Uruguayan, and Chilean dictatorships likewise targeted men and women they identified as communists and labor agitators, incidentally sending to their deaths numerous innocents who were in the wrong place at the wrong time. Jews were among those killed by these governments, not for being Jews, but because they were suspected of subversive activity. Only in Argentina was there a distinct anti-Semitic component to the repression. The Argentine military surpassed their colleagues in other countries by their untrammeled acting out of Nazi-style anti-Semitism.

> Many testimonies of Jewish and non-Jewish prisoners document the fact that, from the moment of detention up until the decision to "transfer" and in many cases to execute the victims, there existed a tendency toward negative preferential treatment of Jews. This was manifest, in the first place, in plainly anti-Semitic oral expressions, including references of a religious-traditional type about the Jew as Antichrist; and in a vocabulary of clear Nazi derivation; also in the interrogations about the objectives of Zionism and its anti-Argentine activities. In the second place, the existence of Nazi inscriptions and emblems in the detention centers has been documented; and in the methods used to destroy the personality of the victim, an anti-Jewish dimension played a part in psychological torture as well as in accentuated brutality. Finally, it is possible to establish that, in the selection of victims for sacrifice by means of "transfer," priority was given to the Jewish disappeared.[20]

Moreover, the Argentine military brought the Church hierarchy along with them. A 1966 concordat with the Vatican, initiated by the democratic administration of Illía and confirmed by General Onganía, provided the basis for agreement (convivencia) between the army and the church, and identification of the military with Catholic dogma. Although the struggle for dominance by the one over the other never ceased, the posture of the Argentine church coincided more with the military regime of the proceso than with the Brazilian and Chilean church hierarchies that, in similar circumstances, confronted their own authoritarian regimes over issues of human rights.[21]

The actions of the junta have been scrutinized by foreign observers as well as by the Argentine National Commission on the Disappeared (CONADEP), and the Argentine courts. Appointed in 1983, CONADEP comprised individuals with national and international reputations as defenders of human rights; it included two Jewish human rights advocates, Professor Gregorio Klimovsky and Rabbi Marshall Meyer. Their report, as well as subsequent judicial proceedings against members of the junta, proved that thousands of people had been illegally deprived of their freedom, tortured and killed in secret prisons and concentration camps. Atrocities were the common practice, the normal method of daily operation that could not have occurred without the approval of top commanders. Moreover, the commission of the most heinous crimes against Jewish Argentines was licensed and condoned by the anti-Semitic ideology at the top of the military hierarchy.[22] The response of nacionalistas was to describe the published report as a Jewish conspiracy aimed at besmirching the honor of the Argentine military.

The role of the DAIA during the Dirty War quickly became, and has remained, a focus of bitter controversy. Accused of passivity in the face of anti-Semitic outrages, the kehillah leadership was able to point to the fact that the Catholic Church had not been able to protect its own people; and that the DAIA had at least protected its member institutions from physical invasion.

Without verbally expressing the distinction, DAIA may be said to have eschewed responsibility for Jewish Argentines who were not affiliated with the kehillah and who were thus (in the words of one kehilla president) "not even Jewish." Defined out of the community by proprietary criteria of membership and by their own choice, unaffiliated Jews fell victim in significant numbers to the military's paranoid delusions regarding Jewish proclivities toward subversion.

Falklands War

By 1982, the repression had succeeded in eliminating political dissent but Argentina's economy was a shambles. In a desperate gamble to regain public approval, the generals played the irredentist card, invading the islands that Argentines call the Malvinas. Under their English name, the Falklands had been ruled by the British for a century, but the Argentines had never given up their claim. Britain, the United States, and the European Community all froze arms shipments to Argentina when the invasion took place, and requested that other trading partners do the same. Israel, however, continued making deliveries of goods already contracted for.

The war held up a funhouse mirror to the political alignments of the day. Though Argentina had suppressed her own leftists, her chief military suppliers were the USSR and Cuba. Israeli arms deliveries established rapport with the most anti-Semitic elements in Argentina. Perhaps as a quid pro quo, the army for the first time permitted the appointment of Jewish army chaplains (no one of Jewish origin had been commissioned above the rank of captain in the Argentine army since 1934). In the atmosphere of chauvinist exhilaration that characterized the first days of the war, the kehillah became the first ethnic community officially to express loyalty to the junta. The DAIA was quick to pledge allegiance in a statement linking Argentina's drive to recover the Malvinas with the Jewish people's desire to recover the land of their ancestors.

Jews in Argentine Politics

In Argentina, the notion of Jews in public office is still viewed by nacionalistas as a betrayal of traditional values, a reversal of natural law. The idea of Jews exercising power over Christians has been taboo in Spanish culture since the fifteenth century. Nacionalistas who remain enthralled by the preconciliar past view the ascension of Jews to positions of public trust as prima facie evidence of a worldwide Jewish conspiracy, beachheads for the advancement of foreign, subversive ideas. Thus the election or appointment of Jews to public office, and their retention there, tests the readiness of these sectors to break from the medieval past.

When President Frondizi assumed office in 1958, he appointed a number of Jews to his administration, including the country's first Jewish cabinet minister, David Blejer, as minister of labor. Santiago Nudelman, a physician, lawyer, and national deputy, was an important figure in the Unión Cívica Radical. Four Jewish delegates were elected to the Argentine House of Representatives in the same election; two other Jews were elected governors that year, in Neuquén and Formosa. At the very same time, the anti-Semitic demonstrations described above were taking place without attracting Frondizi's attention or concern. More Jews were elected to national office in 1963, but officeholders were removed arbitrarily by the military coup of 1966.[23] No Jewish official survived the purges that took place under the presidency of Juan Carlos Onganía. The record shows that Jews attain official positions during democratic interludes but are removed by right-wing and military governments, as much for their Jewishness as for their politics.

In 1973, with the advent of the peronista government of Hector Campora, two Jews were appointed to top positions: one as undersecretary of interior, the other as finance minister. However, following the death of Perón, finance minister José Ber Gelbard, a former peddler and the second Jew to reach cabinet rank, became the focus of an anti-Semitic campaign launched by López Rega, adviser to President Isabel Perón. After being dismissed from his position, Gelbard was stripped of his citizenship and deported. Attacks on Gelbard also targeted the Jewish businessmen's association that he had headed. The anti-Semitism that surfaced at this time shook the confidence of the Jewish community that the excesses of the Onganía period had ended.

No Jew was elected or appointed to public office during the proceso. When the junta dissolved in disarray, the election of Raúl Alfonsín to the presidency in October 1983 marked a watershed in Argentine history. In that election, six Jews elected to the Chamber of Deputies. Two years later, Jewish candidates won 11 of 254 seats, or 4.3 percent, higher than the proportion of Jews in the Argentine population. Increased acceptability of Jewish candidates was demonstrated by the fact that these deputies were elected from various provinces and from both the Radical and Justicialista (peronist) parties. Both the Chamber of Deputies and the Senate chose Jews to serve among its leadership: César Jaroslavsky was elected majority leader of the Chamber, and Senator Adolfo Gass became chair of the Senate Foreign Relations Committee. Only two of fourteen competing political parties did not include Jews on their ballots, and Jewish identity did not become an issue during the campaign. "Overall, the Argentine electorate displayed a much more sophisticated and rational understanding of candidates and issues than in the past."[24]

President Alfonsín appointed a number of Jews to his administration, including Bernardo Grinspun as minister of finance and later as minister of planning; Leopoldo Portnoy as vice-president of the Central Bank, Mario Brodersohn as treasury secretary, Oscar Oszlak as undersecretary of research and administrative reform, and Roberto Schteingart as undersecretary of state for information and development. Adolfo Stubrin as minister of education, Manuel Sadosky as secretary of state for science and technology; Oscar Shuberoff as rector of the University of Buenos Aires, as well as the appointment of Jewish deans, and especially the appointment of Marcos Aguinis, a well-known Jewish psychoanalyst and writer, to the post of undersecretary of culture, signified recognition of the multicultural reality of the country but enraged the Catholic Church and its allies.[25] These appointments aroused a campaign to discredit the administration as "la sinagoga Radical" ("Radical" is the name of Alfonsín's centrist party; *sinagoga* is defined by Spanish-language dictionaries as "conspiracy") and Jewish officials were accused of infiltrating the government on behalf of "international Zionism." General Ramon Camps, the "hero" of the military repression in Buenos Aires responsible for gross human rights violations during the proceso, published a book in which he charged that Jewish banking interests were subverting the state and warning of Zionist infiltration. Nevertheless, these appointments held, and prepared the way for amendment of the constitution so as to eliminate the requirement that the president of the nation be a communicant of the Catholic Church.

Peronista Carlos Saúl Menem, a Catholic born into a Muslim family that originated in Syria, followed Alfonsín in the presidency. Menem showed sensitivity to Jewish issues, becoming the first Argentine president to send his foreign minister on a visit to Israel. He apparently utilized his special relationship to ask the government of Syria to look into the fate of missing Israeli prisoners of war. He is known to have close advisers who are Jews (such as Samuel Muzykanski and Moises Ikonicoff) and has appointed Jewish peronistas to important posts in his administration, including Carlos Vladimiro Corach as minister of interior and Deputy Justice Minister Elias Jassan.

Disintegration

It was in this democratic period that Argentine Jewry suffered its most devastating blow. On Monday morning, 18 July 1994, at a few moments before ten, a bomb destroyed the AMIA building in downtown Buenos Aires, bringing to an end a decade of hope that had begun with the elections of 1983. Eighty-six persons were killed, hundreds maimed, and the building itself was destroyed.[26] The terrorists who planned and carried out the attack—like those who had destroyed the embassy of Israel two years earlier—knew exactly what they were doing. They had struck at the functioning heart of the Jewish community.

The damage caused by destruction of the building and loss of life was compounded by a surge of hoaxes perpetrated against survivors and telephoned threats of "we'll get you next." Perhaps the unkindest cut came from sympathizers who regretted that "not just Jews but innocent people" had been killed. Thousands of citizens came out to demonstrate against race hatred and terror, but others responded by distancing themselves emotionally and geographically from the hazard they perceived as emanating from too close association with the victims. Jewish institutions now had difficulty renewing their leases, Jewish soccer teams found themselves canceled out of league competitions, and the erection of concrete barriers in front of Jewish schools created the atmosphere of a ghetto, something that had never existed in Argentina. To the suggestion that a motive for the attack may have been to destroy Nazi archives which President Menem had recently handed over to the DAIA for analysis, one

AMIA—Comunidad
Judía de Buenos
Aires—is the principal
organization of
Argentine Jewry. Its
building at 633 Pasteur,
in the heart of the old
Jewish district of Once,
housed a library,
archives, social welfare
agencies, a labor
exchange, publishing
and cultural activities.

researcher responded, "In Argentina, no one would be embarrassed to be publicly revealed as a Nazi."

To date, the perpetrators have not been apprehended, leading to the suspicion that they never will be. The perpetrators of the earlier attack on the Israeli Embassy, which left 30 dead and 250 injured, have never been caught. Suspicion in both cases focused on pro-Iranian Hezbullah, but this was never proved; in any event, terrorism experts believe the attacks could not have succeeded without local help, possibly from among disgruntled soldiers and police who believed themselves unjustly accused of criminal behavior for having followed orders to torture or assassinate prisoners during the Dirty War. Such persons likewise have never been identified or apprehended.

The long-run outcome of the bombing of AMIA has yet to unfold. The Jews of Argentina, who had had ample reason for discontent with their major institution, rallied to renovate and rebuild the AMIA. A process of communal self-evaluation got under way. Conceivably, public revulsion at the massacre of innocents may lead to a moderation of anti-Semitic rhetoric as the legacy of

On 18 July 1994, the AMIA building was destroyed by an explosive device. The perpetrators were never apprehended. Eighty-nine persons were killed and dozens more maimed. Most of the victims were Jews, but others, the radio reported, "were innocent."

relentless nacionalista propagandizing is held up for examination. President Menem, whose first reaction to the AMIA bombing was that the attack had been carried out to embarrass him, has displayed neither the capacity nor the will to solve the crime.

Jews in Politics: Beyond Argentina

The path by which Jewish Latinos might participate in national politics was never clearly marked. The electoral process functions only partially and inter-mittently in Latin America. Where it functions, it does so in a manner that does not necessarily enfranchise individuals or small interest groups; and Jews are nowhere numerous enough seriously to affect an electoral outcome. Power-ful corporate bodies are usually the chief political actors: the armed forces, associations of urban or rural entrepreneurs, labor unions, the church. Each views its own interests as paramount; each defends its turf from "meddling" by the larger society, an attitude that has been called "the politics of anti-politics." The military is quite explicit about its mandate to interpret the "will of the people," regardless of what the constitution or the electorate may have to say about the matter, a view that is widespread in Latin America.[27] Political parties are forced to maneuver within extremely limited space. Jews, who are unrepresented in the church, landed oligarchy, army, labor unions, or peasant syndicates, wield no influence within these institutions.

Chile in the years of the Unidad Popular government (1970–73) tested the limits of acceptability of Jews in high public office. The Chileanization policies of Dr. Salvador Allende Gossens, which aimed at creating a socialist society through law, were in part designed by Senator Volodia Teitelboim, chief strate-gist of Chile's Communist party who as a youth had belonged to Hashomer Hatzair, the left wing of the Zionist movement. Allende appointed other Jews as well to key posts in his administration, including David Baytelman in Agrarian Reform, David Silberman in Copper Administration, Jaime Faivovich in the city government of Santiago, Jacobo Schaulsohn on the Constitutional Court, Enrique Kirberg at the Technical University, Enrique Testa at the Defense Ministry, and Luis Vega at the Ministry of Interior.[28] The policies they designed and implemented conformed both to the traditional Jewish demand for social justice and to the Chilean people's demand for social and economic equity, as reflected in the election of Allende to the presidency.[29] But their participation had the effect of intensifying attacks on the president as the pawn of Jewish Bolsheviks. The upsurge of anti-Semitism that accompanied the introduction of Allende's program took as its target not just those Jews who were members of his administration but the entire community, which was held responsible for the fact that some Jews are Marxists.

Given Chile's tradition of tolerance, the effort failed to arouse popular passions against Jews. But right-wing agitation was just one horn of the dilemma. The election of Allende on a Marxist platform had triggered mass abandonment of the country by middle-class entrepreneurs who feared expropriation of their property, as had happened ten years before in Cuba. Among those who departed were some 8,000 of Chile's 30,000 Jews. These were mainly the wealthy, property owners, and members of the communal establishment, and they left despite friendly overtures by the new administration. The flight of the wealthiest members of the Jewish community and the loss of their financial contributions damaged Jewish institutions, a blow the now smaller and poorer community had difficulty absorbing. This was one minor element in the whirlwind of chaos that overtook Chile. In September 1973, a military junta, encouraged by the United States government, overthrew Allende and set about reestablishing a reassuring climate for business.

Once the climate stabilized, many middle-class persons, Jews among them, returned to the country. They were encouraged by the tactics of General Augusto Pinochet, who explicitly rejected anti-Semitism and made a point of attending Rosh Hashanah services in a Santiago synagogue. But Jews were now more aware than ever of their dependence on the goodwill of the powers that be, and were apprehensive that they would pay the price of social experimentation. That a considerable cohort of Jewish individuals had worked for Allende, and that other Jews returned to Chile under Pinochet underscores the fact that Jews are influenced by the same ideologies as motivate non-Jews and that most Jews behave like other members of their economic class. Jews lived in Chile under violent swings of government from right to left and back again, but leaders of the organized community might well conclude that in circumstances that are likely to degenerate into civil war, a studied neutrality offers the best protection.

Jews are more diffused politically through the governing structures of Brazil than any other of the republics. The record shows far greater openness to Jewish political initiative than exists in the Spanish-speaking republics. Individuals from the important commercial families Lafer, Klabin, Moses, Bloch, and Levy have entered politics as ministers of state, bankers, and presidential advisers. There are Jews in numerous government posts and in significant military positions. By 1977, there were three Jews in the Chamber of Deputies, as well as several Jewish state legislators and councilmen. Two federal agencies—the National Housing Bank and the Brazilian Institute for Statistics and Geography—were headed by Jewish individuals. Curitiba, capital of the state of Paraná, has elected itself two Jewish mayors. The state secretary of transport for Rio de Janeiro, the state secretary of planning for São Paulo, and the state secretary of science, culture and technology are posts that have been held by Jews.[30] The administration of President Fernando Collor de Melo reversed the Brazilian position at the United Nations to cancel its acquiescence in Resolution 3379 equating Zionism with racism. The succeeding administration of Fernando Henrique Cardozo, a renowned economist, gained the confidence and support of the Jewish community. In recent years, Jaime Lerner beat back an attempt to rouse anti-Semitic feeling against him to be elected governor of the state of Paraná.

In Mexico, electoral outcomes have been predetermined within the hegemonic Partido Revolucionario Institucional. PRI, its revolutionary credentials somewhat tainted by its fifty-year monopoly of power, is only now beginning to be effectively challenged by rivals. It can be surmised that Jewish Mexicans first achieved some political influence after 1975, as a result of the threat by United States Jews to boycott Mexican goods if the government did not rescind its affirmative vote on the United Nations resolution equating Zionism with racism. That did not happen officially until 1992, but in the interim, relations between the government and the Jewish community measurably improved, despite frequent sackings and desecrations of Jewish cemeteries by persons unknown.[31] Personal contact and discreet financial contributions may take the place of the ballot, which is as ineffective for Jews as a group as it is for other would-be power contenders who cannot control a mass of "voters." As a small urban minority, Jews cannot compete with landowners who truck their peons to the polling station to cast their open ballots.

The growing acceptance of cultural pluralism in Mexico (manifested by government funding for publication of books on Mexican Jewish history and sponsorship of an international conference on Latin American Jewry), and perhaps also the government's recognition of the importance to the national economy of Mexican Jewish businessmen and industrialists with connections to the United States, has led to the appointment of Jews to government positions. Most of these are technical in nature. A series of modernizing Mexican presidents have relied increasingly on technocrats, including Jewish ones, and Ernesto Zedillo's government includes Arturo Warman, secretary of agrarian reform; Santiago Levy, undersecretary for expenditures; Jaime Zabludovsky, undersecretary for communications; and Jacques Rogozinsky, director of tourism. These appointments, as well as the election of Esther Koleteniuk to the city council of Mexico City, mark a clear departure from the past.[32]

The 1990s have been a breakthrough decade for the acceptance of Jews in public office in Peru. As is well known, that country already had elected a Nisei president, Alberto Fujimoro; it next acquired a Jewish prime minister, Efraín Goldenberg-Schreiber. The son of Russian Jewish immigrants, Goldenberg was born in the Pacific coast town of Talara, where he was the only Jewish child in his primary school. He attended high school and San Marcos University in Lima, earning a law degree before entering his family's export business. He also served on the board of the Lima Jewish community association.[33] While Jewish political appointees have commonly been chosen from among businessmen, political activism was the background for selection of Moisés Jarmusz Levy as Bolivia's minister of development and environment by the president of Bolivia in 1992. Jarmusz Levy had been executive secretary of a Bolivian political party allied with the government.[34] In Santiago de Chile, Marcos Libedinsky became the first Jew to be named to that country's Supreme Court and Benjamin Teplitzky Lilyavetzky was appointed minister of mining. Both men are active members of the Santiago Jewish community. Milos Alcalay was appointed director general of the Venezuelan foreign ministry. In Costa Rica, while Sandra Piszk and Saul Weisleder were elected to Parliament and

German Weinstok was appointed minister of health, Rebeca Grynspan was elected vice-president of the country.[35]

The fact that many current appointees are active in their local Jewish community marks a departure from past practice, when nearly all those who entered public life had previously dropped any connection to Jews and Judaism. Furthermore, until the 1980s, Jewish individuals were appointed exclusively to offices involved with finance, conforming to the nacionalista mystique that "Jews are good with money." This situation is now changing, with greater numbers of Jewish individuals being appointed to a wider range of offices, while retaining their identification as Jews.

Jews in Politics: A Schematic View

This roster of non-hispanic names in Latin American politics announces a significant change in social attitudes, one that acknowledges the citizenship rights of Jews. A meaningful future for Jews is difficult to envision without admittance to political participation. It may therefore be a useful exercise to review the conditions under which Jews are able to participate in politics in Latin America. This question can be viewed from three different perspectives: that of society at large, the organized Jewish community, and politically active Jewish individuals; and in three different contexts: democracies, authoritarian states, and under revolutionary conditions.[36]

From the standpoint of society at large, Argentina, Brazil, Chile, Uruguay, Costa Rica and Panama have all elected respectable numbers of Jewish candidates to public office during democratic periods. No legal barriers to their election or appointment are known to exist, but ancient hatreds may surface when partisanship becomes heated, or may be deliberately employed in order to drive a wedge through the ranks of the opposing party. The periods 1958–62 and 1983–85 in Argentina and 1970–73 in Chile demonstrated this political schizophrenia: Jews were elected to office, but nacionalistas attacked the government for being "under the control of Jews."

Authoritarian regimes restrict political participation by all citizens, often converting political interests to financial ones. Robert Levine records an instructive incident from 1930s Cuba. "Relations between the Jewish colony and officialdom followed the rather personalistic formula required by the fact that Batista was de facto the head of state. When anti-Semitic broadcasts on one radio station increased in bellicosity in 1935, representatives from the UHC [United Hebrew Congregations] paid a visit to Batista during which they pledged ten thousand dollars toward the campaign to build a new national library; and they used the opportunity to ask that something be done about the broadcasts. Batista denied that he had any power to influence things but . . . within a few days unknown vandals smashed the radio station, and the offensive broadcasts were stilled."[37] Jews are not found in nacionalista administrations, though presumably these accept emoluments as well. Revolutionary regimes tend to be more puritanic, since they come to power on a platform of cleansing corruption. Furthermore, nations in turmoil face problems of such magnitude that there is usually a desire to avoid complications arising from concern for the status of Jewish citizens; in Castro's Cuba as in Allende's Chile, care was taken to protect the regime against charges of anti-Semitism. Sandinistas too reacted quickly to the perception that their actions might have been prejudicial to Nicaraguan Jews.

In considering the political process from the perspective of the organized Jewish communities, it should be remembered that the kehillot originated in the desire to develop a base for working out coherent policies on issues that concern Jews specifically. Representative bodies such as the Argentine DAIA are organized for the purpose of presenting a Jewish point of view to the government on such issues as the free exercise of religion, lay education, and the situation of Jews abroad. As in the United States and many European countries, governments find it useful to have a single channel of communication, and may even request that one be formed; they may also require that the community name a chief rabbi to fill this role, as did General Pinochet in Chile.[38]

Transactions between a kehillah and an authoritarian regime cannot be completely known because of the closed nature of such regimes. With unsanctioned political initiative suppressed, everyone's principal concern is survival, if possible with one's human, cultural, and economic characteristics intact. In the absence of regular political channels, evidence points to a considerable exercise of *shtadlanut,* or recourse to back channels. The strategy dates to the Middle Ages, when Jewish communities, politically immobilized by laws incarcerating them in ghettos, depended on the king to guarantee their safety. Shtadlanut may have been called into play in both Argentina and Chile in the 1970s, enabling Jewish institutions to escape physical invasion by government forces.

Shtadlanut would appear to have no place in postrevolutionary societies such as Castroite Cuba or Sandinista Nicaragua, where the victors are in rebellion against traditional patterns of behavior. As a practical matter, all the wealthy and politically sophisticated individuals who might conceivably fill the role of *shtadlan* (the intermediary) will have left the country by the time their talent is required. Under conditions of democracy, the kehillah loses authority and can no longer speak for its members, who pour out into general society via employment, education, intermarriage, and political engagement.

For individuals, being Jewish confers no advantage to a Latin American politician, which is why ambitious persons drop their relationship to the community. One thinks of Nestor Perl, peronista governor of the Argentine province of Chubut. But identification with Judaism is less of a handicap now than formerly, and increasing numbers of self-identified Jews are accepting the challenge of public service. The need of modernizing elites for educated, technically competent individuals can override residual prejudice; working relationships erode inherited prejudicial attitudes. Modernizers who recognize the need to make use of available talent appoint Jews to office on the basis of their technical qualifications rather than their ancestry, and Jewish emphasis on education positioned thousands to take advantage of the new openness.

Under conditions of liberal democracy, the number of Jews holding public office rises dramatically, demonstrating enhanced acceptability of Jewish candidates among liberals as well as the existence of a reservoir of political talent and desire for public service that previously were locked up within the kehillah or confined to the business world. Jewish appointees appear to outnumber Jews who are elected to public office, though this observation has not been tested by research.

No Jews have been identified as serving right-wing authoritarian regimes. There are no doubt highly conservative Jews, some of whom may sympathize with the goals of such regimes, but the anti-Semitism inherent in the nacionalista orientation precludes their appointment to government office and mandates the expulsion of any who may already occupy a position. In revolutionary times, some Jews join the revolution, others leave the country, and the remainder stay put but adopt a low political profile. This happened in Cuba and Nicaragua, where the majority of community members left the country but individual Jews remained and continued with their lives.

Overall, one may say that individual Jews are motivated politically by the same forces that motivate non-Jews, but conditioned by the presence or absence of anti-Semitism. The kehillot have adapted to the entire range of governments that have exercised power in Latin America, but they have never been able to control the actions of individual Jews, who are free to drop their association with the community. Adaptation takes place through the increased acceptance of Jews in public life, and the emergence of politically sophisticated community leaders who have grown up in the national political system and learned how to work with it. As Latin as they are Jewish, these leaders adapt Jewish institutions to the exigencies imposed on them. So the communities have survived under every conceivable type of government, but they are diminishing in size as different socioeconomic classes, buffeted by left-wing revolution or right-wing repression, find they cannot survive under the prevailing regime and choose reluctantly to emigrate.

Integration

There were at all times in the history of Latin America individuals and classes who were uninterested in scapegoating and more concerned with the modernization of social attitudes. Masonic lodges, with their history of opposition from the church, were receptive to Jews as allies. Positivists in Brazil and Mexico welcomed European Jews as modernizers. Anticlericals deplore the teachings of the church with respect to Jews and sometimes become pronounced philo-Semites, collecting Jewish and converso memorabilia and endowing themselves retroactively with Sephardic ancestors. It has been noted that individual nonconformists and rebels sometimes identify spontaneously with the ultimate nonconformity of Jews. In recent years, important elements within the hierarchy of the Catholic Church, particularly in Peru, Brazil, and Chile, have collaborated with the organized Jewish communities to reduce the level of free-floating anti-Semitism in the spirit of the enlightened encyclicals of John XXIII. Nevertheless, those who are most actively involved with ecumenical initiatives acknowledge that their efforts have not thus far penetrated popular consciousness.[39]

An optimistic view of relations between Jews and non-Jews was projected by a survey sponsored by the American Jewish Committee in 1992. Attitudes toward Jews and other immigrant groups were surveyed in five regions of Argentina (federal capital, Greater Buenos Aires, and Córdoba, Tucumán, and Santa Fe provinces) a decade after the junta's dismissal from power. In order to distinguish between specifically anti-Semitic sentiments and generalized xenophobia aimed at all immigrants, the poll asked respondents to rate five immigrant groups—Italians, Paraguayans, Koreans, Jews, and Arabs. The survey found that 82 percent of respondents considered ethnic origin, nationality, and religion either "not very important" or "not important at all" in dealing with neighbors or colleagues at work. An even higher percentage had no objection to a son or daughter marrying a member of any of the five immigrant groups; only Italians scored higher than Jews. Seventy percent of respondents rejected the idea that the country would be better off without these ethnic groups, and 80 percent upheld the right of Jews, Protestants, Muslims, Evangelicals, and Buddhists to practice their religion freely. Jews were rated by 62 percent as the "most achievement-oriented" group; Italians were seen as the most devoted to family, with Jews running a close second. Ambivalence showed up in response to the question: "Would you say that in Argentina today, (group) or their descendants are part of the Argentine people or belong to a separate people?" On this, respondents split almost evenly. Forty-seven percent felt that Jewish immigrants and their descendants are separate peoples (Koreans appeared even more alien); while 49 percent responded that Jews are a part of the Argentine people.

The highest levels of anti-Semitism were found in the province of Tucumán, where traditional attitudes privileging cultural and religious homogeneity are most persistent. Also, the lower a person's position on the socioeconomic ladder, the less likely was he or she to endorse cultural or religious pluralism.

> While negative feelings toward Jews . . . are a minority phenomenon in Argentine society, they do increase the lower one goes on the socioeconomic ladder, to the point that the lowest groups show a considerable degree of negativity. In general, for every one respondent at the high or middle levels expressing some form of rejection of Jews, four respondents on the lowest level do so.
>
> Hostility toward Jews is also related to educational level: the more educated the individual, the less likely he or she is to manifest negative feelings toward Jews. Thus, while only 2 percent of college-educated

respondents assert that Jews are undesirable as immigrants, among those who have only an incomplete primary education such belief reaches 15 percent. Not surprisingly, the same applies to a pluralistic outlook in general, with college educated-respondents being most open to cultural and religious diversity. It is important to note that the less educated sectors show a greater hostility toward Jews than toward other minority groups.[40]

The generally positive perception of Jews found by this survey is surprising in the light of Argentine history and in view of other surveys that have been conducted periodically since at least 1919 and that have found higher levels of anti-Semitism.[41] It points either to a reversal of historic beliefs (perhaps inspired by acknowledgment of the excesses to which these beliefs have led) or else to flaws in the design of the survey. Only time will tell which interpretation is nearer the truth. "In a violent society where public constraints against defamation are not very well institutionalized, the political culture of Argentina is ill-equipped to neutralize anti-Semitism, despite the enactment of anti-discrimination laws."[42]

During democratic interludes, not only Jewish politicians but Jewish intellectuals and artists become visible in the public sphere. Jews occupy faculty positions at institutions of higher learning in numbers that apparently exceed their proportion in the population, although many intellectuals of Jewish origin no longer consider themselves Jewish. Perhaps the area of greatest achievement by self-identified Jews has been literary. Fictional works by Jewish authors, widely sold throughout Latin America as well as in translation abroad, no longer portray the idealized landscape painted by Alberto Gerchunoff in his centenary homage to Argentina, *Los gauchos judíos*. The next generation of authors such as Mario Szichman, Germán Rozenmacher, Mario Goloboff, and Pedro Orgambide expressed disillusionment at Jewish marginalization and the ingenious ways in which the marginalized attempt to accommodate to their capricious, often malevolent, circumstances. Contemporary Latin American Jewish authors such as Angelina Muñiz, Esther Seligson, Ilan Stavans, and Margo Glantz (Mexico), Victor Perera (Guatemala), Isaac Goldemberg (Peru), Ricardo Feierstein, Manuela Fingueret, Alicia Steimberg, Eliahu Toker, and Marcos Aguinis (Argentina) elaborate on "multiple exiles," "zones of marginality," "cultural mestizaje," and "dual identities," the latter being a more serious affliction than "dual loyalties" because it attacks one's inner self. Samuel Rawet, Clarice Lispector, and Moacyr Scliar, each with a different response to their Jewish heritage, are all respected Brazilian writers. Scliar turned his Jewish protagonist into a centaur to express the ambiguous status of Jew as Brazilian and human being. These artists' breadth of imagination, willingness to experiment with traditional genres, and creativity in inventing new ones have attracted a general readership while also revealing a profound insecurity; disillusionment is the hallmark of their work. And this very hispanic *desengaño* has won them public acceptance. Through fiction, poetry, and literary criticism (one thinks of María Rosa Lida, David Viñas, Daniel Muchnik) Jewish sensibilities and Jewish authors are winning a place in the Latin American literary canon.[43]

Many Jewish immigrants turned to journalism as a profession, and a considerable number founded their own journals of opinion. The total number of periodicals emanating from identifiably Jewish sources that have circulated in Buenos Aires at one time or another probably comes to as many as 250.[44] With the acculturation of the second generation and attrition of the communal press, journalists who are Jewish emerged into the wider, multimedia, Spanish- and Portuguese-language world. Bernardo Verbitsky of *El Mundo,* Antonio Portnoy of *La Gaceta* and others introduced a substantial presence of Jewish journalists into the Argentine press. The most famous of practicing journalists outside the country may be Jacobo Timerman of *La Opinión;* but equally provocative inside Argentina was the non-English-speaking Hernán Schiller, ousted editor of *Nueva Presencia,* who championed human rights during the worst days of the proceso. The current president of Argentine PEN is a Jew, and so is the first Latin American to be elected president of the Federation of International Association of Journalists.

We have already seen that Jews were among the pioneers of Argentine films: Aida Bortnik's *The Official Story* dramatized the infamy of the proceso for non-Argentine audiences. Paloma Efron ("Blackie") and a host of other entertainers achieved fame on the Argentine radio and stage despite their "exotic" origins. Participation by individuals of Jewish origin in the cultural life of Latin American societies, tentative at the start and largely confined to the world of Yiddish, accelerated in the years between the world wars, with the coming of age of a generation for whom Spanish and Portuguese were native languages. Actors occupy several pages in recent books about Jewish Argentina and Mexico.[45] As writers and performers, Jews present in socially acceptable ways the tensions, humors, and aspirations they share with their audiences. They perform on club and concert circuits, compose tangos, and join the society for the preservation of *lunfardo* (the porteño dialect).

Dissemination abroad of works by these writers and artists is partly attributable to the fact of their emigrations and exiles. Exile sensibility is a major element in postmodern literature, and in this respect, Jews had a two-thousand-year head start. Emigration gave Latin American Jewish writers access to publishers and audiences beyond the Spanish-speaking world. One thinks of the Chilean Jewish social critic (*The Empire's Old Clothes*) and dramatist (*Death and the Maiden*), Ariel Dorfman. Chile, Argentina, Uruguay, and Brazil have all suffered serious diminution of their intellectual and artistic capital as large numbers of talented men and women, Jews among them, were exiled or fled repression. Many were attracted to the United States, owing to its freer intellectual atmosphere, economic incentives, and the existence of New York as a major cultural center. Others, especially Sephardim, made new homes in Spain. The Asociación Internacional de Escritores Judíos en Lengua Hispana y Portuguesa (International Association of Jewish Writers in Spanish and Portuguese Languages) is based in Israel and its principal literary journal, *Noaj* (Noah) is published from Jerusalem, replicating in an uncanny way the experience of fifteenth-century Sephardim, many of whose greatest achievements were accomplished beyond the borders of Spain in Egypt or Turkey.

Some performing artists find it necessary to quit their native lands for less dramatic reasons: to acquire the training they need, or in search of an international career. Bolivian Jaime Laredo, the Argentine composer Lalo Schifrin and the pianist and conductor Daniel Barenboim all made their reputations in the United States. Schifrin was born in Buenos Aires to Latino parents with roots in Russia. His father was concertmaster at Buenos Aires' Teatro Colon and his first piano teacher was Enrique Barenboim (father of Daniel). After studying with Olivier Messiaen, Schifrin formed a jazz band that attracted the attention of Dizzy Gillespie, who brought him to the United States in 1958.[46] Daniel Barenboim, born in Buenos Aires in 1942, debuted in the United States in 1957 and went on to an international career. In 1996 he made a nostalgic trip down memory lane with a cassette of tangos titled "Mi Buenos Aires Querido." The title comes from a Carlos Gardel tango, which itself may owe something to a Yiddish song.

The underground survival of Jewish culture during periods of repression was demonstrated in 1983, when, within a month of the resignation of the military regime, Buenos Aires audiences were treated to a production of *The Diary of Anne Frank* and a recital of Mozart songs sung in Yiddish. The arena within which artists and intellectuals of Jewish origin may function—theatres, universities, art galleries, radio and television—has expanded dramatically in recent years, a fact worth noting because their success depends not only on talent but on their acceptability to the public.

The roster of Jewish scientists who have emerged from Latin cultures to play a role in the evolution of scientific knowledge is distinguished and should be the subject of a separate monograph. A not atypical life history is that of César Milstein, son of a Jewish farmer from Villaguay, Entre Ríos, and a Russia-born peddler who founded the first Yiddish school in Bahía Blanca. César graduated in biochemistry from the University of Buenos Aires, where he founded the first cooperative bookstore. His doctoral thesis was awarded a prize by the Argentine Society of Biochemists, and he went on to win a fellowship to study at Cambridge. Returning to Argentina to make his career, he became director of the Department of Molecular Biology at the National Institute of Microbiology. He resigned his position in 1963 because of turmoil in the institutions of higher learning. Thereafter, he returned to Cambridge. He was awarded a Nobel prize in medicine in 1984.[47] He is just one of the hundreds of intellectuals who were lost to Argentina due to the brutalization of politics in that country.

The integration of Jews into Latin American societies is taking place in an amazing variety of ways. Jewish gauchos continue to exert their charm: in 1995, two Buenos Aires plays dealt with that vanished tribe. Countless colombianos wear a six-pointed Star of David on a chain around the neck as a good luck charm. At another level, in 1992, Uruguay issued a postage stamp commemorating five hundred years of a Jewish presence in the Americas; the stamp was designed by Raquel Orsuj, daughter of the founder of a Yiddish-language daily. In a meaningful symbolic act, Peruvian President Alberto Fujimori prepared for Efraín Goldenberg's swearing in as prime minister by removing the crucifix that usually presides over such ceremonies. In a cemetery in Manaus, Christians make pilgrimage to pray at the grave of Rabbi Salon Moyal, who died on the banks of the Amazon in 1910. The saint, it is said, miraculously confers health and fertility on those who pray here and leave a pebble on his tomb. Not all the mythology is unfavorable to Jews.

Reorienting Jewish Life

Events of the 1970s and 1980s demonstrated that the accommodation Jews had made to Latin American life—a secular minority attached to Zionism as a substitute for its ancestral religion—had reached its limit. The close relationship with the State of Israel, originally a source of pride, presented dangers as Zionism came under attack from the right (as a form of dual loyalty) and the left (Israel as an ally of imperialist powers). Originally, the Jewish state had enhanced the security of insecure immigrants. A generation down the road it was clear that Israel was driven by its own needs, not by the difficulties of Latin American diaspora communities. Mutuality of interest between Israel and Latin American Jewry could no longer be taken for granted. Most important, the original goal of Zionism had been achieved. Not only does the State of Israel exist, but it has emerged as a political force beyond the control of its supporters in the diaspora. Attention could now be turned to local problems.

The secular option had also played itself out. Secularism had been sufficient to sustain Jewish life among immigrants who carried their Judaism within them, for whom Zionism, memorializing the Holocaust, and campaigning for the release of Soviet Jews provided adequate spiritual sustenance. But secularism proved itself inadequate to the task of transmitting Judaism to succeeding generations who had never been exposed to the all-embracing Jewish life of the European, Asian, or African kehillot, and to whom the Holocaust seemed as distant as the Expulsion from Spain. Absence of a religious core to Jewish life came to be seen as a principal reason for the accelerating rate of intermarriage, which brought with it the prospect of disappearance of Judaism from the continent entirely. Furthermore, governments that repressed other aspects of Jewish life, such as Zionism or Bundism, had a record of respecting religious observance. Interest in Judaism as a religion increased as commitment to Zionism waned.

As noted earlier, Argentine synagogues, sports clubs, and cultural institutions all gained membership during the repressive military regime of 1976–83 as they were perceived to be safe havens. With the return of democracy, some parents feared that their children would bolt from their protective custody and return to the national political maelstrom, once more exposing themselves to danger. At this juncture, a species of religious revival began, influenced by global as well as regional developments.[48] Religious commitment is evidently increasing throughout the Christian, Muslim, and Jewish worlds. Within Judaism, the phenomenon of the *baal t'shuva* (one who returns to belief) has gained importance. Orthodox rabbis with a mission of outreach to the lost Jews of Latin America took up the challenge in the 1980s. Missionaries of Agudat Israel, as well as Lubavitcher and Satmar Hasidim were sent to principal cities all over Latin America; founding *yeshivot* (religious schools) to attract the sons of the unaffiliated. Rejecting efforts to modernize the ancient religion, Orthodoxy receives considerable financial and moral support from Jews who lack religious formation themselves but are now seeking their spiritual roots. It detracts nothing from their spiritual motivation to note that the choice of Orthodoxy sometimes originates in the desire to inoculate their children against assimilation and keep them out of reach of another round of rebellion and repression.

As described earlier, the Buenos Aires rabbinical seminary has prepared several classes of Spanish- and Portuguese-speaking rabbis capable of presenting Judaism in a modern vernacular. Their Progressive congregations attract parents who may themselves be agnostic but who want to give their children a Jewish identity without entering into the Orthodox world. These congregations have acquired social status, as upwardly mobile families exchange their Yiddish-speaking schools and clubs for modernized religious congregations. By 1988, some fifty Conservative congregations were functioning in Argentina, Chile, Peru, Brazil, Venezuela, Colombia, and Mexico, thirty of these with Seminario-trained rabbis, and embracing about one hundred thousand congregants whose enthusiasm can achieve lyrical heights.[49] Progressive rabbis also engage in dialogue with Catholic and Protestant clergy where such initiatives are possible, advancing into territory Orthodox Jews avoid. The dialogue is probably most advanced in Brazil; in Argentina, engagement with the church was foreclosed by the hierarchy's involvement with the military repression. Interfaith dialogue could begin only in the postdictatorship period of the 1980s, when it was jump-started by officials of the World Jewish Congress, Anti-Defamation League, and American Jewish Committee. Today, dialogue and the publishing of guidelines for activating the 1952 reforms of Vatican II proceed at a dignified pace. But the principal spokesmen for Jewish and Catholic rapprochement reside in the United States.[50]

Possibly the most spectacular instance of a revival of religion among Jews is taking place in Cuba. Under the Revolution, *creyentes*— religious believers of any faith— were not accepted as members of the Communist party, and therefore could not be admitted to a university or a professional career. Even so, five synagogues survived in Havana, although most Jews abandoned the island and few of those remaining were interested in religion.

When the government's religious policy was relaxed by decision of the Fourth Congress of the Cuban Communist party in 1991, synagogues revived along with churches. As Cubans were relieved of the necessity of suppressing their religious beliefs, Jewish life revived. There were still holes in its roof, but the Patronato de la Casa de la Comunidad Hebrea de Cuba resumed functioning as a synagogue and community center. Leadership was assumed by a physician, Dr. José Miller. Lubavitcher rebbes began visiting the country, bringing prayerbooks. Argentine youth groups visited, taught their songs and dances to local teenagers, and started a youth movement at the Patronato that drew from all the ethnic and religious congregations. Rabbi Shmuel Szteinhendler traveled to Havana monthly from Guadalajara, Mexico, in order to teach, perform marriages, and preside over *brit milah* (ritual circumcision), performed in a government hospital. In a community where by 1990 almost everyone married in the preceding thirty years had married a non-Jew, interest was now aroused in the conversion of non-Jewish spouses to Judaism. Rabbi Szteinhendler, a graduate of the Buenos Aires Seminario Rabínico, was religiously prepared to carry out the conversions, and the tiny community of 809 almost doubled in size.[51] In the drab days of the winding down of Communist society in 1994, while teenagers were leading a group in perfectly articulated Hebrew songs upstairs at the Patronato, downstairs a visitor chartered a Havana chapter of Hadassah. That none of the new members had ever before heard of the largest organization of Jewish women in the world was a measure of their isolation. The new chapter's first president was Dr. Susana Bleifisch, an Argentine who earned her medical degree at the University of Buenos Aires and taught otolaryngology there until 1966. That was the year General Onganía assaulted the universities, provoking the brain drain that has afflicted Argentina ever since. When faculty were dragged from their offices and labs and beaten up on the street, Dr. Bleifisch transferred her knowledge and her family to Cuba.

Kehillot mirror the societies in which they operate. A closed regime cannot tolerate a democratic polity in its midst, and kehillot necessarily adopt the reigning political style. With the renewal of democracy throughout Latin America in the 1980s, opportunity was created for democratizing the kehillot. A new generation assumed leadership, reformed electoral procedures, and developed agendas relating to local needs as well as those of the State of Israel. Energetic young researchers turned their analytic sights on their own history, and books on Jewish subjects found publishers. Sponsorship of international conferences opened the windows of the Jewish world to global winds of change. Advertisements for events of Jewish interest were posted in public places for the first time, and Jews who ran for public office incurred less criticism for endangering the community. These changes could not have come about without the growth of tolerance in the body politic.

The alternation of anti-Semitic razzias during democratic periods with the repressions of militarized periods demonstrates the vulnerability of Jews to political and economic pressures. As a largely middle-class population living in polarized societies, Jews are inordinately affected by social dislocation. Those engaged with Jewish life may be somewhat shielded from repressive actions, but they are marginalized by societies that demand their total immersion in the non-Jewish milieu. Those who have abjured Judaism and won acceptance within liberal and progressive sectors find themselves defenseless against repression from the right. The experiences of the 1970s and 1980s ended the dream of integration into a secular society. The destruction of the AMIA, compounded by the impunity allowed the terrorists, brought into question the future of the largest of the Jewish communities of Latin America and underscored the need to rethink the strategy for Jewish survival in Latin America.

The ideal of a secular Latin American Jewish identity foundered on the rock of nacionalismo. In this situation, a turn to religion could be seen as a way of gaining acceptance as a tolerated minority. It was not the path originally chosen by the Ashkenazic immigrants; it is not the liberalizing solution sought by the immigrant generation. But it is close to the path historically followed by Sephardim, whose culture and whose survival skills were developed in a thousand years of living in hispanic societies. During the Columbus quincentenary year the governments of both Spain and Portugal abjured the anti-Semitism that led to persecution and expulsion of the Jews five hundred years ago. If the Latin American republics follow a similar path, religion could become a way to satisfy both the Jewish quest for survival and the proscriptions that these societies lay upon their nonconformists.

NOTES

Complete references will be found in the Bibliography.

Chapter 1

1.   Benzion Netanyahu, in *The Marranos of Spain*, estimated the number of forced conversions in 1391 at two hundred thousand, with an equal number converting voluntarily in the years 1412–15 (pp. 241–43). He maintains this estimate against the challenges of other historians in his recent *The Origins of the Inquisition in Fifteenth Century Spain*, pp. 1095–1102.

2.   Historians traditionally estimated the number of Jews who went into exile at this time at from 150,000 to 400,000. The numbers were challenged by Henry Kamen, who believes that no more than 80,000 Jews lived in all Castile and Aragon at that date, of whom possibly 40,000 to 50,000 actually left Spain in 1492. ("The Mediterranean and the Expulsion of Spanish Jews in 1492.") Some view this minimalization of the numbers exiled from Spain as a threat to Jewish history comparable to contemporary denial of the numbers of Jews killed in the Holocaust of World War II. See, for example, "Subverting Jewish History," *Latin American Jewish Studies* 13:1 (January 1993):7. However, Martin A. Cohen comes close to agreeing with Kamen: "The number of Jews who left the Peninsula in the wake of the Edict may have exceeded 50,000, although it is possible that only a minority left." "The Sephardic Phenomenon: A Reappraisal," in *Sephardim in the Americas: Studies in Culture and History*, edited by Martin A. Cohen and Abraham J. Peck, p. 2

3.   Netanyahu, *Marranos of Spain*, pp. 211–15.

4.   Ibid., p. 4.

5.   Antonio José Saraiva, *A Inquisição Portuguesa* (Lisbon, 1956).

6.   Martin A. Cohen, "Some Misconceptions about the Crypto-Jews in Colonial Mexico," p. 281.

7.   Netanyahu, *Origins of the Inquisition*, p. 982.

8.   Martin A. Cohen, *Usque's Consolation for the Tribulations of Israel*, p. 5. In 1995, citizens of the island of São Tomé began an organized inquiry into their Judaic heritage. *Latin American Jewish Studies* 16:1 (January 1996): 5.

9.   Albert Sicroff, *Les controverses des statuts de "pureté de sang" en Espagne du Xve au XVIIe siècles*, p. 25.

10. Ibid., pp. 296–97.

11. Ronald Sanders, *Lost Tribes and Promised Lands,* p. 16. Sanders's provocative proposal of a converso agenda to the voyages was probed by J. H. Eliot in his review of this book in the *New York Review of Books* for 1 June 1978.

12. Arguments pro and con are summarized in Elkin, "Columbus: Was He or Wasn't He?" and analyzed by Jonathan Sarna in terms of the meaning of this debate for American Jews in his article "Columbus and the Jews."

13. Charles Gibson, *The Spanish Tradition in America,* pp. 55–57.

14. Richard E. Greenleaf, *The Mexican Inquisition of the Sixteenth Century,* pp. 26–40. See also Seymour B. Liebman, "Hernando Alonso," 291–96.

15. Martin A. Cohen, "The Sephardic Phenomenon," pp. 47–48.

16. Henry Charles Lea, *The Inquisition in the Spanish Dependencies,* p. 193.

17. Seymour B. Liebman, *The Inquisition and the Jews in the New World,* pp. 50–54.

18. The literature on the Carvajal family is extensive. For modern renderings and for extensive bibliography, see Martin A. Cohen, *The Martyr,* and Seymour B. Liebman, *The Enlightened.*

19. Günter Friedlander, *Los héroes olvidados,* pp. 24–25.

20. Martin A. Cohen, ed., *The Jewish Experience in Latin America* 1:xlv–xlvi.

21. Judith Laikin Elkin, "Imagining Idolatry: Missionaries, Indians, and Jews," pp. 89–90.

22. Boleslao Lewin, "Esbozo de la historia judía de la Argentina," p. 39.

23. A full-length biography of Maldonado de Silva was written by Günter Böhm under the title *Historia de los judíos en Chile, vol. 1 Período Colonial: El Bachiller Francisco Maldonado de Silva.*

24. Charles R. Boxer, *Salvador de Sá and the Struggle for Brazil and Angola,* 1602–1686, pp. 80–81.

25. Elias Lipiner, *Gaspar da Gama: Um Converso na Frota de Cabral,* passim.

26. Arnold Wiznitzer, *Jews in Colonial Brazil,* p. 32.

27. "Como letrado, conhecedor dos subterfúgios da linguagem, Bento Teixeira utilizou a escrita como forma de protesto." Lucia Helena Costigan, "A experiencia do converso letrado Bento Teixeira," p. 82.

28. Wiznitzer, *Jews in Colonial Brazil,* p. 146.

29. Anita Novinsky, *Cristãos Novos na Bahía,* p. 145.

30. Ibid., pp. 59–60.

31. Novinsky, "A Historical Bias," p. 132.

32. Novinsky, *Cristãos Novos,* p. 201.

33. Martina Cohen, *Jewish Experience,* 1:lviii.

34. Ibid., 1:lviii-lix.

35. George Alexander Kohut wrote about da Silva and other "Jewish Martyrs of the Inquisition in South America" in a now outdated article that was reprinted in Cohen, *Jewish Experience,* 1:1–87. The article includes bibliographies of works by and about the dramatist.

36. Wiznitzer, *Jews in Colonial Brazil,* pp. 43–62.

37. Novinsky, "A Historical Bias," pp. 146–53.

38. Stuart Schwartz, "The Voyage of the Vassals: Royal Power, Noble Obliga-

tions, and Merchant Capital before the Portuguese Restoration of Independence, 1624–1640," p. 751.

39.   Cohen, *Jewish Experience*, 1:xlv.

40.   Wiznitzer, *Jews in Colonial Brazil*, pp. 129–30.

41.   Wiznitzer, "The Exodus from Brazil and the Arrival in New Amsterdam of the Jewish Pilgrim Fathers, 1654," 1:329.

42.   Frances P. Karner, *The Sephardics of Curaçao*, p. 9.

43.   Isaac S. Emmanuel, *Jewish Education in Curaçao*, p. 1.

44.   There are three major groups within the Jewish people: the Sephardim, who are descendants of those expelled from Spain and Portugal and who preserve their ancient homelands in their languages, Portuguese and Ladino (a compound of Hebrew and of fifteenth-century Castilian); Oriental or Arabic-speaking Jews who are often, in the Latin American context, grouped together with the Sephardim; and Ashkenazim, Yiddish-speaking Jews from eastern and central Europe, the basic stock of the Jewish community of the United States and Canada.

45.   Isaac S. Emmanuel and Suzanne A. Emmanuel, *History of the Jews of the Netherlands Antilles*, 1:115.

46.   Karner, *Sephardics of Curaçao*, p. 12.

47.   For Brazil, see Gilberto Freyre, *The Masters and the Slaves;* for Sephardim in New York, see Steven Birmingham, *The Grandees*.

48.   Harry Hoetink, *The Two Variants in Caribbean Race Relations*, p. 115. The term "La Nación" is still used to denote Caribbean Jewry.

49.   Robert Cohen, *Jews in Another Environment: Surinam in the Second Half of the Eighteenth Century*, p. 1.

50.   Emmanuel and Emmanuel, *Netherlands Antilles*, 1:99.

51.   Ibid., 1:831.

52.   Harry Hoetink, *El Pueblo Dominicano, 1850–1900*, pp. 49–50.

53.   Harry Hoetink, "The Dominican Republic in the Nineteenth Century," p. 101.

54.   Robert Cohen, "Early Caribbean Jewry: A Demographic Perspective," p. 123.

55.   Ibid., p. 132.

56.   Yosef Haim Yerushalmi, "Between Amsterdam and New Amsterdam: The Place of Curaçao and the Caribbean in Early Modern Jewish History," p. 178.

57.   Ibid., p. 181.

58.   Mordecai Arbell, *La Nación: The Spanish and Portuguese Jews in the Caribbean* (unpaged).

59.   Luis Kardúner, "La eliminación de las acepciones peyoritivas del diccionario de la lengua española," *Comunidades judías* (1971–72): 256. These definitions were removed from Spanish-language dictionaries only in 1993.

60.   For a book-length exposition of this phenomenon, see Joshua Trachtenberg, *The Devil and the Jews*.

61.   For analysis of a representative sample of sixteenth-century sermons, see Elkin, "Imagining Idolatry," passim.

62.   Emmanuel and Emmanuel, *Netherlands Antilles*, 2:822.

63.   Hoetink, *Variants*, p. 114.

64.   Antonio de León Pinelo, *El paraíso en el nuevo mundo*.

65. This is a game anyone can play. One Jewish savant has published a book purporting to prove Jewish ancestry for most of the anti-Semitic politicians and generals in Argentina.

Chapter 2

1. For an examination of positivism, see the works of Leopoldo Zea.

2. Magnus Mörner, *Race Mixture in the History of Latin America*, pp. 141–42.

3. Karl Solberg, *Immigration and Nationalism*, p. 20.

4. Judith Laikin Elkin, "The Colonial Origins of Contemporary Anti-Semitism," pp. 134–37.

5. Jacob Lestschinsky, "Jewish Migrations, 1840–1956," p. 1538.

6. Arthur Ruppin, "The Jewish Population of the World," p. 349.

7. Leib Hersch, "Jewish Migrations during the Last Hundred Years," p. 407.

8. Mark Wischnitzer, *To Dwell in Safety*, p. 4.

9. Victor A. Mirelman, "Sephardic Immigration to Argentina Prior to the Nazi Period," pp. 13–15.

10. *Registro oficial de la República*, Buenos Aires, 1879, 1:92, Item 189.5.

11. Bernard Ansel, "The Beginnings of the Modern Jewish Community in Argentina, 1852–1891," pp. 9–12.

12. Juan Bautista Alberdi, *Organización política de la confederación argentina*, p. 27.

13. Ansel, "Beginnings," p. 94.

14. Solberg, *Immigration and Nationalism*, pp. 4 and 26.

15. Ibid., p. 8

16. Juan A. Alsina, *La inmigración en el primer siglo de la independencia*, p. 222.

17. Solberg, *Immigration and Nationalism*, p. 29.

18. Gino Germani, "Mass Immigration and Modernization in Argentina," p. 292.

19. Torcuato di Tella and Gino Germani, *Argentina, sociedad de masas*, pp. 26–28.

20. Gino Germani, *Política y sociedad en una época de transición*, p. 183.

21. Ansel, "Beginnings."

22. Ibid., p. 101.

23. Ibid., p. 117ff.

24. Mirelman, "Sephardic Immigration," pp. 17–19.

25. Mirelman, *Jewish Buenos Aires*, pp. 34–37.

26. Bernard Ansel, "European Adventurer in Tierra del Fuego."

27. Solberg, *Immigration and Nationalism*, pp. 35–36.

28. Günter Böhm, "Judíos en Chile durante el siglo XIX," p. 341.

29. Moshe Nes-El, *Historia de la Comunidad Israelita Sefaradí de Chile*, pp. 35–45.

30. After the French Revolution, French Freemasonry followed the example of the Republic in cutting all ties with institutional Christianity. From that time forward, there was no bar to the entry of Jews into lodges. Freemasonry facilitated

the emancipation of European Jews, providing a channel by means of which they could enter society without passing through the fire of the Catholic Church. We have already seen that Sephardim migrating from Curaçao to Santo Domingo utilized Freemasonry to integrate themselves into society, and the same process appears to have been at work in Chile.

31.   J. Lloyd Mecham, *Church and State in Latin America,* pp. 343–44.

32.   Corinne Azen Krause, "The Jews in Mexico," pp. 17 ff.

33.   Ibid., pp. 49–58.

34.   Guadalupe Zárate Miguel, *México y la diáspora judía,* p. 62.

35.   Krause, "Jews in Mexico," pp. 83–92. A reproduction of the front page of the first issue appears on page 43 of Judit Bokser de Liwerant, ed., *Imágenes de un encuentro.*

36.   Linda Dabbah de Lifshitz, "La inmigración de los judíos de Alepo," p. 116.

37.   Krause, "Jews in Mexico," p. 65.

38.   Jeffrey Lesser, "Immigration and Shifting Concepts of National Identity in Brazil during the Vargas Era," p. 23.

39.   Salamão Serebrenick, *Quatro séculos de vida judaica no Brasil,* p. 95.

40.   Morner, *Race Mixture,* p. 140.

41.   Kurt Loewenstamm, *Vultos judaicos no Brasil,* 2:25.

42.   Egon and Frieda Wolff, *D. Pedro II e os Judeus,* passim.

43.   Anita Novinsky, "Os Israelitas em São Paulo," p. 118.

44.   Loewenstamm, *Vultos,* 2:99–100.

45.   Novinsky, "Os Israelitas," p. 118.

46.   Robert J. Nachman, "Positivism, Modernization, and the Middle Class in Brazil," p. 23.

47.   Mecham, *Church and State,* p. 274.

48.   Mecham, p. 160.

49.   Francis Merriman Stanger, "Church and State in Peru during the First Century of Independence," p. 150. In his *Judíos en el Perú durante el siglo XIX,* p. 52, Günter Böhm relates the saga of the 1863 burial of Max Hahn, director of a Lima bank. Ecclesiastical authorities denied permission to bury the dead man. Thereupon, a friend of the deceased, having made a substantial contribution to the church, arranged for the corpse to be baptized. The remains were publicly displayed in the church for twenty-four hours, dressed in the *sambenito* (the penitential garment condemned heretics were forced to wear on their way to the auto-da-fé), following which Mr. Hahn was at last buried.

50.   Böhm, *Judíos en el Perú durante el siglo XIX,* pp. 46–48.

51.   *Breve reseña historiográfica: Cien años de vida judía en el Perú, 1870–1970,* pp. 11–12.

52.   Böhm, *Judíos en el Perú,* p. 60.

53.   Yaacov Hasson, "Iquitos," p. 367.

54.   William J. Griffith, "Attitudes toward Foreign Colonization," p. 78.

55.   Ibid., p. 75.

56.   Jacob Shatzky, *Comunidades judías en Latinoamérica,* p. 133.

57.   Harry Hoetink, *El Pueblo Dominicano, 1850–1900,* p. 53.

58.   Hans Kohn, "The Jew Enters Western Culture," p. 291.

59.   For an anecdotal account of Arab-Jewish migration, see Liz Hamui de Halabe, *Los judíos de Alepo en México.*

60.   Andre N. Chouraqui, *Between East and West,* p. 120.

Chapter 3

1.   Victor A. Mirelman, "Sephardim in Latin America after Independence," pp. 251–55.

2.   Haim Avni, *Argentina and the Jews,* p. 12.

3.   Juan A. Alsina, *La inmigración en el primer siglo de la independencia,* pp. 49–50.

4.   Bernard D. Ansel, "The Beginnings of the Modern Jewish Community in Argentina," p. 237.

5.   Iaacov Rubel, "Argentina, ¿sí o no?," p. 290.

6.   Haim Avni, *Argentina and the Jews,* pp. 47–48.

7.   Ansel, "Beginnings," p. 289 ff.

8.   Ira Rosenswaike, "The Jewish Population of Argentina," p. 197.

9.   The Jewish Colonization Association entered Jewish history as the "IKO," Yiddishe Kolonizatsie Organizatsie, but the English initials are used in the present study.

10.   Jewish Colonization Association, *Report.*

11.   But not all *rusos* were Jews.

12.   Pinie Wald, "Di Yiddishe Arbeter-Bavegung in Argentina," p. 119.

13.   Harry O. Sandberg, "The Jews of Latin America," p. 45.

14.   This phenomenon was paralleled in the United States. One-fourth of all immigrant and skilled industrial workers who came to this country were Jews, who supplied almost half of immigrant craftsmen in tailoring and watchmaking, a third of all printing workers, and more than 40 percent of all immigrant leather workers (Jacob Lestchinsky, "Jewish Migrations, 1840–1956," pp. 1569–70).

15.   Wald, "Arbeter-Bavegung," pp. 118–19.

16.   Edgardo Bilsky, *El movimiento obrero judío en la Argentina,* pp. 60–61.

17.   Victor A. Mirelman, *Jewish Buenos Aires, 1890–1930,* p. 62.

18.   Ricardo Feierstein, *Historia de los judíos argentinos,* pp. 314–15.

19.   Victor A. Mirelman, "The Semana Trágica of 1919 and the Jews of Argentina," p. 62.

20.   Ricardo Rojas, Preface to *La condición del extranjero en América,* by Domingo F. Sarmiento, pp. 11–12.

21.   *Los gauchos judíos* consists of a series of sketches of eastern European Jewish life on the Argentine pampas, as these religious town dwellers come to grips with life in the "desert." Gauchesque elements of eroticism and violence intrude upon them as they grapple with their strange surroundings. A mounted gaucho snatches a Jewish bride out from under the wedding canopy. She goes willingly. Love conquers fear of the unknown. Her elders, who celebrate Argentine holidays and march behind the Argentine flag, cannot make this leap with her, but the implication is that her sisters will. This Argentine variant of *Abie's Irish Rose* consummates the marriage of two cultures through kidnapping and rape, probably

the only way it could have been done under the circumstances. Gerchunoff himself came into the heritage of the pampas through violence: his father was murdered by a gaucho.

22.   Francisco Luis Bernardez, "Gerchunoff, clásico de verdaderos," p. 32.

23.   For insight into the dynamics of the book's popularity, see Edna Aizenberg's essays, "Sephardim and Neo-Sephardim in Latin American Literature" and "Parricide on the Pampa: Deconstructing Gerchunoff and his Jewish Gauchos."

24.   Hymen Alpern and José Martel, *El teatro hispano-americano,* p. 76.

25.   Silvano Santander, "Tres personalidades judeo-argentinas," p. 75.

26.   See the biographical sketch of Rosenwasser by Manuel Mújica Lainez, pp. 65–83.

27.   Robert Alan Goodman, "The Image of the Jew in Argentine Literature as Seen by Argentine Jewish Writers," p. 38.

28.   For these and other originators of Argentine Jewish literature, see Naomi Lindstrom, *Jewish Issues in Argentine Literature from Gerchunoff to Szichman.*

29.   Helmut Waszkis, "Dr. Moritz (Don Mauricio) Hochschild."

30.   Moisés Senderey, *Di Geshikhte fun dem Yiddishn Yishuv in Chile,* p. 71.

31.   Bruce Chatwin tells of meeting the assassin Simon Radowitzky, in his book, *In Patagonia.*

32.   Sandberg, "Jews of Latin America," pp. 62–63.

33.   Moshe Nes-El, *Historia de la comunidad israelita sefaradí de Chile,* pp. 35–36.

34.   The lower estimate by Jacob Shatzky, *Comunidades judías en Latinoamerica,* p. 113; the higher by Sandberg, "Jews in Latin America," p. 89.

35.   The most complete account of this period is to be found in the 1970 doctoral dissertation of Corinne Krause, "The Jews in Mexico," subsequently published in 1987 as *Los judíos in México.*

36.   N. S. Stern, *Baja California. Jewish Refuge and Homeland.*

37.   So speculates Guadalupe Zárate Miguel in her *México y la diáspora judía,* p. 71.

38.   Harriet Sara Lesser, "A History of the Jewish Community of Mexico City, 1912–1970," p. 11.

39.   Corinne Azen Krause, "The Jews in Mexico," p. 98.

40.   Salomão Serebrenick, *Quatro séculos de vida judaica no Brasil, 1500–1900,* p. 99.

41.   Itzhak Z. Raizman, "Yidn in Brazil," p. 147.

42.   Frida Alexandr, *Filipson: Memorias da primeira colonia judaica no Río Grande do sul.*

43.   Testimony of Carlos Hubermann, born in Quatro Irmãos, child of Russian immigrants who arrived in 1913. Instituto Cultural Judaico Marc Chagall, *Histórias de Vida,* p. 81.

44.   Jeff Lesser, *Jewish Colonization in Rio Grande Do Sul, 1904–1925,* p. 12.

45.   Eliahu Lipiner, "A nova imigração judaica no Brasil," p. 115

46.   Sandberg, "Jews of Latin America," p. 56

47.   Mirelman, "Sephardim in Latin America after Independence," p. 246.

48.   S. Leon Trahtemberg, *Los judíos de Lima y las provincias del Peru,* p. 25.

49.   Ibid., pp. 205–6.

50. The life of Jewish peddlers in Peru is painfully re-created in Isaac Goldemberg's *The Fragmented Life of Don Jacobo Lerner.*

51. Comité Judío Americano, *Comunidades judías de Latinoamérica, 1971–72:* 188.

52. J. Lloyd Mecham, *Church and State in Latin America,* p. 339.

53. Eliahu Trotsky, "Yidn in Uruguay," p.1.

54. Sandberg, "Jews of Latin America," pp. 69–70.

55. Alfredo M. Seiferheld, *Los judíos en el Paraguay,* p. 75.

56. *Comunidades judías, 1971–72:* 228.

57. Sandberg, "Jews of Latin America," p. 67

58. Jacob Shatzky, *Yiddishe yishuvim in Lateyn America,* p. 88.

59. Marco Pitchon, *José Martí y la comprensión humana, 1853–1953.*

60. Leizer Ran, "Cuba," p. 423.

61. Robert M. Levine, *Tropical Diaspora: The Jewish Experience in Cuba,* p. 21; and Margalit Bejarano, "Los sefaradíes, pioneros de la inmigración judía a Cuba," pp. 108–9.

62. *Comunidades judías, 1971–72:* 226.

63. Isidoro Aizenberg, "Coro, Venezuela," p. 386.

64. *Comunidades judías, 1971–72:* 228.

65. Haim Avni, *Argentina and the Jews,* p. 197.

66. Sandberg, "Jews of Latin America," p. 37.

67. A sociological study of the shtetl may be found in Mark Zborowsky, *Life is with People.* The novels of Sholom Aleichem portray this world sympathetically; those of Isaac Bashevis Singer undertake its rediabolization.

68. Isaac Goldemberg, *The Fragmented Life of Don Jacobo Lerner,* p. 157.

69. Edna Aizenberg, describing a novel by Sergio Chejfec, in *"Lenta Biografía:* Chejfec's Post-Holocaust, Postcolonial *Had Gadya,"* p. 53.

70. Sandberg, "Jews of Latin America," p. 43.

Chapter 4

1. Haim Avni, *Argentina and the Jews,* pp. 170–72.

2. Leonardo Senkman, "Argentina's Immigration Policy during the Holocaust (1938–1945)," p. 188.

3. Ronald C. Newton, "Indifferent Sanctuary: German-Speaking Refugees and Exiles in Argentina, 1933–1945," pp. 395–420.

4. "The rich irony, however, is that just as a larger proportion of Dutch Jews perished as a result of the Nazi occupation (in contradistinction to those in western European countries that were more unfriendly to Jews than the Netherlands), so most of the European Jews who found a Latin American haven did so in Argentina, notwithstanding the closer alignment with the United States of nearly all other countries south of the Rio Grande." Ignacio Klich, "Jewish Settlement in Argentina," p. 105 (footnote omitted)

5. Jeffrey Lesser, *Welcoming the Undesirables: Brazil and the Jewish Question,* appendix 5.

6. Wischnitzer, *To Dwell in Safety,* p. 293.

7. Carl Solberg, *Immigration and Nationalism,* p. 93.

8. Solberg, pp. 132–33.

9. Senkman, "Argentina's Immigration Policy," p. 156

10. Haim Avni, "Latin America and the Jewish Refugees: Two Encounters, 1935 and 1938," pp. 50–52.

11. Cited in Senkman, "Argentina's Immigration Policy," p. 179.

12. Jeffrey Lesser, *Welcoming the Undesirables*, pp. 179–80.

13. Ibid., p. 3.

14. Lesser, p. 1 and Appendix 5.

15. Ibid., pp. 48–54. Japanese immigrants, who likewise could not be assigned to the "white race," experienced graver social discrimination than did Jews. However, they had a powerful government behind them, as well as native Brazilian landowners who prized them as a labor force. For these reasons, they experienced less discrimination in the application of immigration law.

16. Arthur D. Morse, *While Six Million Died*, p. 275.

17. Robert M. Levine, *Tropical Diaspora*, chapter 4, passim.

18. Ibid., pp. 129–30; footnotes omitted.

19. Haim Avni, "Latin America and the Jewish Refugees," p. 66–68.

20. Wischnitzer, *To Dwell in Safety*, p. 198. HICEM was a Jewish relief organization dedicated to finding new homes for refugees from Nazism. It was formed by cooperation between three existing organizations: the Hebrew Immigrant Aid Society (HIAS), Jewish Colonization Association (JCA), and Emigdirect.

21. José Kierszenbaum, "El caso del Conte Grande: inmigración y antisemitismo en el Uruguay," in Abel M. Bronstein, et al, eds., *Vida y Muerte en comunidad: ensayos sobre judaísmo en el Uruguay*, p. 111.

22. Wischnitzer, *To Dwell*, pp. 198–99.

23. The lower figure from *Medio siglo de vida judía en La Paz*, p. 20, the higher from Leo Spitzer, "Andean Two-Step: The Encounter between Bolivians and Central-European Jewish Refugees."

24. Spitzer, "Andean Two-Step." See also Spitzer, "Invisible Baggage on an Emigration to the Edge of the Holocaust."

25. Jerry W. Knudsen, "The Bolivian Immigration Bill of 1942."

26. *Comunidades judías, 1973–95*:58.

27. As Lesser has shown, not all Catholics were considered to be equal. Guaranteed Brazilian visas for Catholic Assyrians and European Catholic non-Aryans were annulled. "Immigration and Shifting Concepts of National Identity in Brazil during the Vargas Era," pp. 24–25.

28. Salo Baron, "Jewish Emancipation," p. 396.

29. Haim Avni, "Los judíos y Franco en 1949: un desencuentro mistificado," p. 412.

30. Haim Avni, *Argentina and the Jews*, pp. 188–91.

31. Holger M. Meding, "Refugio seguro. La emigración alemana de la posguerra al Rio de la Plata," pp. 254–55.

32. Luca de Tena, *Yo, Juan Perón*, p. 86, cited in Meding, "Refugio," p. 257.

33. Newton, "Indifferent Sanctuary," p. 408.

34. Gurevich and Escudé, *El Genocidio* . . .

35. Haim Avni, *Argentina and the Jews*, p. 185.

36. Avni, *Argentina and the Jews*, p. 188.

37.   U. O. Schmelz and Sergio DellaPergola, *Hademografia shel hayehudim be-argentina ube-artzot aherot shel America halatinit* [The demography of the Jews in Argentina and in other countries of Latin America], p. 5.

38.   Rattner, Henrique. *Tradição, e mudança: A Comunidade Judaica en São Paulo,* pp. 189–90.

39.   Ira Rosenswaike, "The Jewish Population of Argentina," p. 212.

40.   Raphael Patai, *Tents of Jacob,* p. 288.

41.   Suzana Pasternak Taschner and René Decol, *População Judaica no Brasil: Um Estudo Demográfico,* Table 7.

42.   Jacob Beller, *Jews in Latin America,* passim. That these impressions are based in reality is confirmed by such studies as that by Jacobo Schifter Sikora, Lowell Gudmundson, and Mario Solera Castro, *El judío en Costa Rica.* Schifter identifies a community of shoemakers from the town of Zellochow in Poland as the progenitors of the present-day Jewish community of Costa Rica.

43.   Harriet Sara Lesser, "A History of the Jewish Community of Mexico City, 1912–1970," pp. 40–55.

44.   Patai, *Tents,* p. 160.

45.   Gino Germani, "Mass Immigration and Modernization in Argentina," p. 291.

46.   Boris Sapir, *The Jewish Community of Cuba,* p. 22

47.   Sander M. Kaplan, "Jewish Robinson Crusoes," *Havaner Lebn,* 12 October 1934. What does a Jewish editor write on El Día de la Raza? With what element of Cuba's "race" does he identify?

48.   Margalit Bejarano, "The Deproletarization of Cuban Jews." AMILAT 1:65–66.

49.   Y. O. Pinis, *Hatuey.*

50.   D. M. Hermelin, *Clara.*

51.   Eliezer Aronowsky, *Maceo—poema.*

52.   Abraham M. Matterin, *Martí y las discriminaciones raciales.*

53.   Marco Pitchon, *José Martí y la comprensión humana, 1853–1953.*

54.   Sapir, *Jewish Community,* p. 34.

55.   Leizer Ran, *Cuba,* p. 435.

56.   Cited in Levine, *Tropical Diaspora,* p. 236. Levine's video *Hotel Cuba* surveys the Cuban Jewish community in its heyday.

57.   Moisés Asis, "Situación actual y perspectivas para el judaísmo en Cuba." *Ensayos sobre . . .*p. 21.

58.   Abraham J. Dubelman, "Cuba," pp. 481–85. The video *Havana Nagila* presents interesting interviews with Jewish Cubans who stayed with the revolution.

59.   Harry O. Sandberg, "The Jews of Latin America," p. 56; and Eliahu Lipiner, "A nova imigração judaica no Brasil," p. 118.

60.   Rattner, *Tradição e mudança,* p. 98.

61.   *Gerações/Brasil* 1:2 (May 1995):7.

62.   Memo from Cecilia Rozovsky Davidson, 11 October 1937, p. 23, Brazilian file, American Joint Distribution Committee Archives, New York.

63.   Jeffrey Lesser, *Welcoming the Undesirables,* p. 180, appendix 2.

64.   See his introduction to *Tristes Tropiques: A World on the Wane.*

65. Jeff H. Lesser, "Continuity and Change within an Immigrant Community," pp. 48–50.

66. Robert M. Levine, "Brazil's Jews during the Vargas Era and After," pp. 48–54.

67. Kurt Lowenstein, *Brazil under Vargas*, p. 181.

68. Jeff H. Lesser, "Continuity and Change within an Immigrant Community," p. 51.

69. Moacyr Scliar, *Caminhos da Esperança*, p. 104.

70. Ruth Leftel, "Os sefarditas de São Paulo, O renascimento de uma comunidade," p. 55.

71. *Jerusalem Post*, 14 June 1991, p. 18.

72. Leftel, "Os sefarditas," pp. 50–51.

73. Henrique Rattner, "Economic and Social Mobility of Jews in Brazil," p. 199.

74. *Weekend, The Jerusalem Post Magazine*, 31 August 1990, p. 15.

75. Henrique Rattner, "Economic and Social Mobility," pp. 187–88.

76. Here I must register my protest against the commonly used term, "white slavery," or "trata de blancas." While it is true that the women imported into Argentina were mostly "white," the reason for their enslavement was not their color but their sex. "Woman slavery" would be a more appropriate designation. For prostitution in Argentina, see Donna Guy, *Sex and Danger in Buenos Aires*, and Alberto Londres, *The Road to Buenos Ayres*. For Jewish participation in the trade, see Victor A. Mirelman, "The Jewish Community Fights White Slavery," chapter 9 of *Jewish Buenos Aires, 1890–1930*, and Gerardo Brá, "La mutual de los rufianes." Nora Glickman explores the dynamics of master-slave relations in several plays and in her book, *La trata de blancas*. For a fictionalized portrayal of prostitution in Rio de Janeiro, see Esther Largman, *Jovens Polacas*.

77. Eugene Sofer, *From Pale to Pampa*, pp. 125–26.

78. Mirelman, "The Jewish Community Versus Crime: The Case of White Slavery in Buenos Aires," pp. 150–51.

79. Ibid., p. 163.

80. José Luis Imaz, *Los que mandan*, p. 216.

81. John Raymond Hebert, "The Tragic Week of January, 1919, in Buenos Aires," p. 172.

82. Ibid., p. 174.

83. *Encyclopedia Judaica*, "Argentina."

84. Hebert, "Tragic Week," p. 225.

85. Mirelman, *Jewish Buenos Aires*, p. 65.

86. Ibid., p. 73.

87. Natan Lerner, "Anti-Semitism and the Nationalist Ideology in Argentina," pp. 135–38.

88. Sandra McGee Deutsch, "The Argentine Right and the Jews," p. 122.

89. Mirelman, *Jewish Buenos Aires*, p. 74.

90. Ibid., 179.

91. Ibid., 177.

92. The individuals singled out in this and the following paragraphs are no more than representatives of a much larger cohort. Their names, achievements,

and brief biographic notes are to be found in *Judíos y argentinos, judíos argentinos,* Martha Wolff and Myrtha Schalom, eds. and in Ricardo Feierstein, *Historia de los judíos argentinos.*

93. Mirelman, *Jewish Buenos Aires,* pp.182–83.

94. Alicia Steimberg, lecturing at Northwestern University in October 1994. My thanks to Lois Barr for bringing this statement to my attention.

95. Mario Schteingard, *Mis Memorias.*

96. Boris Blank, *La Mujer judía en la ciudad de Córdoba a comienzos del siglo XX,* p.19–20.

97. José A. Itzigsohn, "La atención médica en las colonias agrícolas . . .," p. 17.

Chapter 5

1. James R. Scobie, *Revolution on the Pampas,* p. 31

2. Haim Avni, *Argentina and the Jews,* p. 36.

3. Baron Maurice de Hirsch, "My Views on Philanthropy," p. 416.

4. Kurt Grunwald, *Turkenhirsch,* pp. 76–77.

5. Haim Avni, *Argentina and the Jews,* p. 38.

6. Scobie, *Revolution,* p. 124. For detailed analysis of the role of JCA in the context of total Jewish immigration to Argentina, see Haim Avni, *Argentina and the Jews.*

7. Lázaro Schallman, "Dramática historia de los 'Pampistas' o 'Stambuler,'" p. 154.

8. Ellen Eisenberg, "Argentine and American Jewry: A Case for Contrasting Immigrant Origins," pp. 7–8.

9. Morton D. Winsberg, "Jewish Agricultural Colonization in Entre Ríos," part 1, p. 286.

10. Haim Avni, "Argentine Jewry," part 1, pp. 137–38.

11. Jacob Lestschinsky, "Economic and Social Development of the Jewish People," p. 377.

12. Jewish Colonization Association, *Su obra en la Argentina,* 1891–1941, p. iii.

13. Arieh Tartakower, *Hahityashvut hayehudit bagolah,* p. 167.

14. This was common practice in all the colonies; the colonist did not receive actual title to the land until all payments were completed and all debts with the company were canceled (Scobie, *Revolution,* p. 58).

15. S. Y. Horowitz, "Di cooperativn in di yiddishe kolonies in Argentina," p. 81.

16. Winsberg, "Entre Ríos," part 3, p. 180.

17. Ibid., part 2, p. 423.

18. Tartakower, *Hahityashvut,* p. 167.

19. Haim Avni, *Argentina and the Jews,* p. 117.

20. Ibid., p. 136.

21. Winsberg, "Entre Ríos," part 1, pp. 287–88.

22. This strange symbiosis is depicted in the video *Yidishe Gauchos.*

23. Scobie, *Revolution,* p. 128.

24. Gino Germani, "Mass Immigration and Modernization in Argentina," p. 298.

25. Oscar E. Cornblit, "European Immigrants in Argentine Industry and Politics," pp. 223–24.

26. Winsberg, *Colonía Baron Hirsch,* pp. 54–55.

27. U. O. Schmelz and Sergio DellaPergola, *Hademgrafia shel hayehudim be-argentina ube-artzot aherot shel America halatinit,* p. 132.

28. Ira Rosenswaike, "The Jewish Population of Argentina," p. 204.

29. Schmelz and DellaPergola, *Hademografia,* pp. 132–35.

30. As it was, considerable hostility was directed at JCA schools as centers of alien influence. See Solberg, *Immigration and Nationalism,* pp. 148–49.

31. Mark Wischnitzer, *To Dwell in Safety,* p. 65.

32. Harry Hoetink, *El Pueblo Dominicano, 1850–1900,* p. 75.

33. The motive for this offer has been the subject of speculation. Perhaps it was a move to counter unfavorable publicity generated by Trujillo's slaughter and expulsion of Haitians the year before.

34. Hyman Kisch, "The Jewish Settlement from Central Europe in the Dominican Republic," pp. 1–20.

35. Minifundia are defined as holdings of five hectares or less.

36. Harriet Taub and Harry Kafka, *Sosua.*

37. Jacob Shatzky, *Yiddishe Yishuvim in Lateyn America,* p. 89.

38. Hochschild was a German Jew who came to Bolivia in the 1920s by way of Chile (see Chapter 3). Starting as a broker of tin sales, he went on to become one of the "big three" of Bolivian tin mining, only to be nationalized, along with his competitors, in 1952.

39. Information on the Bolivian settlement was found in unlabelled files of the American Joint Distribution Committee in New York.

40. Círculo Israelita de La Paz, "SOCOBO: Sociedad colonizadora de Bolivia," mimeo.

41. Edelmann, *Government and Politics,* p. 197.

42. Jerry W. Knudsen, "The Bolivian Immigration Bill of 1942," p. 139.

43. Memo by J. B. Lightman and T. Berelejis, "Report on Bolivia," 21 July 1948, JDC Archives, New York.

44. Círculo Israelita, *Medio siglo de vida judía en La Paz,* pp. 20, 312, and private correspondence with David Sheinin.

45. Haim Avni, *Argentina and the Jews,* p. 66.

46. Ibid., p. 89.

Chapter 6

1. This deprecated figure recently achieved scholarly apotheosis through the dedication of an entire issue of *The Americas* to his life and times. "Turco Immigrants in Latin America" was the subject of the journal's issue for July 1996.

2. Simon Guberek, *Yo ví crecer un país,* p. 29.

3. Haim Avni, "Argentine Jewry," part 1, p. 144.

4. *Havaner Lebn,* 26 April 1935.

5. Eliahu Trotzky, "Yidn in Uruguay," p. 5.

6. *Havaner Lebn,* 5 April 1935.

7. Jeff H. Lesser, "From Pedlars to Proprietors: Lebanese, Syrian and Jewish Immigrants in Brazil," p. 400.

8. Moisés Senderey, *Historia de la colectividad israelita de Chile,* p. 217.

9. Harriet Sara Lesser, "A History of the Jewish Community of Mexico City, 1912–1970," p. 23.

10. Tovye Meisel, "Yidn in Meksike," in *Algemeine Entsiclopedia,* p. 409.

11. Memo from Noel Aronovici, 20 August 1940, Bolivia file, Joint Distribution Committee Archives, New York.

12. Boris Sapir, "Jews in Cuba," p. 112.

13. *Havaner Lebn,* 12 October 1934.

14. Ibid., 12 April 1935.

15. Eugene Sofer, "From Pale to Pampa," chapter 4.

16. Pinie Wald, "Di Yiddishe Arbeiter-Bavegung in Argentina," p. 124.

17. Sofer, "From Pale to Pampa," pp. 163–66.

18. Ibid., p. 178.

19. Sandra McGee Deutsch, "Women: The Forgotten Half of Argentine Jewish History," pp. 49ff.

20. For a memoir of tenement life and homage to his immigrant mother, see Argentino S. Liniado, *Recuerdos Imborrables.*

21. Sofer, "From Pale to Pampa," p. 285.

22. Ibid., p. 163

23. Ibid., p. 130.

24. Henrique B. Veltman, "Crónica do judaísmo carioca," p. 54.

25. Alfred Hirschberg, "The Economic Adjustment of Jewish Refugees in São Paulo," pp. 37–38.

26. Boris Sapir, *The Jewish Community of Cuba,* pp. 29–30.

27. Leizer Ran, "Cuba," p. 426.

28. Sapir, *Jewish Community of Cuba,* p. 34.

29. Moisés Senderey, *Chile,* pp. 218–19.

30. Ibid., p. 219.

31. Ibid., p. 224.

32. Harriet Sara Lesser, "Mexico City," pp. 158–59.

33. Celia Zack de Zukerman, "Colectividad y kehila," p. 6:20.

34. Memo by S. Lipschitz, "The Jewish Situation in Mexico," May–June 1931, American Jewish Committee Archives, New York.

35. Haim Avni, "Antisemitism under Democratic and Dictatorial Regimes, pp. 13–14.

36. Jacob Levitz, "The Acculturation of East European Jews in Mexico City, 1920–1946," p. 83.

37. Meisel, "Yidn in Meksike," p. 410.

38. Memo by Max Weiser, "Report of the Anti-Semitic Current in Ecuador," 29 December 1948, American Joint Distribution Committee Archives, New York.

39. Ran, "Cuba," p. 426.

40. Margalit Bejarano, "Deproletarization of Cuban Jewry," pp. 64–65.

41. The diamond industry subsequently migrated to Tel Aviv and New York City.

42. Veltman, "Carioca," p. 58.

43. Simon Kuznets, "Economic Structure and Life of the Jews," pp. 1598–1603.

44. Gino Germani, "Mass Immigration and Modernization in Argentina," pp. 297–98.

45. José Luis de Imaz, *Los que mandan,* p. 143.

46. Carl Solberg, *Immigration and Nationalism,* p. 64.

47. Aaron Lipman, "Social Backgrounds of the Bogotá Entrepreneur," p. 231.

48. Eugene E. Sofer, "From Pale to Pampa," p. 283.

49. José Luis de Imaz, *Los que mandan,* p. 145.

50. U. O. Schmelz and Sergio DellaPergola, *Hademografia shel hayehudim be-Argentina ube-artzot aherot shel America ha latinit,* pp. 106–7.

51. Ibid., p. 111.

52. Ibid., p. 128.

53. Ibid., p. 130.

54. Ibid., pp. 119–20.

55. Maritza Corrales Capestrany, "Comportamiento Económico y espacial," p. 18.

56. Henrique Rattner, *Tradição e mudança,* p. 43.

57. Rattner, "Occupational Structure of Jews in Brazil," pp. 8–9.

58. Moshe Syrquin, "The Economic Structure of the Jews in Argentina and other Latin American Countries," p. 8.

59. Ibid., p. 9 and Table 1.

60. Deutsch, "Women: The Forgotten Half," p. 54.

61. Tuba Teresa Ropp, *Un colono judío en la Argentina.*

62. DellaPergola, "The Demography of Latin American Jewry," *American Jewish Year Book* 85:89–92.

63. Rattner, *Tradição,* p. 180, Table 8.

64. Smith, "Jewish Education in Colombia," p. 29.

65. DellaPergola and Lerner, *La población judía de México,* p. 63 and Table H.

66. Maritza Corrales Capestrany, "Comportamiento Económico y espacial," Table 1.

67. Ibid., pp. 16–18.

68. *Jerusalem Post International Edition,* 2 June 1990.

69. Leon Trahtemberg, *Demografía judía del Peru,* pp. 14 and 26.

70. Jacobo Kovadloff, paper delivered at LASA, Washington, D.C., 28 September 1995.

Chapter 7

1. Günter Böhm, "Judíos en Chile durante el siglo XIX," p. 360.

2. Zvi Beitner, "Origins and Development of the Ashkenazic Jewish Community of Montevideo," p. 8.

3. Alicia Backal, *Generaciones judías en México,* vol. 2, *De un minyan a una comunidad,* p. 149.

4. David Schers, "Argentina," in *American Jewish Year Book* 89:278.

5. Corinne Azen Krause, "The Jews in Mexico," p. 167

6. S. Y. Horowitz, "Di cooperativn in di yiddishe kolonies in Argentina," pp. 79–80.

7. Ibid., pp. 90–95.

8. Morton D. Winsberg, "Jewish Agricultural Colonization in Entre Ríos," part 3, p. 189.

9. Memo by Noel Aronovici, "Interim Report on Bolivia," 20 August 1940, AJDC Archives.

10. In 1898, in the absence of Hebrew type, the publisher of *Viderkol* engraved his four-page newspaper on stone. The paper went just three issues. A descriptive list of early periodicals appears in Lázaro Schallman, "Historia del periodismo judío en la República Argentina," *Comunidades judías* (1970): 149–73.

11. A guide to approximately 300 Latin American Jewish periodicals was compiled by Analya Sater. Elkin and Sater, *Latin American Jewish Studies: An Annotated Guide to the Literature.*

12. Haim Avni, "Argentine Jewry: Its Socio-Political Status and Organizational Patterns," part 3, p. 162.

13. Moisés Senderey, *Historia de la colectividad israelita de Chile,* pp. 58–60.

14. Harriet Sara Lesser, "A History of the Jewish Community of Mexico City, 1912–1970," pp. 40–55.

15. Haim Avni, "Argentine Jewry," p. 158.

16. Irving Louis Horowitz, "The Jewish Community of Buenos Aires," p. 212.

17. Marshall Meyer, "Una década de judaísmo conservador en Latinoamerica," p. 182.

18. Henrique Rattner and Gabriel Bolaffi, "Jewish University Students in Face of Judaism," p. 21.

19. "25 Aniversario del Seminario Rabínico Latinoamericano," *Maj'shavot/Pensamientos* 27:1 (Enero/Marzo 1988)80–81.

20. Moshe Zemer, "The Rabbinic Ban on Conversion in Argentina."

21. *Havaner Lebn,* 12 February 1933.

22. Daniel Levy, "Jewish Education in Latin America," pp. 160–61.

23. Ultimately, no fewer than seventy-eight were established.

24. The report is quoted in full in Horowitz, "Di cooperativn," p. 77 ff.

25. Victor A. Mirelman, *Jewish Buenos Aires, 1890–1930,* pp. 56–58.

26. Iejiel Harari, "Yahadut Argentina," p. 28.

27. Rabbi Shmuel Eliezer Dan, cited in Backal, *Generaciones judías en México,* vol 2, *De un minyan a una comunidad,* p. 43. English translation by the author.

28. Tzila Chelminsky, "La educación judía en México," p. 221.

29. Chelminsky, and Tovye Meisel, "Yidn in Meksike," *Algemeine Entsiclopedia,* pp. 415–19.

30. Adina Cimet de Singer, "A War of Ideas: The Struggle for Ideological Control of Jewish Schools in Mexico City," p. 203.

31. Benny Bachrach, "Hayishuv hayehudi ba-Valparaíso, Chile," pp. 45–47.

32. Rattner, *Tradição,* p. 131

33. For a full-scale examination of the Jewish school system in Argentina, see Efraim Zadoff, *La educación judía en Argentina, 1930–1957.*

34. Simja Sneh, "La red escolar judía en la República Argentina," pp. 136–37.

35. Yaacov Rubel, "The Jewish Educational Network of Buenos Aires . . .," pp. 3–8.

36. Figures from the *First Census of Jewish Schools in the Diaspora,* carried out by the Government of Israel, the Jewish Agency, and the World Zionist Organization. Cited by David Schers, "Argentina," in *American Jewish Year Book,* 89:280.

37. Rattner, *Tradição,* p. 66.

38. David Schers, "Brazil," in *American Jewish Year Book,* 89:288.

39. S. Leon Trahtemberg, *Demografía judía del Perú,* p. 25. Trahtemberg is the principal of Lima's Jewish school, Colegio León Pinelo.

40. John Kenneth Smith, "Jewish Education in Colombia," p. 102.

41. Efraim Zadoff, "La educación judía en pequeñas y medianas comunidades de América Latina," p. 154.

42. Levy, "Jewish Education in Latin America," p. 158. Levy's calculations are based on Harold S. Himmelfarb and Sergio DellaPergola, *Enrollment in Jewish Schools in the Diaspora, Late 1970s* (Jerusalem: Hebrew University, Institute of Contemporary Jewry, 1982).

43. *The Reporter.* Women's American ORT (Fall 1994): 22. Founded in Russia to provide technical training to Jews confined in the Pale of settlement, ORT now translates its acronym as "Organization for Rehabilitation through Training."

44. See, for example, Bernard Ansel, "Discord among Western and Eastern European Jews in Argentina."

45. This remark was made to me by the president of one of the largest kehillot on the continent.

46. Rattner and Bolaffi, "Jewish University Students," pp. 4–5.

47. Nissim Elnecavé, "Sephardic Jews in Argentina," p. 56. For an assessment of neo-sefardismo thirty years later, see Elkin, "Centaur on the Roof."

48. Zárate, *México y la diáspora judía,* p. 102.

49. Schatzky, *Comunidades judías,* pp.143–44

50. DellaPergola and Lerner, *La población judía de México,* Table 1. A survey of Jewish households in metropolitan Santiago de Chile carried out in the same year found that 15 percent of married couples include Ashkenazic and Sepharadic partners, to which must be added the 12 percent of couples in which one or both are themselves the offspring of "mixed" marriages between Ashkenazic and Sephardic parents (*Estudio Sociodemográfico de la Comunidad judía de Chile*). So "traditional" Mexico is following the pattern of "modernized" Chile in this respect.

51. Adina Cimet de Singer, "A War of Ideas: The Struggle for ideological Control of Jewish Schools in Mexico City, 1940–1951," p. 203.

52. Perla Reicher, "Hapoalim hayehudim ba-Uruguay," pp. 105–8.

53. Zvi Gitelman, *Jewish Nationality and Soviet Politics,* pp. 34–35.

54. Dieter Schonebohm, "The Utility of a Life History Approach for Understanding the Interaction between Jewish Immigrants and the Uruguayan Left (1920–1955)," and "Mujeres trabajadoras, mujeres judías, mujeres."

55. Beitner, "Montevideo," p. 12–13.

56. Reicher, "Hapoalim," p. 107.

57. The evolution of the organized community is analyzed against a back-

ground of national events in Victor A. Mirelman, *Jewish Buenos Aires, 1890–1930: In Search of an Identity.*

58.   Teresa Kaplanski de Caryevschi, "The Organized Jewish Community of Buenos Aires—AMIA," pp. 154–55.

59.   AMIA claimed 53,487 members (presumed heads of families) in 1974. Of this number, 38,200 paid dues, 200 were in arrears, and 19,000 had dropped out of sight. See Natan Lerner, *Jewish Organizations in Latin America,* p. 29.

60.   Couples who apply to be married by a rabbi are obliged to become members of AMIA. But a 1974 sample of Jews not affiliated with AMIA showed that 42 percent of them had married under civil law only. Large numbers of Jewish names also showed up in municipal cemetery records but not in the AMIA register. Lerner concludes, "If we bear in mind that one of the main motivations for registration as a Community member is to have a burial place in the Jewish cemetery, then we may draw regrettable conclusions as to the interest shown in the Jewish community" (Natan Lerner, p. 29).

Chapter 8

1.   Sergio DellaPergola, "World Jewish Population, 1994." *American Jewish Year Book* 96:441.

2.   Sergio DellaPergola, "Demographic Trends of Latin American Jewry," p. 88.

3.   *Hademografia shel hayehudim be-argentina ube-artzot aherot shel America halatinit* [The Demography of the Jews in Argentina and in other countries of Latin America], 1974.

4.   Henrique Rattner, *Tradição e mudança.*

5.   Anita Brumer, *Identidade em Mudança: Pesquisa sociológica sobre os judeus do Rio Grande do Sul.*

6.   Sergio DellaPergola, *Población judía de México*

7.   Schmelz and DellaPergola in *American Jewish Year Book* 85:76.

8.   Rattner, *Tradição,* pp. 32–33.

9.   Brumer, *Identidade,* 75–76.

10.   Taschner and Decol, "População judaica no Brasil," p. 7.

11.   DellaPergola and Lerner, *Población judía de México,* p. 56.

12.   Ibid., p. 56 and Table 6.

13.   Schmelz and DellaPergola, *Hademografia,* p. 54.

14.   DellaPergola in *American Jewish Year Book* 85:67 and p. 76, Table 8.2.

15.   Schmelz and DellaPergola, "World Jewish Population, 1994," *American Jewish Year Book* 96:445.

16.   Eduard E. Arriaga, *New Life Tables for Latin American Populations in the Nineteenth and Twentieth Centuries,* pp. 1–4.

17.   Brumer, *Identidade,* p. 64.

18.   Meisel, "Yidn in Meksike," p. 407.

19.   James M. Malloy and Eduardo A. Gamarra, eds., *Latin America and Caribbean Contemporary Record* 7: 1987–1988. See entries for these countries.

20.   This phenomenon is not restricted to the southern Americas. High rates of infant and maternal mortality prevail in United States inner cities.

21.   Rattner, *Tradição,* pp. 23–24.

22.   Brumer, *Identidade,* p. 64.

23.   Eugene F. Sofer, *From Pale to Pampa,* pp. 12–13.

24.   Schmelz and DellaPergola, *Hademografia,* p. 45.

25.   AMIA, *Censo de la comunidad judía de Quilmes,* pp. 34–35.

26.   Rattner, *Tradição,* pp. 24 and 178.

27.   Schatzky, "Guatemala," p. 302.

28.   Schmelz and DellaPergola, *Hademografia,* p. 65.

29.   Comité Judío Americano, *Comunidades judías de Latinoamérica,* 1972–72, p. 193.

30.   DellaPergola, "World Jewish Population, 1994," *American Jewish Year Book* 96:445.

31.   DellaPergola, "Demographic Trends of Latin American Jewry," p. 100.

32.   Schatzky, *Comunidades judías en Latinoamérica,* p. 11.

33.   AMIA, *Primer censo de la población de la provincia de Tucumán,* p. 18.

34.   DellaPergola in *American Jewish Year Book* 85:72.

35.   Taschner and Decol, p. 3.

36.   Brumer, *Identidade,* p. 74.

37.   Schatzky, *Comunidades,* p. 138.

38.   Uriah Z. Engelman, "Sources of Jewish Statistics," p. 1531.

39.   Malloy and Gamarra, *Latin America and the Caribbean,* p. D3.

40.   AMIA, *Censo de la comunidad judía de Quilmes,* p. 69.

41.   Schmelz and DellaPergola, *Hademografia,* p. 102.

42.   Benny Bachrach, "Hayishuv hayehudi ba-Valparaíso, Chile," pp. 44–45.

43.   Rattner, *Tradição,* p. 75.

44.   Brumer, *Identidade,* p. 86.

45.   AMIA, *Quilmes,* p. 68.

46.   Smith, "Jewish Education in Colombia," p. 29.

47.   Rattner, *Tradição,* p. 72.

48.   Brumer, *Identidade,* p. 88.

49.   Leon Trahtemberg, "Comunidad judía de Lima . . ." in Haim Avni and Florinda Goldberg, eds., *Estudios Judaicos en Universidades Latinoamericanos,* p. 41.

50.   AMIA, *Quilmes,* p. 70.

51.   Nora Scott Kinzer, "Women Professionals in Buenos Aires," pp. 163–64.

52.   Bernardo Kliksberg, "Elementos de juicio respecto de la realidad universitaria venezolana," in Avni and Goldberg, *Estudios Judaicos,* p. 69.

53.   Schmelz and DellaPergola, *Hademografia,* pp. 46–47.

54.   Schmelz and DellaPergola, "The Demography of Latin American Jewry," *American Jewish Year Book* 85:79–80.

55.   Ibid., p. 100.

56.   Rosa R. Kráusz, "Some Aspects of Intermarriage in the Jewish Community of São Paulo, Brazil," p. 219.

57.   DellaPergola and Lerner, *Población judía de México,* p. 117.

58.   Ibid., Table 2.

59.   For life stories of the assimilating, see Elkin, "A Gallery of Former Jews."

60.   *Haaliá le-Israel 1986.* Publicación No. 808, Central Office of Statistics,

Jerusalem, 1987, Table 5. Cited in Goldberg and Rozen, *Los latinoamericanos en Israel,* p. 250.

61.   *Statistical Abstract of Israel 1996.*

62.   DellaPergola, "Demographic Trends," pp. 120–21.

Chapter 9

1.   Louis D. Hartz, *The Founding of New Societies,* p. 28.

2.   Denunciations of Jews as idolators and cannibals beyond the saving grace of God animate sermons delivered to Native American congregations in Peru and Mexico in the sixteenth century. See Elkin, "Imagining Idolatry: Missionaries, Indians, and Jews."

3.   Charles S. Bernheimer, *The Russian Jew in the United States*, pp. 256–61.

4.   Stephen D. Isaacs, *Jews and American Politics,* p. 11.

5.   *American Jewish Year Book* 94:117.

6.   Leonardo Senkman, "Los usos políticos del antisemitismo bajo el peronismo, 1974–75," 1:105–6.

7.   Milton M. Gordon, *Assimilation in American Life,* pp. 71–76.

8.   Mörner, *Race Mixture in the History of Latin America,* p. 5.

9.   Elkin, "Centaur on the Roof: Can a Neo-Sephardic Culture Emerge in Latin America?"

Chapter 10

1.   According to Mexican political scientist Judit Liwerant, just 7 percent of the funds raised in annual campaigns remains locally. In the United States, the proportion ranges from 35 to 70 percent for overseas needs (including Israel and all other countries), with 30–65 percent being kept for support of local institutions.

2.   The author was present in the Buenos Aires office of the principal of the Jewish school system when he placed a call to the Israeli embassy urgently requesting the transmission of promised funds.

3.   Florinda Goldberg and Iosef Rozen, *Los LatinoAmericanos en Israel: Antología de una Aliá,* p. 250.

4.   *Statistical Abstract of Israel 1996,* p. 87.

5.   The story of the operation is told in *The House on Garibaldi Street,* by Isser Harel, the man who commanded it.

6.   Jeffrey Lesser, *Welcoming the Undesirables,* p. 119.

7.   Lesser reports Aranha's alleged comment to the effect that creation of the State of Israel meant that Copacabana could be returned to the Brazilians. *Welcoming the Undesirables,* p. 2.

8.   Edy Kaufman, Yoram Shapira, and Joel Barromi, *Israel-Latin American Relations,* p. 213.

9.   Ibid., p. 118–23.

10.   Michael Rubner, "Israel and Latin America: The Politics of Bilateral Economic Aid," pp. 459–60.

11.   Cited by Rubner, p. 278.

12.   Kaufman, Shapira, Barromi, *Israel-Latin American Relations,* p. 105 and note 48.

13.   Yoram Shapira, Edy Kaufman. "Cuba's Israel Policy: The Shift to the Soviet Line." pp. 22–35.

14.   *Latin American Weekly Report,* WR 87–19, 21 May 1987.

15.   Ibid., WR-82–32, 13 August 1982.

16.   "Equidistance and gradualism have been the hallmarks of Argentine foreign policy in the Arab-Israeli conflict. . ." Klich, "The Peronist Challenge," p. 15.

17.   *Latin American Newsletters. Special Report,* "Latin America's Relations with Israel and the Arab World," SR 85–05, November 1985.

18.   The depth reached by anti-Zionist and anti-Semitic rhetoric at this time has been described by Robert M. Levine in "Anatomy of a Brazilian Anti-Semite: Paulo Francis and the Israel-Arab Conflict."

19.   Figures from International Monetary Fund, cited in Klich, "The Peronist Challenge in the May 1989 Presidential Election," p. 14, Table 2.

20.   Widely reported in the press in the early 1980s, Israeli arms sales were subjected to in-depth treatment in Aaron Klieman, *Israel's Global Reach: Arms Sales as Diplomacy* (New York: Pergamon-Bassey, 1985); Bishara Assad Bahbah, *Israel and Latin America: The Military Connection,* Foreword by Stanley Hoffmann (New York: St. Martin's Press, 1986); Milton Jamail and Margo Gutierrez, *It's No Secret: Israel's Military Involvement in Central America* (Belmont, MA, Association of Arab-American University Graduates, 1986); and Damián J. Fernández, ed., *Central America and The Middle East: The Internationalization of the Crises* (Miami: Florida International University Press, 1990), in addition to the Kaufman, Shapira, Barromi volume cited above.

21.   Data from *Latin American Newsletters. Special Report,* SR-85–05, November 1985.

22.   Edy Kaufman, "Israel and the Contras."

23.   This account relies on a report by Joel Barromi, a former official of the Israeli Foreign Affairs Ministry, who reconstructed events from government archives and interviews. "Israel Frente a la Dictadura Militar Argentina," pp. 327–30.

24.   Senkman, "Israel y el rescate de las víctimas . . . ," p. 300.

25.   Barromi, "Argentina: twenty years afterwards. An appraisal of Israeli policies toward Argentina and the Argentinian Jewry during the epoch of the military junta (1976–1983)," p. 10.

26.   Ibid., p. 11, and Senkman, "Israel y el rescate," p. 303–4.

27.   *Latin American Newsletters. Special Report,* SR-85–05, November 1985.

28.   Barromi, "Argentina: twenty years," p. 14

29.   Senkman, "Israel y el rescate," p. 315.

30.   The essence of the Iran-Contra scandal was summarized by Lawrence A. Walsh, the independent counsel appointed to investigate the matter, in the executive summary of his book *Iran-Contra: The Final Report.* "In October and November 1986, two secret U.S. Government operations were publicly exposed, potentially implicating Reagan Administration officials in illegal activities. These operations were the provision of assistance to the military activities of the Nicaraguan Contra rebels during an October 1984 to October 1986 prohibition on such aid, and the sale of U.S. arms to Iran in contravention of stated U.S. policy and

in possible violation of arms-export controls. In late November 1986, Reagan Administration officials announced that some of the proceeds from the sale of U.S. arms to Iran had been diverted to the Contras" (xiii). Investigation revealed that Israel had been one of the channels utilized by Reagan operatives under the control of Col. Oliver North to sell weapons to Iran in exchange for U.S. hostages, and to use profits from the sale to transmit weapons to the Nicaraguan Contras.

31.   The 1975 figure, from *Comunidades judías de latinoamérica, 1973–75;* the 1982 figure, by Sergio DellaPergola, "Population Trends of Latin American Jewry," in Elkin and Merkx, *The Jewish Presence.*

32.   Ignacio Klich, "Latin America, the United States, and the Birth of Israel: The Case of Somoza's Nicaragua," pp. 429–30.

33.   Cited in JoAnn Fagot Aviel, "The Enemy of My Enemy," in Fernández, *Central America,* pp. 17–18.

34.   See reports and editorials in *Christian Science Monitor, New York Times, Latin America Weekly Report,* etc., throughout the year.

35.   These and other insights are developed by Damián J. Fernández in his essay "Central America, the Middle East, and the Spiderweb Theory of Conflict," in Fernández, ed., *Central America and the Middle East.*

36.   Peter Kornbluh and Malcolm Byrne. *The Iran-Contra Scandal: The Declassified History,* pp. 59–60.

37.   Ibid., p. 59.

38.   *New York Times,* 13 January 1985, p. 1, "Nicaragua Rebels Reported to Have New Flow of Arms."

39.   Edy Kaufman, "Israel and the Contras," pp. 14–17.

40.   Edy Kaufman, "The View from Jerusalem," p. 45.

41.   The report of the delegation, sponsored by the now-defunct New Jewish Agenda, was circulated in mimeographed form. It was signed by, inter alia, Rabbi Marshall Meyer, who had established his human rights credentials by opposing the Argentine military junta. The report was debated in the pages of *Moment* 9, no. 9 (October 1984):12–24.

42.   SIPRI, *Armaments, Disarmament and International Security, 1995:* Table 13.1.

Chapter 11

1.   For recent scholarly analysis of anti-Semitism in Latin America, see Haim Avni, "Postwar Latin American Jewry: An Agenda for the Study of the Last Five Decades," in *The Jewish Diaspora in Latin America: New Studies on History and Literature,* edited by David Sheinin and Lois Baer Barr (New York: Garland Publishing, 1996). For analysis of the phenomenon, see especially Haim Avni, "Antisemitism under Democratic and Dictatorial Regimes: The Experience of Latin American Jewry" (Jerusalem: Hebrew University, 1985); Judith Laikin Elkin, "Antisemitism in Argentina: The Jewish Response," in *Living with Antisemitism: Modern Jewish Responses,* edited by Jehuda Reinharz (Hanover, NH: University Press of New England, 1987); and José María Ghio, "La cuestión nacional y la cuestión judía," in *El genocidio ante la historia y la naturaleza humana,* edited by

Beatriz Gurevich and Carlos Escudé (Buenos Aires: Universidad Torcuato DiTella, 1994), p. 235.

2.   Alberto Spektorowski, "La imágen del judío en las corrientes integralistas y populistas del nacionalismo argentino," in AMILAT II, p. 112.

3.   Haim Avni, "Antisemitism in Argentina: The Dimensions of Danger," p. 69.

4.   Ibid., pp. 68–69.

5.   Leonardo Senkman, "El antisemitismo bajodos experiencias democráticas," p. 7.

6.   Ibid., pp. 13–18.

7.   David Rock, *Argentina, 1516–1982,* p. 340.

8.   Senkman, "El antisemitismo bajo," pp. 90–92.

9.   Ibid., 91.

10.   Robert M. Levine, "Anatomy of a Brazilian Anti-Semite."

11.   Figures from Bernardo Kligsberg, "La juventud judía en la Argentina," cited in Robert Weisbrot, "Jews in Argentina Today," p. 396.

12.   Haim Avni, in "Antisemitism in Argentina: The Dimensions of Danger," pp. 62–63, asserts that "The affiliation of Jews with either organization (ERP and Montoneros) required the renunciation of Jewishness." A similar statement by the present author in the first edition of this book aroused a passionate denial from a Jewish former member of the Montoneros who asserted that Jews were accepted on equal terms with non-Jews among leadership, middle echelon, and action cadres alike. My informant also claimed that Jewish radicals were effective within the Uruguayan Tupamaros despite the anti-Israel stance of that group.

13.   Testimony of Laura Bonaparte de Bruschtein, from exile in Mexico. In *Exigimos justicia porque queremos la paz,* pp. 7–8.

14.   Kaufman, "Jewish Victims of Repression in Argentina under Military Rule (1976–1983)," p. 489.

15.   Barromi, "Argentina: twenty years afterwards"; and Senkman, "Israel y el rescate de las víctimas de la represión," pp. 283–93.

16.   Mirelman, "Las organizaciones internacionales judías ante la represión y el anti-Semitismo en Argentina," p. 243.

17.   The Anti-Defamation League of B'nai B'rith, American Jewish Committee, and the World Jewish Congress all tracked these incidents. Reference may be made to their numerous publications for details.

18.   See, inter alia, Jacobo Timerman, *Prisoner without a Name, Cell without a Number;* CONADEP, *Nunca Más: The Report of the Argentine National Commission on the Disappeared;* Carlos Gabetta, *Todos somos subversivos;* Centro de Estudios Legales y Sociales, various publications reproducing testimony of victims.

19.   Kaufman, "Jewish Victims of Repression," p. 491 and appendix.

20.   Edy Kaufman, "Introducción," p. 194, in *Legado.* My translation.

21.   Paúl Warszawski, "Régimen militar, iglesia católica y comunidad judía en la república argentina," pp. 221–23.

22. . *Nunca Más (Never Again): The Report of the Argentine National Commission on the Disappeared,* passim.

23.   Haim Avni, "Argentine Jewry," part 1, p. 152.

24. Jacobo Kovadloff and Susan Rothblatt, "The Argentine Jewish Community under Alfonsín."

25. Leonardo Senkman, "The Restoration of Democracy and the Impunity of Antisemitism in Argentina," p. 42.

26. A moving memorial to the victims will be found in Eliahu Toker, *Sus nombres y sus rostros: Album recordatorio de las víctimas del atentado del 18 de julio de 1994.*

27. By way of example, here is Gen. Juan Velasco Alvarado, on the first anniversary of the military takeover in Peru. "I want to repeat that not one of us has political ambitions. We are not interested in competing in the electoral arena. We have not come to play the game of politics . . . . Some people expected very different things and were confident, as had been the custom, that we came to power for the sole purpose of calling elections and returning to them all their privileges. The people who thought that way were and are mistaken." Cited in Loveman and Davies, *The Politics of Anti-Politics,* p. 211.

28. Mario Sznajder, "Judaísmo chileno y el gobierno," in AMILAT II, p. 143.

29. Despite Chile's international reputation as a democratic society, in the 1950s the country had the second highest infant mortality rate in the hemisphere, exceeded only by Haiti.

30. *American Jewish Year Book* 77:356.

31. Alicia Backal and Gloria Carreño, *Parte de México,* 7:144–46, *Generaciones judías en México.*

32. *American Jewish Year Book* 96:226.

33. *Washington Jewish Week,* 3 November 1994.

34. World Jewish Congress, *Dateline,* 1992.

35. Names and offices were reported in successive issues of World Jewish Congress *Dateline* and OJI (Buenos Aires).

36. A more detailed analysis is to be found in my essay "Is There a 'Jewish Interest' in Latin American Politics?"

37. Robert M. Levine, "Cuba," in *The World Reacts to the Holocaust,* pp. 786–87.

38. Interview, Rabbi Angel Kreiman, at the time chief rabbi of Chile.

39. Interview, Rabbi Henry Sobel, Congregação Israelita Paulista, São Paulo, 1996.

40. Edgardo Catterberg, "Argentina Survey." Nineteen hundred individuals were interviewed face-to-face in their homes between 12 November and 3 December 1992.

41. The three most influential studies are Gino Germani's class-based "Antisemitismo ideológico y antisemitismo tradicional," *Comentario* 39(1962); Enrique Pichon Riviére's comparison of civilian with military opinion, "Los perjuicios raciales en Argentina," in *Nueva Sion* for 31 January 1964; and Joaquín Fischerman's "Etnocentrismo y antisemitismo," *Indice* 1 (December 1967). All were reprinted in Sebreli, *La cuestión judía en la Argentina.*

42. Senkman, *Impunity,* p. 54.

43. See, for example, Lois Baer Barr, *Isaac Unbound: Patriarchal Traditions in the Latin American Jewish Novel;* Ana E. Weinstein and Miryam E. Gover de Nasatsky, eds., *Escritores judeo-argentinos. Bibliografía 1900–1987;* Ilan Stavans,

ed., *Tropical Synagogues: Short Stories by Jewish–Latin American Writers;* Robert DiAntonio and Nora Glickman, eds., *Tradition and Innovation: Reflections on Latin American Jewish Writing;* David William Foster and Naomi Lindstrom, "Jewish Argentine Authors: A Registry." Ricardo Feierstein, ed., *Cien años de narrativa judeoargentina 1889/1989;* Naomi Lindstrom, *Jewish Issues in Argentine Literature. From Gerchunoff to Szichman;* Saúl Sosnowski, *La orilla inminente. Escritores judíos argentinos;* Robert and Roberta Kalechovsky, *Echad: An Anthology of Latin American Jewish Writings.*

44.   Ricardo Feierstein, *Historia de los judíos argentinos,* p. 330.

45.   Biographic sketches of hundreds of Argentine Jewish personalities will be found in Feierstein, *Historia de los judíos argentinos,* and in Martha Wolff and Myrtha Schalom, eds., *Judíos y argentinos, judíos argentinos.* For Mexico, see Judit Bokser de Liwerant, *Imágenes de un encuentro: La presencia judía en México durante la primera mitad del siglo XX.*

46.   Wolff and Schalom, eds., *Judíos & Argentinos,* p. 225.

47.   Ibid., *Judíos & Argentinos,* p. 246.

48.   Research into the practice of Judaism in Latin America is almost non-existent. A rabbinic thesis on "The Emergence of the Progressive Judaism in South America" was submitted to Hebrew Union College by Clifford Kulwin in 1983.

49.   *Maj'shavot/Pensamientos,* 27:1 (Jan-March 1988): 16.

50.   Rabbi Leon Klenicki (Anti-Defamation League) and Eugene J. Fisher (National Conference of Catholic Bishops) have jointly published instructional materials in Spanish for putting into practice the principles of *Nostra Aetate,* the 1982 document in which the Second Vatican Council spelled out the spiritual bonds between the church and the Jewish people.

51.   In 1991 the number of persons registered to receive matzo at Passover was 809.

BIBLIOGRAPHY

Reference Works

Algemeine Entsiclopedia. Vol. 5. New York: Dubnow Fund and Encyclopedia Committee, 1957.

American Jewish Committee. *American Jewish Year Book. (AJYB)*. New York: American Jewish Committee. Vol. [1]–(1899–1900–).

AMIA (Asociación Mutual Israelita Argentina). *Pinkus fun der kehilla in ihr 75stn aniversar*. Buenos Aires, 1969.

———. *Yohrbuch fun yiddishn yishuv in Argentina*. Edited by Nehemia Zucker. Buenos Aires, 1945–46.

———. *Yohrbuch fun der yiddisher kehillah in Buenos Aires, 1953–54*. Edited by Abraham Mittelberg. Buenos Aires, 1953.

———. *Yohrbuch fun der yiddisher kehillah in Buenos Aires, 1954–55*. Edited by Abraham Mittelberg. Buenos Aires, 1954.

Argentiner IWO Schriftn. Buenos Aires. Vol. 1–(1941–).

Arriaga, Edward E. *New Life Tables for Latin American Populations in the Nineteenth and Twentieth Centuries*. Population Monograph Series no. 3. Berkeley: University of California Press, 1968.

Bachi, Roberto. *Population Trends of World Jewry*. Jerusalem: Institute of Contemporary Jewry, Hebrew University, 1976.

Central Yiddish Culture Organization. *The Jewish People: Past and Present*. 3 vols. New York: Marstin Press, 1946–48.

Comité Judío Americano. *Comunidades judías de Latinoamérica*. Buenos Aires: Editorial Candelabro, 1966, 1968, 1970, 1971–72, 1973–75.

Elkin, Judith Laikin, and Ana Lya Sater, compilers. *Latin American Jewish Studies: An Annotated Guide to the Literature*. Westport, CT: Greenwood Press, 1992.

Encyclopedia Judaica. 16 vols. New York: Macmillan Co., and Jerusalem: Keter Publishing House, 1971–72.

Finkelstein, Louis, ed. *The Jews: Their History, Culture, and Religion*, 3d ed. 2 vols. New York: Harper & Bros., 1960.

Foster, David William, and Naomi Lindstrom. "Jewish Argentine Authors: A Registry." Part 1. *Revista Interamericana de Bibliografía* 41,3 (1991):478–503. Part 2. *Revista Interamicana de Bibliografía* 41,4 (1991):655–82.

Hebrew University. *Jews in Latin America*. Bibliography and Exhibition Catalogue. Jerusalem, 1972.

Israel, Government of. *Statistical Abstract of Israel*, Jerusalem 1996.

League of Nations. *Statistical Year Book*. Geneva, various years.

Liebman, Seymour B. *Mexican Jewry: A Guide to Jewish References in Mexico—Colonial Era, 1521–1821*. Philadelphia: University of Pennsylvania Press, 1964.

Marcus, Jacob Rader. *The Colonial American Jews, 1492–1776.* Vol. 3, *Bibliography.* Detroit: Wayne State University Press, 1970.

Malloy, James M., and Eduardo A. Gamarra, eds. *Latin America and Caribbean Contemporary Record.* Vol. 7. New York and London: Holmes & Meier, 1990.

Pan American Union and New York Public Library. *Indice general de publicaciones periódicas latinoamericanas: Humanidades y ciencias sociales.* 8 vols. New York, 1960. *Supplement.* 1961–65.

Sable, Martin H. *Latin American Jewry: A Research Guide.* Cincinnati: Hebrew Union College Press, 1978.

Shatzky, Jacob. *Comunidades judías en Latinoamérica.* Buenos Aires: American Jewish Committee, 1952. Also published as *Yiddishe yishuvim in Lateyn America.* Buenos Aires, 1952.

SIPRI (Stockholm International Peace Research Institute). *Armaments, Disarmament and International Security, 1995.* New York: Humanities Press, 1995.

Taylor, Charles L., and Michael C. Hudson. *World Handbook of Political and Social Indicators.* New Haven: Yale University Press, 1972.

United Nations. *Demographic Year Book.* New York: United Nations, various dates.

Weinstein, Ana E., and Miryam E. Gover de Nasatsky, eds. *Escritores judeo-argentinos: Bibliografía 1900–1987,* 2 vols. Buenos Aires: Editorial Milá, 1994.

Books and Pamphlets

Alberdi, Juan B. *Organización de la confederación Argentina.* New ed. 2 vols. Buenos Aires: P. García y Cia., 1913.

Alexandr, Frida. *Filipson: Memorias da primeira colonia judaica no Rio Grande do Sul.* São Paulo: Editôra Fulgor, 1967.

Alpern, Hymen, and José Martel. *El teatro hispano-americano.* New York: Odyssey Press, 1956.

Alsina, Juan A. *La inmigración en el primer siglo de la independencia.* Buenos Aires, 1910.

AMIA (Asociación Mutual Israelita Argentina), Instituto de Investigaciones Sociales. *Censo de la comunidad judía de Quilmes, 1963.* Buenos Aires, 1968.

———. *Primer censo de la población judía de la provincia de Tucumán: Datos y comentarios.* Buenos Aires, 1963.

AMILAT. *Judaica Latinoamericana: Estudios Histórico-Sociales* I. Edited by Margalit Bejarano, Rosa Perla Raicher, et al. Jerusalem: Magnes Press, 1988.

———. *Judaica Latinoamericana: Estudios Histórico-Sociales* II. Edited by Silvia Schenkolewski-Kroll and Leonardo Senkman. Jerusalem: Magnes Press, 1993.

Arbell, Mordechai. *La Nación: The Spanish and Portuguese Jews in the Caribbean.* Tel Aviv: The Nahum Goldmann Museum of the Jewish Diaspora, 1981.

Aronowsky, Eliezer. *Kubaner Lider.* Havana: Oifgang Presse, 1928.

———. *Maceo–poema.* Havana: Ediciones Bené Brith Maimonides, 1950.

Asamblea Permanente por los derechos Humanos. *Extimimos justicia porque queremos la paz.* Neuquen Capital, n.d.

Asociación Feminina Hebrea de Cuba. *Almanaque conmemorativo de la caja de préstamos.* Havana, Centro 1952.

Avni, Haim. *Antisemitism under Democratic and Dictatorial Regimes.* Jerusalem: Hebrew University, Institute of Contemporary Jewry, 1986.

————. *Argentina and the Jews: A History of Jewish Immigration.* Translated from the Hebrew by Gila Brand. Tuscaloosa: University of Alabama Press, 1991.

————. *Jewish Students and the Argentinian Jewish Community.* Jerusalem: Seminar in the home of the President of Israel, 1971.

————, Asher Dov Glick, Nathaniel Lorch, and Moshe Lazar. *Yahadut america halatinit be'idan shel temurot.* [Latin American Jewry in a changing world.] Symposium. Jerusalem: Hebrew University, Institute of Contemporary Jewry, 1972.

————, and Florinda Goldberg. *Estudios judaicos en universidades latinoamericanas.* Jerusalem: Centro para Estudios Universitarios, 1985.

Backal, Alicia Gojman de, coordinator. *Generaciones judías en México. La Kehilá Ashkenazi (1922–1992).* 7 vols. Mexico: Comunidad Ashkenazí de México, 1993.

Bahbah, Bishara Assad. *Israel and Latin America: The Military Connection.* Foreword by Stanley Hoffmann. New York: St. Martin's Press, 1986.

Barr, Lois Baer. *Isaac Unbound: Patriarchal Traditions in the Latin American Jewish Novel.* Tempe: Arizona State University Press, 1995.

Beller, Jacob. *Jews in Latin America.* New York: Jonathan David Publishers, 1969.

Bernheimer, Charles S. *The Russian Jew in the United States.* Philadelphia: John C. Winston Co., 1905.

Blank, Boris. *La mujer judía en la ciudad de Córdoba a comienzos del siglo XX.* Córdoba: Junta Provincial, 1994.

Blejmar, Bernardo, and Ana E. Weinstein, eds. *Ensayos sobre Judaísmo Latinoamericano.* V Congreso Internacional de Investigadores sobre Judaísmo Latinoamericano (LAJSA). Buenos Aires: Editorial Milá, 1990.

Böhm, Günter. *Historia de los judíos en Chile.* vol. 1. *Período Colonial: El Bachiller Francisco Maldonado de Silva 1592–1639.* Santiago: Editorial Andrés Bello, 1984.

————. *Nuevos antecedentes para una historia de los judíos en Chile colonial.* Santiago: Editorial Universitaria S.A., 1963.

————. *Los sefardíes en los dominios holandeses de América del Sur y del Caribe, 1630–1750.* Frankfurt: Vervuert Verlag, 1992.

Boxer, Charles R. *Salvador de Sá and the Struggle for Brazil and Angola, 1602–1686.* London: Athlone Press, 1952.

Brumer, Anita. *Identidade em Mudança: Pesquisa sociológica sobre os judeus do Rio Grande do Sul.* Pôrto Alegre: Federação Israelita do Rio Grande do Sul, 1994.

Breve reseña historiográfica: Cien años de vida judía en el Perú, 1870–1970. Lima, 1970.

Bronstein, Abel M., et al., eds. *Vida y Muerte en comunidad: ensayos sobre judaísmo en el Uruguay.* Montevideo: Comunidad Israelita del Uruguay, 1990.

Brookings Institution. *Refugee Settlement in the Dominican Republic.* Washington, DC: Brookings Institution, 1942.

Castanien, Donald B. *El Inca Garcilaso de la Vega.* New York: Twayne Publishers, 1969.

Castro, Américo. *The Spaniards: An Introduction to Their History.* Berkeley: University of California Press, 1971.

Centro de Estudios Legales y Sociales. "El secuestro como metodo de detención," "Muertos por la represión," "Un caso judicial revelador," "Conscriptos detenidos-desaparecidos," "Uruguay/Argentina: coordinación represiva," "Adolescentes detenidos-desaparecidos." Buenos Aires, 1982.

Chatwin, Bruce, *In Patagonia*. New York: Penguin Books, 1988.

Chouraqui, Andre N. *Between East and West: A History of the Jews of North Africa*. Philadelphia: Jewish Publication Society, 1968.

CJL. *See* Comité Judío Americano. *Comunidades judías de Latinoamérica*.

Cohen, Martin A. *The Martyr. Luis de Carvajal: The Story of a Secret Jew and the Mexican Inquisition in the Sixteenth Century*. Philadelphia: Jewish Publication Society, 1973.

———. *Usque's Consolation for the Tribulations of Israel*. Translated from the Portuguese by Martin A. Cohen. Philadelphia: Jewish Publication Society, 1965.

———, ed. *The Jewish Experience in Latin America*. 2 vols. Philadelphia: American Jewish Historical Society, 1971.

Cohen, Robert. *Jews in Another Environment: Surinam in the Second Half of the Eighteenth Century*. Leiden: E. J. Brill, 1991.

Comité Judío Americano. *Estudio demográfico-piloto de la comunidad judía de Guadalajara*. Mexico City: 1970.

Comité Representativo de las Entidades Judías. *Estudio Sociodemográfico de la comunidad judía de Chile*. Santiago de Chile, 1995.

Cúneo, Dardo, Julio Mafud, Amalia Sánchez Sívori, and Lázaro Schallman. *Inmigración y nacionalidad*. Biblioteca de Psicología y Sociología. Buenos Aires: Editorial Paidós, n.d.

DellaPergola, Sergio, and Susana Lerner. *La población judía de México: perfil demográfico, social y cultura*. Jerusalem: Instituto Avraham Harman de Judaísmo Contemporáneo, Universidad Hebrea de Jerusalén, 1995.

Deutschman, Paul, et al. *Communication and Social Change in Latin America*. New York: Praeger, 1968.

DiAntonio, Robert, and Nora Glickman, eds. *Tradition and Innovation: Reflections on Latin American Jewish Writing*. Albany: SUNY Press, 1993.

Dickmann, Enrique. *Recuerdos de un militante socialista*. Buenos Aires: Editorial de Vanguardia, 1949.

Di Tella, Torcuato, Gino Germani, Jorge Graciarena, et al. *Argentina, sociedad de masas*. Buenos Aires: Editorial Universitario de Buenos Aires, 1965.

Dominican Republic Settlement Association (DORSA). *Sosua, Haven for Refugees in the Dominican Republic*. Pamphlet no. 4. New York, 24 September 1941.

Dubelman, Abraham J. *Oif Kubaner Erd*. Havana, 1953.

Eisenstadt, Shmuel N. *The Absorption of Immigrants*. London: Routledge & Kegan Paul, 1954.

———. *Modernization: Protest and Change*. Englewood Cliffs, NJ: Prentice-Hall, 1966.

Elbogen, Ismar. *A Century of Jewish Life*. Philadelphia: Jewish Publication Society, 1953.

Elkin, Judith Laikin. *Jews of the Latin American Republics*. Chapel Hill: University of North Carolina Press, 1980.

————, and Gilbert W. Merkx, eds. *The Jewish Presence in Latin America*. Boston: Allen & Unwin, 1987.

Emmanuel, Isaac S. *Jewish Education in Curaçao*. Philadelphia: American Jewish Historical Society, 1955

————. *The Jews of Coro, Venezuela*. Monographs of the AJA, no. 8. Cincinnati: American Jewish Archives, 1973.

————. *Precious Stones of the Jews of Curaçao, 1656–1957*. New York: Bloch Publishing Co., 1957.

————, and Suzanne A. Emmanuel. *History of the Jews of the Netherlands Antilles*. 2 vols. Assen: Royal Van Gorcum, 1970, and Cincinnati: American Jewish Archives, 1970.

Experts Conference on Latin America and the Future of Its Jewish Communities. *Proceedings*. New York, 3–4 June 1972. London: Institute of Jewish Affairs, 1973.

Estudio Sociodemográfico de la Comunidad judía de Chile. Comité Representativo de las Entidades Judías. Santiago de Chile, 1995.

Federação Israelita do Estado de São Paulo. *Guia das Instituições Israelitas do Estado de São Paulo*. São Paulo, 1967.

Feierstein, Ricardo. *Historia de los judíos argentinos*. Buenos Aires: Planeta Espejo de la Argentina, 1993.

————, ed. *Cien años de narrativa judeoargentina 1889/1989*. Buenos Aires: Editorial Milá, 1990.

Feingold, Henry L. *Zion in America*. New York: Hippocrene Books, 1974.

Fernández, Damián J., ed. *Central America and The Middle East: The Internationalization of the Crises*. Miami: Florida International University Press, 1990.

Fillol, Thomas Roberto. *Social Factors in Economic Development: The Argentine Case*. Cambridge: M.I.T. Press, 1961.

Friedlander, Günter. *Los héroes olvidados*. Santiago: Editorial Nascimiento, 1966.

Gabetta, Carlos. *Todos somos subversivos*. Buenos Aires: Editorial Bruguera, 1983.

Garfunkle, Boris. *Narro mi vida*. Buenos Aires, 1963.

Gerchunoff, Alberto. *Jewish Gauchos of the Pampas*. New York: Abelard-Schuman, 1955.

Germani, Gino. *Estructura social de la Argentina: Analisis estadistico*. Buenos Aires: Editorial Raigal, 1955.

————. *Política y sociedad en una época de transición*. Buenos Aires: Editorial Paidós, 1962.

Gibson, Charles. *The Spanish Tradition in America*. Columbia: University of South Carolina Press, 1968.

Ginzberg, Eli. *Kavim le-heker haye hakalkalah shel yehudei hatefutsot*. [Notes for the study of the economic life of the Jews of the diaspora.] Study Circle on Diaspora Jewry in the home of the President of Israel. Jerusalem: Hebrew University, Institute of Contemporary Jewry, 1972.

Glickman, Nora. *La trata de blancas*. Buenos Aires: Editorial Pardes, 1984.

Goldberg, Florinda, and Iosef Rozen, eds. *Los LatinoAmericanos en Israel: Antología de una Aliá*. Buenos Aires: Editorial Contexto, 1988.

Goldemberg, Isaac. *The Fragmented Life of Don Jacobo Lerner*. New York: Persea Books, 1976.

Gonçalves Salvador, José. *Cristãos-Novos, Jesuítas e Inquisição*. São Paulo: Libraria Pioneira Editôra, 1969.

Gordon, Milton M. *Assimilation in American Life*. New York: Oxford University Press, 1964.

Gori, Gaston. *Inmigración y colonización en la Argentina*. Buenos Aires, 1964.

Greenleaf, Richard E. *The Mexican Inquisition of the Sixteenth Century*. Albuquerque: University of New Mexico Press, 1969.

Grunwald, Kurt. *Turkenhirsch: A Study of Baron Maurice de Hirsch*. New York: Transaction Books, 1966.

Guberek, Simon. *Yo ví crecer un país*. Bogotá: self-published, 1974.

Gurevich, Beatriz, and Carlos Escudé, eds. *El genocidio ante la historia y la naturaleza humana*. Buenos Aires: Universidad Torcuato Di Tella, 1994.

Guy, Donna. *Sex and Danger in Buenos Aires*. Lincoln: University of Nebraska Press, 1991.

Hagen, Everett E. *On the Theory of Social Change: How Economic Growth Begins*. Homewood, IL: Dorsey Press, 1962.

Hamui-Halabe, Liz, ed. *Los judíos de Alepo en México*. Mexico: Maguén David, 1989.

Hanke, Lewis, ed. *Do the Americas Have a Common History?* New York: Alfred A. Knopf, 1964.

Haring, Clarence. *Empire in Brazil*. Cambridge: Harvard University Press, 1958.

Hartz, Louis D. *The Founding of New Societies*. New York: Harcourt, Brace and World, 1964.

Havaner Lebn. *Un cuarto siglo de vida habañera, 1932–57*. Edited by Sander M. Kaplan and Alexander J. Dubelman. Havana, 1958.

Hermelin, D. M. *Clara: An Historical Romance*. A novel serialized in *Havaner Lebn* beginning 18 November 1932.

Hertzberg, Arthur. *The French Enlightenment and the Jews*. New York: Columbia University Press, 1968.

Hirschberg, Alice Irene. *Desafio e resposta: A história da Congregação Israelita Paulista*. São Paulo, 1976.

Hoetink, Harry. *El Pueblo Dominicano, 1850–1900: Apuntes para su sociología histórica*. 2d ed. Santiago de los Caballeros: Universidad Católica Madre y Maestra, 1971.

―――. *The Two Variants in Caribbean Race Relations*. London: Oxford: University Press, 1967; New York, 1971.

Imaz, José Luis de. *Los que mandan*. Translated and with an introduction by Carlos A. Astiz. Albany: State University of New York Press, 1970.

Instituto Cultural Judaico Marc Chagall. *Histórias de Vida*. Pôrto Alegre, 1989.

Isaacs, Stephen D. *Jews and American Politics*. New York: Doubleday, 1974.

Jamail, Milton, and Margo Gutierrez. *It's No Secret: Israel's Military Involvement in Central America*. Belmont, Mass.: Association of Arab-American University Graduates, 1986.

Jewish Colonization Association. *Report*. Buenos Aires, 1909.

―――. *Su obra en la Argentina, 1891–1941*. Buenos Aires, 1942.

Jews on the Banks of the Amazon. Photographs by Sergio Zalis. Text by Rahel Arbel. Tel Aviv: Museum of the Diaspora, 1987.

Johnson, John J. *Political Change in Latin America: The Emergence of the Middle Sectors*. Stanford: Stanford University Press, 1958.

Kahl, J. A. *Measurement of Modernism: A Study of Values in Brazil and Mexico*. Austin: University of Texas Press, 1970.

Kahn, Solomon. *Meksikanishe refleksn*. Mexico City: Farlag "Selbsthilf," 1954.

————. *Yidish-Meksikanish*. Mexico City: Farlag "Selbsthilf," 1945.

Kalechovsky, Robert and Roberta. *Echad: An Anthology of Latin American Jewish Writings*. Marblehead, MA: Micah Publications, 1980.

Karner, Frances P. *The Sephardics of Curaçao: A Study of Sociocultural Patterns in Flux*. Assen: Van Gorcum & Co., 1969.

Katz, Jacob. *Jews and Freemasons in Europe, 1723–1939*. Translated from Hebrew by Leonard Oschry. Cambridge: Harvard University Press, 1970.

Kaufman, Edy, Yoram Shapira, and Joel Barromi. *Israel–Latin American Relations*. New Brunswick, NJ: Transaction Books, 1979.

Klieman, Aaron. *Israel's Global Reach: Arms Sales as Diplomacy*. New York: Pergamon-Bassey, 1985.

Kornbluh, Peter, and Malcolm Byrne. *The Iran-Contra Scandal: The Declassified History*. New York: The New Press, 1993.

Krause, Corinne A. *Los judíos en México*. Mexico: Universidad Iberoamericana, 1987.

Kuznets, Simon. *Economic Structure of U.S. Jewry: Recent Trends*. Jerusalem: Hebrew University, Institute of Contemporary Jewry, 1972.

Lapide, Pinchas. *Three Popes and the Jews*. New York: Hawthorn Books, 1967.

Largman, Esther. *Jovens Polacas*. Rio de Janeiro: Editôra Rosa dos Tempos, 1993.

Lea, Henry Charles. *The Inquisition in the Spanish Dependencies*. New York: Macmillan Co., 1908.

Lee, Samuel James. *Moses of the New World*. Cranbury, N.J.: A. S. Barnes, 1970.

Leite Filho, Solidonio. *Os judeus no Brasil*. Rio de Janeiro: J. Leite & Cia., 1923.

Lerner, Ira T. *Mexican Jewry in the Land of the Aztecs*. Mexico City: B. Costa-Amic, 1973.

Lerner, Natan. *Jewish Organizations in Latin America*. Tel Aviv: David Horowitz Institute, Tel Aviv University, 1974.

Lesser, Jeffrey M. *Jewish Colonization in Rio Grande do Sul, 1904–1925*. São Paulo: Estudos CEDHAL 6, 1991.

————. *Welcoming the Undesirables: Brazil and the Jewish Question*, Berkeley: University of California Press, 1995.

Lestschinsky, Jacob. *Di lage fun yidn in lateyn-amerikaner lender*. [The situation of Jews in Latin America.] New York: World Congress for Jewish Affairs, 1948.

Levine, Robert M. *Tropical Diaspora: The Jewish Experience in Cuba*. Gainesville: University Press of Florida, 1993.

Lewin, Boleslao. *El judío en la época colonial: Un aspecto de la historia rioplatense*. Buenos Aires: Colegio Libre de Estudios Superiores, 1939.

————. *Martíres y conquistadores judíos en Latinoamérica*. Also published as *Yidishe deroberer un martiren in lateyn-america*. Buenos Aires: Asociación pro-cultura judía, 1968.

Liebman, Seymour B. *The Enlightened: The Writings of Luis de Carvajal, El*

Mozo. Translated, edited, and with an introduction and epilogue. Coral Gables: University of Miami Press, 1967.

―――. *The Inquisition and the Jews in the New World: Summaries of Procesos, 1500–1810, and Bibliographic Guide.* Coral Gables: University of Miami Press, 1974.

―――. *The Jews in New Spain: Faith, Flame, and the Inquisition.* Coral Gables: University of Miami Press, 1970.

Liniado, Argentino S. *Recuerdos Imborrables.* Prólogo por Marcos Aguinis. Buenos Aires: Editorial Milá, 1994.

Lindstrom, Naomi. *Jewish Issues in Argentine Literature: From Gerchunoff to Szichman.* Columbia: University of Missouri Press, 1989.

Lipiner, Eliahu. *Gaspar da Gama: Um Converso na Frota de Cabral.* Rio de Janeiro: Editora Nova Fronteira, 1986.

―――. "A nova imigração judaica no Brasil." Part 2 of *Breve historia dos judeus no Brasil.* Rio de Janeiro: Ed. Biblos, 1962.

―――. *Os Judaizantes nas Capitanias de Cima.* São Paulo: Editôra Brasiliense, 1969.

Liwerant, Judit Bokser de, ed. *Imágenes de un encuentro: La presencia judía en México durante la primera mitad del siglo XX.* Mexico: UNMA, Tribuna Israelita, Comité Central Israelita de México and Multibanco Mercantil Probursa, 1993.

Loewenstamm, Kurt. *Vultos judaicos no Brasil.* Vol 1, *Tempo colonial, 1500–1822.* Vol. 2, *Imperio, 1822–1899.* Rio de Janeiro: 1949 and 1956.

Loewenstein, Kurt. *Brazil under Vargas.* New York: Macmillan, 1942.

Londres, Alberto. *The Road to Buenos Ayres.* New York: Blue Ribbon Books, 1930.

Loveman, Brian, and Thomas M. Davies, Jr. *The Politics of Anti-Politics: The Military in Latin America.* Lincoln: University of Nebraska Press, 1978.

Luca de Tena, Torcuato, et al., eds. *Yo, Juan D. Perón: Relato autobiográfico.* Barcelona: 1976.

Matterin, Abraham M. *Martí y las discriminaciones raciales.* Havana, 1953.

McClelland, David. *The Achieving Society.* Princeton, NJ: Van Nostrand, 1961.

Mecham, J. Lloyd. *Church and State in Latin America.* Rev. ed. Chapel Hill: University of North Carolina Press, 1966.

Medio siglo de vida judía en La Paz. La Paz: Círculo Israelita, 1987.

Mirelman, Victor A. *Jewish Buenos Aires, 1890–1930: In Search of an Identity.* Detroit: Wayne State University Press, 1990.

Monk, Abraham, and Eduardo I. Rogovsky. *Survey of Attitudinal Trends of the Buenos Aires Jewish Community: Attitudes of Young Jewish Married Couples.* Buenos Aires: American Jewish Committee, 1964.

Mörner, Magnus. *Race Mixture in the History of Latin America.* Boston: Little, Brown, 1967.

―――. ed. *Race and Class in Latin America.* New York: Columbia University Press, 1970.

Morse, Arthur D. *While Six Million Died.* New York: Random House, 1967.

Nes-El, Moshe. *Historia de la Comunidad Israelita Sefaradí de Chile.* Santiago de Chile: Editorial Nascimiento, 1984.

Netanyahu, Benzion. *The Marranos of Spain.* Millwood, NY: Kraus Reprint Co., 1963.

————. *The Origins of the Inquisition in Fifteenth Century Spain.* New York: Random House, 1995.

Nicolaiewsky, Eva. *Israelitas no Rio Grande do Sul.* Pôrto Alegre: Editôra Garatuja, 1975.

Novinsky, Anita. *Cristãos novos na Bahía.* São Paulo: Editôra Perspectiva, 1972.

Nunca más: The Report of the Argentine National Commission on the Disappeared. New York: Farrar, Straus and Giroux, 1986.

Oddone, Juan Antonio. *La formación del Uruguay moderno—La inmigración y el desarrollo económico-social.* Buenos Aires: Editorial Universitaria, 1966.

Omegna, Nelson. *Diabolização dos judeus: martírio e presença dos sefardins no Brasil colonial.* Rio de Janeiro: Distribuidora Record, 1969.

Patai, Raphael. *Tents of Jacob.* Englewood Cliffs, NJ: Prentice-Hall, 1971.

Pinelo, Antonio de Leon. *El paraíso en el nuevo mundo.* Biographic prologue by Raúl Porras Barrenechea. Lima: Imprenta Torres Aguirre, 1943.

Pinis, Y. O. *Hatuey: An Epic Poem.* Havana, 1931.

Pitchon, Marco. *José Martí y la comprensión humana, 1853–1953.* Havana, 1957.

Ramagem, Sônia Bloomfield. *A Fênix de Abraão: Um Estudo sobre cristãos novos retornados ao judaísmo de seus ancestrais.* Brasília: Universidade de Brasília, 1994.

Ran, Leizer, ed. *Continuidad hebrea en tierra Cubana.* Almanaque conmemorativo del 25 aniversario del Centro Israelita de Cuba, 1925–50. Havana: *Havaner Lebn, 1951.*

Rattner, Henrique. Tradição e mudança: A comunidade judaica em São Paulo. São Paulo: Atica, 1970.

————, ed. *Nos caminhos da diaspora.* Sao Paulo: Centro Brasileiro de Estudos Judaicos, 1972.

Reicher, Perla. "Hapoalim hayehudim ba-Uruguay." [Jewish workers in Uruguay.] Tel Aviv University, Institute for Zionist Research, 1971.

Rock, David. *Argentina, 1516–1982.* Berkeley: University of California Press, 1985.

Rojas, Ricardo. *La restauración nacionalista.* Buenos Aires: Ministerio de Justicia e Instrucción Pública, 1909.

Ropp, Tuba Teresa. *Un cólono judío en la Argentina.* Buenos Aires: IWO, 1971.

Sanders, Ronald. *Lost Tribes and Promised Lands: The Origins of American Racism.* Boston: Little, Brown, 1978.

Sapir, Boris. *The Jewish Community of Cuba.* Translated by Simon Wolin. New York: Jewish Teachers' Seminary Press, 1948.

Sapolnik, Jaime. *A contribução judaica a independencia do Brasil.* Bahia: Sec. Ed. e Cultura, Estado de Bahia, 1973.

Saraiva, Antonio José. *A inquisição portuguesa.* Lisbon, 1956.

Sarmiento, Domingo F. *La condición extranjero en América.* Preface by Ricardo Rojas. Buenos Aires: Librería "La Facultad," 1928.

Schallman, Lázaro. *Historia de los "pampistas."* Biblioteca Popular Judía. Buenos Aires: Congreso Judío Latinoamericano, 1971.

————. *Los pioneros de la colonización judía en la Argentina.* Buenos Aires: Congreso Judío Latinoamericano, 1969.

Schifter Sikora, Jacobo, Lowell Gudmundson, and Mario Solera Castro. *El judío en Costa Rica.* San José: Editorial Universidad Estatal a Distancia, 1979.

Schmelz, U. O., and Sergio DellaPergola. *Hademografia shel hayehudim be-Argentina ube-artzot aherot shel America halatinit.* [The demography of the Jews in Argentina and in other countries of Latin America.] Tel Aviv: Tel Aviv University, 1974.

Schteingard, Mario. *Mis memorias.* Buenos Aires: self-published, 1956.

Scliar, Moacyr. *Caminhos da Esperança: A Presença Judaica no Rio Grande do Sul.* Pôrto Alegre: Riocell, n.d. (1995?).

Scobie, James R. *Revolution on the Pampas.* Austin: University of Texas Press, 1964.

Sebreli, Juan José, ed. *La cuestión judía en la Argentina.* Buenos Aires: Editorial Tiempo Contemporáneo, 1968.

Seiferheld, Alfredo M. *Los judíos en el Paraguay.* Asunción: Universidad Católica Nuestra Señora de la Asunción, 1981.

Senderey, Moisés. *Historia de la colectividad israelita de Chile.* Santiago: Editorial "Dos Yidische Wort," 1956. Also published as *Di Geshikhte fun dem Yiddishn Yishuv in Chile.* Santiago, 1956.

Senkman, Leonardo, and Mario Sznajder, eds. *El Legado de autoritarismo: Derechos humanos y antisemitismo en la Argentina contemporánea.* Jerusalem: Hebrew University, Harry S. Truman Institute; and Buenos Aires: Nuevohacer, 1995.

Serebrenick, Salomão. *Quatro séculos da vida judaica no Brasil, 1500–1900.* Part 1 of *Breve historia dos judeus no Brasil.* Rio de Janeiro: Edições Biblos, Ltda., 1962.

Sheinin, David, and Lois Baer Barr, eds. *The Jewish Diaspora in Latin America.* New York: Garland Publishing, 1996.

Sicroff, Albert. *Les controverses des statuts de "pureté de sang" en Espagne du XVe au XVIIe siècles.* Paris: Didier, 1960.

Sklare, Marshall. *The Jew in American Society.* New York: Behrman House, 1974.

Solberg, Carl. *Immigration and Nationalism: Argentina and Chile, 1890–1914.* Austin: University of Texas Press, 1970.

Sosnowski, Saúl. *La orilla inminente: Escritores judíos argentinos.* Buenos Aires: Editorial Legasa, 1987.

Sourasky, Leon. *História de la comunidad israelita de México (1917–1942).* Mexico City: self-published, 1965.

Stavans, Ilan, ed. *Tropical Synagogues: Short Stories by Jewish–Latin American Writers.* New York: Holmes & Meier, 1994.

Stern, Norton B. *Baja California: Jewish Refuge and Homeland.* Los Angeles: Dawson's Book Shop, 1973.

Tartakower, Arieh. *Hahityashvut hayehudit bagolah.* [Jewish colonization in the Diaspora.] 2 vols. Tel Aviv: M. Neuman, 1969.

Timerman, Jacobo. *Prisoner without a name, Cell without a number.* New York: Alfred A. Knopf, 1981.

Toker, Eliahu, ed. *Sus nombres y sus rostros: Album recordatorio de las víctimas del atentado del 18 de julio de 1994.* Buenos Aires: AMIA, 1995.

Trachtenberg, Joshua. *The Devil and the Jews.* New Haven: Yale University Press, 1943.

Trahtemberg, S. Leon. *Demografia judía del Perú.* Lima: Union Mundial ORT, 1988.

———. *Los judíos de Lima y las provincias del Perú.* Lima: Union Israelita del Perú, 1989.

Varon, Benjamin. *Si yo fuera paraguayo.* Asunción: self-published, 1972.

Vieira, Nelson. *Jewish Voices in Brazilian Literature: A Prophetic Discourse of Alterity.* Gainesville: University Press of Florida, 1995.

Walsh, Lawrence A. *Iran-Contra: The Final Report.* New York: Random House, 1993.

Weill, Simon. *Población israelita en la república Argentina.* Buenos Aires, 1936.

Willems, Emilio. *Latin American Culture: An Anthropological Synthesis.* New York: Harper and Row, 1975.

Williams, Eric E. *From Columbus to Castro: The History of the Caribbean, 1492–1969.* New York: Harper and Row, 1971.

Winsberg, Morton D. *Colonía Baron Hirsch: A Jewish Agricultural Colony in Argentina.* University of Florida Monographs, Social Sciences no. 19. Gainesville: University of Florida Press, 1964.

Wischnitzer, Mark. *To Dwell in Safety.* Philadelphia: Jewish Publication Society, 1948.

Wiznitzer, Arnold. *Jews in Colonial Brazil.* New York: Columbia University Press, 1960.

———. *Records of the Earliest Jewish Community in the New World.* Philadelphia: American Jewish Historical Society, 1954.

Wolff, Egon and Frieda. *D. Pedro II e os Judeus.* Rio de Janeiro: Editora B'nai B'rith, 1983

Wolff, Martha, and Myrtha Schalom, eds. *Judíos y argentinos, judíos argentinos.* Buenos Aires: Manrique Zago Ediciones, 1988.

World Jewish Conference. *Judíos en el Uruguay.* Montevideo, 1968.

Yerushalmi, Yosef Hayim. *From Spanish Court to Italian Ghetto. Isaac Cardoso: A Study in 17th Century Marranism and Jewish Apologetics.* New York: Columbia University Press, 1971.

Yidishe Zaitung, Di. Yovl Bukh. Sakh ha-koln fun 50 yohr yidish lebn in Argentina. [Jubilee Book: Account of 50 Years of Jewish Life in Argentina.] Edited by Hirsch Trivacks. Buenos Aires, 1940.

Zadoff, Efraim. *Historia de la educación judía en Buenos Aires (1935–1957).* Buenos Aires: Editorial Milá, 1994.

Zárate Miguel, Guadalupe. *México y la diáspora judía.* Mexico: Instituto Nacional de Antropología, 1986.

Zborowsky, Mark. *Life Is with People: The Culture of the Shtetl.* New York: Schocken Books, 1962.

Zea, Leopoldo. *The Latin American Mind.* Norman: University of Oklahoma Press, 1963.

———. *Positivism in Mexico.* Austin: University of Texas Press, 1974.

Articles and Chapters in Books

Aizenberg, Edna. "*Lenta Biografía:* Chejfec's Post-Holocaust, Postcolonial *Had Gadya.*" In *The Jewish Diaspora in Latin America,* edited by David Sheinin and Lois Baer Barr, pp. 53–60. New York: Garland Publishing, 1996.

———. "Parricide on the Pampa: Deconstructing Gerchunoff and his Jewish Gauchos." *Folio* 17 (September 1987):24–39.

————. "Sephardim and Neo-Sephardim in Latin American Literature." *The Sephardic Scholar.* Series 4 (1979–82):125–32.

Aizenberg, Isidoro. "Coro, Venezuela: Primera corriente de inmigración al país." In *Comunidades judías (1971–72):379–87.*

Angel, Marc D. "The Sephardim of the United States: An Exploratory Study." *American Jewish Year Book* 74 (1973):77–138.

Ansel, Bernard D. "Discord among Western and Eastern European Jews in Argentina." *American Jewish Historical Quarterly* 60 (December 1970):151–58.

————. "European Adventurer in Tierra del Fuego: Julio Popper." *Hispanic American Historical Review* 50 (February 1970):89–110.

Asamblea Permanente por los Derechos Humanos. "Exigimos justicia porque queremos la paz." Neuquen Capital, Argentina, n.d.

Asis, Moíses. "Situación actual y perspectivas para el judaísmo en Cuba." *Ensayos sobre judaísmo latinoamericano,* edited by Bernardo Blejmao and Ana E. Weinstein, pp. 15–25. Buenos Aires: Editorial Milá, 1990.

Austri-Dan, Isaiah. "The Jewish Community of Mexico." *Dispersion and Unity* 2 (1963): 51–73.

Avni, Haim. "Antisemitism in Argentina: The Dimensions of Danger." In *Approaches to Antisemitism: Context and Curriculum,* edited by Michael Brown, pp. 57–77. New York: American Jewish Committee, 1994.

————. "Argentine Jewry: Its Socio-Political Status and Organizational Patterns." *Dispersion and Unity* 12 (1971):128–62; 13/14 (1971–72):161–208; 15 (1972–73):158–215.

————. "Jewish Communities in Latin America." In *World Politics and the Jewish Condition,* edited by Louis Henkin, pp. 256–74. New York: Quadrangle Books, 1972.

————. "Latin America and the Jewish Refugees: Two Encounters, 1935 and 1938." In *The Jewish Presence in Latin America,* edited by Judith Laikin Elkin and Gilbert W. Merkx (Boston: Allen & Unwin, 1987), pp. 45–68.

————. "Los judíos y Franco en 1949: Un desencuentro mistificado." *Encuentros en Sefarad.* Instituto de Estudios Manchegos, 1987.

————. "Postwar Latin American Jewry: An Agenda for the Study of the Last Five Decades," in *The Jewish Diaspora in Latin America,* edited by David Sheinin and Lois Baer Barr, pp. 3–19. New York: Garland Publishing, 1996.

Bachrach, Benny. "Hayishuv hayehudi ba-Valparaíso, Chile." [The Jewish community of Valparaíso, Chile.] *Dispersion and Unity* 2 (June 1960):40–47.

Backal, Alicia Gojman de, "Minorías, estado y movimientos nacionalistas de la clase media en México. Liga Antichina y Antijudía (siglo XX)." In AMILAT I, *Judaica Latinoamericana,* pp. 174–91. Jerusalem: Magnes University Press, 1988.

Baron, Salo. "Jewish Emancipation." *Encyclopedia of the Social Sciences.* New York: Macmillan Co., 1937.

————. "Who Is a Jew?" In *History and Jewish Historians. Essays and Addresses by Salo Wittmayer Baron.* Compiled with a foreword by Arthur Hertzberg and Leon A. Feldman, pp. 5–22. Philadelphia: Jewish Publication Society of America, 1964.

Barromi, Joel. "Israel frente a la dictadura militar argentina: El episodio de Córdoba y el caso Timerman." In *El Legado del autoritarismo,* edited by Leonardo Senkman and Mario Sznajder, pp. 325–51. Jerusalem: Hebrew University, 1995.

Becker, Larry M. "The Jewish Community of Cuba." *Congress Bulletin* (U.S.), May–June 1971.

Bejarano, Margalit. "The Deproletarization of Cuban Jews." AMILAT I, *Judaica Latinoamericana: Estudios Histórico-Sociales,* pp. 57–67. Jerusalem: Magnes Press, 1988.

———. "Los sefaradíes, pioneros de la inmigración judía a Cuba." *Rumbos* 14 (1985):107–22.

Benítez, Fernando. "Domingo de Ramos." *Siempre* (Mexico, D.F.) 414(14 January 1970):2–16. Reprinted as CIDOC 70/201, Cuernavaca.

Bernardez, Francisco Luis. "Gerchunoff, clásico de los verdaderos." *Comentario* (Buenos Aires) 63 (November–December 1968):32–33.

Bilsky, Edgardo. "El movimiento obrero judío en la Argentina." In *Bibliografía temática sobre judaísmo argentino.* Vol. 1, no. 4. Buenos Aires: Centro de Documentación e Información sobre Judaísmo Argentino Marc Turkow, 1987.

Blecher, J. "Hastatistika shel hayehudim be-Argentina." [Statistics of Argentine Jewry.] In *Am yisroel b'doreynu,* edited by Shaul Esh, pp. 34–40. Jerusalem: Hebrew University, 1964.

Böhm, Günther. "Judíos en Chile durante el siglo XIX." In CJL (1971–72):340–66.

Brá, Gerardo. "La mutual de los rufianes." *Todo es Historia* (Buenos Aires) (June 1977):75–92.

Bustamente, Norberto R., et al. "Discriminación y marginalidad social en latino-américa." *Comentario* 72 (May–June 1970):3–23.

Chacon, Vamireh. "Consciéncia nacional e judaísmo no Brasil." *Revista do Instituto de Estudos Brasileiros* (São Paulo), no. 10 (1971), pp. 7–26.

Chelminsky, Tzila. "La educación judía en México." In Comité Judío Americano. *Comunidades judías de Latinoamérica.* Buenos Aires:Editorial Candelabro CJL (1970):221–29.

Cimet de Singer, Adina. "A War of Ideas: The Struggle for Ideological Control of Jewish Schools in Mexico City, 1940–1951." *YIVO Annual* 22 (1995):203–28.

Cohen, Martin A. "Antonio Díaz de Cáceres: Marrano Adventurer in Colonial Mexico." *American Jewish Historical Quarterly* 60 (December 1970):169–84.

———. "Some Misconceptions about the Crypto-Jews in Colonial Mexico." *American Jewish Historical Quarterly* 61 (December 1972):278–93.

———. "The Sephardic Phenomenon: A Reappraisal." In *Sephardim in the Americas: Studies in Culture and History,* edited by Martin A. Cohen and Abraham J. Peck, pp. 1–79. Cincinnati: American Jewish Archives and Tuscaloosa: University of Alabama Press, 1993.

Cohen, Robert. "Early Caribbean Jewry: A Demographic Perspective." *Jewish Social Studies* 45:2 (Spring 1983):123–34.

Cornblit, Oscar E. "European Immigrants in Argentine Industry and Politics." In *The Politics of Conformity in Latin America,* edited by Claudio Veliz, pp. 221–48. London: Oxford University Press, 1967.

Costigan, Lucia Helena. "A experiencia do converso letrado Bento Teixeira: Um *Missing Link* na história intelectual e literária do Brasil-Colônia." *Revista de*

Critica Literaria Latinoamericana 20:40 Lima-Berkeley (250 semestre de 1994):77–92.

Cukierkorn, Jacques. "Discovering Brazilian Marranos." *Latin American Jewish Studies* 15:1 (January 1995):4.

Dajes, Marta de. "Los estudiantes judíos universitarios de Bogotá." CJL (1971–72): 307–22.

DellaPergola, Sergio. "Demographic Trends of Latin American Jewry." In *The Jewish Presence in Latin America,* edited by Judith Laikin Elkin and Gilbert W. Merkx, pp. 85–133. Boston: Allen & Unwin, 1987.

Deutsch, Sandra McGee. "The Argentine Right and the Jews." *Journal of Latin American Studies* 18:1 (May 1986):113–34.

——. "Women: The Forgotten Half of Argentine Jewish History." *Shofar* (Spring 1997):49–65.

Dijour, Ilya M. "Jewish Migration in the Post-war Period." *Jewish Journal of Sociology* 4 (June 1962):72–81.

Dubelman, Abraham J. "Cuba." *American Jewish Year Book* 63 (1962):481–85.

Eisenberg, Ellen. "Argentine and American Jewry: A Case for Contrasting Immigrant Origins." *American Jewish Archives* 47:1 (Spring–Summer 1995):1–16.

Judith Laikin Elkin, "Antisemitism in Argentina: The Jewish Response," in *Living with Antisemitism: Modern Jewish Responses,* edited by Jehuda Reinharz (Hanover, N.H.: University Press of New England, 1987), pp. 333–48.

——. "Centaur on the Roof: Can a Neo-Sephardic Culture Emerge in Latin America?" *Shofar* 13:2 (Winter 1995):1–15.

——. "The Colonial Legacy of Anti-Semitism." *NACLA Report on the Americas* 25:4 (February 1992):4–7.

——. "The Colonial Origins of Contemporary Anti-Semitism." In *The Jewish Diaspora in Latin America,* edited by David Sheinin and Lois Baer Barr, pp. 127–41. New York: Garland Publishing, 1996.

——. "Columbus: Was He or Wasn't He?" *Hadassah Magazine* 73:5 (January 1992):49–50.

——. "A Gallery of Former Jews." *Commentary* 92:6 (1992).

——. "Imagining Idolatry: Missionaries, Indians, and Jews." In *Religion and the Authority of the Past,* edited by Tobin Siebers, pp. 75–97. Ann Arbor: The University of Michigan Press, 1993.

——. "Is There a 'Jewish Interest' in Latin American Politics?" *Patterns of Prejudice* 24:2–4 (Winter 1990):60–74.

Elnecavé, Nissim. "Sephardic Jews in Argentina." *Dispersion and Unity* 2 (June 1960): 56–57.

Engleman, Uriah Z. "Sources of Jewish Statistics." In *The Jews: Their History, Culture and Religion,* edited by Louis Finkelstein, pp. 1510–35. 2 vols. 3d ed. New York: Harper & Bros., 1960.

Gann, Lisa. "Israeli Arms Sales to Nicaraguan Rebels." *Jewish Frontier* (May 1985):5–6, 22.

Germani, Gino. "Antisemitismo ideológico y antisemitismo tradicional." In *La cuestión judía en la Argentina,* edited by Juan José Sebreli, pp. 177–90. Buenos Aires: Editorial Tiempo Contemporáneo, n.d.

——. "Mass Immigration and Modernization in Argentina." In *Masses in Latin*

America, edited by Irving Louis Horowitz, pp. 289–330. New York: Oxford University Press, 1970.

Ghio, José María. "La cuestión nacional y la cuestión judía." In *El genocidio ante la historia,* edited by Beatriz Gurevich and Carlos Escudé, pp. 209–247. Buenos Aires: Universidad Torcuato Di Tella, 1994.

Gillin, John. "Ethos Components in Modern Latin American Culture." *American Anthropologist* 57 (1955):488–500.

Glauert, Earl T. "Ricardo Rojas and the Emergence of Argentine Cultural Nationalism." *Hispanic American Historical Review* 43 (1963):1–13.

Griffith, William J. "Attitudes toward Foreign Colonization." In *Applied Enlightenment: Nineteenth Century Liberalism,* edited by Margaret Harrison and Robert Wauchope, pp. 71–110. New Orleans: Tulane University Press, 1972.

Gudiño Kramer, Luis. "Colonización judía en el litoral." *Davar* (Buenos Aires) 14 (November 1947).

Harari, Iejiel, "Yahadut Argentina." [Argentine Jewry.] *Dispersion and Unity* 2 (June 1960):16–34.

———, and Itzjak Lewin. "Resultado de la encuesta sobre profesiones, idiomas, y crecimiento de la colectividad judía." *Nueva Sion* (Buenos Aires), 24 February 1950 and 14 July 1950.

Hasson, Yaacov. "Elementos para el estudio histórico y pedagógico de la educación judía en el Perú." CJL (1970):240–44.

———. "Iquitos: Alma judía en la Amazonia peruana." CJL (1971–72):367–73.

Hernández, Frances. "The Secret Jews of the Southwest." In *Sephardim in the Americas: Studies in Culture and History,* edited by Martin A. Cohen and Abraham J. Peck, pp. 411–54. Cincinnati: American Jewish Archives and Tuscaloosa: The University of Alabama Press, 1993.

Hersch, Leib. "Jewish Migrations during the Last Hundred Years." In Central Yiddish Culture Organization, *The Jewish People: Past and Present,* 1:407–30. New York: Marstin Press, 1946–48.

Hexter, Maurice Beck. "The Jews in Mexico." *Jewish Social Service Quarterly* 2 (March–June 1926):188–96, 274–86.

Hirsch, Baron Maurice de. "My Views on Philanthropy." *North American Review* 2 (July 1891): 416.

Hirschberg, Alfred. "The Economic Adjustment of Jewish Refugees in São Paulo." *Jewish Social Studies* 7 (January 1945):31–40.

Hochstein, Joshua. "La colaboración hispano-israelita en la América." *América: Revista de la Asociación de escritores y artistas americanos.* Havana, September 1939.

———. "La inmigración judía de la postguerra." *América: Revista de la Asociación de escritores y artistas americanos.* Havana, October 1939.

Hodara, Joseph. "Hayehudim ba-Córdoba." [The Jews of Córdoba.] *Dispersion and Unity* 2 (June 1960): 34–51.

Hoetink, Harry. "The Dominican Republic in the Nineteenth Century: Some Notes on Immigration, Stratification, and Race." In *Race and Class in Latin America,* edited by Magnus Mörner, pp. 96–121. New York: Columbia University Press, 1970.

Horowitz, Irving Louis. "The Jewish Community of Buenos Aires." *Jewish Social Studies* 24 (October 1962):195–222.

———. "Jewish Ethnicism and Latin American Nationalism." *Midstream* 18 (November 1972):22–28.

Horowitz, S. Y. "Di cooperativn in di yiddishe kolonies in Argentina." *Argentiner IWO Schriftn* 1 (1941):59–116.

Hurvitz, Nathan. "Sources of Motivation and Achievement of American Jews." *Jewish Social Studies* 23 (October 1961):217–34.

Itzigsohn, José A. "La atención médica en las colonias agrícolas judías de la Argentina." In AMILAT II, *Judaica Latinoamericana: Estudios Histórico-Sociales II*, pp. 17–27. Jerusalem: Hebrew University, 1993.

Kahan, Arcadius. "A Note on Methods of Research on the Economic History of the Jews." In *For Max Weinreich on his Seventieth Birthday*, pp. 173–82. The Hague: Mouton, 1964.

Kamen, Henry. "The Mediterranean and the Expulsion of Spanish Jews in 1492." *Past & Present* 119 (May 1988):30–55.

Kaplan, Sander M. "Jewish Robinson Crusoes." *Havaner Lebn*, 12 October 1934.

Kaplanski de Caryevschi, Teresa. "The Organized Jewish Community of Buenos Aires—AMIA." *Dispersion and Unity* 11 (1970):147–78.

Kardúner, Luis. "La eliminación de las acepciones peyoritivas del diccionario de la lengua española." *Comunidades judías* (1971–72):251–72.

Kaufman, Edy. "Introducción: Derechos humanos en Argentina: La perspectiva judía y la visión desde Israel." In *El Legado de Autoritarismo*, edited by Leonardo Senkman and Mario Sznajder, pp. 193–96. Jerusalem: Hebrew University, and Buenos Aires, 1995.

———. "Jewish Victims of Repression in Argentina under Military Rule (1976–1983)." *Holocaust and Genocide Studies*, 4:4 (1989):479–91.

———. "The View from Jerusalem." *Washington Quarterly* 7:4 (Fall 1984):40–51.

———, and Nadir Tsur. "Israel and the Contras." *Present Tense* 14, no. 4 (May–June 1987):14–17.

Kierszenbaum, José. "El caso del Conte Grande: inmigración y antisemitismo en el Uruguay," in Abel M. Bronstein, et al., eds., *Vida y Muerte en comunidad: ensayos sobre judaísmo en el Uruguay*, pp. 111–28.

Kinzer, Nora Scott. "Women Professionals in Buenos Aires." In *Female and Male in Latin America*, edited by Ann Pescatello, pp. 159–90. Pittsburgh: University of Pittsburgh Press, 1973.

Klich, Ignacio. "Argentina." *American Jewish Year Book 1996*: 227–37.

———. "Jewish Settlement in Argentina: A View from Jerusalem" (review of Haim Avni, *Argentina and the Jews: A History of Jewish Immigration*). *American Jewish Archives* 46:1 (Spring–Summer 1994):101–26.

———. "Latin America, the United States, and the Birth of Israel: The Case of Somoza's Nicaragua." *Journal of Latin American Studies* 20(1988):389–432.

———. "The Peronist Challenge in the May 1989 Argentine Presidential Election." London: Institute of Jewish Affairs *Research Report*, no. 2, 1989.

———. "Towards an Arab-Latin American Bloc? The Genesis of Argentine-Middle East Relations: Jordan, 1945–54." *Middle Eastern Studies* (London), 31:3 (1995).

Knudsen, Jerry W. "Anti-Semitism in Latin America." *Patterns of Prejudice* (London) 6 (September–October 1972):1–10; and 6 (November–December 1972):22–30.

———. "The Bolivian Immigration Bill of 1942: A Case Study in Latin American Anti-Semitism." *American Jewish Archives* 22 (November 1970):138–58.

Kochanski, Mendel. "The Jewish Community in Cuba." *Jewish Frontier* 18 (September 1951):25–27.

Kohn, Hans. "The Jew Enters Western Culture." *Menorah Journal* 18 (April 1930):291–302.

Kovadloff, Jacobo. "La sociedad Hebraica Argentina de Buenos Aires." *Comunidades judías* (1966):180–85.

Krause, Corinne Azen. "Mexico—Another Promised Land? A Review of Projects for Jewish Colonization in Mexico: 1881–1925." *American Jewish Historical Quarterly* 61 (June 1972):325–41.

Krausz, Rosa R. "Some Aspects of Intermarriage in the Jewish Community of São Paulo, Brazil." *American Jewish Archives* 34:2 (1982):219.

Kriesberg, Louis. "Entrepreneurs in Latin America and the Role of Cultural and Situational Processes." *International Social Science Journal* 15 (1963):581–94.

Kritschmar, Najum. "Der itztiker matzav fun di yidishe kolonies." In AMIA, *Pinkus fun der kehillah*, pp. 282–95. Buenos Aires, 1969.

Kuznets, Simon. "Economic Structure and Life of the Jews." In *The Jews: Their History, Culture, and Religion*, edited by Louis Finkelstein, pp. 1597–1666. 2 vols. 3d ed. New York: Harper & Bros, 1960.

Lat, Netam. "From Sosua to Azua." *Hadassah Magazine* 53 (November 1971):16–17, 38–39.

Latin American Newsletters. Special Report, "Latin America's Relations with Israel and the Arab World." SR 85–05. November 1985.

Leftel, Ruth. "Os sefarditas egípcios de São Paulo, O renascimento de uma comunidade." In *Ensayos sobre Judaísmo Latinoamericano*, edited by Bernardo Blejmar and Ana E. Weinstein, pp. 45–56. Buenos Aires: Editorial Milá, 1990.

Lemle, Henrique. "Jews in Northern Brazil." *Reconstructionist*, 3 March 1967.

Lerner, Natan. "Anti-Semitism and the Nationalist Ideology in Argentina." *Dispersion and Unity* 17/18 (1973):131–39.

———. "Argentina's First Anti-Semitic Novel." *Patterns of Prejudice* 5 (September–October 1971):25–27.

Lesser, Jeffrey H. "Continuity and Change within an Immigrant Community: The Jews of São Paulo, 1924–1945" *Luso-Brazilian Review* 25:2 (1988):45–58.

———. "Immigration and Shifting Concepts of National Identity in Brazil during the Vargas Era." *Luso-Brazilian Review* 31:2 (Winter 1994):23–44.

———. "From Pedlars to Proprietors: Lebanese, Syrian and Jewish Immigrants in Brazil." *The Lebanese in the World: A Century of Emigration*. Albert Hourani and Nadim Shehadi, eds. London: I. B. Tauris and St. Martins Press, 1992, pp. 393–410.

Lestschinsky, Jacob. "The Economic Development of the Jews of the United States." In Central Yiddish Culture Organization, *The Jewish People: Past and Present* 1:391–406. 3 vols. New York: Marstin Press, 1946–48.

———. "Economic and Social Development of the Jewish People." In Central

Yiddish Culture Organization, *The Jewish People: Past and Present* 1:361–90. 3 vols. New York: Marstin Press, 1946–48.

———. "Jewish Migrations, 1840–1956." In *The Jews: Their History, Culture, and Religion,* edited by Louis Finkelstein, 2:1536–96. 2 vols. 3d ed. New York: Harper & Bros., 1960.

Levine, Robert M. "Anatomy of a Brazilian Anti-Semite: Paulo Francis and the Israel-Arab Conflict." University of Miami Institute of InterAmerican Studies: *Occasional Paper,* n.d. (1983?).

———. "Brazil's Jews during the Vargas Era and After." *Luso-Brazilian Review* 5 (Summer 1968):45–58.

———. "Cuba." In *The World Reacts to the Holocaust,* edited by David S. Wyman, pp. 782–808. Baltimore: The Johns Hopkins University Press, 1996.

———. "Jews under the Cuban Revolution: 1959–1995." In *The Jewish Diaspora in Latin America,* edited by David Sheinin and Lois Baer Barr, pp. 265–87. New York: Garland Publishing, 1996.

Levy, Daniel. "Jewish Education in Latin America." In *The Jewish Presence in Latin America,* edited by Judith Laikin Elkin and Gilbert W. Merkx, pp. 157–84. Boston: Allen & Unwin, 1987.

Lewin, Boleslao. "Esbozo de la historia judía de la Argentina desde 1580 hasta 1889." AMIA, *Pinkus fun der Kehillah,* pp. 37–66. Buenos Aires, 1969.

———. "The Struggle against Jewish Immigration into Latin America in Colonial Times." *YIVO Annual of Jewish Social Science* 7 (1952):212–28.

Liebman, Seymour B. "Hernando Alonso: The First Jew on the North American Continent." *Journal of Inter-American Studies* 5 (April 1963):291–96.

———. "The Jews of Colonial Mexico." *Hispanic American Historical Review* 43 (February 1963):95–108.

———. "Latin American Jews: Ethnicity and Nationalism." *Jewish Frontier* 40 (July–August 1973):8–13.

———. "The Mestizo Jews of Mexico." *American Jewish Archives* 19 (November 1967):144–74.

———. "Research Problems in Mexican Jewish History." *American Jewish Historical Quarterly* 54 (December 1964):165–80.

Lifshitz, Linda Dabbah de. "La inmigración de los judíos de Alepo." In *Los judíos de Alepo en México,* edited by Liz Hamui de Halabe, pp. 61–79. Mexico: Maguén David, 1989.

Lipiner, Eliahu. "Yidn in Brazil." *Algemeine Entsiclopedia* 5 (1957):385–404.

Lipman, Aaron. "Social Backgrounds of the Bogotá Entrepreneur." *Journal of Inter-American Studies* 7 (1965):227–35.

Lipset, Seymour Martin. "The Study of Jewish Communities in a Comparative Context." *Jewish Journal of Sociology* 5 (1963):156–60.

Litvinoff, Norberto. "Estudio de actitudes en la comunidad judía Argentina." *Indice* (Buenos Aires) 2(April 1969):88–102.

Lleras Camargo, Alberto. "A Humble Jewish Revolution." *Visión* (Bogotá 1972).

Luftig, Roman. "La comunidad israelita de San Pablo." CJL (1970):156–59.

———. "Sistema y extensión de la asistencia social en San Pablo." CJL (1968):156–59.

Maller, Julius B. "The Role of Education in Jewish History." In *The Jews: Their*

History, Culture, and Religion, edited by Louis Finkelstein, 2:1234–53. 2 vols. 3d ed. New York: Harper & Bros., 1960.

Meding, Holger M. "Refugio seguro. La emigración alemana de la posguerra al Rio de la Plata." In *El genocidio ante la historia y la naturaleza humana,* edited by Beatriz Gurevich and Carlos Escudé, pp. 249–61. Buenos Aires: Universidad Torcuato Di Tella, 1994.

Meisel, Tovye. "Yidn in Meksike." *YIVO Bletter* 27 (1946):213–330.

———. "Yidn in Meksike." *YIVO Annual of Jewish Social Science* 2–3 (1947–48):295–312.

———. "Yidn in Meksike." *Algemeine Entsiclopedia* 5 (1957):405–20.

Meyer, Marshall. "Una década de judaísmo conservador en Latinoamérica." CJL (1970): 182–93.

Mirelman, Victor A. "A Note on Jewish Settlement in Argentina, 1881–1892." *Jewish Social Studies* 33 (January 1971):3–12.

———. "The Semana Trágica of 1919 and the Jews of Argentina." *Jewish Social Studies* 37 (January 1975):61–73.

———. "Sephardic Immigration to Argentina Prior to the Nazi Period." In *The Jewish Presence in Latin America,* edited by Judith Laikin Elkin and Gilbert W. Merkx, pp. 13–32. Boston: Allen & Unwin, 1987.

———. "Sephardim in Latin America after Independence." In *Sephardim in the Americas: Studies in Culture and History,* edited by Martin A. Cohen and Abraham J. Peck, pp. 235–308. Tuscaloosa: University of Alabama Press, 1993.

Mújica Lainez, Manuel. "Discurso de recepción del Señor Academico don Abraham Rosenvasser." *Boletín de la Academia Argentina de Letras,* 45, no. 175–78 (January–December 1980), pp. 65–83. Buenos Aires, 1980.

Nachman, Robert G. "Positivism, Modernization, and the Middle Class in Brazil." *Hispanic American Historical Review* 57 (February 1977):1–23.

Newton, Ronald C. "Indifferent Sanctuary: German-Speaking Refugees and Exiles in Argentina, 1933–1945." *Journal of Interamerican Studies and World Affairs* 24:4 (November 1982):395–420.

Novinsky, Anita. "Fontes para a historia economica e social do Brasil. Inventários dos bens de condenados pela Inquisição. (Brasil, século xviii)." *Revista de História* (São Paulo), no. 98 (1974), pp. 359–92.

———. "A Historical Bias: The New Christian Collaboration with the Dutch Invaders of Brazil (Seventeenth Century)." Jerusalem: Fifth World Congress of Jewish Studies, 1972.

———. "Os israelitas em São Paulo." In *São Paulo: Espírito, povo, instituiçãos,* edited by J. V. Freitas Marcondes and Osmar Pimentel, pp. 109–26. São Paulo: Livraria Pioneira Editora, 1974.

———. "Uma fonte inédita para a história do Brasil." *Revista de História* (São Paulo) no. 94 (1973), pp. 563–72.

Nun, José. "A Latin American Phenomenon: The Middle-Class Military Coup." In *Latin America: Reform or Revolution?* edited by James Petras and Maurice Zeitlin, pp. 145–85. Greenwich, Conn.: Fawcett Publications, 1968.

Patai, Raphael. "Indios Israelitas of Mexico." *Menorah Journal* 38:1 (1950):54–67.

Perera, Victor. "Growing up Jewish in Guatemala." *Present Tense* 1 (Winter 1974):55–59.

Perez, Leon S. "The Problems of Jewish University Youth in the Argentine." *Dispersion and Unity* 2 (1963):89–98.

Pessah, Alberto. "La Asociacíon Comunidad Israelita Sefardí de Buenos Aires." CJL (1970): 194–96.

Raizman, Itzhak Z. "Yidn in Brazil." *Jewish Review* 4 (October 1946):139–53.

Rattner, Henrique. "Economic and Social Mobility of Jews in Brazil." In *The Jewish Presence in Latin America,* edited by Judith Laikin Elkin and Gilbert W. Merkx, pp. 187–200. Boston: Allen & Unwin, 1987.

———. "Persistencia de padrões tradicionais." *Sociologia* (São Paulo) 27:2 (June 1965).

———. "Sociological Research & Census of the Jewish Community in São Paulo, 1968." Preliminary Report. *American Jewish Year Book* 70 (1969): 382.

Reicher, Perla. "Safrut, itoniyot, ukruzim shel yahadut Uruguay." [Books, newspapers, and posters of Uruguayan Jewry.] University of Tel Aviv, Institute for Zionist Research, 1970.

Ricard, Robert. "L'emigration des Juifs marocains en Amérique du Sud." *Société de Géographie du Maroc* (Casablanca) 8:7 (1928):237–40.

Rischin, Moses. "The Jewish Labor Movement in America: A Social Interpretation." *Labor History* 4:3 (Fall 1963):227–47.

Rivkin, Ellis. "The Utilization of Non-Jewish Sources for the Reconstruction of Jewish History." *Jewish Quarterly Review* n.s., 48 (October 1957):183–203.

Rosen, Joseph A. "New Neighbors in Sosua." *Survey Graphic* (September 1941).

Rosenswaike, Ira. "The Jewish Population of Argentina." *Jewish Social Studies* 22 (October 1960):195–214.

Rosenthal, Celia S. "The Jews of Barranquilla." *Jewish Journal of Sociology* 18 (1956): 262–74.

Rubel, Iaacov. "Argentina, ¿sí o no?" In CJL (1971–72): 273–91.

Ruppin, Arthur. "The Jewish Population of the World." In Central Yiddish Culture Organization, *The Jewish People: Past and Present,* 1:348–60. New York: Marstin Press, 1946–48.

Sandberg, Harry O. "The Jews of Latin America." *American Jewish Year Book* 19 (1917–18): 35–105.

Santander, Silvano. "Tres personalidades judeo-argentinas." In AMIA (Asociación Mutual Israelita Argentina) *Pinkus fun der kehilla in ihr 75stn aniversar.* Buenos Aires, 1969, pp. 75–82.

Sapir, Boris. "Jewish Organizations in Cuba." *Jewish Review* 4 (January–March 1947): 263–81.

———. "Jews in Cuba." *Jewish Review* 5 (July–September 1946):109–44.

———. "Tsu der geshikhte fun yidn in Cuba." *YIVO Bletter* 25:3 (May–June 1945): 335–66.

Sapolinsky, Asher. "The Jewry of Uruguay." *Dispersion and Unity* 2 (1963): 74–88.

Sarna, Jonathan. "Columbus and the Jews." *Commentary* 94:5 (November 1992):38–41.

Schallman, Lázaro. "Dramática historia de los 'pampistas' o 'stambuler.'" Comunidades judías (1966):151–72.

———. "Historia del periodismo judío en la Republica Argentina." Comunidades judías (1970):149–73.

————. "Orígenes de la colonización agrícola judía en la república Argentina." *Comentario* (Buenos Aires) 40 (1964):23–34.

————. "Proceso histórico de la colonización agrícola." In *Inmigración y nacionalidad,* edited by D. J. Cúneo et al., pp. 145–209. Buenos Aires: Editorial Paidós, n.d.

Scharfstein, Zevi. "Jewish Education in Latin America." In Central Yiddish Culture Organization, *The Jewish People: Past and Present,* 2:172–78. 3 vols. New York: Marstin Press, 1946–48.

Schers, David. "Argentina." In *American Jewish Year Book.* 89 (1989): 270–81.

————. "Brazil" In *American Jewish Year Book.* 89 (1989): 282–89.

————, and Hadassa Singer. "The Jewish Communities of Latin America: External and Internal Factors in Their Development." *Jewish Social Studies* 39 (Summer 1977):241–58.

Schmelz, U. O. "Critical Assessment of Jewish Population Estimates for Argentina and Latin America." In *Studies in Jewish Demography: Survey for 1969–1971,* edited by U. O. Schmelz et al., pp. 25–52. Jerusalem: Hebrew University, 1975.

————, and Sergio DellaPergola. "The Demography of Latin American Jewry." *American Jewish Year Book.* Vol. 85:51–102.

————. "World Jewish Population, 1982." *American Jewish Year Book.* Vol. 85: 324–29. New York: American Jewish Committee, 1985.

————. "World Jewish Population, 1990." *American Jewish Year Book.* Vol. 92: 484–512.

————. "World Jewish Population, 1994." *American Jewish Year Book.* Vol. 96: 434–63.

Schneider, Joseph. "Shpurn fun di Yiddisher fargangenheit in der alter Havana." *Havaner Lebn,* 12 October 1934.

Schonebohm, Dieter. "Mujeres trabajadoras, mujeres judías, mujeres." Unidentified press clipping of 21 April 1991.

Schusheim, A. L. "Tsu di geschichte fun der antsteiung fun dem idishn kibuts in Buenos Aires." *Yohrbuch 5714* (1953–54). Buenos Aires: AMIA, 1954.

————, and J. Bottachanski. "The Jewish Community in Argentina." *Algemeine Entsiclopedia* 5 (1957) 342:84.

Schwartz, Stuart. "The Voyage of the Vassals: Royal Power, Noble Obligations, and Merchant Capital before the Portuguese Restoration of Independence, 1624–1640." *Hispanic American Historical Review* 96:3 (1991):735–62.

Senkman, Leonardo. "Argentina's Immigration Policy during the Holocaust (1938–1945)." Jerusalem: *Yad Vashem Studies* 21 (1991).

————. "El antisemitismo bajo dos experiencias democráticas: Argentina 1915–19 y 1973–76." In *El antisemitismo en la Argentina* 1:9–104. Buenos Aires: Centro Editor de América Latina, 1986.

————. "Israel y el rescate de las víctimas de la represión." In *Legado del autoritarismo,* edited by Leonard Senkman and Mario Sznajder, pp. 283–324. Jerusalem: Hebrew University, 1995.

————. "The Restoration of Democracy in Argentina and the Impunity of Antisemitism." *Patterns of Prejudice* 24:2–4 (Winter 1990): 34–59.

Shapira, Yoram, and Edy Kaufman. "Cuba's Israel Policy: The Shift to the Soviet Line." *Cuban Studies/Estudios Cubanos* 8:1 (January 1978):22–35.

Sharot, Stephen. "Minority Situation and Religious Acculturation: A Comparative Analysis of Jewish Communities." *Comparative Studies in Society and History* 16 (June 1974):329–54.

Shatzky, Jacob. "Guatemala." *Jewish Journal of Sociology* 7 (December 1965):302–3.

Sidicaro, Luis. "La comunidad sefardí de habla española de Buenos Aires." CJL (1970):197–202.

Smith, T. Lynn. "Changing Functions of Latin American Cities." *Américas* 24 (July 1968): 70–83.

Sneh, Simja. "La red escolar judía en la república Argentina." In CJL (1968):129–42.

Sobel, Louis H. "Jewish Community Life in Latin America." *American Jewish Year Book.* 47 (1945–46):119–40.

Spektorowski, Alberto. "La imágen del judío en las corrientes integralistas y populistas del nacionalismo argentino." In AMILAT II, *Judaica Latinoamericana: Estudios histórico-sociales,* 2:99–114. Jerusalem: Magnes Press, 1993.

Speist, Robbie. "Jews of Cuba." *Morgn Freiheit,* 14 June 1970.

Stanger, Francis Merriman. "Church and State in Peru during the First Century of Independence." In *The Conflict between Church and State in Latin America,* edited by Frederick B. Pike, pp. 143–53. New York: Alfred A. Knopf, 1964.

Steinberg, I. N. "Jewish Colonization in the Americas: Argentina." In Central Yiddish Culture Organization, *The Jewish People: Past and Present,* 2:81–87. 3 vols. New York: Marstin Press, 1946–48.

Strassman, Paul W. "The Industrialist." In *Continuity and Change in Latin America,* edited by John J. Johnson, pp. 161–85. Stanford: Stanford University Press, 1964.

Syrquin, Moshe. "The Economic Structure of the Jews in Argentina and Other Latin American Countries." Discussion Paper no. 7507. Department of Economics, Bar Ilan University, May 1975.

Szajkowski, Zosa. "Baron Hirsch's bamiyungen l-teives di rusishe yidn un der crisis in der ICA kurz far zein toit." *Davke* (Buenos Aires), no. 2 (1950–51), pp. 401–16.

Sznajder, Mario. "Judaísmo chileno y el gobierno." In AMILAT II, *Judaica Latinoamericana: Estudios Histórico-Sociales,* pp. 137–48. Jerusalem: Magnes Press, 1993.

Trahtemberg, S. Leon. "Comunidad judía de Lima," In *Estudios Judaicos en Universidades Latinoamericanos,* edited by Haim Avni and Florinda Goldberg, pp. 21–63. Jerusalem: Centro para Estudios Universitarios de la Cultura Judía, 1985.

Uslar-Pietri, Arturo. "La escuela y el destino de América Latina." *Cuadernos* (Paris) 76 (September 1963):3–8.

Vasertzug, S. "La kehilla de Buenos Aires y el vaad hakehillot de la Argentina." CJL (1966):143–55.

Veltman, Henrique B. "Crônica do judaísmo carioca." *Comentario* (Rio de Janeiro) 13 (1972):51–59.

Wald, Pinie. "Di Yiddishe Arbeter Bavegung in Argentina." In AMIA, *Pinkus fun der Kehilla,* pp. 109–43. Buenos Aires, 1954–55.

Warszawski, Paúl. "Régimen militar, iglesia católica y comunidad judía en la República Argentina." In *Legado del Autoritarismo,* edited by Leonardo Senkman and Mario Sznajder, pp. 217–38. Jerusalem: Hebrew University, and Buenos Aires, 1995.

Weisbrot, Robert. "Jews in Argentina Today." *Judaism* 25 (Fall 1976):390–401.

Weiser, Benno. "Ecuador: Eight Years on Ararat." *Commentary* 3 (June 1947):531–36.

Winsberg, Morton D. "Jewish Agricultural Colonization in Entre Ríos." *American Journal of Economics and Sociology* 27 (July 1968):285–95; 27 (October 1968): 423–28; 28 (April 1969):179–91.

Winter, Olga M. de. "La educación judía en la Argentina." In CJL (1966): 133–42.

Wischnitzer, Mark. "Historical Background of Settlement of Jewish Refugees in Santo Domingo." *Journal of Social Studies* 4:1 (1942):50–58.

———. "Jewish Communal Organization in Modern Times." In Central Yiddish Culture Organization, *The Jewish People: Past and Present*, 2:201–16. 3 vols. New York: Marstin Press, 1946–48.

———. "The Sosua Settlement." *ORT Economic Bulletin* 2:3 (1941).

Wiznitzer, Arnold. "Crypto-Jews in Mexico during the Sixteenth Century." *American Jewish Historical Society Quarterly* 51 (1961–62):168–214, 222–68.

———. "The Exodus from Brazil and Arrival in New Amsterdam of the Jewish Pilgrim Fathers, 1654." In *The Jewish Experience in Latin America*, edited by Martin A. Cohen, 2:313–30. 2 vols. Philadelphia: American Jewish Historical Society, 1971.

Yerushalmi, Yosef Haim. "Between Amsterdam and New Amsterdam: The Place of Curaçao and the Caribbean in Early Modern Jewish History." *American Jewish History* 72:2 (December 1982):172–211.

Zack de Zukerman, Celia. "Colectividad y kehila." *Generaciones Judías en México*, vol. 6, edited by Alicia Gojman de Backal. Mexico: Comunidad Ashkenzaí de Mexico, 1993.

Zadoff, Efraim. "La educación judía en pequeñas y medianas comunidades de America Latina." *Rumbos* 14 (October 1985):154.

Zemer, Moshe. "The Rabbinic Ban on Conversion in Argentina." *Judaism* 37:145 (Winter 1988):84–96.

Zenner, Walter P. "International Networks in a Migrant Ethnic Group." In *Migration and Anthropology. Proceedings of the 1970 Annual Spring Meeting of the American Ethnological Society*. Seattle: University of Washington Press, 1971.

Dissertations

Ansel, Bernard D. "The Beginnings of the Modern Jewish Community in Argentina, 1852–1891." University of Kansas, 1969.

Bejarano, Margalit. "The Jewish Community of Cuba 1898–1939. Communal Consolidation and Trends of Integration under the Impact of Changes in World Jewry and Cuban Society." [Hebrew] Hebrew University, 1992.

Goodman, Robert Alan. "The Image of the Jew in Argentine Literature as Seen by Argentine Jewish Writers." State University of New York, 1972.

Hebert, John Raymond. "The Tragic Week of January, 1919, in Buenos Aires: Background, Events, Aftermath." Georgetown University, 1972.

Hordes, Stanley M. "The Crypto-Jewish Community of New Spain, 1620–1649: A Collective Biography." Tulane University, 1980.

Kisch, Hyman. "The Jewish Settlement from Central Europe in the Dominican Republic." Jewish Theological Seminary, 1970.

Krause, Corinne Azen. "The Jews in Mexico: A History with Special Emphasis on the Period from 1857 to 1930." University of Pittsburgh, 1970.

Kulwin, Clifford M. "The Emergence of Progressive Judaism in South America." Hebrew Union College–Jewish Institute of Religion, 1983. Rabbinic thesis.

Lesser, Harriet Sara. "A History of the Jewish Community of Mexico City, 1912–1970." Jewish Teachers' Seminary and Columbia University, 1972.

Levitz, Jacob. "The Jewish Community in Mexico: Its Life and Education." Dropsie College, 1954.

Mirelman, Victor A. "The Jews in Argentina (1890–1930): Assimilation and Particularism." Columbia University, 1973.

Rubner, Michael. "Israel and Latin America: The Politics of Bilateral Economic Aid." University of California, Berkeley, 1975.

Smith, John Kenneth. "Jewish Education in Colombia: Group Survival versus Assimilation." University of Wisconsin, 1972.

Sofer, Eugene F. "From Pale to Pampa: Eastern European Jewish Social Mobility in Gran Buenos Aires, 1890–1945." University of California, 1976.

Periodicals Cited

Havaner Lebn
Jerusalem Post
Latin American Jewish Studies
Latin American Weekly Report
Majshavot/Pensamientos
OJI—Boletín Informativo
World Jewish Congress Dateline

Videotapes

Freeman, Mark, director. *The Yidishe Gauchos.* National Center for Jewish Film, 1989.

Levine, Robert M., and Mark D. Szuchman. *Hotel Cuba.* University of Illinois Film Center, 1985.

Paull, Laura. *Havana Nagila: The Jews in Cuba.* Ergo Media, 1995.

Taub, Harriet, and Harry Kafka. *Sosua.* Ergo Media, 1987.

Unpublished Papers

Barromi, Joel. "Argentina: Twenty years afterwards. An appraisal of Israeli policies toward Argentina and the Argentinian Jewry during the epoch of the military junta (1976–1983)." Paper presented at the Eighth International Research Conference, LAJSA, Mexico City, 12 November 1995.

Bolaffi, Gabriel. "Socialização e resocialização num grupo juvenil informal." Mimeographed. São Paulo, 1960s.

Catterberg, Edgardo, and Associates. "Argentina Survey, 1992." For the American Jewish Committee and Delegación de Asociaciones Israelitas Argentinas. Buenos Aires.

Corrales Capestrany, Maritza. "Comportamiento Económico y espacial de los comercios e industrias judías en La Habana: 1902–1959." Paper delivered at the Eighth International Research Conference of the Latin American Jewish Studies Association, Mexico City, 14 November 1995.

Kovadloff, Jacobo. Paper presented at meeting of the Latin American Studies Association, Washington, DC, 28 September 1995.

———, and Susan Rothblatt. "The Argentine Jewish Community under Alfonsín." New York: American Jewish Committee, 1986.

New Jewish Agenda. "Report of the Jewish Human Rights Delegation to Nicaragua, August 12–17, 1984." 6 September 1984.

Rattner, Henrique, and Gabriel Bolaffi. "Jewish University Students in Face of Judaism" (mimeo), São Paulo, 1966.

Rieier, Jacques. "The Jewish Colony of Cuba." Typescript. N.p. 1942.

Schonebohm, Dieter. "The Utility of a Life History Approach for Understanding the Interaction between Jewish Immigrants and the Uruguayan Left (1920–1955)." Paper presented at the Sixth Research Conference of the Latin American Jewish Studies Association, University of Maryland, 6–8 October 1991.

Segal, Ariel Freilich. "Self-Exile in the Earthly Paradise: One Hundred Years of Solitude for the Jewish Mestizos of Iquitos (1890s–1990s)." Unpublished dissertation proposal.

Spitzer, Leo. "Andean Two-Step: The Encounter between Bolivians and Central-European Jewish Refugees." Paper presented at the University of Michigan, 31 October 1994.

———. "Invisible Baggage on an Emigration to the Edge of the Holocaust." Paper delivered at the Seventh International Research Conference of the Latin American Jewish Studies Association, Philadelphia, 7 November 1993.

Taschner, Suzana Pasternak, and René Decol. "População Judaica no Brasil: Um Estudo Demográfico." Projeto de Pesquisa do Arquivo Histórico Judaico Brasileiro e Casa da Cultura de Israel. N.d. [1995?]

Waszkis, Helmut. "Dr. Moritz (Don Mauricio) Hochschild." Paper presented at the Eighth International Research Conference, LAJSA, Mexico City 11–14 November 1995.

INDEX

Açâo Integralista Brasileira, 94

Agricultural colonization, 105–30; in Argentina, 58, 70, 74, 100, 105–20, 127–30, 163; in Bolivia, 124–30; in Brazil, 61–62, 70, 92–93, 130; in the Dominican Republic, 120–24, 128–30, 239; evaluation of, 127–30; ideal of, 106; in Uruguay, 70, 130. *See also* JCA

Agro-Joint, 121, 125

Alianza Monte Sinai, 169

Allende, Salvador, 224, 247, 268, 269

Alliance Israélite Universelle, 29, 107, 108, 120–21; education and, 174

Alonso, Hernando, 9

American Jewish Committee, 62, 66, 68, 144, 194, 274, 279

AMIA (Asociación Mutual Israelita Argentina), 186–88, 201; bombing, 265–68, 281; budget, 161; record keeping, 138; social services, 155

Anarchism, 56–57, 77, 98, 99, 166, 232

Anticlericalism, 21, 38, 48, 87, 169, 273

Anti-Defamation League, 279

Anti-Semitism, 87–88, 237–38, 281; in Argentina, 54, 77–78, 83–85, 98–100, 163, 186, 234, 241–43, 252–68, 274–75; in Bolivia, 81, 124–26; in Brazil, 78–79, 94; Catholicism and, 274; in Chile, 36, 60, 268–69, 272; in Cuba, 89, 271–72; in Ecuador, 145; *La Bolsa*, 256; in medical schools, 101; in Mexico, 143–44; nationalism and, 273; origins of, 73; publishing, 227–28; survey of, 274; in the United States, 248; west of Russia, 72; and Zionism, 248–50. *See also* Nazism; Semana Trágica

Arabic-speaking Jews, 49, 55, 73, 170; in Cuba, 53; in Mexico, 40, 53, 85–86

Argentina, 74, 96–102, 252–68; agricultural colonization, 58, 70, 74, 100, 105–20, 127–30, 163; anti-Semitism, 77–78, 83–85, 98–100, 163, 186, 234, 241–43, 252–68, 274–75; arms trade, 249; Ashkenazim in, 53, 181; demography, 191–92, 195–98, 201, 251; economic policy, 133, 139; education, 174–75, 177; emigration from, 210–11; fascism, 225, 255; higher education, 205–6; immigration policy, 29–35, 53–59, 77–78, 82–85, 98, 118, 175; intermarriage, 172, 188, 207–8, 226; Jewish youth, 256; Jews in politics, 263–65; *kehillot*, 186–88; longevity, 199; military juntas, 225, 240–45, 257–63; *nacionalismo*, 263; natural increase rate, 202; occupations, 34, 149–51; racism, 27; religious observance, 168, 170–72, 279; Sephardim, 181; settlement patterns, 74–75; sports clubs, 188–89; terrorism, 220, 265–68; urbanization, 117–19, 203–4; xenophobia, 30, 34. *See also* AMIA; DAIA; Dirty War; Gauchos; Semana Trágica

Arms sales, 236, 238–40, 244–50. *See also* Falklands War

Ashkenazim, 29, 47–48, 51–53, 68–71, 76, 85, 86, 166; in Argentina, 53, 181; assimilation, 48, 209; in Brazil, 53, 61; burial practices of, 160; in Chile, 36; ethnic rivalry, 180; family size, 201; intermarriage with Sephardim, 35, 190; in Mexico, 85–86, 160, 176, 183; in Paraguay, 65; as peddlers, 134; in Peru, 63; religious education of, 174; religious observance, 169–70; in Uruguay, 185

Assimilation, 71, 101, 180, 209–10, 219–20, 228, 251–52, 273–78; in Argentina, 56, 59, 112, 120; of Ashkenazim, 48, 209; in Bolivia, 127; in Chile, 143; in Cuba, 154; danger of, 231; of first generation, 146–49; of Jewish youth, 188; in Peru, 45; pressure for, 87; resistance to, 77; in Santo Domingo, 47; of

JUDITH LAIKIN ELKIN is the founding president of the Latin American Jewish Studies Association and a historian associated with the Frankel Center for Judaic Studies at the University of Michigan. She is the author of *Krishna Smiled: Assignment in Southeast Asia*, co-editor of *The Jewish Presence in Latin America* (with Gilbert W. Merkx) and *Latin American Jewish Studies: An Annotated Guide to the Literature* (with AnaLya Sater), and has written articles for *Commentary, Hadassah, Hispanic American Historical Review*, and *Latin American Research Review*. During the Quincentenary Year, she directed a federally funded project, "Jews and the Encounter with the New World 1492/1992," and served as consultant for several exhibits and a video, *The Yiddishe Gauchos*. A former United States Foreign Service Officer, she currently lives in Ann Arbor, Michigan, where she edits *Latin American Jewish Studies*.